"For decades, British Foreign Secretaries have wrestled with the great challenges of dealing successfully with Iranian leaders. Jack Straw has gone beyond that to develop the rich understanding of the country's culture, psychology and history revealed in this book. It will be required reading for anyone who wants to understand how to improve relations with Iran in the coming years, and is an accurate record of the attempts many of us have made to do so."
WILLIAM HAGUE

"Jack Straw was in the frontline of negotiations with Iran. This vivid account links his early diplomatic successes on the nuclear file with the harsh reality of the Iranian system. Iran remains a strategic flashpoint, as the Americans replace diplomacy with sanctions. Jack's book is essential reading for those with a thirst for deeper understanding of the Middle East's most complex and fascinating nation."
SIR JOHN SAWERS, CHIEF OF THE SECRET
INTELLIGENCE SERVICE 2009–2014

"A book that is both highly readable and refreshingly personal. Jack Straw's analysis of what shaped Iran's tangled relations with Britain is lucid; his deep affection for the country shines through; and his first-hand account of the highs and lows of his adventures in Iran, both while British Foreign Secretary and afterwards, makes for a gripping yarn."
BRIDGET KENDALL, BBC DIPLOMATIC
CORRESPONDENT 1998–2016

"It's rare for a Foreign Secretary to become so engrossed in the challenges of dealing with a single country that he decides to write a history of Britain's involvement with it. But that is what Jack Straw has done. Cleverly linking his own experiences with the bigger picture, he gives us a splendid, engrossing account of the remarkable relationship that developed over the centuries between Iran and the UK, and ends with some wise advice for both sides on how to move on from the present, seemingly interminable, exchange of recriminations."
SIR PETER WESTMACOTT, FORMER UK AMBASSADOR
TO THE US, FRANCE AND TURKEY

THE ENGLISH JOB

UNDERSTANDING IRAN
– AND WHY IT DISTRUSTS BRITAIN

JACK STRAW

Biteback Publishing

First published in Great Britain in 2019 by
Biteback Publishing Ltd
Westminster Tower
3 Albert Embankment
London SE1 7SP

ISBN 978-1-78590-399-1

10 9 8 7 6 5 4 3 2

A CIP catalogue record for this book is available from the British Library.

Set in Adobe Garamond Pro and Baskerville

Printed and bound in Great Britain by
CPI Group (UK) Ltd, Croydon CR0 4YY

For William and Charlotte

CONTENTS

INTRODUCTION

Iran is too large and too strategically situated to be so misunderstood outside its borders, by policy-makers and the public alike. Its population of 80 million is equal to Germany's, well above the UK's. Its hydrocarbon reserves are vast. It is middle income. Its economy, though held back for years by sanctions, is surprisingly resilient – and, partly because of sanctions, self-sufficient in many areas.

Iran has had a distinguished history, stretching back three millennia. It has a high culture, whose influence can be seen and felt in India, in Turkey, and on Islam itself. Its connections with European civilisation and Western philosophy are profound. But Iran has suffered grievously in its past from foreign domination, and today craves international respect and recognition.

In a region being torn apart by ethnic and religious strife, Iran appears on the surface to be relatively stable, though there are serious tensions ready to erupt. Whatever fantasies President Trump may have that squeezing Iran will cause the Islamic Republic to crumble, it is nonetheless likely to survive. Iran is hugely influential, for good or ill, in the politics of Lebanon, Syria, Iraq, in Yemen, in many Gulf States, and Afghanistan.

At times since the 1979 Islamic Revolution it has been as brutally repressive in its own way as was the regime of the Shah which it replaced. Yet the constitution of the Islamic Republic provides an arena for intense political argument, which in better periods is larger than many outside might think.

During my time as British Foreign Secretary, I became fascinated, bewitched, infuriated, perplexed by this singular country. I strived to understand it better, and have done ever since. In 2001, I was the first British Foreign Secretary to visit the country after the 1979 Islamic Revolution, and have visited it many times since. I count many Iranians as my friends.

The purpose of this book is to provide some illumination of this country. As I show, Britain's entanglement with Iran goes back five centuries – far longer than most people may realise. Iran has a powerful sense of exceptionalism, and of its national identity. It is Muslim, but never Arab, Shi'a not Sunni. And it has the most extraordinary system of government, in which factions as disparate as the Tea Party and Bernie Sanders's left-wing Democrats are in office at the same time.

I have great affection for its people, notwithstanding the unwelcome experiences to which my wife and I, with two close friends, were subject in October 2015.

Jack Straw
June 2019

CHAPTER 1

'ENGLISH IS NOT THE ENEMY'

'Cross the dual carriageway at that gap,' Mohammed, our interpreter, shouted to the driver, taking instructions from his phone, 'and pull up behind that white car.'

In the dark, we (my wife and I and two friends) saw three large men in plain clothes get out of the white car as we braked behind it. One, shorter, was better-dressed than the other two. He was wearing an immaculately pressed suit, buttoned-up shirt, no tie, and had an enamel insignia in his lapel, with the Iranian emblem on it. He was obviously in charge.

He opened our driver's door and shouted at him in Persian. The blood visibly drained from the driver's face. He was bundled into the back of the unmarked white car. One of the other men got into our driver's seat. Mohammed, who had got out to talk to the other officers, had to scramble back into the people carrier as it was about to drive off.

Our driver had quickly worked out who these men were and knew not to argue. I hoped that they were police officers of some kind, and on our side, but this was far from self-evident. Three decades before, there had been a hard stop in north Tehran on a British diplomat, Edward Chaplin, driving with his wife and young child, with Edward bundled handcuffed and hooded into another car and driven off. I decided not to share this information with the rest of our party. They were already fearing that this was a kidnap.

We sped along the Shiraz ring road again. We had been round and round this road system, which circles the great city, at least three times already and were now very familiar with it. Close to the Botanic Gardens, we abruptly turned into a dimly lit side street to pull up behind another people carrier, identical in make and model to ours. The only differences were that this one had different plates and smoked-glass windows. We were told to be very quick, to transfer all our luggage and ourselves into the new vehicle. A third officer joined us in the back seats, this one carrying an unconcealed pistol.

Off we drove again at high speed for yet another scenic tour of Shiraz's ring road. As we approached one roundabout, a uniformed police motorcyclist, with a plain-clothes pillion passenger carrying a large sub-machine gun that looked like a Heckler & Koch MP5, drew alongside and had a conversation with the senior official.

We finally arrived not at our booked hotel but at the brash, five-star Shiraz Hotel, which commands a high position on the northern hills overlooking the city. We were put into rooms at the end of the ninth floor, told to lock them and open them to no one. It was then that we learnt that the well-dressed man was an official of the Fars province, and that the others were police officers of varying ranks.

By now, I was assuming that these officers were indeed on our side, and that we were not under house arrest. But could I be certain? As for my emotions, I was doing my best not to have any, though in truth I was in a great muddle about them. I'd had 24-hour police protection throughout my thirteen years in Cabinet, and I kept telling myself that these men were not that different from the British police officers who had kept me safe. On the other hand, I knew enough about Iran, and its competing organs of government, to know that it could be dangerous and unpredictable. I also felt a strong sense of responsibility for the anxiety that had so plainly been caused to the other members of the party. It was I who had prompted the trip, and organised it.

Later, we were let out of our rooms for dinner. In the hotel restaurant, the lugubrious owner of the hotel, who spoke perfect American English, introduced himself and told us how happy he was to have us as unexpected guests. On the way back to our rooms, we were told to stay in them until instructed otherwise. We noticed that the complement of police officers had meanwhile grown to eight.

This was day seven of our Iranian holiday.

'We' were my wife Alice and me, with two close friends, Julia and Dan, whom we had known for almost forty years. Alice, Julia and Dan had heard me rabbit on about my interest in Iran over many years. A Foreign Office diplomat who had served in Tehran had commented to me, 'Once you've got the Iran bug, there's no known cure.' I had the bug. I had already visited Iran six times before, but only ever to Tehran, and always in an official capacity. I'd devoured every volume I could about Iran. I wanted to see and learn more. So did Alice, and our friends. Once I'd retired from the House of Commons in May 2015, I had the time and space to take a holiday in Iran.

Our first mistake was to decide to visit in the last two weeks of October. This suited us, and the weather was likely to be tolerable across the country. But, as we discovered after fixing our dates, this was the period of Muharram, the sacred month in the Shi'a calendar. This commemorates the assassination – 'martyrdom' – of Husayn ibn Ali, the grandson of the Holy Prophet Muhammad, at the Battle of Karbala in what is now southern Iraq on 10 October 680 AD, cementing the growing schism that had disrupted early Islam from the death of the Prophet in 632 AD and which continues to this day.

The mourning is very public. Men everywhere were dressed in black clothing, with black flags, marching in processions, with some flagellating themselves. It made for such a stark contrast with us, despite our respectful clothing, including Alice and Julia in headscarves, and

3

no doubt the disparity heightened the suspicions that some (though by no means all) Iranians have of outsiders.[1]

The climax of Muharram is the tenth day, Ashura: 'the great feast of mourning, remembrance, and atonement' which 'most emphatically' sets the Shi'a apart from the Sunni, according to the Iranian-American scholar Vali Nasr.

In retrospect, I should have guessed that we might face difficulties once in Iran given the problems we had encountered in having our promised visas issued.

Normal diplomatic relations between Iran and the UK had been suspended in November 2011 when the British Embassy in Tehran had been invaded and sacked by hooligans – and intelligence officers – almost certainly under the direct control of the Islamic Revolutionary Guard Corps (IRGC) and its powerful, shadowy militia, the Basij, which counts some millions amongst its volunteers. The IRGC had been established soon after the 1979 revolution by the newly installed Supreme Leader, Ayatollah Khomeini, as a counterweight against the regular armed forces, about whose loyalty he was very suspicious. The Basij was established in November 1980. Originally independent, it came under the IRGC in 1981.

By the 1990s, the IRCG (with the Basij) had become the strongest organ of all within the Iranian security apparatus, and so its position remains. The IRGC has established itself as a political force in its own right, with a closely associated political party and media outlets. Major-General Qasim Soleimani, the commander of its Quds Force, responsible for its non-conventional warfare and extraterritorial operations, is by far the best-known military leader in Iran. It is he, working directly to the Supreme Leader, and not the elected government, who has been in the lead on Iran's military and foreign policy in its neighbourhood. The IRGC has extensive business networks under its control. Most of its leaders have been strongly opposed to President Rouhani's nuclear negotiations, partly for ideological reasons but not least because it has done so well from the supervision of sanction-busting smuggling.

Once reformist President Rouhani had taken office in the summer of 2013, relations between Iran and the United Kingdom began gradually to be restored. The British Embassy was partially reopened in 2014. But the then UK Home Secretary, Theresa May, had been reluctant to allow the provision of a full visa service, on the mistaken belief that this supposed bargaining chip would somehow pressure Iran into agreeing to the easier readmission of failed asylum seekers and other illegal immigrants who had been detained in the UK. Thus, at this time, any Iranian national wanting a visa to visit the UK had to go to Istanbul or Abu Dhabi, and any UK national wanting an Iranian visa had to go to an Iranian Embassy abroad.

I'd got to know the new Iranian chargé (the diplomat in charge of the Embassy), Hassan Habibollahzadeh, and liked him. He knew from experience that he could trust me. I had talked to him about the idea of our holiday some eight months in advance. He had assured me that there would be no problems in my securing visas for my party – and later received our completed application forms himself.

Weeks went past, with me regularly checking on progress. 'Inshallah' (Arabic for 'if God wills') was usually the reply. 'So, Mr Habibollahzadeh, is that Inshallah yes, or Inshallah no?' I asked him. I was met with a nervous chuckle and a promise that it should all be all right. I was initially told that I'd be able to collect our visas from Iran's Oman Embassy when I happened to be there at the end of September. I took all four passports with me, but was told the visas were not ready.

We were due to fly out to Iran on Friday 16 October 2015. At the beginning of that week, Mr Habibollahzadeh said that the 'relevant permissions' had now been granted – but there was no precision whatever about how these 'permissions' might be translated into visas in our passports. I called Mr Habibollahzadeh and told him politely that I was going to turn up at his Embassy on Wednesday 14 October and would not be leaving until I had written confirmation of the visas.

After I had sat around in the Embassy for two hours, one of the staff finally came in with an email from Tehran with the magic serial numbers for our visas. I then had to book the Eurostar to Brussels for the following day, since the London Embassy could not formally issue me with the visas. I was accompanied on that trip by a young, bright British-Iranian, Kasra Aarabi, who had been working for me part-time in the Commons on Iran, who spoke fluent Persian and who has helped me greatly with this book. The Iranian Ambassador to Belgium and the EU received me royally, and the visas were quickly pasted into our passports.

Before I left his Embassy in London, however, I asked Mr Habibollahzadeh why there had been such delay in granting us our visas. There had first, he said, been a problem with an invitation I'd accepted to attend and speak at an official conference run in Tehran by a think tank directly attached to the Ministry of Foreign Affairs, on the day before our holiday was due to begin. Despite the fact that this invitation had only been made to me because they knew I'd be in Iran anyway, and despite the fact that it had come from an Iranian government institution, 'some others' had said that I'd be compromising the terms of my tourist visa. So I'd abandoned the conference. 'Someone else' had complained that I had 'not been very helpful in 2003 over the nuclear dossier' – a bit rum, since I had been extremely helpful, and many, especially in the US government, thought I'd been far too helpful. Then Mr Habibollahzadeh dropped into the conversation that an Iranian deputy foreign minister was due to visit London the following week for official meetings and he was furious that the British government were requiring him to go to Istanbul to collect his visa. I didn't blame this deputy foreign minister his anger about his treatment by Theresa May's Home Office. I'd opposed Mrs May's policy, as they well knew. However, the Iranians are always reciprocal.

Having acquired the visas, we had to travel on Turkish Airlines via Istanbul because British Airways had suspended their direct, almost daily flights to Iran when our Embassy had been invaded in November 2011. We arrived in Tehran in the small hours of the following morning, where we were met by our tour guide and interpreter.

Mohammed (not his real name) had been recommended to us by Kasra's auntie, who had been senior in a large, semi-state Tehran travel agency. He proved to be one of the best tourist guides and interpreters there was. As events transpired, we were more grateful than we could ever have imagined for this recommendation.

Once we had obtained our visas, the other practical problem we faced was money. US banking restrictions mean that international credit cards do not work in Iran. We had to stuff our pockets with thousands of US dollars and pounds sterling to cover the whole trip. Changing money in Iran was simplicity itself – there were scores of exchange kiosks in every large city, who operated with remarkably little paperwork or delay.

The holiday began like any other sightseeing trip. There's plenty to see in Tehran, though it's been the country's capital only since 1786. Tehran is known to its residents as the city of paradox. Surprises are everywhere – none better than the Museum of Contemporary Art. With its contemporary, concrete spiral design, the building is rather like the Guggenheim in New York City. The museum was established by 1977 by Empress Farah Pahlavi, wife of the last Shah, with an as-tonishing collection of modern art from around the world. The most risqué is stored, but a lot is on display. During the more puritanical periods of the Islamic Republic, most of the contents had been put in storage. I asked one of the curators why the museum had not been closed altogether. 'We just carried on,' he said, 'and tried to keep out of sight.' But how no one could have noticed the two large Henry Moore sculptures displayed on public view in the museum's garden, in full view from one of Tehran's major thoroughfares, remains a mystery.

As we left the museum, Mohammed said to me, 'Never forget, Jack. Iran is the end of the West.' Iran's singular sense of itself, its pride in its three millennia of history, and its resentment that its European heritage is not appreciated beyond its borders are themes with which one is constantly assailed across this intriguing country.

I interrupted our tourist programme for one piece of official business – to pay a call on my old friend Dr Kamal Kharrazi, who was Foreign Minister of Iran for four of the five years that I served as British Foreign Secretary. Kamal remained an important influence on Iranian foreign policy as President of the Strategic Council on Foreign Relations and, more significantly, as an adviser to Khomeini's successor, the present Supreme Leader, Ayatollah Ali Khamenei. Kamal was a great representative for his country: tough and single-minded.

On one famous occasion when I had complained, 'Kamal, you have no idea how difficult it is to do business with the government of Iran,' he had shot straight back, in his fluent English, 'But you, Jack, have no idea how difficult it is to do business *within* the government of Iran.' Touché. That riposte speaks volumes for the complexity of Iran's governments within governments, as we were to discover, in technicolour, on this trip.

One small surprise was the penetration of social media. If you ever think that the British are obsessed with their mobile phones, try Iran. There seemed to be more phone shops than in any of the scores of other countries I have visited. The iPhone 6 had got to Iran six months before it got to the UK, the full force of sanctions notwithstanding. When I had asked a very senior Iranian diplomat shortly before our trip whether the upcoming elections to the Majlis, the Iranian Parliament, might lead to disturbances and repression, as had happened in 2009, he replied, 'Very unlikely: 10 million iPhone 6s have now been purchased in Iran.'

The much larger surprise, however, was how almost everyone knew who I was. My recognition rate not just on the streets of Tehran but in provincial centres was almost as high as it was in my Blackburn parliamentary constituency, which I had served for thirty-six years. 'Jack E-Straw' would go the cry,* pointing – with the inevitable request for

---

* The Iranians have great difficulty in pronouncing a word that begins with the consonants S and T without putting an E in front, leading to this pronunciation, which sounds to English ears very much like 'Jackie Straw'.

a selfie. Julia decided to start a selfie count, which reached thirty in a few days.

On day three, Mohammed showed me a blog with a picture, taken from a car, of our group walking towards the Museum of Contemporary Art. The caption was not flattering, but I took no more notice of it.

The second stage of our journey was by train, from Tehran Station to Yazd, the isolated desert city in the centre of the country. Whilst we waited for our train in the secure area between two control points, a bearded, thick-set man in his thirties engaged me in conversation. He was, he said, studying for a PhD in Ethics in the holy city of Qom – a two-hour commute every day. Was it true, he asked, that 'money controlled everything' in America, and why did the UK and Germany always agree with the US? As I did my best to explain, we were joined by others. An old man asked if I thought Tehran was safe – and did I like it. Yes to both, I replied; I'd be happy to see my daughter walk around the city. She'd come to no harm.

The train journey turned into a public meeting, complete with selfies. One man asked about setting up a youth parliament; another told me that the forthcoming Majlis elections would result in no change. He was going to see his family during Muharram, but he was not religious. For those who were, the train stopped at Mohammadieh, Qom, for twenty minutes to allow passengers to get off and pray. About two-thirds did so.

Yazd proved to be delightful and well-ordered, with a strong sense of civic society. Its isolation had meant that it had avoided much of the conflict that had raged across this part of Asia for centuries, enabling it to continue as a Zoroastrian stronghold. Its temple has had a fire burning continuously in it since 470 AD. It has the most exquisite and functioning wind towers (known in Persian as '*badger*', windcatchers), which act naturally as air conditioners, and a remarkable system of *qanats*, underground water channels for irrigation.

One night, as families were gathering for communal eating and entertainment as part of Muharram, we went off to a *zur khaneh*, a special circular gym pit, where ritual martial arts with huge weights are practised by all generations. It's a tradition which reaches back to Iran's Zoroastrian roots. Big strong men have long played an influential part in street politics in Iran.

After three nights in Yazd, still unsuspecting as to what lay in store, we set off by people carrier to the southern city of Shiraz. About 100 miles from Yazd, in the middle of nowhere, we had a scheduled stop to visit the Cypress of Abarkuh, a venerated tree estimated to be between 4,000 and 5,000 years old, which, myth has it, was planted by Japheth, son of Noah.

Close to the tree was a group of young men in their twenties, all in Muharram black, neatly dressed with trimmed beards, waiting for me. They presented me with a document formally tied with green ribbon. It was two A4 pages in Persian, personally addressed, and explaining why I was not welcome in Iran.

Mohammed, our guide, gave me a quick translation. The full text (see appendix) began:

> To be honest with you, we are not at all happy with your presence in our town. Not only are we not happy, we're negative and suspicious! … During these days [of Muharram] the blood of the young Shi'a is boiling because of the injustices caused to the Prophet's family and several times a day they cry 'Harb laman harabokom', therefore we are annoyed and hurt by the fact that someone like you is on holiday enjoying yourself.

Later, it asked, 'In your presence what sedition is planning to occur?'

The rest of the leaflet was a comprehensive charge sheet against Britain, 'the old colonial fox', and against me by extension. It explained why we 'will never have a good feeling about the presence and appearance of the English in [our] country'.

Part of the leaflet asserted my direct culpability, as the British Foreign

Secretary involved with the nuclear negotiations and the imposition of sanctions during the Ahmadinejad presidency. Part asserted my guilt by association – for being British, and therefore responsible for a long list of humiliations of Iran, from the 1857 Paris Treaty, the Reuters (1872) and the tobacco (1890) monopolies, the 'stealing and looting [of] Iran's oil' (1901 onwards), our malign intervention in the 1906 Constitutional Revolution, our occupation of part of their country during and im-mediately after the Second World War (1941–46), through to the 1953 coup against Prime Minister Mossadegh, our support for the Shah, our arms to Saddam Hussein in the Iran–Iraq War, and our 'support' for 'terrorist groups against the Islamic Republic'. The indictment con-cluded by asserting that I had supported the 'heads of the sedition' behind the 2009 Green Movement in the disturbances which followed the disputed 2009 election, which were brutally repressed by the IRGC and the Basij. The leaflet was signed by seventeen groups, including 'The Students of Yazd's Basij' – useful confirmation of who was behind the campaign to ensure that ours was a holiday to remember.

Once I'd moved away from the black-clad group, an Iranian tourist said to me, in good English, how sorry he was that these Basij men had been disrupting our enjoyment. He commented that they did not like President Rouhani or Foreign Minister Zarif, and spat out 'Basij' as though it was the most profane word in the Persian lexicon. Basij they were. There is no way they could have known almost exactly when I would arrive, least of all with enough time to produce such a document, unless they'd been given a lot of advance information.

Mohammed Javad Zarif had been appointed as Foreign Minister following President Rouhani's election on a reformist platform in June 2013. Zarif is the most accomplished of Iran's career diplomats. With a PhD from a US university, he is completely fluent in English. He served as Iran's Ambassador to the United Nations from 2002 to 2007, and was the principal negotiator for Iran from 2013 to 2015, leading to the successful nuclear deal with the US and other world powers, the Joint Comprehensive Plan of Action (JCPOA).

The encounter with the black-clad young men by the Cypress tree was only the start of a determined campaign by the Basij and their allies to make our trip as little like a holiday as possible, and much more like our forced conscription into a thriller. It was a campaign that would see one part of the Iranian state, along with its police force, trying to protect us, pitted against another part of the same state, backed by its security apparatus.

It was a further five hours by road from the Cypress tree to Shiraz. On the way, we were able to visit the tomb of Cyrus the Great at Pasargadae. Later, Mohammed made a routine call to the Hotel Homa, the downtown Shiraz hotel where we were due to stay, to let them know that we were on our way. All was fine. Soon afterwards, Mohammed was called back by the hotel to say that there was a group of five men waiting in the lobby for my arrival. They were evidently colleagues of the Basij group we'd encountered at the Cypress tree, as it would have been impossible for the Cypress group, even driving madly as only Iranians can, to have compressed the trip into two hours.

Mohammed told the hotel to call the local police. The police then phoned Mohammed and told him to have us drive round the ring road whilst they sorted out a safe passage through the hotel's rear entrance. Within a few minutes that plan was off too. There were, the police told Mohammed, a hundred demonstrators at the front of the hotel and twenty at the rear. We'd have to carry on round and round the ring road.

After another half-hour, Mohammed stopped the vehicle and disappeared into a mobile phone kiosk, returning with two new phones. He started working both. He beckoned Dan and me out onto the pavement. He couldn't speak in front of our driver, he explained – he might be on the wrong side. It was the police who had told him to change his phones. They were sure that Mohammed's had been intercepted by the IRGC, and they thought that our vehicle had also been bugged. We should give no detail to our wives in the car, as the driver understood more English than he let on.

Anxiety levels were rising in the people carrier.

'There's only one thing for it,' said Dan, chuckling. 'Jane Austen.'

'Jane Austen what?' came our reply.

'I've got Lindsay Duncan reading *Pride and Prejudice* on my iPad. That will take our minds off whatever's going on.'

The plan now was that we would switch hotel. Whilst that was being arranged, it was back along the ring road, diverted by Mr Bennet and Elizabeth. It was after another twenty minutes and more animated phone calls that Mohammed shouted to the driver to cut across the central reservation and stop behind the unmarked white car.

* * *

We were due to spend three nights in Shiraz, to include a visit on our final day to Persepolis,* the ceremonial capital of the Achaemenid Persian Empire.

The police said that we couldn't visit Persepolis when it was open to the public – and the following day it, like all other public monuments, would be closed for Ashura itself. 'But that's fine,' the senior official told us. 'I have arranged for it to be opened just for you and your party, but on one condition: none of you goes too close to the perimeter of the site, where you could be spotted by picnickers in the adjacent public park.'

Persepolis, a UNESCO World Heritage site, covers a vast area. At the height of the Achaemenid Empire, it not only contained all the imperial buildings but housed a small city as well. We had it to ourselves. It was an astonishing privilege, and a mark of the efforts being made by one part of the Iranian state to compensate for the disruption of our trip by another.

Late that afternoon, Dan and I went for a swim in the hotel's pool. It was a men-only session, and two of the senior officials were

---

* From the Greek *perses* for Persian and *polis* for city; Takht-e-Jamshid in Persian.

in the pool with us. I thanked them for all their help. One of them replied that this had been given because I had 'so long supported the BARJAM' – as the JCPOA nuclear deal is known in Persian. Most Iranians viewed me in a very friendly way, but some did not and saw me as a 'representative of the English, with malign intent'. I had indeed long supported the BARJAM, along with my French and German Foreign Minister colleagues. We three had started the nuclear negotiations with Iran in 2003 and had come frustratingly close to a deal in 2005.

Early on our last day in Shiraz, we went to pay homage to Hafez at his shrine in the Musalla Gardens, again opened specially for us. Hafez was a poet and a son of Shiraz, rarely leaving the city. The Iranians are mad about poetry. It's something never to forget when negotiating with them – their love of words, their poetic appreciation of ambiguity. It was a golden morning, with the birds chittering and early autumn scents in the air; the best of Iran.

It was late by the time we arrived at our next stop, Isfahan, because we had been told by the police that we had to arrive after dark. We were staying at the Abbasi Hotel, which must be one of the most beautiful in the world. Its core is a 300-year-old caravanserai – a lodging house for travellers – on a spectacular scale, with an astonishing Persian garden at its heart.

There was a plain-clothes policeman waiting for us in the lobby. All was quiet overnight.

Isfahan had been the capital of Iran on two occasions: in the Seljuk period around the eleventh century, and then during the Safavid era of 1501–1736. It is the Seljuks and Safavids who have left their mark on the city, with the blue-tiled Jameh Mosque, the Naqsh-e Jahan Square (reputed to be one of the largest city squares in the world) and the 33-arch Allahverdi Khan Bridge.

In the morning, it was off to visit the sights. The mosques were heavenly, with the sublime atmosphere a stark contrast to what was to follow. We were trailed the whole time by a young man. We were never quite sure whose side he was on – Basij or that part of the police that was on our side?

Lunch was in a very old restaurant which had water channels between the tables. These required very careful navigation – too careful for Julia, who managed to trip into one of them, though without damage to herself. Having eaten, we were waiting for a signal from Mohammed to leave. But he was first on one phone, then on the other. After about an hour, he came over and told us mournfully that about a hundred Basij were holding a demonstration outside our hotel.

The police sent us to an empty, anonymous hotel about twelve miles away in an industrial park in Shahin Shahr to await developments. Two hours went past. There was no news at all about what might happen next. We were all outraged that we were being sequestered in this soulless place, deprived of time to enjoy exquisite Isfahan.

Alice and Julia had had enough. This was not the holiday they had signed up for, nor did they find especially tolerable the Boys' Own attitude of their spouses that this was an interesting adventure, that we were sure we'd come to no physical harm, and on no account should we allow ourselves to be seen off by the Basij.

Our new chargé in the just-reopened British Embassy in Tehran, Ben Fender, knew of our trip, but up to this point I had seen no point in bothering him with our local difficulties, hoping that the diversions in Shiraz would be the beginning and end of them. It was, however, now plain that the Basij would be at us wherever we went. I called Ben for advice, though knowing before he told me that what he could do – talk to the Ministry of Foreign Affairs (MFA) – would make little difference, since, like the local police, they were on our side anyway. The problem was with other parts of the Iranian state, over which the MFA had no effective influence.

After two more hours in limbo, we got word that the demonstration had been cleared and it was safe to return to the Abbasi Hotel. We dropped in there briefly and then went off to the Shahrzad restaurant, where we received a warm welcome from the distinguished elderly gentleman who ran it. He insisted on wearing a tie, an unusual sight in Iran, where the absence of a tie has long been regarded as one essential mark of being a good (male) citizen of the Islamic Republic.

On Monday 26 October, we checked out of the Abbasi early to visit the Blue Mosque and two others, equally exquisite, and then to have breakfast at the Kowsar Hotel, across the city, where we were told we could eat in peace. A professional football team were also having breakfast. More selfies.

But peace was not on the menu. We got word that the Basij had 'found out' where we were, and were organising yet another demonstration for my benefit. It was only a small group, but on the way out, as we were bundled into our people carrier and were driving off, one man, puce in the face, began shouting and then threw a large tomato at the van. We were given a plain-clothes escort and were later told that two cars of Basij had been turned around by the police.

A visit to Kashan, an ancient city halfway between Isfahan and Tehran, had been scheduled, but we were now warned off that too. I agreed with the rest of the party that we'd have to cut our losses and truncate our 'holiday'. We weren't due to leave until the Saturday, but we'd thankfully booked fully flexible tickets. Back in Tehran on the Monday evening, we took our dinner in our hotel. Across the restaurant was a middle-ranking government minister with his family. He came over to greet us in good English. He knew exactly what had happened to us at the hands of the Basij without us saying a word about it. He was sympathetic but brushed our experience off with a chuckle, as though this was one of those hazards in a tourist trip that could happen to anyone. It was another reminder that those nominally in charge of the government of Iran have no control whatever over its security apparatus, nor a sense of responsibility for the consequences of its actions – or, in this case, its failure to act.

When my daughter read this account, she asked, 'What is it about Iran and your relationship with it that meant you were so desperate to pretend to yourself and your dear wife and friends that everything was fine and would just go away?' I dearly wanted our problems to go away – and my experience with the country suggested that often they did. On this occasion, however, I was wrong.

Dan and I visited Turkish Airlines and changed our return flights to Wednesday 28 October.

That evening, we had a relaxed dinner inside the British Embassy compound with Ben Fender and his newly arrived, and very small, team. I'd last been inside the compound on a British parliamentary visit in January 2014. At that stage, little of the damage caused by the Basij and associated thugs when they had invaded the Embassy two years before had been repaired. Now the perimeter was secure, with razor wire everywhere, and the main residence was serviceable.

After the Embassy dinner, we were driven straight into the base-ment car park of our hotel to avoid any Basij who might be hanging around in the lobby. The others took the lift direct to our rooms on the thirteenth floor, but I needed to go to the front desk to retrieve our passports. As Mohammed and I got into the lift in the lobby, a large, sinister-looking man dressed all in black squeezed in just as the doors were closing. When asked which floor, he signalled that he wanted the same one as us, all the while speaking on one phone and texting into another. Basij. He trailed us round the corridor. Moham-med called the hotel security and then spent the whole night outside our rooms in case this man, plus compatriots, decided to return. It was yet another reminder of the astonishing decency and sense of duty of most Iranians.

The plan was that on the way to the airport we would visit Ayatol-lah Khomeini's shrine, but on police advice that was cancelled too. As our plane finally left Iranian air space, the four of us ordered large alcoholic drinks – our first for eleven days – and celebrated, if that's the word, our safe departure.

I had had one enquiry from a UK paper asking whether it was correct that we were having to stay overnight in a safe house outside Isfahan because of demonstrations. I was able to answer accurately,

if economically, that although there had been a demonstration outside our hotel, that had been dispersed and we were staying there as
planned. The last thing that any of us wanted was to give the Basij
the satisfaction of international publicity. We were always clear that
we were simply the means by which the Basij could attack their real
target: the Rouhani government, and its wish to open Iran up to the
outside world. The hardliners did not like me, for sure, but they hated
the reformists for what they might do to rein in the militia's unaccountable power.

The demonstrations against our trip did receive some limited
publicity within Iran. One website carried a large colour photograph
showing demonstrators holding placards with complaints against me
in both Persian and English. The Persian text told the reader, 'The
City of Martyrs is not the place to cater for the English enemy.'

Thanks to the vagaries of Google Translate, the English version carried the immortal lines:

> City martyr catering
> English is not the enemy

CHAPTER 2

IT'S ALWAYS AN ENGLISH JOB

Kar kareh ingilisee hast – *the job is always an English one.*
Ubiquitous saying in common use in Iran

It is a huge mistake to trust evil Britain.
Ayatollah Ali Khamenei, Supreme Leader of Iran,
televised address, 3 June 2016

The Basij demonstrators protesting against my presence in Iran were not alone in describing the English as 'the enemy'. High suspicion of the British is ingrained in Iranian society, and for good reason. This distrust springs from the malign experiences that Iran suffered at Britain's hands during almost all of the nineteenth century and much of the twentieth. There's an old joke amongst British diplomats that Iran is the only country in the world that still thinks the UK is a superpower. To the Iranians, it's not a joke.

It's routine for conservative elements in the regime to blame outsiders, usually the British, when faced with protests against the restrictions of the Islamic Republic, or other manifestations of discontent. Thus, in their eyes, foreign agents, including the UK, were primarily responsible for the serious street protests that occurred in Iran in December 2017 and January 2018.[1]

When, in February 2016, elections to the Iranian Parliament

produced the 'wrong' answer, with a victory for allies of reformist President Rouhani, the then Chief Justice of Iran, Ayatollah Sadeq Larijani, complained that the moderates had formed a 'British list' of successful candidates and had worked with 'American and English media outlets' during the campaign.[2]

Whether someone as worldly as Ayatollah Larijani – he comes from one of the most powerful families in Iran and is fluent in English – really believes the fantastic idea that in 2016 British agents could have manufactured voter discontent in Iran amongst an electorate otherwise sublimely content with their lot is impossible to say. What is certainly true is that the notion that we are some unseen, all-pervasive influence on life and events in Iran is very deep-seated. It is not just a convenient alibi for the unaccountable conservative elements amongst the Iranian elite but a truism amongst much of Iranian society.

This neurosis about the British extended to the last Shah. As we will see, in 1953 the UK and the US were planning a *coup d'état* against the incumbent, elected, Prime Minister Mohammad Mossadegh. The Shah was to be the beneficiary of the coup: it would enable him to rule untrammelled by the will of the people. He was, however, so intensely neurotic that he was being set up by the 'hidden hand' of the British that the most extraordinary measures had to be taken to reassure him.*

A few years ago, whilst President Ahmadinejad was in office, a Persian-speaking British academic flagged down a taxi at Tehran Airport. On the way into the city, the cab driver confided in his passenger, 'We all know that it was Margaret Thatcher who removed the Shah and put the Ayatollahs in power.' But he added, 'Now we're really cheesed off with the mullahs, so would you ask the British Prime Minister, Mr Brown, to get rid of them?'[3]

This notion of blaming the British (almost always described as 'the English' by Iranians) and endowing them with superhuman powers

---

* See Chapter 10.

was brilliantly satirised by Iraj Pezeshkzad in his novel (later a popular television series) *My Uncle Napoleon*.[4] It's the story of a pathetic and pathological man who, depressed by his failures, turns himself into a Napoleon in his fantasies and becomes convinced of a British plot to destroy him. As the book explains, there was no such plot. Uncle Napoleon was small fry. But the novel was set in the early 1940s. Britain and the Soviet Union had invaded Iran in 1941 and jointly occupied it until 1946. It was we, the occupying powers, who effectively ran the country in this period, and locked up a number of prominent figures on suspicions of their pro-Nazi sympathies. So Uncle Napoleon's paranoia was not entirely misplaced.

Few Londoners would be able to say where the German, French or even US Embassies are situated. Everyone in Tehran knows where the British Embassy is. The main compound in downtown Tehran occupies a large twelve-acre site – and there's another residential compound, Gholhak Garden, four times bigger, in less-polluted northern Tehran.*

These compounds are seen as potent symbols of the disproportionate power that many Iranians feel the British exercised over their country for nearly two centuries – right up to the Islamic Revolution in 1979 – and our alleged continuing efforts to subvert the Iranian nation.

Colloquial sayings in everyday use emphasise this. '*Poshteh pardeh hamisheh yek ingilsee hast*' – 'Behind the curtain there's always an Englishman' – goes one. '*Ingilisee 'ha ba pambeh sar miboran*' – 'The English cut heads with cotton' – runs a second, a back-handed compliment to our diplomatic skills. And, most ubiquitous of all, '*Kar kareh ingilisee hast*' – 'The job is always an English job' – hence the title of this book.

* * *

---

*   By way of comparison, St James's Park in central London is fifty-seven acres.

As I explained in my introduction, the principal aim of this book is to try to provide readers with a better understanding of this country and of Britain's role in it. But that understanding also requires an appreciation of three aspects of the singular nature of modern Iran.

The first is the multifarious ethnic composition of Iran. True Persian speakers make up less than two-thirds of its population. Nearly one-sixth are Azeris, who have a Turkic mother tongue (Supreme Leader Ali Khamenei is one). Kurds in the north-west are a tenth. There are then Arab minorities in the west and south-west, and Baluchs near the Pakistani border. Ninety per cent of the population is Shi'a, around 8 per cent Sunni and the remainder Christians, Baha'is, Jews, and Zoroastrians.

The second aspect is the antiquity of Iran's civilisation, which informs its profound and secular sense of Iranian nationalism.

The third, and most important, element is the fundamental role that Shi'ism has played, and continues to play, in underpinning Iranian identity and politics.

Former US Secretary of State Henry Kissinger has argued that Iran has to decide 'whether it is a nation or a cause'.[5] It's a curious observation for such a distinguished American statesman to make, since the United States itself only became the immensely powerful nation it is today because of the ideals, the cause, that the Founding Fathers set out, and which are now so embedded in the Americans' sense of self-belief. For Iran, disentangling 'cause' and 'nation' is a well-nigh hopeless task. I argue in my concluding chapters that if Iran wants the international respect it craves (and deserves), it has to follow agreed international norms of behaviour. But an understanding of Iran today requires an appreciation of the very strong cultural and ideological forces – the causes – that have moulded its history and its people today. Even as most Iranians become more secular in their daily lives, this remains the case. It's not just another country: it's Iran.

My story begins with one of Iran's most powerful leaders, Cyrus the Great.

CHAPTER 3

FROM FIRE TO ALLAH

Iran was indeed Islamized, but it was not Arabized.
Persians remained Persians.
BERNARD LEWIS, *IRAN IN HISTORY*[1]

In 1879, a British Museum archaeological expedition in Babylon, in modern-day Iraq, found a cylinder covered with Babylonian cuneiform script. Now known as the Cyrus cylinder, it was originally inscribed and buried in the foundations of a wall after the Persian Emperor Cyrus the Great (c. 600–530 BC) captured Babylon in 539 BC. The text of the cylinder was probably a proclamation that was widely distributed across the Persian Empire.

The cylinder records that, aided by the god Marduk, Cyrus had captured Babylon without a struggle, restored shrines dedicated to different gods, and repatriated deported peoples who had been brought to Babylon. It was this decree that allowed the Jews to return to Jerusalem and rebuild the Temple. Because of these enlightened acts, which were rare in antiquity, the cylinder has acquired a special resonance and is valued by people all around the world as a symbol of tolerance and respect for different peoples and faiths. These are the qualities for which Cyrus is revered in the Hebrew Bible.* The Cyrus

---

* 'Thus saith Cyrus, king of Persia. The Lord God of heaven hath given me all kingdoms of the earth, and he hath charged me to build him a house at Jerusalem' – Ezra, 1:2.
   'That saith of Cyrus, He is my shepherd and shall perform all my pleasure: even saying to Jerusalem, Thou shalt be built; and to the temple, Thy foundation shall be laid' – Isaiah, 44:28.

cylinder has been owned by and displayed in the British Museum ever since its discovery in 1879.

In an important act of 'cultural diplomacy', the cylinder was loaned by the British Museum to the National Museum of Tehran in 2010, at a difficult period in our relationship with Iran. Neil MacGregor, then director of the British Museum, commented that the cylinder was 'the first attempt we know about running a society, a state with different nationalities and faiths – a new kind of statecraft', adding that it is 'often referred to as the first bill of human rights'.

When the cylinder was inscribed, Britain was in its pre-history, divided by warring territories, savage, poor and possessed of no written language. In contrast, Persia at that period had centuries of experience of civilisation, of complex urban settlements. United in the seventh century BC, by the time of Cyrus the Persian Empire covered the Balkans, north Africa and central Asia – 44 per cent of the world's population at the time. It is considered the first 'world empire' in human history.

Its capital was Persepolis, about forty miles to the north of Shiraz, in the south-west province of Fars. To visit the vast site is to gain an understanding of the extraordinary sophistication of the Achaemenid dynasty that built the city, from which it controlled its empire. The Achaemenids took control of Greece in the first of the Greco-Persian wars but lost control in the second war, with a decisive victory by the (outnumbered) Greeks in the naval Battle of Salamis in 480 BC. In 330 BC, Persepolis, and with it the whole Achaemenid dynasty, fell with its defeat by Alexander the Great – known to the Zoroastrians as 'the accursed Alexander', and never referred to by Iranians as 'Great', only, at best, as 'Alexander the Macedonian'. In a drunken rage, Alexander laid waste to Persepolis.

Despite the Iranians' revulsion for the destruction Alexander wreaked on their empire and civilisation, Greek influence has been a powerful force in Persian literature, culture and philosophy. In *Persian Fire*, the author Tom Holland comments that the impact of Persia and Greece upon history cannot be entirely confined within rigid notions of East and West. Monotheism and the notion of the universal state, democracy and totalitarianism: all can trace their origins back to the period of the Persian wars. Justifiably it has been described as the axis of world history.[2]

As former diplomat Gerard Russell notes, 'the classical philosophers who had inspired the European Enlightenment [are] fashionable with the reactionary clergy of Iran'.[3] To this day, theological students training for the clergy at the key Shi'a seminaries in the holy city of Qom are examined on Aristotle and Plato. But it also needs to be remembered, especially in the West, that Iranian culture itself has had a striking influence thousands of miles beyond Iran's borders.

One of those abiding influences has been Zoroastrianism. Cyrus made this the official state religion of his empire. Zoroastrianism is the religion of followers of Zoroaster (also known as Zarathustra). The nineteenth-century German philosopher Friedrich Nietzsche observed: 'Zarathustra was the first to consider the fight of good and evil the very wheel in the machinery of things: the transposition of morality into the metaphysical realm, as a force, cause, and end in itself, is *his* work.'[4] Followers of Zoroastrianism hold that fire is sacred, and their temples have fires of 'eternal flame'.[*] But they are not 'fire-worshippers': their faith is much more sophisticated than that. It asserts that the individual has a personal responsibility for their behaviour. Associated with the imperative of moral choice in this life is the notion of Paradise, from the Persian *fardis*, meaning a walled garden, well-watered and lush, with flowers, fruit, trees and domestic animals, filled with beauty, in sharp contrast to the world beyond the garden's walls. It is a messianic faith. The final saviour of the world, Saoshyant, will be born to a virgin impregnated by the seed of Zoroaster whilst bathing in a lake.

On the Arab invasion of Iran in the seventh century AD,

---

[*] In the large *Ateshkadeh* – fire temple – in the desert city of Yazd, the priests claim that the fire has been burning continuously for at least 2,500 years.

Zoroastrianism was quickly and brutally replaced as the principal religion of Iran. But its ideas of divine justice have powerful echoes in the Abrahamic faiths, including Islam; there is a continuity of its tenets to the present day. The monarchs who practised this faith in the pre-Islamic period asserted that church and state were one, 'brothers born of one womb and never to be parted'. Once the authority of the chief priests had been asserted, deviance was not only heresy but treason.[5]

There is a reflection of this notion in the current constitution of the Islamic Republic. As we will see, the church – Shi'ism and its interpretation by the clerics perpetually in power – trumps the secular authority of the elected government.*

Some explicitly Zoroastrian traditions have survived and prospered in Iranian culture to this day, most notably Nowruz, the two-week celebration of the Zoroastrian New Year. Ayatollah Khomeini made an effort to abolish this but failed.

The continuing hold that aspects of Zoroastrianism have on the minds of Iranians is to a significant degree due to the influence of some key Iranian poets – notwithstanding that they wrote some centuries after the Arab conversion of their land to Islam. The world's longest epic poem by a single author, and Iran's greatest, *Shahnameh* (*The Book of Kings*), by Abu 'I-Qasim Ferdowsi was written in the tenth century. It celebrates much of Iran's pre-Islamic history and continues to have great resonance today. It is considered to be one of the principal factors that allowed Persian to flourish, whilst local languages elsewhere in the lands conquered by the Muslim invaders from the south were subsumed into Arabic.

* * *

After Alexander's conquest of Iran in 330 BC, the Seleucid Empire ruled for six decades, followed by the Arsacid Parthians. One of the

---

* See Chapter 12.

founders of the latter dynasty, Mithridates, revived the Archaemenid title of Shahanshah, meaning King of Kings. These people came from the north-east of Iran and had some difficulty in establishing their rule over their subjects to the west and south. It was a people who came from 'Persis' (or 'Persia proper'), the Sassanians, who finally defeated the Seleucids in about 224 AD. They ruled for four centuries over a large empire (though smaller than the Archaemenids').

Through these changes of dynasty, Iran was intermittently locked into conflict with the Romans for nearly 700 years, from 69 BC to 629 AD. These Roman–Persian wars were the longest in human history.

The almost continuous conflict, and periodic internal divisions, profoundly weakened the Sassanians and their hold over Iran. It was in a state of decay and lawlessness. After a disastrous defeat by Byzantium in about 624 AD, the ruler, Khosrow, was deposed, blinded and later killed by his son Shiruyeh. Rulers then followed one after another, killed or blinded by their successors.

Taking advantage of this disarray, a force of Muslim Arabs under Umar, the second caliph, took a small army to invade part of what is now Iraq in 637 AD, and despite inferiority in numbers defeated a Sassanian army near Hilla. The Arabs then moved into Iran itself. The Sassanian Empire collapsed in 651 AD. By the end of the seventh century, Muslim Arabs were in control of virtually the whole of Iran, along with an area from the Atlantic to the Indian Ocean.

The Umayyad dynasty was replaced in the middle of the eighth century by the Abbasids, under their new caliph, Abu 'l-Abbas. They had been able to forge alliances with the old Iranian landowning classes in Khorasan, in what is now north-east central Iran. Though the capital of their empire was Baghdad, the new rulers fused much of Iranian culture with their own practices, as well as absorbing some of the language. They were also wise enough not to follow their conquests by mass murder and forced conversion, provided their subjects accepted the reality of their rule. Critically, and unlike their predecessors, they established the principle of equality for all Muslims, rather than the supremacy of the Arabs.

As the author and former diplomat Michael Axworthy puts it:

The Abbasid period was a time of enormous human achievement, in political terms as well as in terms of civilisation, art, architecture, science and literature. The release of new ideas and the exchange of old ones within a huge area held together by a generally benign and tolerant government brought about a dynamic and hugely influential civilisation, way ahead (it need hardly be said) of what was going on in Europe at the time.[6]

From the beginning of the eleventh century, migrations and local revolts by people of Turkic origin known as the Seljuks gradually conquered Iran. They governed in a similar manner to the Abbasids, from around 1038 AD to about 1220 AD.

The Mongol Genghis Khan was the leader not of a simple band of thugs but of a highly effective and disciplined army, which from a base far in the eastern Asian steppe had conquered China and then moved westwards. What distinguished the Mongols from both the Abbasids and the Seljuks was their utter ruthlessness. When they arrived at the major desert oasis city on the Silk Road, Merv (in what is now Turkmenistan), they massacred virtually all the residents they could find – hundreds of thousands, according to contemporary claims. They had a practice of leaving pyramids of skulls.

The Mongols made Tabriz their capital, and did something that had defeated their predecessors. High in the Alborz mountains, the Assassins, a dissident Ismaili sect, had made their base in impregnable fortresses. From there they went in for the targeted killing of rulers, sometimes on a contract basis. The Mongols destroyed them.

The Mongols ruled from about 1220 to 1375, when they were progressively dislodged by the Timurids, under their leader Tamerlane. He built up his army on the model of Genghis Khan, but his methods were if anything worse. He razed city after city, parading the heads of thousands of those whom he had killed, *pour encourager les autres*.

In contrast to the Mongols, Tamerlane was explicit that he was conquering in the name of Sunni Islam. Following his death in 1405, his son ruled eastern Iran for a period, whilst in the west two Shi'a confederations, the White Sheep and the Black Sheep, took control. But they were defeated by the Ottomans in 1473, leaving a power vacuum – to be filled by the end of the century by the Safavids (1501–1736), whose period marks the beginning, in many eyes, of modern Iranian history to which I now turn.

CHAPTER 4

SHAH ISMAIL I – IRAN'S HENRY VIII

With some degree of historical latitude, the state-sponsored Shi'ism that came about with the rise of the Safavids can be compared to the Reformation of northern and central Europe, and the Sunni reaction to it with the Counter-Reformation.
ABBAS AMANAT, *IRAN: A MODERN HISTORY*[1]

The Shias' historical experience is akin to those of Jews and Christians in that it is a millennium-long tale of martyrdom, persecution, and suffering. Sunnis, by contrast, are imbued with a sense that immediate worldly success should be theirs.
VALI NASR, *THE SHIA REVIVAL*[2]

Under the Observance of 5 November Act 1605, annual commemorations were ordered to mark the deliverance of King James I of England, and his nation, from the attempt by

many malignant and devilish papists, Jesuits, and seminary priests much envying and fearing, conspired most horribly ... upon the fifth day of November in the year of our lord 1605 suddenly to have blown up the ... House [of Lords] with gunpowder, an invention so inhuman, barbarous and cruel, as the like was never before heard of.[3]

England itself had been a 'papist state' until Henry VIII broke with the

Church of Rome in 1534 to found the Church of England. From the 1558 Act of Supremacy onwards, the British monarch has been the 'Supreme Governor', and 'Defender of the Faith' of the Anglican Church, as new Anglican bishops have to acknowledge in their oath of homage to the Queen, and our own coinage still recites. Though in its early days the Church of England remained Catholic in its liturgy, it gradually subsumed strong elements of Protestantism. The Anglican Church not only became the religious embodiment of the nation of England, and a means by which its identity could be anchored, but until the end of the nineteenth century helped to underpin the secular authority of the state.

In Iran, it's not an annual Bonfire Night that serves to underline the distinctive nature of the practice of its religion, but something much more profound: the mourning month of Muharram, which we witnessed on our trip. Muharram culminates in Ashura, when some Shi'a followers beat their breasts and flagellate their backs to mark the assassination of Husayn ibn Ali.

In England, the sectarian purpose of Bonfire Night has largely been forgotten, though England's sense of exceptionalism, which is reflected in the foundation of the Church of England, remains a powerful force even in this secular age. Its failure over forty years of membership ever fully to embrace the supranational (and in many ways Catholic Christian democracy) European Union is but one example.

Iran has an even stronger sense of exceptionalism. Its nationalism, its pride in its two and half millennia of history, is interwoven with the particular, distinctive faith that is Shi'ism.

All the Muslim dynasties that had ruled Iran from the seventh century through the fifteenth were Sunni. The Safavid dynasty which replaced them were Shi'a. The Safavids came from the north. Their first ruler, Shah Ismail I, reigned from 1501 to 1524. Born a Shi'a, he loathed Sunnis and murderously oppressed them. But his conversion of the whole of the Persian Empire to make Shi'ism the state religion had a cold strategic purpose as well: to rid the empire of the supranational power exercised over Muslim followers by Mecca, Medina and increasingly by Istanbul, capital of the Ottoman Empire, and to establish a practice of religion that would reinforce Iran's sense of nationhood.

The parallels between the rise of Shi'ism in Iran and of the Reformation in northern Europe can be taken too far. But they do serve as a reference point to our understanding of this faith, without which little comprehension of Iran today is possible.

*   *   *

Husayn ibn Ali, the grandson of the Holy Prophet Muhammad, was killed by the Sunni forces of the Umayyad caliphate at the Battle of Karbala in 680, along with seventy-two of his followers.

The Battle of Karbala was the culmination of the succession crisis which followed the death of Muhammad in 632 AD. Most Muslims at the time followed the tribal traditions by which a new leader would be chosen by a council of elders. The majority, the Sunnis, chose Abu Bakr, the Prophet's close friend and father-in-law. A small group, however, argued that Muhammad's cousin and son-in-law Ali ibn Abi Talib was both more qualified for the position and the Prophet's preferred successor.

Ali initially acquiesced in Abu Bakr's leadership as caliph, and later became the fourth caliph. Sunnis call these four the Rightly Guided, or *Rashidun* caliphs. But whether rightly guided or not, this period was characterised by internecine strife which turned into a civil war. This war ended when Ali was assassinated in 661 AD in his capital, Kufa (now in southern Iraq, near Najaf). The victors, led by Muawiya, assumed the caliphate and established the Umayyad dynasty in the same year, with its centre in Damascus. However, Ali's younger son Husayn* refused to accept the writ of the Umayyads. Many of Husayn's compatriots were liberated slaves and Iranian prisoners of war who had resented the Arab

---

* The elder son was Hasan. After a series of skirmishes, he accepted the authority of Muawiya and retired to Medina, where he was murdered by his wife in 670.

character of Umayyad rule. The Umayyads sent a powerful army to crush Husayn and his followers. In desperation, vastly outnumbered and deprived of water, Husayn and his group bravely charged the much larger force against them. They were cut down and beheaded.

It was thus that martyrdom became a key tenet of Shi'ism.

Although both traditions, Sunnism and Shi'ism, draw their theological authority from the Prophet Muhammad, and the Quran, there are also very significant differences of belief and practice between them. Not least, there is the obvious difference between the two traditions in the narratives they have adopted and nurtured. Unlike the Sunni, Shi'ism is a messianic faith, similar in this regard to Judaism and Christianity.

Iranian Shi'as are overwhelmingly 'Twelver Shi'as', meaning that they revere twelve imams. These twelve imams are considered to have special spiritual qualities, reflecting those of the Prophet himself. They were (and are) seen as the trustees of the Prophet's light, able to understand the inner meaning of his teaching. In other words, in contrast to ordinary believers (including clerics), they had a special authority in respect of the interpretation of sharia law. Muhammad's and the imams' words and deeds are a guide and model for the community to follow; as a result, they must be free from error and sin (a concept known as *ismah*, or infallibility) and must be chosen by divine decree, or *nass*, through the Prophet.

For Shi'a, the first imam was Ali, cousin and son-in-law of the Prophet. The third was Husayn, who was murdered at Karbala in 680 AD. The dates of death of the first eleven imam (in the seventh to ninth centuries) are recorded. So is the date of birth of the twelfth imam, in about 868 AD. However, to Twelver Shi'a, the twelfth imam has never died, but is 'occulted' or hidden. Shi'a believe that God hid this imam from physical access to preserve his life. During his occultation, the twelfth imam is the unseen Lord of the Age (*imam al-zaman*), permanent until the Day of Judgment. With his second coming, there will be a reign of justice until the return of Jesus Christ (revered in the Quran as a prophet), when the world will end. The occultation of the twelfth imam is the theological justification for the authority of Iran's Supreme Leader today, and holds pride of place in the Islamic Republic's constitution, as we shall see.*

The authority of the Supreme Leader, and the *ulema* (the body of clerical scholars practised in the study and interpretation of holy texts), and the particular influence that they hold in the polity of Shi'a countries, especially Iran, also derives from a different view of the role to be played by the congregation in understanding religious truths.

In the Sunni tradition (much to the frustration of Western politicians, because there is no obvious chief with whom to communicate), there is no Pope, no College of Cardinals, not even a Bishops' House of the Church of England. Sunnism can be compared with the Presbyterian Protestant tradition, by which there is a parity between ministers of the church and their congregation. No special intermediaries between the believer and God are deemed necessary. As Vali Nasr explains,

> Shiism is based on a more pessimistic assessment of human fallibility. Just as humans could not find salvation until the Prophet took up the task of guiding them toward it, so after him people need the help of exceptionally holy and divinely favoured people in order to live in accord with the inner truths of religion ... The imams ... provide that continual help, renewing and strengthening the bond between man and God. The *ulema* ... carry on the project of the imams in safeguarding and sustaining the faith. Without the right leadership, Shias insist, the true meaning of Islam will be lost.[4]

One such divinely favoured person was Husayn ibn Ali: 'Shi'a' is a contracted form of 'Shiite-Ali', or 'partisan for Ali'.

This different view of the role of the senior clergy is much more akin to that of the doctrine and hierarchy of the Catholic Church.

---

* See Chapter 6.

The priest is the intermediary between God and man. In the Catholic Church there is a clear hierarchy, culminating in the Pope, whose office rests upon its infallibility.

There is no single Pope in the Shi'a hierarchy. Rather, there are a number of senior legal experts – *mujtahids* – (these days, Ayatollahs) who might be compared to the College of Cardinals, who have the task of ministering to the social and political needs of their community, as well as their spiritual needs.

For many centuries the Catholic Church was heavily involved in the politics of the countries of its faith; in some, it still is. Similarly, from the Safavids onwards, the Shi'a religious establishment has played a key role in the politics of Iran, though exactly how much temporal power they have been able to exercise has varied over time.

There are three other parallels with the Catholic Church that are worthy of note. First, Catholics, particularly when they were oppressed, were permitted by doctrine to 'dissimulate'. Believers were thus allowed to conceal their real intentions, provided this was for a morally justified purpose. Since secrets had to be kept, the argument ran, their preservation may at times require dissimulation. In the Shi'a tradition there is a similar doctrine, called '*taqiya*'. (The doctrine also exists in the Sunni tradition, but is much less central than in Shi'ism, not least because Shi'a were and are the minority within the Muslim world, and therefore more vulnerable to oppression.)

Second, the political Islam espoused by Ayatollah Khomeini and many other Shi'a clerics is similar in some respects to the Catholic movement in Latin America known as liberation theology, by which a number of leading clerics* argued that their church's duty was to improve the living standards and civic rights of their communities.

Third, and most important, local clerics in Iran are usually drawn from their locality and are embedded in the community, in the way that Catholic priests in, for example, Ireland have been. This gave

---

* Such as the Peruvian priest Gustavo Gutiérrez and the Brazilian friar Leonardo Boff.

them a natural authority with the masses which from the late nineteenth century was to make the clerics an important political force.

*   *   *

In the sixteenth century in the Middle East, as across Europe, spiritual and secular power was completely intertwined. The Safavids were sincere and devout in their belief in Twelver Shi'ism. At the same time, their ruthless pursuit of religious uniformity reinforced their temporal control of their state. They combined both objectives by stunning, monumental architecture, designed to strengthen piety, impress their subjects and intimidate – as Shah Abbas I, aka Abbas the Great, who ruled from 1588 to 1629, did in Isfahan, to which he moved the capital of Iran in 1598.

A wise administrator and a fine soldier, Abbas built the most exquisite mosques, covered bridges, boulevards and what is thought to be one of the largest public squares in the world. He placed his palace so he could watch over the mosques and the bazaars at the same time – both potential sources of trouble.

After Abbas's death, Iran stagnated, with its elite corrupt and decadent. By 1722, they were under attack from the north by Tsar Peter the Great and from the east by an Afghan army. This army besieged and took Isfahan, where its leader, Mahmud, proclaimed himself Shah of Persia.

A native Iranian warlord from Khorasan, Nader Shah, then defeated and banished the Afghans and temporarily restored the Safavids to the throne. By 1736, Nader had become so powerful he was able to depose the Safavids and have himself crowned as Shah.

Nader was assassinated in 1747. Thereafter, Iran fell into a half-century of turmoil and civil war, culminating at the end of the eighteenth century with a victory for the Qajars, a Turkic Iranian tribe. They gradually restored Iran's territorial integrity, and ruled Iran from 1796 until 1925, when they were officially replaced by Reza Khan (though their authority was rapidly eroded after Reza Khan's *coup d'état* in 1921).* As we will see, Khan came from a lowly background; by dint of his own determination and character, with help from the British General Sir Edmund Ironside, he rose rapidly from sergeant to brigadier-general, and then to Shah.

* * *

By Abbas the Great's reign in the late sixteenth century, 'Iran's geopolitical identity was curiously tied up with Europe's', as Abbas Amanat notes. 'Safavid rulers' correspondence with European courts often rhetorically questioned the futility of the religious schism which divided Christian Europe while the Turkish threat was at hand'⁵ – despite the Sunni–Shi'a schism, of which they were the main protagonists. Inevitably, the greatest contact between the Safavids and Europe was with the countries closest to Iran. Nonetheless, there was some contact between the Iranians and the British, but in the early days this was, with important exceptions, overwhelmingly about trade, and not about interference in Iran's internal affairs.

One of the first British visitors, Anthony Jenkinson, received a very frosty reception from Shah Tahmasp on his arrival in 1561. Jenkinson was a cloth merchant, sent by the Muscovy Company of London to explore opening up direct trade with Iran through Russia. He arrived in Qazvin, in the north-east of Iran (at that time the Safavids' capital), with samples of cloth and a letter from Queen Elizabeth I, drawn up in Latin, English, Italian and Hebrew. The Shah and his court spoke none of these languages; luckily for Jenkinson, he was able to make himself understood in Turkish, which was the main language of the Safavid court. He left an amusing record of his encounter with the Shah. He was made to exchange his shoes for

a pair of the Sophie's [Shah's] own shoes, [so] I might not be suffered

---

* See below, Chapter 7.

to tread upon his holy ground, being a Christian … unbeliever and unclean: esteeming all to be infidels and pagans which does not believe as they do, in their false filthy prophets Mahomet and Murtezallie [Ali, the first Shi'a imam]. … I delivered the Queen's majesties letters with my present, which he, accepting, demanded of me of what country of Franks* I was … 'Oh thou unbeliever,' said he, 'we have no need to have friendship with unbelievers' and so willed me to depart.[6]

The Shah's main reason for rejecting Jenkinson's offer was not that he was an unclean infidel, as Jenkinson had reported, but that he did not wish to discomfort the Ottoman Turks, with whom he had just made a peace. However, Jenkinson's journey was not all in vain. Four years later, the Shah did grant trading privileges to the Muscovy Company.

Three decades later, two high-born British adventurers, the brothers Anthony and Robert Shirley, hearing that they might receive a favourable reception from the Safavids, travelled to the Safavid court to offer their services, with a retinue of about twenty other of their countrymen. It was the younger brother, Robert, who had the greatest involvement in Iranian affairs. It is claimed, not least by his brother in his memoir, that he was responsible for training the Safavids' army along more efficient English lines, and that this was a key factor in the Iranians' successes in the Ottoman–Safavid wars of 1603–18,[7] though the significance of Shirley's efforts is now disputed.[8]

Both brothers were emissaries for the Shah to foreign courts. Robert also accompanied the English diplomat Sir Dodmore Cotton to Qazvin when Cotton was appointed as the first Ambassador to Iran by King Charles I, though this was not with a view to establishing a permanent Embassy. In the event, Cotton's mission was very short-lived. He fell ill a few months after his arrival in Iran and died in Qazvin on 23 July 1628. It was to be a long while before another English Ambassador was appointed.

Although the Muscovy Company was the first English chartered

---

* All Europeans were called 'Franks' by the Iranians.

company to be granted trading privileges, it was the greatest of them all, the East India Company, that began to establish permanent posts along the Iranian coast in the Gulf, in return for military assistance to the Shah.

The Portuguese had also been active traders in the Gulf, but they incurred the Shah's enmity by their occupation of the port of Gambrun – renamed Bandar Abbas when it was recovered. In 1622, the Shah sought to capture the strategically important island of Hormuz, also held by the Portuguese. Lacking the sea power to do so, the Shah pressed the East India Company's ships to help, transporting Iranian troops who successfully drove away the Portuguese.

*　*　*

The East India Company, in return for the naval assistance they had given the Shah to take the port of Bandar Abbas, had been allowed to set up a trading station there. But its isolation, on the southern border of Iran by the Straits of Hormuz, and its climate led the Company to move their main headquarters in the Gulf to Basra (then in Ottoman territory, now Iraq). It also established a subsidiary base in the Iranian port of Bushehr, much further up the Gulf (almost opposite Kuwait), with better access to Shiraz, Isfahan and Tehran (Iran's capital from 1796). From 1778, Bushehr replaced Basra as the principal base for the Company's operations throughout the Gulf area.

Initially, the interests of the Company were commercial. But as the Company strengthened its hegemony over India, against both local rulers and the French, so its interests in Iran became political as well. The Afghans, the French and the Russians all viewed Iran as the back door into India. Keeping these three out of Iran then became a strategic imperative which dominated Britain's approach to Iran throughout the nineteenth century.

When, in 1798, the Afghans first tested this imperative, the die was cast. Britain's and Iran's interest had become indissolubly linked. They were to remain entwined for most of the next two centuries.

CHAPTER 5

THE BRITISH
MONOPOLIES THAT
TRIGGERED DEMOCRACY

*Mr Straw! The people of Iran do not have good memories [of] you and
the British regime ... You know better than us about the crimes and
ample plots that were orchestrated by your country against the people of
this Holy Land. We have not forgotten the 'Paris Treaty' and the separation of Afghanistan from Iran. The cunning contracts of D'Arcy, Talbot,
Reuters, Reji [and others] are still fresh in our history.*
BASIJ LEAFLET, 2015

The British national narrative deals overwhelmingly with victories. Defeats (of which there have been many) are shrugged
off (the American War of Independence, for one) or converted into
triumphs of the national will (Rorke's Drift, Dunkirk). Iran's national
narrative is different. It's much more about humiliations and defeats
at the hands of foreigners (the UK especially), which in turn fits
well with the profound sense of victimhood which is a key element
of Shi'ism.

The Treaty of Paris which the Yazd Basij remembered so well was
signed in 1857, between the UK and Iran, mediated by the French
Emperor Napoleon III. It marked the third attempt in less than
twenty years by the Iranians to take back the key western Afghan city
of Herat. It ended, as usual, in an inglorious withdrawal and defeat for

the Iranians when, in their eyes, all that they were seeking to do was to retake what was theirs.

Herat and its surrounding region was a bread basket, linked by geography, ethnicity and faith to the Khorasan province in the north-east corner of Iran. It was strategically placed on the key trade routes from China and India through Iran to the west and the north. It had close links with the holy Iranian city of Mashad, 230 miles away. For the first two centuries of the Safavid dynasty it had been firmly in Iranian hands. Most of its residents spoke a dialect of Persian.

As we have seen, around the beginning of the eighteenth century, Safavid power weakened. In consequence, Herat came under the control of the Afghans.

In 1798, the Afghan ruler Zaman Shah was threatening to move east to the rich lands of the Punjab (now in Pakistan and India). The Governor-General of India, Lord Wellesley, sent the East India Company's acting Resident in Bushehr to Tehran to 'persuade' the new Qajar Shah, Fath-Ali, to invade Herat, on Afghanistan's western border. When, not long afterwards, it seemed that Napoleon might invade India through Iran, Wellesley sent the same able young officer, Captain John Malcolm, with a large entourage to Tehran to encourage the Iranians to attack the Afghans, with promises of 'as many canons and war-like stores' as possible for the Iranians should the Afghans or the French invade them. By 1801, Malcolm had succeeded in negotiating two treaties with the Iranians: one commercial; the other political.*

For Iran, the greater preoccupation about its own territorial integrity was not France but Russia, its enormously powerful northern neighbour which had expansionist designs on the parts of the Iranian Empire in the southern Caucasus – Georgia, Armenia, Azerbaijan and Dagestan. When Britain's formal diplomatic relations with Iran in the modern era were established in 1800, the Iranians compared us favourably to the Russians, whom they regarded as brute aggressors. The

---

* Britain's first formal diplomatic envoy, Sir Harford Jones Brydges, was sent to Iran in 1807. He served until 1811, when Sir Gore Ouseley was appointed as Ambassador.

British, they felt, were shrewd, far-sighted and careful – but worrying too, given the scale of the military and naval forces at our command.

Whilst Britain's view at this stage was that we might encourage the Iranians to take over the west of Afghanistan against its ruler, Zaman Shah, this was the precise reverse of the policy we were to follow later in the century, when Britain severely punished the Iranians for trying to do exactly that. A draft treaty offered by Captain John Malcolm ran into the ground over British reluctance to guarantee sufficient funds to Iran in the event of foreign aggression.

The French, then riding high from their successes in the Napoleonic Wars, seized their chance, offering a frustrated Fath-Ali Shah a better deal in the 1807 Treaty of Finckenstein. This promised Iran the return of Georgia upon Napoleon's defeat of Russia – but also demanded that Iran expel all English from Iran, declare war on the UK, and order its subjects in Herat and Kandahar, still considered roughly speaking under Iran, to attack British possessions in India, whose north-west frontier was only the other side of Afghanistan.

Just two months after the Treaty of Finckenstein had been signed, Napoleon temporarily found a new ally in the Russian Tsar, with whom a new peace treaty was concluded. This was wholly contrary to the interests of Iran, who feared further domination by a Russia no longer fighting the French. The Iranians felt betrayed. They turned again to Britain and negotiated a new treaty – the Anglo-Persian Definitive Treaty of Defensive Alliance, finally ratified in 1814, six years after it had been negotiated.

For neither the first nor the last time, what Iran actually received from this deal with Britain was less than it had first appeared.

From 1804, Iran had been locked in a war with Russia in the southern Caucasus following Russia's annexation of what is now Georgia a few years before. Early successes by Iran in its wars with Russia were not sustained.

As Iran's losses mounted, the British began to make common cause with the Russians. After Napoleon's catastrophic retreat from Moscow over the winter of 1812–13, we had no wish to aggravate our rekindled alliance with Russia. The latter's victory had greatly strengthened its territorial ambitions in the southern Caucasus. Britain 'mediated' in the treaty negotiations which followed, arguing that if Iran continued fighting it could suffer a worse fate. But the deal was humiliatingly one-sided. Under the October 1813 Treaty of Gulistan, Iran had to cede to Russia much of its Caucasian territory north of the river Aras.

Thirteen years later, egged on by prominent Shi'a clerics (who were safely behind the front line), Iran engaged in yet another war with the Russians. This predictably ended in defeat for the Iranians. So abject were the losses that the British envoy, John Macdonald Kinneir, had to lend the Crown Prince some cash for his subsistence.

The British were of more positive help in the treaty negotiations which followed than they had been in 1813. Even so, in the Treaty of Turkmenchay, signed in February 1828, Iran lost its remaining territory north of the river Aras, in what is today Georgia, Armenia and Azerbaijan. With this, it lost about 10 per cent of its population (from a total of around 5 million), and significantly more in terms of its economy and government revenue. A war indemnity 'agreed' by the treaty was twice that of the Iranian government's total annual income. An eccentricity in an annexe to the treaty declared that the scarlet stockings and green slippers that the Iranian monarchy had demanded that all foreign envoys should wear in the royal presence would be replaced by galoshes. From a British perspective, it was thanks to its negotiating skill that Iran did not lose any more territory under this treaty. Iran's western and northern borders have remained intact ever since. Nonetheless, this treaty has been considered one of the most disastrous in Iranian history, and helps to explain some of the Iranians' mixed emotions towards the British. It is part of their contemporary political lexicon. For example, a headline in a Tehran newspaper in September 2018 sought to reassure readers by saying of a proposed agreement about the Caspian Sea that it was 'not Turkmenchay'.[1]

In the decade following the Treaty of Turkmenchay, the Qajar

Shahs turned their attention again to Herat. They tried to lay siege to the city in 1833 – against the strong advice of the British envoy – and made a more sustained attempt in 1838. Again, they ran up against the ire of the British, who were not willing to allow such a takeover, which would now adversely affect their strategic interests in Afghanistan. Diplomatic relations were broken off by Britain in the summer of 1838. A force from the British Indian Army was sent to occupy Kharg Island in the Persian Gulf, ready to invade the mainland if necessary. Relations were restored in 1842, but ten years later the Iranians were back fighting for Herat. Diplomatic relations were not severed this time, but Indian Army troops reoccupied Kharg Island until the adventure reached its by now predictable conclusion.

By 1856, Britain and its allies had been engaged in a bloody and costly war with the Russians over the Crimea for more than two years. There were also early indications of the instability and insurgency in India which were to lead, the following May, to what we know as the Indian Mutiny. This insurrection (known to the Indians as their first war of independence) was directed against the East India Company, which operated as a sovereign power on behalf of the UK. The new Shah of Iran, Naser al-Din Shah, who had succeeded in 1848 and was to last until assassinated in 1896, believed that Britain was likely to be too preoccupied in the Crimea and India to intervene again over Herat. He was wrong.

Herat fell to the Iranians in 1856. Even before this, Britain had issued a declaration of war against Iran, claiming that its action was in breach of the Herat Agreement signed with the British envoy after Iran's previous attempt on the city. This time, Britain sent a large force of around 5,000, which occupied Kharg Island and then moved to the mainland, where Iranian forces were routed in two key engagements. Iranian losses were significant; British and Indian Army ones slight.

The Treaty of Paris, signed in March 1857, marked the formal end of this conflict. Iran gave up all claims to Herat and elsewhere in the territory of Afghanistan, exactly as the Basij claimed in their leaflet.

They could have added, as a further example of British perfidy, that in 1879, Britain reversed the policy on which it had been so insistent for five decades and offered the Iranians the 'guardianship' of the city of Herat. The Iranians rejected this offer, partly under pressure from the Russians.

It was a separate clause in this treaty that helped greatly to expand Britain's influence on, and interference in, Iran, about which the Basij may also have been complaining.

It had long rankled with the British that the Russians had far more extensive trading and diplomatic rights in Iran than did we. Our trading position had been somewhat improved in 1841 by a treaty that allowed for the UK to establish Consuls responsible for commercial relations in Tabriz and Tehran. However, in the 1828 Treaty of Turkmenchay, the Russians had forced the Iranians to include provision allowing them to establish as many consular posts as they wished across Iran. By the 1857 Treaty of Paris, the UK extracted the same 'most favoured nation' treatment. In time (as discussed in more detail below), the number of British consular posts rose to twenty-three – an astonishing level of penetration for a country whose population in 1875 was only an estimated 5 million and had not reached 12 million by the end of the Qajar period in 1925.*

The same treaty also allowed Britain to establish, as Russia had already done, a 'capitulatory' system by which Britain exercised extraterritorial jurisdiction in criminal and civil matters over any British nationals, including Indian subjects of the Raj, ousting the control of the local Iranian courts. This was to become yet another source of understandable resentment by the many Iranians (as did similar provisions extracted to the east from the Chinese).

The Anglo-Persian War over Herat of 1856–57 was the last occasion

---

* This representation consisted of four Consulates-General, seven Consulates, eight Vice-Consulates and four consular agents. See Sir Denis Wright, *The English Amongst the Persians*, second edition (I. B. Tauris, 1977), p. 191.

in the nineteenth century when Britain took military action against Iran. By then, the Shah had come to understand that there was little point in attempting to use force of arms against the most powerful nation on earth, nor in engaging the great bear to their north, Russia. Instead, the governments of Iran sought to preserve the independence of their state, and wherever possible by playing Russia and Great Britain off against each other. They were successful in this first aim, if only nominally. Iran never went the way of so many nations in Asia and Africa and became a colony. But the price they paid for this supposed freedom was increasing interference in their internal affairs, with neither Britain nor Russia having any compunction whatever in demanding the removal of ministers whom they found inconvenient, and otherwise seeking to influence the conduct of government in their interests. For Russia and the UK, it was all part of the 'Great Game'. It was no game for the Iranians.

Both powers were helped by the decrepit state of Iran throughout the century. There were very few paved roads outside the centre of the main cities, which made journeys between the main centres of population long, tortuous and often unsafe – and in practice greatly reduced the authority of the central state.

Edward Granville Browne was a lecturer in Persian at Cambridge University, and is one of the few Britons still revered in Iran in an unqualified way, with a Tehran street named after him. He went to Iran in late 1887, and spent a year there writing a celebrated volume, *A Year Amongst the Persians*.[2] On his journey out, he had to travel from the north-west city of Tabriz to Tehran, a distance of about 390 miles. It took him seventeen days, by horse and by foot.

By this stage in the nineteenth century, India and Russia were running railway services over thousands of miles of track. Even the Ottoman Empire, to Iran's west, was operating a significant railway system. But, other than a six-mile track from Tehran to a shrine, Iran had no railways until the First World War, because of an arrangement between Russia and the UK which gave each power a veto over railway development in Iran.*

* * *

Naser al-Din had become Shah in 1848. He understood that without a railway system, and lacking much else, there was no chance of bringing industrial development and wider modernisation to his country. The Shah made three foreign tours, in 1873, 1878 and 1889. On these, he was apparently astonished by the difference between his own country and the modernity of Western Europe, not least the United Kingdom, where science and technology had been so successfully harnessed to make the UK both the workshop of the world and its superpower.

One of the Shah's problems was that although he knew, even before he left for his first tour, how much development his country needed, his country lacked the necessary resources. He concluded that it would only be by encouraging foreign investment that he could make the improvements required. He also calculated that if Britain had long-term investments in his country, this might strengthen their commitment to his country above its use as a pawn in the Great Game with Russia.

This approach by the Shah was, in the circumstances, understandable. But it led to the granting of the most extraordinary and rapacious business concessions, which have gone down in Iranian history as further evidence that foreigners, especially British, have only malign intentions for their country.

Thus the second charge by the Yazd Basij against Britain that 'the cunning contracts of D'Arcy, Talbot, Reuters, Reji etc. are still fresh in our history'. The Reuters concession was chronologically the first, in 1872. Talbot's tobacco concession came next, in 1890. William Knox

---

* It was not until Reza Khan became Shah in 1925 that a serious programme of railway building began. Even today, the legacy of the Anglo-Russian veto on railway development is clear. Tehran, with a population of nearly 9 million, has one railway station, about the size of London's smallest, Marylebone.

D'Arcy's oil concession, which led to the establishment of the Anglo-Persian Oil Company (APOC, later British Petroleum), was the third, in the early twentieth century. The latter is dealt with in the next chapter. I can find no reference to 'Reji', but it may have been a transliteration of 'Régie', referring to the tobacco concession.

*   *   *

Baron Julius de Reuter was a German-born Jew who had emigrated to the UK and had become a naturalised British citizen. It is said that he had purchased his title from a minor German principality.

Reuter's interest in Iran appears to have been prompted by the success of the Indo-European Telegraph Department, another subject that should certainly have been on the Yazd Basij's list. The Telegraph Department was, in turn, one of the consequences of the Indian Mutiny in 1857.

The mutiny cost 150,000 Indian lives and many thousands of British lives too. The scale of the uprising, though ultimately unsuccessful, sent shock waves through the British establishment. The East India Company was stripped of its governmental responsibilities, to be replaced by direct British rule. The need for swifter communications between the Raj and London now became urgent. Submarine cabling over any distance was unreliable, so the view was taken that the best route for a British–Indian telegraph connection was across Iran – a route of 1,250 miles. First, the Shah and his ministers had to be squared. There was a well-founded anxiety that a British-controlled communication system across the country could result in the UK having even more influence over Iran. There was also opposition from conservative clerics about the importation of any Western technology, and a worry – again well-founded – by the provincial authorities that the autonomy they enjoyed because internal communications were so poor would be undermined by the speedier instructions from Tehran that a telegraph system would facilitate.

Lengthy and difficult negotiations ensued. The Iranians were to gain valuable royalties, but under the usual veneer of Iranian involvement the British would be firmly in control. By the end of the 1860s, the lines across Iran were working, with repeater stations every sixty miles or so, staffed mainly by the British and Indians.* What Baron de Reuter spotted, before almost anyone else, was how the telegraph systems that were gradually spanning the globe, including between the UK and India, could be exploited by providing timely market-sensitive information, including general news. He linked up share information between the London and Paris stock exchanges, and was the first to bring the news of Abraham Lincoln's assassination to Europe in 1865. He made his fortune from the news agency that still bears his name.

It's a further mark of how underdeveloped was Iran that until the last quarter of the nineteenth century the country had no postal system of its own. (In contrast, Britain's postal service dates from 1660.) To fill this void, the extensive network of British telegraph stations, together with the expanding network of British consular posts across Iran, was used by Britain to run its own, relatively reliable, postal service within Iran – using Indian Post Office stamps with the head of Queen Victoria on them, an additional indignity for the Iranians trying vainly to assert their independence as a nation.

Even as late as 1919, the Foreign Office concluded that Britain's commercial interest in the telegraph across Iran was more important than the (British-owned) central bank, the Imperial Bank of Persia, or the Anglo-Persian Oil Company. Britain's control of Iran's telegraph system did not end until 1931. When it did, Sir Arnold Wilson, former British Commissioner in Baghdad, and later a manager with the Anglo-Iranian Oil Company, wrote in *The Times* that this 'episode ... reflects nothing but credit on the participants'.[3] That is not quite how the Iranians saw it.

---

* The reliability of the service was greatly enhanced when Siemens and Co., then a British–German company, established the Indo-European Telegraph Company to provide a more secure connection across southern Russia and Germany to the UK.

Reuter had become friendly with the Persian Minister (Ambassador) in London, General Hajü Mohsen Khan, who was seeking on behalf of his head of state to interest British entrepreneurs in investment opportunities in Iran. Khan found that established City grandees were not particularly keen. In Reuter, an outsider (because of his being both German and a Jew), he found an eager partner. With encouragement from Khan, and £200,000* in bribes to key figures in Tehran, including the then Prime Minister, Moshir al-Dowleh, Reuter secured the most breathtaking of concessions from the Shah. It was so astonishing in its breadth that even the arch-imperialist George Nathaniel, Viscount Curzon, declared the Reuter concession 'the most complete and extraordinary surrender of the entire industrial resources of a kingdom into foreign hands that has ever been dreamed of'.

Under the 1872 agreement, for an official down payment of £40,000[†] (a fifth of what he had spent in bribes), Reuter gained the monopoly right to build railways, tramways, canals, irrigation systems and most of the mines, and to develop all of the government's forests and all future industries for a period of seventy years. On top of this, Reuter was to be allowed to establish banks to issue Iranian banknotes, to change Iran's silver-backed currency to an internationally accepted gold standard at a future date, and to sell on any part of his monopoly when and to whom he pleased.

In return, apart from the measly down payment, Reuter was to pay 20 per cent of the net income from the railways and 15 per cent from all the other concessions. There was just one proviso – which in the event proved almost fatal to Reuter's schemes: that the construction of the proposed railway from Bushehr in the Persian Gulf to the Caspian had to begin within fifteen months of the start of the concession.

As news of this incredible arrangement emerged, along with suspicions that it could only have been negotiated by senior ministers if their concern for their nation's interests had been subordinated to

---

* £200,000 in 1870 would be worth approximately £23 million in today's money.
† Now worth about £4 million.

their own personal greed, the Shah had embarked on the first of the three official visits he was to make to Europe.

When the Shah got to St Petersburg, the Tsar explained that such a concession was completely unacceptable to Russia, because of the way it would unduly strengthen Britain's influence in Iran and give the UK direct access to the Caspian and to Russia itself.

When the Shah returned to Tehran, he found that resistance to the deal was at boiling point, both within his own court and amongst influential members of the clerical establishment. The Prime Minister, Moshir al-Dowleh (who personally had done so well from the negotiations), was formally dismissed. He was brought back shortly afterwards as Foreign Minister, with instructions to abrogate the concession. To do so, Moshir al-Dowleh latched onto the requirement in the agreement that the railway's construction had to be started within fifteen months. Since it was claimed that this had not happened, the Shah cancelled the agreement in November 1873. Once he had heard of the outcry against his concession, Reuter had in fact started a little work on the railway within the stipulated fifteen-month deadline. But this disingenuous gesture was not enough. The cancellation was confirmed and Reuter's demand for compensation rejected.

Reuter was down, but not out. In a master stroke, he threatened to sell his concession to the Russians. The Tsar's vocal opposition to the concession was not because it would place much of Iran's economy in the hands of a foreigner but because it would place much of Iran's economy in the hands of the wrong kind of foreigner – the British and not the Russians. The Shah continued to resist. The Foreign Office, which up to this point had distanced themselves from Reuter, now felt that they had to intervene. When a horde of racketeers and chancers from elsewhere in the West arrived in Tehran to obtain concessions offered by the Shah on other matters, the Foreign Office lodged vigorous protests that these had to be rejected as long as Iran had failed to honour the Reuter concession.

Reuter's obduracy, and his patience, paid off. In 1889, the Shah granted him another concession, not quite as generous as his original one, but still lucrative. The principal element was banking – not just any bank, but effectively Iran's central bank.

Reuter's Imperial Bank of Persia was allowed to establish branches across the country. It was granted a monopoly over the issue of bank-notes (previously Iran's currency had been in coinage alone), giving this British bank direct control over Iran's monetary policy. An initial share capital of £6 million* was issued on the London Stock Exchange, dwarfing the resources of Iran's domestic financial institutions. As collateral, Reuter was granted mining rights across Iran. These rights were sold off to a separate company, floated in London, with Viscount Curzon as one of its directors. This went bust four years later, when geology, and hostility from the local inhabitants, defeated those seek-ing a new Klondike in Iran.

The new bank did produce some benefits to the Iranian economy, facilitating trade and commerce across the nation and forcing down the interest payments previously charged by the *bazaaris*. The *bazaaris* were the businessmen based in Iran's main bazaars. They served as moneylenders and traders as well as shopkeepers and were a powerful political lobby with strong links to the clerical establishment.

Despite some of the practical benefits from the Imperial Bank's establishment, it was nonetheless widely seen as 'an agent of British imperialism, and with reason'.[4] It was criticised by Iranian nation-alists, who objected profoundly to having the nation's central bank owned and controlled from London. It was claimed that the bank often discriminated against Persians in giving credit, and that it did not employ locals as managers.[†]

In these endeavours, Reuter was greatly assisted by Sir Henry

---

* Now worth about £750 million.
† Under Reza Shah, who ruled between 1925 and 1941, the bank's position was rapidly eroded. It lost its facility to issue Iranian banknotes in 1933. In 1952, during the premiership of Mohammad Mossadegh, who was violently hostile to Britain and its policy towards his country, the bank abandoned Iran, renaming itself the Bank of the Middle East (later incorporated into HSBC), though it returned in 1958, remaining there until the Islamic Revolution.

Drummond Wolff, the British Minister (Ambassador), who had been appointed in 1887. Wolff was extraordinarily well-connected. He had started as a clerk in the Foreign Office, but before he went to Tehran, he had had experience as a financier and had served for ten years as a Conservative Member of Parliament.* He was a friend of Lord Salisbury, who combined the roles of Prime Minister and Foreign Secretary at the time, and well acquainted with Reuter and many other City figures.

Wolff was dangerously impetuous, driven by a short-sighted desire to extend Britain's commercial involvement in Iran with little regard for the consequences for Britain's wider reputation and influence, or for the Iranian people themselves – a concern about which he evinced not a flicker of interest.

*   *   *

Ironically, Wolff's most abiding legacy is in his unwitting contribution to the radicalisation of the Iranian clergy. He helped lay the foundations which ninety years later culminated in the Islamic Revolution.

Wolff's successor, Sir Frank Lascelles, reportedly confided in the French Ambassador to Tehran that the rise of *ulema*, the clerics, as a powerful political force in Iran was 'the heritage of the baneful influence of Sir Drummond Wolff. This man thinks only of making a noise and fame for himself.'⁵

The trigger was yet another exclusive monopoly offered to a well-connected Briton, the second listed in the Basij charge sheet against me, and this time over the production, distribution, domestic sale and export of tobacco.

The earlier concession to Reuter had undoubtedly been extraordinary in its scope and had aroused intense opposition from Iran's elite because it so offended their sense of national dignity. But its fact was

---

*   For Christchurch from 1874 to 1880 and for Portsmouth from 1880 to 1885.

distant for the vast majority of the Iranian public, who were unaffected by it in their personal lives.

Tobacco was different. In the nineteenth century in Iran, as across the world, smoking tobacco was seen as an innocent pleasure. No evidence was available about its effects on people's health. The climate in Iran was such that the country was able to grow all the tobacco it consumed, and export large quantities too.[6] Major production centred in the north-west and the south-west of the country. Thousands depended on the industry for their livelihood. Virtually all adults in the country – women and men – smoked. Removing control of the totality of the chain of production from thousands of Iranians to a single foreigner was asking for trouble.

Major Gerald Talbot was a friend of Wolff from his City days and a distant cousin of Lord Salisbury. With Wolff's help, Talbot secured an audience with the Shah. Lubricated by some personal 'down payments' (bribes) of £25,000 to the Shah and £15,000 to the Prime Minister,* the arrangement was agreed on 8 March 1890. The Shah was later to claim, in a panicky letter to his heir apparent, and to the *ulema*, that he had had to grant the concession, along with that for the Imperial Bank of Persia, in order to annul the original Reuter concession. But it is hard to see how a concession to Talbot, an unrelated third party, though friends with Reuter, could possibly have offset Reuter's claims, which in any event had already been satisfied by the establishment of his Imperial Bank.

The terms of the agreement with Talbot were just as disadvantageous to Iran as the Reuter concession, if not more so. The Iranian exchequer would receive £15,000 per year in 'rent', plus a quarter of the profits. The concessionaires knew that they were on to a good thing. They boasted about it in the prospectus they issued in London for the 'Imperial Tobacco Company of Persia'. The Régie, as it was known (after the French for a state-controlled company), had taken

---

* Now worth about £3.1 million and £1.8 million respectively.

'advantage … of the experience gained in the working and administration of the Turkish Tobacco Régie'. The latter had paid £630,000
to the Turkish (Ottoman) government, whereas the Persian Régie
would be paying 'only £15,000'. Net annual profits from the Iranian
concession to be remitted to the Company in London were estimated
precisely at £371,875[*] – a more than 50 per cent annual return on the
capital invested of £600,000.

'To sum up, the Régie has a very brilliant future before it,' extolled
Talbot. 'It will realise large profits from the beginning; and all the
parties interested, such as the Government, your Company, the consumers and the growers, will certainly find their share in the profits.'

'Thus everybody was to be happy and pleased,' Edward Browne
acidly commented, 'except the wicked Persian tobacco-vendors who,
"with the small capital they possess" were apparently regarded as un-
worthy of serious consideration.'[7]

Every wise politician with a care for their own survival knows that
the 'losers' in any policy change always feel their loss far more intensely than the 'winners' appreciate their gain. What is taken away is real
and present; what may be given in the future is more abstract.

The tobacco vendors were one, fairly large, group who would be
directly worsted by the Régie. But there were thousands of others
who feared a loss of income and position from the new arrangements.
The disingenuous words from Talbot about how much the ordinary
growers and the nation would benefit were dismissed as no more than
cynical guff, especially once the boasts in the London prospectus
about the return on capital and how little the Régie was to pay to
the Iranian government were translated and published in unofficial
newspapers and leaflets distributed across Iran.

But there was a larger objection to the Persian Régie than its adverse material effect on indigenous Iranian growers, distributors and
consumers. The tobacco that was smoked would be rendered impure

---

[*]   Approximately £46 million in today's money.

by passing through the hands of Christian infidel. It was *haram* – forbidden.

It might be thought that by this time the British had learnt something from the Indian Mutiny about cultural and religious differences. This mutiny had in part been provoked by the issue of cartridges for the new Enfield rifle which required the soldier to bite the end to release the powder. The cartridges were pre-greased, with tallow made from beef fat (highly offensive to Hindus) and pork fat (equally offensive to Muslims). Britain had in the end been able to crush this mutiny, but at huge cost of lives lost and property destroyed.

However, so blinded were the avaricious Britons involved in the tobacco concession, and those in the Iranian court who had been so handsomely bribed to agree to this conceit, that they missed the enormity of the risks they were taking by the complete expropriation of Iran's tobacco industry.

The Shah and his entourage had been nervous about the concession from the start. Initially, they kept it confidential. But details quickly leaked once the Imperial Tobacco Company began to establish itself in Tehran in early 1891.

Into this already toxic situation now stepped Sayyid Jamāl al-Dīn al-Afghānī. Afghānī was a peripatetic thinker and brilliant propagandist who was born a Shi'a in Iran but claimed to be an Afghan Sunni. He had lived in the Indian Raj and had a profound antipathy to Britain because, it was said, of his experiences there. His preoccupation was to secure independence from foreign domination of Muslim states. He was much more a radical reformer than he was a devout follower of the faith. However, as E. G. Browne explains,

> advanced reformers [like Afghānī] were willing to put their own liberal, freethinking or heretical notions into the background ... to achieve an active alliance with the *ulema* leaders against the government. Afghānī and others recognised that only the *ulema* were powerful and influential enough to lead a successful mass movement ...

and that the use of religious language and appeal was necessary to move the masses.[8]

In early 1891, Afghānī issued a lengthy public letter addressed to Mirza Hasan Shirazi, who was recognised throughout the Shi'a world as the *marja-e taqlid*, the source of universal emulation. He was the most senior cleric, the chief *mujtahid* of the two key shrine cities of Karbala and Najaf in southern Iraq. The letter was couched in religious tones – 'an invocation to the spirit of Islamic law'. In paragraph after paragraph, it spelt out the reasons why the Shah should be deposed. The Shah, said the letter, 'has sold to the foes of our faith the greater part of Persian lands and the profits accruing therefrom, to wit the mines, the roads connecting them to the frontiers of the country ... and the gardens and fields surrounding them'.

It added, 'Also the river Karun and the gardens and meadows which adjoin it' – an inclusion apparently provoked by a boast of Prime Minister Lord Salisbury[9] about the benefits to British business of yet another concession, this time the opening to foreigners of Iran's only navigable river, the Karun (which runs from the Gulf near Abadan through Ahvaz to the Zagros mountains, 590 miles to the north). The Shah, added Afghānī, had

similarly disposed of the grapes used for making wine ... likewise soap, candles and sugar and the factories connected therewith. Also the tobacco, with the chief centres of cultivation, the land on which it is grown, and dwellings of the custodians, carriers and sellers wherever these are found.

Lastly there is the Bank [Imperial Bank of Persia] ... It means the complete handing over of the reins of the government to the enemy of Islam [i.e. the United Kingdom] ... Then he [the Shah] offered what was left to Russia ... but they turned up their nose at this offer ... for they are bent on the annexation of Khorasan and the occupation of Azerbaijan and Mazandaran.

Afghānī's conclusion was that the Shah should go. 'He is incapable of governing the land, or of managing the affairs of his people.'[10]

Protests of increasing intensity raged across the country against the Régie from the end of 1890, especially in the main tobacco-growing areas, in the north-west around Tabriz and in the south-west around Isfahan and Shiraz. The Russians hugely enjoyed the discomfort of the British and did all in their power to fan the flames of the discontent. But they were not remotely the cause of the uprisings, which were sparked by the outrageous terms of the Régie itself.

The Shah's reaction was typical of this vacillating incompetent. He swerved between inadequate, complicated 'modifications' of the concession – which, far from assuaging the concerns of the protesters, simply aroused them to further outcry – and brutal repression. In early November 1891, for example, a local revolt in Kelardasht, Mazandaran province, near the Caspian Sea, and led by a local Sayyid (descendant of the Holy Prophet), was put down with 200 of the protesters killed.

Mahatma Gandhi's non-violent approach to fighting servitude has rightly been celebrated across the world. But much less is known about a similar tactic adopted thirty years before Gandhi by the leading clerics in Iran. This was brilliantly simple in its form – and brilliantly successful. It was a *fatwa* banning the use of tobacco in any form until the Régie was cancelled.

There had been local boycotts of tobacco, called by clerics, especially in the Shiraz area, once the tobacco monopoly had been made public. But in December 1891, in what Edward Browne describes as a 'master-stroke', the chief *mujtahid* of the Shi'a, Mirza Hasan Shirazi, issued his very short *fatwa*, which simply said, 'In the name of God, the Merciful, the Forgiving. Today the use of … tobacco in any form is reckoned as war against the Imam of the age (may God hasten his glad Advent!).'

As mentioned earlier, when the telegraph across Iran had first been mooted in the late 1860s, many clerics had objected, not only on the grounds that it was another British project but also because they regarded it as an infidel instrument of 'modernisation' which could undermine their authority and the proper observance of the Shi'a faith.

Two decades later, the clerics took full advantage of the telegraph's facilities. The *fatwa* was widely and quickly distributed across Iran. Amazingly, given the highly addictive nature of tobacco, the ban was almost universally observed. The country simply stopped smoking. The Régie's market disappeared, and with it any chance that the shareholders of the Imperial Tobacco Company of Persia could gain any return.

In early January 1892, in ambiguously worded telegrams, the Shah appeared to give in to the protesters and agree their demand that he should withdraw the concession. But the clerics and their vast following wanted clarity. They refused to lift the *fatwa* until a firm decision was forthcoming.

In exasperation, the Shah did something which in today's climate seems utterly extraordinary. He ordered chief cleric, the *mujtahid*, of Iran, Hajji Mirza Hasan-i-Ashtiani, either to set an example and start smoking again or to go into exile. Hasan-i-Ashtiani refused to do either. The Shah's order provoked increased demonstrations outside his palace, leading to further bloodshed and turmoil.

The Shah continued to haver for three more weeks. Finally, the directors of the Imperial Tobacco Company of Persia bowed to the inevitable and issued their own statement declaring that their concession was at an end.

With that, on 26 January 1892, the *fatwa* was withdrawn. The Iranian people started smoking again. Victory, total and complete, was the clerics' and their millions of followers'. Politics in Iran would never be the same again. The clerics had tasted power.

*   *   *

In his weighty history of Iran, the American-Iranian historian Abbas Amanat challenges this view of the extent of the clerics' involvement. He claims that interventions by the clerics were far less common and far more anecdotal than some modern apologists for the authority of the *ulema* versus the Qajar state would like us to believe ... The few [clerics] who did protest the government's action, such as during the Régie Protest of 1891 and 1892 ... did so at the urging of political activists and only briefly and on specific issues.[11]

It is correct that on the whole the clerical establishment continued to support the monarchy in Iran. For example, thirty-four years later, they successfully opposed Reza Khan's initial proposal to create a republic, and instead had him crowned as Shah. Some key clerics supported the *coup d'état* that led to the fall of Prime Minister Mohammad Mossadegh in 1953, strengthening the Shah's rule.[*] However, Amanat's central argument, downplaying the significance of the *ulema* in the tobacco protests and their assumption of significant political involvement, which dates at least from this time, seems at variance with the facts. As we will see, the clerics' political role was fundamental to the success of the 1906 Constitutional Revolution, and to agitation in the 1960s and 1970s against Mohammad Reza Shah, which culminated in 1979 with his flight from Iran and the foundation of the Islamic Republic of Iran.

Drummond Wolff suffered a nervous breakdown whilst the tobacco protests were beginning and had to be sent home. The pieces were picked up initially by his deputy, Robert Kennedy, and then by his replacement as Minister, Sir Frank Lascelles, in 1891. One of Lascelles's first duties was to negotiate compensation terms for Talbot and his shareholders. The latter had hoped for huge compensation for their prospective loss of profit, but they were persuaded otherwise by Lascelles and in the end settled for a single payment of £500,000. There was a further twist, adding to the Shah's humiliation and the contempt in which he was held by his subjects. The Shah's exchequer

---

[*]   For example, Ayatollah Abul-Qasim Kashani, see Chapter 9.

was broke, so the compensation monies had to be borrowed – from Reuter's Imperial Bank of Persia. The interest set at 6 per cent per annum required annual payments of £30,000; the capital had to be repaid after forty years. The loan was secured on the customs of the Persian Gulf. 'All this', commented Edward Browne, 'for the enrichment of a few greedy English speculators and a handful of traitorous Persian courtiers and ministers!'[12]

The damage from Drummond Wolff's folly was lasting. Britain's reputation with the Iranian people was thereafter always stained, and its influence with the Iranian elite severely reduced for almost a decade. It was inadvertently rescued by the Russians. Savouring their power as the pre-eminent foreign nation in Iran, they overreached themselves, just as we had before.

The Shah himself was assassinated four years later, shot on 1 May 1896 by Mirza Reza Kermani, an acolyte of Afghānī. The Shah had presided over an increasingly introspective and self-serving court. There were virtually none of the improvements in living conditions, industrialisation and urban development that had begun to take place in similar territories, including Turkey and southern Russia. No railways, few paved roads, no gas or electricity supplies, and what little 'improvement' there had been was in the hands of the infidel, including steamers on the Karun River, the telegraph and the central (British-owned) bank.

The new Shah, Muzaffar al-Din Shah, was crowned in early June 1896 and served until his death on 4 January 1907. He was different from his father, the previous Shah, and apparently disliked unpopularity or cruelty (though his regime displayed both). But he was equally ineffective, and the situation in Iran went from bad to worse. In 1900, he had to obtain the first of two large loans from the Russian government, of £2.4 million, followed by one of around £1 million two years later. Some of the proceeds of the first loan were used to pay off the Talbot loan owed to the Imperial Bank, so that Iran was then only indebted to Russia and not to the UK as well.

Much of the money raised was spent by the Shah on two European tours, allegedly to improve his health. On the second of these, in 1902, the Shah visited the UK. Britain, recovering from the costs and political turmoil of the Boer War, was anxious to impress the Shah, with the aim of restoring its influence in Iran.

There then began a pantomime over the award to the Shah of the Order of the Garter, one of the highest honours of the British Crown. His father had been given the Order by Queen Victoria, as had the Turkish Sultan. Muzaffar al-Din Shah had been promised the same by the British Minister in Tehran, Sir Arthur Hardinge. But the new monarch, Edward VII, claimed, against all the evidence, that the Order was reserved for those of the Christian faith alone.

Various consolation prizes were offered the Shah, including the Order of the Bath and a miniature of the King set in a diamond-studded frame. He refused them all, and returned to Tehran in high dudgeon.

Arthur Balfour, the British Prime Minister, anxious that this slight could turn the Shah towards Russia, eventually persuaded the King to climb down. In 1903, a special envoy, Lord Downe, was despatched to Tehran to invest the Shah with his Order of the Garter. What ordinary Iranians would have made of this saga is anyone's guess. In the meantime, conditions in the country continued to deteriorate, boiling over just two years later.

CHAPTER 6

HOW OIL TRUMPED DEMOCRACY

We have not forgotten how you spun the Constitutional Revolution of Iran and in doing so produced a dictator who listened to your orders.

We have not forgotten that for years you had your tentacles engaged in Iran's natural resources, in particular stealing and looting Iran's oil.
TWO MORE CHARGES FROM THE BASIJ LEAFLET

The Qajar dynasty finally collapsed in the first quarter of the twentieth century, though the seeds of its demise had been sown decades before, during the long and dismal reign of Naser al-Din. Things came to a head with the Constitutional Revolution of 1906, which, in turn, had been in part prompted by the popular uprisings the year before in Russia, across Iran's porous north-west border.

Tsar Nicholas II was no less a dictator than were the Iranian Shahs. But his country was more tied into the Western financial and economic system, was more advanced industrially, and had a much larger educated middle class. A contraction of the European money markets in 1899–1900 led to a prolonged economic crisis in Russia. Various lukewarm 'reforms' by the Tsar served only to raise the people's expectations of further changes, which the Tsar was unwilling to concede.

A policy of 'Russification', favouring true-born Russians, alienated the many ethnic minorities living within the Russian Empire, including many Muslims in the southern Caucasus (as well as the Poles, Finns and Ukrainians). In Russian provinces like Azerbaijan, which had been part of the Iranian Empire until the early nineteenth century, there were strong religious, linguistic and cultural ties with Iranians living south of the border. Thousands went on strike in this area, including in Baku, in 1902 and 1903, with the revolutionary leader Rosa Luxemburg claiming that the region was 'aflame'.

In 1904, Russia embarked on perhaps the most disastrous military conflict in its history: the Russo-Japanese War, which culminated in June 1905 in the sinking by the Japanese of virtually the entire Russian Baltic fleet, which had been sent halfway round the world by the Tsar to seal Russia's victory.

By late 1905, civil unrest, strikes and mutinies meant that Russia was in a state of near revolution. The October Manifesto demanded widespread reform, including the establishment of civil rights, free political parties, universal suffrage and an elected Parliament, the Duma.

Although the 1905 revolution was ultimately crushed by the Tsar, he did concede the establishment of the Duma. The uprisings in Russia enhanced the confidence of Iranians who were weary of their country's condition and increasingly angry at the excesses of the Shah and his court.

The Belgians, at the time close allies of the Russians, had ingratiated themselves with the Shah to be appointed to take control of Iranian customs. A Monsieur Naus had been appointed in 1903, initially as Director of Customs. He very soon took on four other senior positions, as Minister for Posts and Telegraphs, High Treasurer, Head of the Passport Department, and Member of the Supreme Council of State.

An authoritarian and unpopular man, the Aynu'd-Dawla, was appointed as Prime Minister, reportedly benefiting (as had his predecessor) from the new Belgian-led customs arrangements. Tariffs were raised and more strictly enforced.

In this imbroglio, it was scarcely surprising that unrest soon began to break out in many of Iran's major urban centres, led by *bazaaris* and other merchants, whose livelihood had been badly affected by the new measures, and supported by some senior clerics. M. Naus, already a target of considerable hatred, added to that discontent and earnt the enmity of the clerical establishment by having himself photographed dressed as a mullah.

The unrest was treated with contempt and repression by the Shah and his Prime Minister.

'*Bast*', or sanctuary, was a long-standing right of Iranians, a counterbalance to the capricious and arbitrary rule of successive Shahs, whose 'law' was, roughly speaking, whatever they said it was at the time. *Bast* could be taken in mosques, or more safely in foreign legations (Embassies), regarded as inviolable foreign territory where the writ of the Shah did not apply.

In 1905, a number of protesters took *bast* in the Royal Mosque in Tehran. At this stage, their demands were limited to the removal of the unpleasant Aynu'd-Dawla as Prime Minister; they later added demands for a 'House of Justice' (a precursor to a Parliament) composed of representatives of the clergy, merchants and landed proprietors, to be headed by the Shah; and to make all the Shah's subjects equal in the eyes of the law.

The Shah responded to these demands by agreeing to them in principle – but failed to implement them. Worse, he claimed that the proposals for a 'House of Justice' had been misunderstood and that all he had agreed to was the institution of a court of law.

The despotism continued. There were shootings of demonstrators, and the infliction on some of the more senior protesters of a particularly sadistic punishment, the 'bastinadoing', or beating on the soles of the feet.

In the middle of June 1906, Grant Duff, the British chargé, reported to London that 300 people, including some Qajar princes, had taken *bast* in the British Consulate in Shiraz and were refusing to leave until the Iranian government resolved their grievances.

'The Mollahs [*sic*] of Tehran are now united against the Grand Vizier [Prime Minister] and are clamouring for reform,' Duff reported to London. He continued that Tehran was in an unsatisfactory state. In Seistan, a plague was raging.

> Luristan, Kurdistan, parts of Azerbaijan and Arabistan may be said to be in a state of chronic rebellion. Such Government as can be said to exist emanates from the Sovereign, without whose assent even the most trivial orders cannot be issued … The orders of the central Government are only obeyed when it happens to suit the convenience of the provincial authorities … The Treasury is empty, [and] most officials and a large proportion of the army have received no pay for months.[1]

The final trigger was the shooting dead of a Sayyid (a descendant of the Holy Prophet Muhammad) who had been protesting the forced exile from Tehran of one of the protest's leaders. The Sayyid's body was paraded through the streets. The bazaars, closed out of respect to the Sayyid, were ordered by the Shah to be opened – or face their looting by his soldiers.

As befitted its global position, Britain's diplomatic premises in Tehran projected its power. The main compound, known as Ferdowsi, was a large, walled twelve-acre site. Outside what were then the city limits, in the cooler northern hills above the capital, was Gholhak, an even larger compound of fifty acres, to which the British legation decamped each summer.

On 19 July, a deputation of merchants and bankers went to see Grant Duff in Gholhak to ask if a group of protesters would be allowed to stay should they take *bast* in the main British compound in Ferdowsi. Duff agreed.

His telegram to the Foreign Secretary, Sir Edward Grey, the following day simply reported that some fifty merchants and Mullahs had 'taken asylum in the British Legation … complaining of oppression'.

Numbers rose rapidly: Duff reported 700 on 21 July, 2,000 in the morning of 24 July and 5,000 that evening. On 25 July, Grey agreed that the legation could hardly turn out this number of protesters; it was a matter for the Iranian government to resolve.

Five days later, on 30 July, there were 12,000 protesters in the compound, and 14,000 three days later – but, said Duff, the 'refugees' had been very orderly. Their demands included the establishment of courts of justice; a National Assembly (Majlis); the return 'with all honours' of those clerics exiled to the holy city of Qom; pensions for the relatives of protesters who had been killed; and a guarantee by the British that they would ensure that the Shah's promises were fulfilled.

On 15 August, the Shah conceded all the protesters' demands, including the removal of the detested Prime Minister. 'I hope before the end of the week to get rid of the remaining refuges,' reported a by now slightly exasperated Grant Duff, adding drolly that 'the members of the Persian Foreign Office, including the head of the British Department, have meanwhile gone on strike'.[2]

The first ever constitution for Iran was approved and the new Majlis was accordingly opened, with members of the clerical establishment in pride of place, emphasising the key role they had played to secure this, the first ever constitution for Iran. Duff reported triumphantly that 'British prestige has been immensely increased' by its role in hosting the *bast* and by helping to persuade the Shah to accept the protesters' demands.[3]

The initial promulgation of the 'Fundamental Laws' of Iran was agreed at the end of December 1906, when the new constitution was based, it was said, on the Belgian constitution. That constitution had been drafted in 1831 on the formation of Belgium and was itself a balanced synthesis of the French and Dutch constitutions and of English constitutional law. To today's eyes, it's boilerplate. In 1906, its provisions in Iran were worthy of the adjective 'revolutionary'. If it was 'Belgian' in most of its text, it was also peculiarly Iranian, and Shi'a too.

An addition to the 1906 constitution made the following year dictated that 'at no time may any legal enactment of [the Majlis] … be at variance with the sacred principles of Islam', and that this article shall continue unchanged until the reappearance from his occultation of the twelfth imam.[4] To enforce this law, a special committee of five *mujtahids* or 'other devout theologians' was to be established. Although, in practice, this committee never met, and appeared to have been forgotten after 1910, its provision illustrated a fundamental tension as representative government began to develop, in the polity of Iran, about how to reconcile allegiance to the laws of God with those made by humankind for the provision of democracy and human rights. (As we will see, there is a similar, though more powerful, provision in the 1979 constitution. There, the drafters sought to resolve this tension, but did so uneasily, with the inevitable consequences now so patent of separate centres of power within what is supposed to be a single system of governance.)

In his telegram reporting on the outcome of the protests, the British chargé, Grant Duff, added that the 'Russian Legation [are] making active efforts to induce the Shah to upset the recently granted constitution'.

By its role in granting *bast* and acting as something of a midwife for the new constitutional arrangements, Britain had greatly enhanced its standing with the Iranian people. But Britain then negligently damaged its own reputation, and the prospects of the constitutional settlement bedding down, by a crude deal with the Russians which inflamed the sensibilities of Iranians of every shade of opinion.

The debacle of Russia's defeat in its war with Japan weakened not only the Tsar's regime internally but also its projection internationally of its influence. As the Tsar moved from concession to suppression to deal with the 1905 rebellion, the last thing he wanted was government of the people, by the people breaking out on his southern border.

Britain's position was much more ambiguous. Empire was always about money and power, and was ultimately enforced down the barrel of a gun. When Britain itself was governed by an undemocratic oligopoly, no huge issue of principle arose when it sought to replace one form of such government, of local monarchs and notables, by another, its own. However, in the latter half of the nineteenth century, as democratic government began to develop in Britain with the extension of the franchise to most adult males, those in favour of our imperial adventure knew that there was a question they could not duck for ever.

This was that if our constitutional monarchy, with its checks and balances, the rule of law, independent courts and a free press, was good enough for Britain, why should it be denied to those over whom Britain exercised power, whether directly within the empire or in those nominally independent countries where it nonetheless held great sway?

Rudyard Kipling's 1899 poem 'The White Man's Burden' provided an answer (albeit, from today's perspective, an unacceptable one), arguing that where the indigenous subjects were not white, the West could plausibly claim that by empire they were 'bringing civilisation' to uneducated peoples who lacked a written language and little known history. Kipling wrote the poem about the indigenous peoples of the Philippines. But it was more difficult to make this case with civilisations much older than our own, including Egypt, India and Iran. British diplomats might, and did, routinely refer to the Iranians as 'natives', but Iran had had an empire centuries before the Romans moved into England; their language, like ours, was Indo-European; and there was that clue in what they called themselves – 'Iranian', meaning 'Aryan', just like us. Moreover, there was a practical complication. For very clear strategic reasons, we wanted an independent and stable Iran. The Qajar dynasty had increasingly shown itself incompetent to deliver that objective.

As we have seen, when the Constitutional Revolution broke out, Britain began well. It was aided in that by two factors. One was that Russia was on the opposing side, seeking to ventriloquise the reactionaries' resistance to any reform. The cancellation of the Talbot tobacco concession was a humiliation for Britain, as were the two Russian loans (part used to pay off Talbot's compensation). As Grant Duff never tired of saying, Britain's stature had been improved immeasurably by its role in providing sanctuary to the leaders and the 14,000 protesters behind the Constitutional Revolution, without which they would not have succeeded.[*]

The other factor was the personality of Muzaffar al-Din Shah, hopeless in many ways, but more accommodating and less inclined to authorise violence than his father – or his son. The Shah was, however, in poor health when the protests broke out in the summer of 1906. He issued his *firman*, or Royal Declaration, initiating the drafting of the constitution; he attended the formal opening of the Majlis; and he signed the first version of the Fundamental Laws on 30 December 1906. But he died just five days later, on 4 January 1907.

Though his son, the Crown Prince, had also applied his seal under his father's signature to the Fundamental Laws of the new constitution, his approach differed markedly from his father's. As Crown Prince he had had his own 'capital', in Tabriz, where he had already made himself unpopular by the savagery with which he had put down unrest. As Mohammad Ali Shah, he was profoundly hostile to the new constitution, which by definition constrained his caprice and the availability of funds. He manifested this displeasure by failing to invite any members of the Majlis to his coronation.

Nonetheless, the Majlis began its work with a will. Their first decision was to refuse to sanction a fresh loan to Iran of £400,000 to be split evenly from Russia and the UK. The Majlis went on to insist, successfully, that the Belgian Director of Customs, M. Naus, be dismissed; that the Shah's Civil List be fixed; that irregular profits be banned, especially those from the farming of taxes; and that a National Bank be established. Its members were assiduous in their complaints

---

[*] Britain's role in the Constitutional Revolution continues to be recorded in photographs displayed in the Majlis.

about ballot stuffing and other irregularities in the conduct of the elections for the provincial members of the Majlis.

Provisional agreement on a joint loan from Russia and the UK to the Shah was by no means the only subject under discussion between these two powers. From 1905, when Russia had suffered its abject defeat at the hands of the Japanese, it had been seeking a rapprochement with the UK, especially in respect of Asian territories – Tibet, Afghanistan and Iran – in which it had had common, if conflicting, interests for decades with the UK. For its part, after the Boer Wars, Britain wanted to avoid another expensive military engagement. Whilst it continued to be exercised about the prospect of a Russian invasion of India, the UK calculated that a diplomatic understanding with Russia was a better, and much less costly, alternative to the stationing of thousands more troops on the north-west frontier of the Raj. Thus, an agreement with Russia appeared to make a great deal of sense.

After two years of negotiation, the Anglo-Russian Agreement was concluded on 31 August 1907. It was full of warm words. Indeed, a naïve Iranian (if such existed) might have been forgiven for believing that the only motive of these two European powers was the welfare and happiness of the Iranian people. The British Minister, Sir Cecil Spring-Rice, sought to explain in syrupy language the view of Foreign Secretary Sir Edward Grey that had the antagonism between Russia and the UK been prolonged, 'suspicion would have arisen on one side or both that the other was interfering in the internal affairs of Persia to prevent its rival from profiting'. He then quoted with approval the words of Alexander Isvolsky, the Russian Foreign Minister, that 'neither of the two Powers demands anything of Persia, so that Persia can devote all her energies to the settlement of her internal affairs'. How considerate.

The Iranians were not, however, reassured by these protestations of selflessness, and for very good reasons. They had never been officially informed of the negotiations over the agreement, still less consulted about its terms. They learnt of its existence only after it was signed. In essence, the agreement carved up Iran between the two powers, with something left for Iran in the middle.

Accompanying the agreement was a map of Iran, showing the country in three sections. A large northern segment, including Tehran, Tabriz and Mashad, was within the 'Russian sphere of influence'; a smaller segment, covering the area from Bandar Abbas on the Persian Gulf to Iran's border with Herat, was the 'British sphere of influence', thus protecting its Indian empire. The section in the centre of the country was labelled 'Neutral'.

It was impossible for any sane Iranian to conclude anything but that Russia and the UK had indeed decided to settle their differences over Iran, not by withdrawing their interference in that country's internal affairs but by better coordinating that interference, to mutual advantage. Many Iranians, Browne commented, might

> assert that Great Britain's real object was to prevent the spread of constitutional ideas in Asia, for fear of the influence they might exert on India and Egypt, to keep Persia weak and distracted, and to maintain in their present deserted and depopulated condition those [south-eastern] provinces of Persia which lay nearest to her Indian frontier.[5]

The Times excused Britain's position by asserting that Iran's condition was 'a signal example of the inability of Orientals to assimilate the principle of self-government'.[6]

Britain's prestige within Iran following the Constitutional Revolution was shattered.

As the new Shah was hardening his opposition to the new constitution, and to the Parliament it had spawned, so Britain came off the fence over whether the 'spread of constitutional ideas' was a good idea or not.

* * *

The first crisis in relations between the Shah and the Majlis was in the closing months of 1907. He imprisoned the moderate Prime Minister and in all likelihood would have had him summarily executed had the British legation not intervened and secured his release.

As explained in Chapter 1, *zur khanehs* – or 'houses of strength' – are a long-standing institution in Iran. They are large gymnasia with circular pits in which men train with huge weights. These houses of strength have provided a large corps of extremely strong men, groups of whom have played a significant role in decisive acts of street politics (as we shall see in relation to the 1953 coup). So it was that in December 1907 the Shah hired some of these men, and a variety of other thugs, to rough up members of the Majlis and to wreck its proceedings. In the event, members of the Majlis, aided by radical clerics, were able to gather a much larger crowd, some of whom were armed, to protect the Parliament. The stand-off forced the Shah to give way and to dismiss some of his most reactionary courtiers.

This truce did not last long. There was an attempted assassination on the Shah in February 1908 and a bombing the next day. At the end of May, the Shah demanded that opposition newspapers, and some charismatic orators, should cease to speak against him. There were counter-demands by the Majlis.

The Russians, deeply alarmed by the rising unrest in the capital, decided to deliver an ultimatum to the government. The message was that there were elements threatening the life of the Shah or seeking to depose him. If that were to happen, Russia would be bound militarily to intervene. The Russian Ambassador added that such action by Russia would come with 'the approval and sanction of England'. This was initially dismissed as a 'fairy-tale' but was indeed true. The British chargé, a Mr Marling, had accompanied the Russian diplomat and had endorsed his remarks.

In June 1908, frightened for his position and emboldened by this ultimatum, the Shah established martial law. He made a series of demands on the Majlis, the effect of which would have been completely to neuter the institution. Crowds gathered within the Majlis and the surrounding area to try to protect it. Troops were sent in by the Shah. These included a large contingent of the Persian Cossacks, the best-trained troops in Iran, which had Russian officers and which were ultimately under Russian control.

The Parliament building, the Baharistan, and an adjacent mosque in which Majlis members and their supporters had sought shelter were then shelled and reduced to ruins. Some key leaders of this nationalist movement were summarily executed. Far from this repression leading to a wholesale defeat of the nationalist and progressive forces in Iran, along with their clerical allies, the Shah's actions only made these forces more determined than ever to regain what they had achieved in the 1906 revolution. Uprisings, close to civil war, broke out across the country, including in Rasht, Lar and Isfahan. There was an appalling siege of Tabriz, one key centre of opposition to the Shah. Russian troops entered north-eastern Iran, and a British gunboat and a small contingent of troops were sent to the southern ports of Bandar Abbas and Bushehr, ostensibly to protect British subjects and other foreigners there.

As this bloody struggle continued, two nationalist 'armies', one from the north and one from the south, began to converge on Tehran. There was intense fighting when they reached the city, with at least 500 killed. Efforts by Russian and British diplomats to seek some kind of accommodation between the nationalists and the Shah failed dismally because of the intense distrust towards the latter. The nationalist forces closed in. On 16 July 1909, in a delicious twist of fate, it was now the Shah himself who sought *bast*, in the Russian diplomatic compound, from where he had to accept that he would now be deposed. This was formally determined by the Majlis later that day. His successor was to be his twelve-year-old son, the Crown Prince, who succeeded to the throne on 18 July 1909 as Sultan Ahmad Shah, with the head of the Qajar family, Azudu'l-Mulk, as regent.

The nationalists, back in power, sought to bring stability to the country, ravaged by a breakdown in the civil order and close to bankruptcy. They were more successful than many of their detractors had hoped. They abolished class representation in the Majlis; created five new seats for the minorities (Armenians got two seats; Jews, Zoroastrians and Assyrians one each); improved the electoral system with a reduction in the dominance of Tehran; and lowered the voting age from twenty-five to twenty.

But the nationalists' policies threatened the deeply entrenched interests of most of the nobility and major landowners. By 1912, the reactionaries were back in the ascendancy, aided by Russia and the UK. The two powers' preoccupation with their own interests far outweighed their empty words in the 1907 agreement about supporting Iran's independent development. Twenty thousand Russian troops had landed in the north and occupied virtually the whole of Russia's 'sphere of influence'. Substantial contingents of the British Indian Army landed in the Gulf and moved up to Shiraz, ostensibly in the 'neutral' zone, and to Isfahan in the Russian zone. Gone was any pretence that Britain sought to nurture the seeds of representative and democratic government. The Basij were broadly correct in their claim that Britain had 'produced a dictator who listened to [our] orders'.

*　　*　　*

In the monumental struggle for representative government in Iran and its immediate aftermath, the one word that was absent from the nationalists' rhetoric was 'oil'. Within a few years, however, oil was to dominate and to define Iran's relationship with the outside world.

Since time immemorial, oil had been seeping out of the ground on the Aspheron Peninsula, protruding into the Caspian Sea near Baku. Until the early nineteenth century, this area – contemporary Azerbaijan – was part of the Iranian Empire. This, in pre-Islamic Iran, was the region of the Zoroastrians, the religion that venerated fire. Maintaining their 'eternal pillars of fire' was easy enough when gases coming out of the ground with the oil seepages could be lit, and kept alight for ever.

Oil seepages had also occurred for centuries in parts of Iran, where the tar was used for the caulking of boats and for brick-making. Baron Julius de Reuter's notorious concessions had included the right to prospect for oil and develop an oil industry, but, as we have seen, these came to nothing, as the concessions had to be withdrawn in the face of overwhelming internal opposition.

One of the more eccentric foreign concessions Shah Naser al-Din had granted was in 1895, at the behest of his personal physician, Dr Joseph Désiré Tholozan, a Frenchman. This arrangement gave France exclusive rights to undertake archaeological excavations in any part of Iran.* The excavations were directed by Jacques de Morgan, who had already conducted extensive geological as well as archaeological missions across many regions of Iran.†

During his work, de Morgan had identified many oil seepages in Iran and was convinced from this that there were oil reserves in Iran suitable for exploitation. In 1900, the Shah, Muzaffar al-Din, duly sent an emissary, General Antoine Kitabgi, to Paris, to seek out entrepreneurs willing and able to invest in Iran in return for a suitable concession.

Kitabgi, together with de Morgan, and a former Reuter's agent from Iran, Edouard Cotte, linked up in Paris with the incorrigible Henry Drummond Wolff, who it must be assumed travelled there for this purpose. In return for a handsome commission, Wolff was asked to nominate a businessman to take on this concession.

Wolff alighted on the exotically named William Knox D'Arcy. D'Arcy, born in Devon, had early in his career emigrated to Australia.

---

* Tholozan served the Shah from 1858. He died in 1897 in Tehran, aged seventy-six. The circumstances of his death were unclear, and there have been suggestions that this could have been the
  result of poisoning ordered by the new Shah, Muzaffar al-Din.
† I am indebted to Prof. Roger Matthews, Professor of Archaeology in the University of Reading,
  for providing me with details of this concession. The concession was terminated by Reza Khan
  in 1927.

There, he qualified as a lawyer, but his main interest was in making a fortune. This he did by leading a syndicate which took over an old, and apparently exhausted, gold mine, which yielded much more of the world's most precious metal. He returned to England a very wealthy man, indulged his passion for horse-racing and sought out other opportunities to make money.

D'Arcy took a punt on the Iranian oil concession. He sent out his own representative to Tehran in early 1901.

For Britain, the prize of a major oil concession in Iran was clear. It was concerned about the increasing dominance of the burgeoning oil market by John D. Rockefeller's Standard Oil and wanted other British players in addition to Shell and Burmah Oil. For equal and opposite reasons, the Russians quickly spotted the potential benefits to the UK of any concession. They protested loud and long to the Shah about the prospect of him granting so favourable a deal to their rivals.

But a month after D'Arcy's representative had arrived in Tehran, assisted greatly by the British Minister, Sir Arthur Hardinge, and lubricated by a bribe of £5,000 direct to the Shah, an agreement was signed on 28 May 1901. It was on half-sheets of foolscap paper, pasted together, one side in Persian, the other in French (the lingua franca of diplomatic agreements). Under the agreement, the Shah was to receive £20,000 in cash, £20,000 worth of shares and 16 per cent of the 'annual net profits' – a term which was ill-defined and was later to become a major bone of contention between the UK and Iran. In return, D'Arcy received a sixty-year concession covering three-quarters of the country (wisely excluding the provinces nearest Russia).

It took another seven years for the D'Arcy Petroleum Company's trial drillings to yield any profitable results. D'Arcy had been advised that it would cost just £20,000 to drill a couple of wells. Within four years he had spent £200,000. He very nearly went bust.

Salvation came from the British Admiralty. In 1904, they cajoled the ascetic and hard-bitten Glaswegian directors of Burmah Oil to make D'Arcy's company a subsidiary. Burmah was promised government

79

contracts and the protection of its interests in India in return. The company was renamed the Anglo-Persian Oil Company (APOC).*

Exploration was shifted from the centre of Iran's border with Iraq to the south-west, the 'Plain of Oil', near a fire temple, Masjid-e-Suleiman. In 1908, seven long years after the concession had been agreed with the Shah, oil in commercially exploitable reserves was found. The area was controlled by the Bakhtiari clan, a powerful tribal confederacy, largely a law unto themselves, remote from Tehran. It was they who had to be squared in the usual way – bribery. In the end, this worked. Roads and a 140-mile pipeline were put in. Abadan, an island in the Shatt al-Arab, at the northern end of the Persian Gulf, was chosen as the site for the refinery.

The project continued, however, to leech money. Again, the British Admiralty stepped in, this time not as midwife but as the company's new owner.

The Royal Navy had gradually started using oil, rather than coal, for its smaller boats, but the huge battleships on which Britain's imperial power and reach depended still used coal. As competition with Germany over the size of their respective navies built up, so the argument intensified within the British government that these ships should use oil, for the additional speed its engines could generate and the greater ease with which oil rather than coal could be moved around.

But there was a major obstacle to this strategy. Coal was available in almost unlimited quantities from British mines. Oil had to come a long way, from abroad. How did Britain, with the prospect of a war looming, ensure secure supplies?

Iranian oil was the answer.

All Royal Navy ships were forthwith to be run on oil. But further security was required. In June 1914, just two months before war

---

* Later it was renamed the Anglo-Iranian Oil Company (AIOC) and then, in 1954, British Petroleum. Despite its name, the latter had originally been owned by the German Deutsche Bank and was a downstream distributor of Romanian oil. It had been taken over as enemy property at the start of the First World War and later transferred to the AIOC. See Chapter 10.

was declared, First Lord of the Admiralty Winston Churchill gained Parliament's agreement to nationalise the Anglo-Iranian Oil Company – or as near as made no difference. Under the Anglo-Persian Oil Company (Acquisition of Capital) Act 1914, the British government acquired 51 per cent of the share capital, in return for an investment of £2.2 million (about £250 million in today's prices). Two government-appointed directors were put on the board, with the right to exercise a veto over government matters, but not over commercial ones.

At a stroke, it was the British government which now had a direct, vested interest in Iran's oil. This was reinforced by a separate, secret agreement which not only provided the British Admiralty with a twenty-year contract for fuel oil, at guaranteed prices, but also gave them a share of the company's profits – to be taken out before the Shah was to receive his 16 per cent cut.

These arrangements, hugely advantageous to Britain, were to dog the country's relationship with Iran for decades to come. The 2015 Yazd Basij leaflet had charged that 'for years you had your tentacles engaged in Iran's natural resources, in particular stealing and looting Iran's oil'. Whether Britain's investment in exploiting Iran's oil reserves was 'stealing and looting' depends on one's standpoint; I certainly understand why this view is so strongly held in Iran. British exploitation of Iran's natural resources, and the concomitant political influence which Britain believed it had to exercise to protect its interests, came to strike deeply at Iranians' sense of national pride.

*　　*　　*

A British diplomat from the Indian Civil Service, Sir Clarmont Skrine, spent both world wars in Iran, endeavouring to enhance Britain's war effort. In his autobiography, published in 1962, he spoke of his mounting contempt for the 'Gang' – the 'oligarchy of wealthy landlords, merchants, entrepreneurs and dishonest officials who batten on the country's economy', and of how the scales gradually fell from his eyes about Britain's role. The conditions he found in Iran, said Skrine, were worse than anything he had left behind him in India apart from in a few princely states.[7]

Of the 1907 Anglo-Russian Agreement, he wrote:

> Never was a nation's goodwill so unnecessarily and uselessly thrown away in pursuit of a will-o'-the-wisp ... The Persians were convinced that Britain's talk about safeguarding their independence was mere hypocrisy. And there was worse to come. In 1915 ... a fresh agreement with Russia was negotiated (but not published) ... The whole neutral zone was ... brought into our sphere of influence. Small wonder that every Persian, save the small minority who stood to gain by our friendship, hailed the Germans and their allies as their deliverers from the Russian menace, and that Britain became Public Enemy Number Two.[8]

The decade before the First World War had been one of hope raised – through the Constitutional Revolution – then dashed as the Shah and that 'Gang' had sought increasingly to regain the autocratic power they had lost. That period looked relatively benign compared to the catastrophe which befell Iran during the war – and for which Britain took much of the blame.

Iran was formally neutral in the war, but that did not mean that it was able to keep out of it. Lacking a defence force large and well-equipped enough to take on any of the belligerent nations, almost the whole of Iran became a war zone. The Ottoman armies battled the Russians in the north. Russian forces were ultimately to move across Iran to Mashad in the far east, to Qom and Hamadan, and almost to Tehran. British (mainly Indian Army) forces moved in large numbers to occupy the south and south-west, not least to protect Britain's crucial oilfields and its refinery. To add to its troops from India, Britain formed the South Persian Rifles, a force of about 10,000 men recruited mainly from local pro-British tribes, with British officers.

The Germans were active too, including with highly organised covert operations in, for example, Shiraz, to undermine Britain's position. Britain and Russia used the pretext that there could be a German-organised coup to justify the extraordinary power both now exercised over the country. The government of Iran and the Majlis were rendered all but impotent. There were twelve changes of government in the four years of the war, none better than its predecessor.

The Bolshevik Revolution in Russia in October 1917 took Russia out of the war, and in many ways saved Iran from partition between Russia and Britain. Once the Treaty of Brest-Litovsk was signed in March 1918 between the Bolsheviks and the German and Ottoman governments, the secret 1915 agreement between Russia and the UK was denounced by the new Bolshevik administration. This did not, however, bring tranquillity to Iran.

The decrepitude of the Qajar dynasty, by now in its death throes, left many parts of the country prey to banditry. Towards the end of the war, a famine ravaged the country, caused by drought, mismanagement of water resources, and the purchase (or sometimes theft) of available food by Russian and British armies. The already weakened population was then even more vulnerable to the next catastrophe it had to face – epidemics of cholera and the Spanish flu, killing millions across the globe. In countries like Iran, with no public health service and little understanding of how to deal with such diseases, the effects were truly terrible. Reliable estimates of the total casualties from the war, famines and disease in this period are not available, but a plausible estimate is that around one in nine of the Iranian population lost their lives during the war and in its immediate aftermath.

Fate, ill luck and a useless government may have been amongst the causes of these disasters. But, unsurprisingly, given the vast areas it controlled, Britain was blamed by many for exacerbating the famine and doing nothing about the epidemics. In a country where dark conspiracy theories rapidly take hold (and with good reason), there were some who believed that Britain had deliberately set out to starve the populace into submission, though there is no evidence to support this.

The First World War was supposed to be the war to end all wars. US President Woodrow Wilson, who tried to set the agenda for the post-war Paris Peace Conference with his famous 'fourteen points', had declared, 'National aspirations must be respected; people may now be dominated and governed only by their own consent. "Self-determination" is not a mere phrase; it is an imperative principle of action.'[9]

The Iranians took Wilson at his word. They sought the restoration of territory which had once been within the Iranian Empire, including Turkish Kurdistan, part of the Caucasus south of Baku, and about 15,000 square miles in what is now Uzbekistan, north of Iran's Khorasan province. More realistically, they asked for compensation for the losses they had suffered during the war through military occupation; above all, they wanted recognition as an independent state.

The Iranians got none of this. They were not even allowed into the chamber of the Paris Peace Conference to present their grievances. An Egyptian nationalist delegation had been allowed in, but manoeuvring by the United Kingdom delegation, on the entirely spurious grounds that Iran had not been a party to the war, was used to prevent their delegates from presenting their case. When the Iranian delegate, Mushavim-el-Mamaulik, then tried to go to London to protest, he was refused entry to the UK. The Iranian humiliation was complete.

The man who refused Iran admission to the peace conference, and its delegate admission to the UK, was the acting Foreign Secretary,[*] George Nathaniel, Viscount Curzon – who, as the Balliol rhyme about him went, was 'a most superior person'. Curzon had spent some months in Iran in 1891, producing a large volume, *Persia and the Persian Question*. With his six-year experience as Viceroy of India, his regard for himself as an expert on all matters Oriental was matched only by his conviction that almost all his colleagues were ignoramuses.

---

[*] In early 1919, Curzon was made acting Foreign Secretary in the absence of Arthur Balfour at the Paris Peace Conference. He formally assumed the post in late 1919.

Curzon's belief was that self-determination for Iran would be a disaster (for Iran, as well as, of course, for Britain). What he wanted, and on paper secured, was

> some arrangement with the Persian Government by which British interests in that part of the world should be safeguarded in future from a recurrence of the recent shocks, and by which Persia, incurably feeble and unable to stand by herself, should be given support that would enable her to maintain her position among the independent nations of the world.[10]

The Anglo-Persian Agreement of August 1919 was negotiated in secret with Sultan Ahmad Shah, and three of his senior ministers. The Shah had been bought off the year before, with agreement to pay him a monthly stipend of 15,000 tumans (about £325,000 today). This was on condition that the Shah would appoint the Anglophile Vossugh al-Dowleh as Prime Minister and two Qajar princes, Firouz Mirza and Akbar Mirza, as senior ministers.

Vossugh al-Dowleh and his two colleagues proved very expensive. Curzon bleated that their demands were 'not merely exorbitant but corrupt' – and duly paid up. (Or, rather the British taxpayer did, from secret funds.) The three of them shared the inducement of £133,000 (around £7 million today), paid direct to them, together with a shrewdly anticipated promise that if necessary the UK would give the three asylum.[11]

With the usual opening weasel words about the absolute respect the United Kingdom had for the 'independence and integrity' of Iran, the agreement provided for the British government to supply financial advisers to Iran's Treasury and military officers to reorganise its army, as well as providing munitions and other materiel. There would be 'advice' on a new customs tariff and assistance with planning new roads and railways, on unspecified routes (not least because for the Iranians the first priority was a rail link from the Caspian via Tehran to the Gulf, whereas for the UK the imperative was to connect up the Baghdad railway system in British-mandated Iraq with Tehran). All the 'advice' and 'assistance' would be paid by Iran. In return (if that's the word), Iran was to receive a loan of £2 million (about £100 million today) at 7 per cent interest, paid from customs revenues.

However prosaic the individual terms of this agreement might have seemed, its intention was to make Iran a British protectorate in all but name. The UK would effectively control its finances, its public administration and its military, and have first refusal on potentially lucrative civil engineering projects for road and rail. Other countries – especially Bolshevik Russia – would be pushed out, and those 'incurably feeble' Iranian people would have even less influence over how they were governed than before.

The agreement could not possibly be kept secret, and nor could the bribes that went with it.* Curzon and the British Minister in Tehran, Sir Percy Cox, had failed to understand that aside from those who objected on principle to another subjugation to an imperial power, there were quite a number of others who were furious that they had not been bribed too. Once this all became public, there was a huge furore.

Curzon had also overlooked one detail about the way in which the Iranian system worked. This may have appeared trivial to him, but it was fundamental to the Iranians. Any such agreement had to be ratified by the Majlis.

There was no prospect of this happening with the existing Majlis. New elections were then called by the Prime Minister, Vossugh al-Dowleh. These were, according to J. M. Balfour, one of the UK's financial advisers in Tehran, 'accompanied by every circumstance of fraud, intimidation, and corruption in which according to local belief, the British legation was concerned'.[12]

---

* One of the three ministers tried to persuade the chief manager of the Imperial Bank of Persia to make false entries in the bank's books to disguise the bribes. See Geoffrey Jones, *Banking and Empire in Iran, Volume 1: The History of the British Bank of the Middle East* (Cambridge University Press, 1986), p. 191.

But there was still a high risk of rejection by the Majlis, so the Prime Minister marked time. Vossugh al-Dowleh and his two collaborators were dubbed 'the robber princes' by their critics, and faced increasing hostility for their role in negotiating the agreement and in making themselves rich in the process. Anxious about the public mood, the Shah dismissed Vossugh al-Dowleh and his government in June 1920.

The agreement had been negotiated at a time when, along with Britain's substantial presence in the south to protect its oil interests, and in the Gulf, British forces were still in the Caucasus and north Iran, a British flotilla was patrolling the Caspian Sea, and it looked as though the White Russian General Anton Denikin might crush the Bolsheviks. However, when Denikin was defeated by the Bolsheviks, everything changed.

Britain could, at considerable expense, have decided vastly to increase its land forces in north Iran. But Iran was already costing the British Exchequer an eye-watering £30 million a year (about £1.5 billion today) on military and diplomatic 'assistance' (including those twenty-three British diplomatic posts). After the ravages of the war, Britain had neither the resources nor the will to spend so much, nor to risk so much blood in Iran, when there were many other more pressing priorities in Ireland, India and Egypt.

Winston Churchill, then Secretary of State for War, shared Curzon's love of empire, but he had nothing but contempt for Curzon the man. Curzon, he said, 'sow[ed] gratitude and resentment along his path with equally lavish hands'. He wrote a withering letter to Curzon in May 1920, in which he said:

> There is something to be said for making peace with the Bolsheviks. There is also something to be said for making war upon them. There is nothing to be said for a policy of doing all we can to help to strengthen them, to add to their influence and prestige, to weaken those who are fighting against them, and at the same time leaving weak British forces tethered in dangerous places [Iran], where they

can be easily and suddenly overwhelmed ... I must absolutely decline to continue to share responsibility for a policy of mere bluff.[13]

Churchill had shown great percipience. A small British garrison in
Enzeli, on the Caspian, was forced to surrender in late May 1920. The
control of the Caspian passed to the Bolsheviks, and, as J. M. Balfour
later wrote, 'British military prestige received such a set-back that [no]
Persian Minister could thereafter have secured confirmation of the
Agreement'.[14] After much argument amongst ministers in London,
the last British forces in northern Iran withdrew in the spring of 1921.
Britain's prized possessions in Iran, the oilfields, and the refinery at
Abadan, could continue to be protected by the South Persian Rifles,
with reinforcements from India when necessary.

Curzon had to accept defeat, but he blamed everyone but himself
for his debacle. The list included his ignorant Cabinet colleagues and
the new British Minister in Tehran, Herman Norman. Norman had
taken over in 1920 from the egregious Sir Percy Cox, who had helped
negotiate the agreement, and he received no thanks from Curzon for
telling him the truth of what the Iranians thought of his neo-protec-
torate for Iran. Curzon's ire was in particular directed to the Iranians
themselves, at the Majlis, 'the desperate and colossal incapacity of the
Shah' and the 'incomparable, incurable, and inconceivable rottenness
of Persian politicians'.[15] He would not consider another agreement
with the Iranians 'unless they came on their knees ... and probably not
then'. With that conceit, and the total absence of self-knowledge for
which he was notorious, Curzon then declared that he had 'devoted
more years of labour in the last 31 years to the cause of Persian integrity
and freedom than most other people have devoted days or hours'.[16]

Curzon had not, however, been wrong about the Shah. In early
1921, Norman telegraphed Curzon to tell him that the 'Shah, mad
with fear, is dead to shame and inaccessible to reason'.[17] It would be
just a few weeks before the Shah lost power, and only a few years
before he lost his throne. Britain had a hand in that, too.

CHAPTER 7

SERGEANT TO SHAH –
WITH BRITISH HELP

I fancy that everybody thinks that I engineered the coup d'état.
I suppose I did, strictly speaking.
MAJOR-GENERAL SIR EDMUND IRONSIDE,
BRITISH COMMANDER OF NORPERFORCE, 1920–21[1]

Norperforce – or the North Persian Force – was what was left of British forces in Iran by 1920. Stationed at Qazvin, its purpose was not so much to protect Britain's oil interests hundreds of miles south as to prevent Bolshevik aggression and guard the back door to the British Indian Raj.

Command of Norperforce in late October 1920 was in the hands of Major-General Sir Edmund Ironside. Ironside was a distinguished soldier who served in the Boer War and both world wars, rising to Chief of the Imperial General Staff in 1939. He had great presence, at 6 feet 4 inches tall and seventeen stone. He also had an extraordinary facility for languages: he could speak fourteen, with complete fluency in five and passable Persian and Urdu.

Despite the surrender of British forces at Enzeli in May 1920, Britain still had 6,000 troops in northern Iran. Ironside was warned by his superiors in Baghdad that he would find things in Iran 'in some disorder'. He was told that he could not be given a military policy because there had been no instructions from London. His main task was to prevent the Bolsheviks from 'reaching the Persian plateau'. His role was later extended to reorganising the Persian Cossack Brigade.

This brigade had been formed in 1879 by Naser al-Din Shah, and was modelled on the Russian Cossacks. Its senior officers were all seconded from the Imperial Russian Army – an arrangement which had ensured that Russia was able to enhance its power and influence within Iran. The brigade was by far the most effective and well-organised military unit available to the Shah. It had played a crucial role in June 1908 in the temporary defeat of the nationalists and in shelling the Majlis building to the ground. By the middle of the First World War, there were about 8,000 men in the brigade. Once the Bolsheviks had seized control in the 1917 Russian Revolution, some of the officers of the Persian Cossack Brigade left to join the White Russians.

Ironside judged that whatever the feelings of the Russian officers who remained with the brigade, their leadership would run counter to British interests. They were 'incompetent and treacherous men'. The British Minister, Herman Norman, added that the presence of White Russian officers in the brigade exposed the Shah, and Britain, to the charge that we were plotting against the new Soviet government, which made the risk of retaliation much higher.

Ironside established a comprehensive wire-tapping operation which confirmed his suspicions about the Russian officers, who were intent on lobbying the Shah to 'get rid of us as soon as he could'. When the orders from the Russian commander of the brigade, one Vsevolod Starosselsky, were transmitted by telegram to his officers, Ironside's wire-tappers were able not only to intercept the signals but to change them. Starosselsky had wanted a group of them to go to the north of Qazvin, but they all ended up being given orders, apparently from him, to go to a different place, a camp at Aga Baba – where British troops were waiting to detain them.[2]

The Shah was persuaded to dismiss Starosselsky and to order all Russian officers and men to be removed from the brigade and leave the country. When Starosselsky then issued further orders to his remaining officers, these too were altered by the wire-tappers. They and Starosselsky fell into Ironside's trap and were taken into custody.[3]

Ironside set about reshaping the brigade, which he said was in a 'pitiable condition', with inadequate equipment, poor clothing and many suffering with cold and fever. The key question was who amongst the Iranian officers had the capacity to command. 'The weak point lay ... in [these] senior ranks ... who had never been allowed to take any responsibility on their shoulders' – decisions having been entirely in the hands of the Russian officers.

> Gradually Colonel Smythe [British liaison officer] and I found our attention being drawn to the work of the Tabriz *otryad* or troop ... The men were cheery and contented. Their Captain was a man of well over six feet in height with broad shoulders and a most distinguished-looking face. His hooked nose and sparkling eye gave him a look of animation which was unexpected ... His name was Reza Khan. Thus gradually came to notice the man who was to affect the fate of his country so greatly ... We decided to make him Commander of the Cossack Brigade at least temporarily, and at once.[4]

Reza Khan came from a poor family in the Mazandaran province of Iran, on the southern shore of the Caspian Sea. Born in 1878, he joined the Persian Cossacks at sixteen as a private soldier. He rose to become a gunnery sergeant, then a lieutenant. He was a captain by the time he was spotted by Ironside – and promptly promoted first to lieutenant-colonel, later to brigadier.

At this stage after the war, Iran was in a terrible condition. There was near anarchy in many parts. By early January 1921, such was the anxiety in Tehran that the British legation advised all European women, children and 'dispensable men' to evacuate as soon as possible. Anti-British feeling rose, assisted by the cack-handed policy of the (British-owned) Imperial Bank of Persia to restrict the sale of European credits to Europeans alone, whilst 'they were absolutely refused to Persians'.[5]

The Shah was close to a nervous collapse. Norman had telegraphed Curzon to say that the Shah

> asserted that he had incurred much unpopularity by identifying himself with our policy and taking my advice. We were now withdrawing our support [our troops] from Persia, which could not continue to exist as a nation without it. He did not complain of our change of policy … but if he were caught by the Bolsheviks, who would come here as soon as British troops left, he would inevitably lose his life. On the other hand, he would fare no better if he fell into the hands of Bakhtiari.[6]

Under continuing pressure from Curzon, the Shah was still trying to resurrect the Anglo-Persian Agreement, though in truth it had been dead for many months. A new Cabinet took over on 3 February. Since this wanted formally to drop the agreement, and was unwilling to convene the Majlis to endorse it, the ever-vacillating Shah forced its resignation three days later. The previous Cabinet was then reinstated. This lasted two days – and meanwhile forty deputies of the Majlis issued a petition against the agreement. Another administration was formed on 16 February. 'By the evening of 20 February,' the British financial adviser J. M. Balfour recorded, 'the situation could not be described as anything but desperate.'[7]

During the months in 1920 and early 1921 that he was commanding Norperforce, Ironside made regular visits to check on the Persian Cossacks, whose morale, equipment and training had hugely improved since he had taken a grip on the situation, expelled the Russian officers and installed Reza Khan as their commander. In one of his last meetings with Khan, in January 1921, Ironside sought two promises in anticipation of Britain's withdrawal of its troops. The first was that the Cossacks did not take any action against British troops as they left the country. The second, he wrote, was that 'I also asked him not to take or allow to be taken any violent measures to depose the Shah. To both these requests he gave me his solemn promise.'

Ironside continues in his diary that Reza Khan

talked very openly to me, expressing his dislike of politicians who controlled the Majlis for their own benefit ... He seemed a strong and fearless man who had his country's good at heart. Persia needed a leader in the difficult times ahead, and here was undoubtedly a man of outstanding value.

Ironside then went to Tehran to pay his respects to the Shah (whom he regarded as 'lazy and timorous, always frightened for his life'). At this meeting, the Shah 'presented a pathetic picture of defeat'. As Ironside was wondering how to bring the audience to an end, the Shah offered him effusive thanks and promptly invested him with one of Iran's highest honours, the Order of the Lion and the Sun. It is more likely that the Shah would have offered Ironside tea laced with poison if he had realised both what Ironside really thought about him and what he had advised Reza Khan to do about it. The undertaking Ironside had sought from Reza Khan was about not deposing the Shah himself 'by violent measures'; neither Ironside nor Khan saw this restraint as extending to the removal of the Shah's incompetent ministers.

Ironside left Iran on 16 February. In the final entry in his diary, he asked himself, 'Would the Shah have the sense to put his trust in this man [Reza Khan]?'[8]

The Shah would not have long to wait before being presented with that choice, which turned out to be no choice at all.

Five days later, on 21 February 1921, Tehran woke to the sound of artillery fire, to discover that 'the Qazvin and Hamadan detachments of Cossack brigade, numbering 2,500 to 3,000 men with eight field guns and eighteen machine guns, under command of Col Reza Khan marched from Kazvin [*sic*] to Tehran and entered the town 21 Feb shortly after midnight'.[9] The Cossacks quickly took control of the city. A coup was in progress.

Reza Khan was head of the military operation for this coup, but he was not its political head. That position was taken by Sayyid Zia al-Din Tabataba'i, described as a 'fiery young political activist known for his pro-British sentiments ... [and] about the only Iranian journalist who consistently advocated the ratification of the Anglo-Persian Agreement' in his newspaper. This association with the UK did Zia no harm, though others with similar views were not so lucky.

The plotters, led by Khan and Zia, moved swiftly, following the playbook of all successful coups. The telegraph and telephone systems were blocked and key roads cordoned off, whilst leading Bolshevik agitators and senior figures of the *ancien régime* were promptly arrested. Amongst the latter was Firouz Mirza, one of the three ministers who had taken British bribes to secure his support for the Anglo-Persian Agreement.

A little difficulty, however, then arose as to what to do with the prisoners who had been implicated in the former administrations. As Balfour put it:

> As many of those arrested were protégés of the British Government, which had already begun to interfere on their behalf, this would have brought about an awkward situation for the new Government, which was strongly Anglophile. Thus, as a result of its lurid past, the Foreign Office was at the very beginning thrown into a position of potential opposition to the only government in Persia which showed a desire for genuine reform.[10]

To avoid this complication, the prisoners were released on promises that they would reimburse the state the sums they had purloined from it. Balfour claims that this was a 'cardinal error'. They all should have been incarcerated a long way from the capital. As it was, the new regime faced the 'inveterate hostility' of some of the most powerful men in the country, who stayed in Tehran to form a 'centre of intrigue'.

Inveterate hostility or not, the Shah was quickly 'persuaded' by Reza Khan, Zia and the British Minister, Norman, to recognise the inevitable and to appoint Zia as his new Prime Minister. He moved swiftly to stabilise the situation in the country and to normalise its external relations, especially with the Soviet Union, with whom it agreed a new Treaty of Friendship on 26 February, just five days after the coup.

The day before the treaty was signed, Zia had told Norman that the 'Anglo-Persian Agreement must be denounced. Without such denunciation the new Government cannot get to work ... [This] implies no hostility to Great Britain.'

*　*　*

How far was Britain instrumental in this coup? Firouz Mirza, who had so benefited from British bribes, now moved from an Anglophile to a dedicated Anglophobe as a result of his incarceration, and claimed vociferously that the coup had been organised by the British legation. Like so much else about Britain's role in Iran, that quickly became the indelible truth for most Iranians.

Balfour, on the spot, had a different view. The coup, he wrote, 'appears to have originated by chance rather than by design ... One thing I believe ... with absolute certainty ... the movement was not engineered either by or with the knowledge of the British Legation.'

My own view, from the sparse available sources, is that the truth lies somewhere in between. There is no evidence that Curzon, the Foreign Secretary, knew anything about the coup. He blocked Norman's request for assistance to the new government, saying, 'I have not the slightest feeling for a Government which simultaneously denounces and fawns'[11] – and which, he might have added, had finally buried his dream to create a 'chain of vassal states stretching from the Mediterranean to the Pamirs [eastern Tajikistan]'.[12]

There is nothing in the published Foreign Office records that implicates Norman or his colleagues in Tehran. But his relations with Curzon were strained – for being the messenger who had brought the bad news that Curzon's plan would never fly. For that transgression, Curzon was to recall Norman and force him into early retirement, without the usual knighthood which every other British Minister in Tehran had received in the final fifty years of the Qajar dynasty.

The absence of incriminating telegrams from Tehran to the Foreign Office may not, however, be the whole story. Abbas Amanat, in his *Modern History of Iran*, claims that 'Norman endorsed Sayyid Zia's plan to stage a coup and subsequently form a national government – perhaps without the Foreign Office's prior knowledge and support',[13] and that Zia had become a 'more viable choice to head the semi-clandestine Iron Committee, a quasi-revolutionary party financed by the British legation to foster popular anti-Bolshevik sentiments'.[14]

What we know for certain, from Ironside's own diaries, is this. He and Norman frequently discussed the dreadful situation in Iran. Both shared complete contempt for the Shah, and could see that Curzon's plan, including his highly selective bribery of only three senior ministers, was doomed to failure.

Ironside did ensure that the Persian Cossacks were reorganised, re-clothed, and re-equipped – with British funds. He did spot Reza Khan as the only man who could credibly lead the Cossacks, and believed that he had the potential to lead the country as well. And he did say in his diary, 'I fancy that everybody thinks that I engineered the *coup d'état*. I suppose I did, strictly speaking.'

But – and it is a very big 'but' – British involvement in this coup was very different in character from its involvement in the 1953 coup against Prime Minister Mohammad Mossadegh.* The latter was originated by

---

* See below, Chapter 10.

the UK and the US, and for their benefit. It would not have happened but for their involvement.

Reza Khan's coup, in contrast, could easily have happened without any direct British involvement or encouragement, apart from its role in modernising the Persian Cossacks. The aim of this coup was the opposite of that of the 1953 coup. It was to establish a coherent national government, able to assert Iran's independence from foreign powers, especially Russia and the UK. Khan may have been trained up by the British, and Zia may have been a known Anglophile. But Reza Khan was far from being a British lackey – and Zia's first (and very wise) demand was to repudiate Curzon's agreement.

*   *   *

In the event, Zia lasted just three months as Prime Minister. He fell victim to the intrigue of the Qajar relics, who were nursing great grievances against him after their incarceration. As he fell from grace, so his influence with Reza Khan, and his usefulness to the British legation, rapidly evaporated. He was sent into exile across the border to the British-mandated territory of Palestine.

Reza Khan's official position in the government was as *Sardar Sepah* – Minister for War. He quickly took control of all of Iran's security apparatus: the gendarmerie, the police, the South Persian Rifles and the regular army. He set about pacifying the country, eliminating the many rebel groups and bandits, bringing recalcitrant tribal chiefs to heel and securing the writ of the state across the whole of the country. By late 1923, he had also become Prime Minister. In the same year, Ahmad Shah left the country, ostensibly on health grounds, never to return.

Reza Khan was hugely influenced by post-war developments elsewhere in the aftermath of the war. Independence movements against European colonial masters were becoming stronger, especially in Egypt and in neighbouring India. Germany was in the chaos of the Weimar Republic, caused in some eyes by a surfeit of democracy. In sharp contrast, strong authoritarian rulers were taking power in other countries and embarking on major programmes of national reconstruction. The 'march on Rome' by 30,000 fascist Blackshirts in October 1922 had led to Mussolini's appointment as Prime Minister. In the Soviet Union, Stalin was gradually centralising all power around him. Most influential of all on Reza Khan were developments in Turkey.

Under the 1920 Treaty of Sèvres, Turkey was to be partitioned to Greece, Italy and Armenia, with much of the remainder becoming 'zones of influence' under French or British control. Turkey proper was to be confined to north central Anatolia, centred on Ankara.

Mustafa Kemal Atatürk, a senior army officer, had distinguished himself as instigator of the Allies' defeat at Gallipoli and very quickly became the most powerful political and military leader in Turkey. He led the Turks in a war of independence against the terms of the Sèvres Treaty – and won. The boundaries of Turkey were reset in the July 1923 Treaty of Lausanne, and remain the same today.

The Republic of Turkey was declared on 29 October 1923, with Atatürk as its first President. His vision, set out in Turkey's constitution, was for a strong, secular state independent of foreign influence. He abolished the caliphate, the religious base of the Ottoman Sultanate, and embarked on a major programme to reduce the influence of Islam on Turkish society. A Latin-script alphabet replaced the old Turkish alphabet. Western dress, including hats, was prescribed by law for male students and civil servants. The female suffrage, extensive social reforms including universal primary education, and major reconstruction programmes were introduced. In 1925, to counter what he saw as subversion from old reactionaries and new enemies alike, Atatürk introduced one-party rule.

Reza Khan sought to model himself on Atatürk, though he had failed fully to comprehend that Turkey was already more influenced by the West and was more advanced in its economy, and that Atatürk had been able to capitalise on the Ottoman Empire's defeat in the First World War, by ruthlessly sweeping away much of the old order.

Reza Khan's first move to emulate Turkey was, in 1924, to propose that Iran too should become a republic, with him as its first President. He overreached himself. He met with vigorous opposition from two sides: from the clerical establishment, who could see how Atatürk's republic was marginalising the clerics there, and from the Majlis, who feared that they would lose influence under an all-powerful President.

Khan resigned as Prime Minister over this defeat and threatened to go abroad. Army commanders instigated disturbances around the country, saying they would march on Tehran if Khan was not reinstated, and soon the Majlis relented. Khan was back in power. He led a campaign in the oil-rich province of Khuzestan in south-western Iran, which had previously been run as a semi-autonomous protectorate by the British government on behalf of the Anglo-Persian Oil Company, in alliance with local tribal chiefs.

Reza Khan's newly asserted central control of this region greatly enhanced his authority and weakened his opponents. He established martial law in order to crush internal opposition further. In October 1925, he 'persuaded' a by now supine Majlis to abolish the Qajar dynasty and amend the constitution to create a new Pahlavi dynasty, with Khan as its first Shah. He was crowned in April 1926, in a ceremony with many reminders of Iran's pre-Islamic Achaemenid heritage, when Iran ruled much of the known world from its ceremonial capital in Persepolis. Not bad for a private soldier from a poor, single-parent family from a remote province of Iran.

Like his neighbour Kemal Atatürk, Reza Khan was above all a nationalist, determined to make a reality of his country's independence, to allow it to follow its own course, not one dictated by foreign powers. He set about a major reconstruction of the country, literally rebuilding much of Tehran, constructing Iran's first major railway, from the Caspian Sea to the Gulf, improving its decrepit road system and building up its industry.

Khan weakened British influence in a number of ways. The British-owned Imperial Bank of Persia lost its exclusive right to issue banknotes, which was handed to a new National Bank. The Indo-European tele-graph system was absorbed into the Iranian one. Two Royal Navy coal-ing stations in the Gulf were closed. The extraterritorial jurisdiction of foreign Consuls, moribund for some time, but long seen as a symbol of Iran's humiliations by foreign powers, was formally abolished.

Nor was Khan's attention directed against British interests alone. The Soviet Union's claims to special influence were similarly whittled away. Even France did not escape. That extraordinary concession, granted at the instigation of the previous Shah's French physician, which gave France a monopoly on all archaeological excavations in Iran was cancelled in 1927.

Much influenced by the economic policies of the Soviet Union and Turkey, Reza Khan greatly expanded the role of the state. State monopolies of sugar, opium and tobacco were established – the latter causing none of the upheavals that Major Talbot's tobacco monopoly had generated three and a half decades earlier. The state's tentacles in the economy became so extensive that it became the largest employer by far – 'a curse on the modern Iranian political economy that contin-ues to the present', comments Abbas Amanat.[15]

The education system was greatly improved, laying the grounds for a major expansion of the middle class, who benefited from the Shah's regime provided they did not involve themselves in opposition poli-tics. Reza Khan also sought to emulate Atatürk's dress laws, but in a more severe manner, forcing women to be unveiled in public places. This emancipated some urban women but had negative consequences for many women in rural areas, who now felt unable to leave the compounds of their own homes. Through land confiscations, Khan became one of the country's major landowners, allying himself to some of the old landowning ruling elites.

As power was more and more concentrated in his hands, Reza Khan became more paranoid and more dictatorial. He preserved a veneer of constitutionality with an elected Majlis, but from the fifth Majlis in

1926 to the thirteenth in 1941, it was he who decided who would sit in Iran's Parliament.

For centuries, the country had referred internally to itself as Iran, though the name Persia continued to be used for external relations. In 1935, Reza Khan formally requested that foreign delegates likewise refer to the country as Iran.

* * *

By the late 1920s, oil revenues from Iran's still small – 16 per cent – share of APOC's profits were the largest source of income to the Iranian state. Reza Khan now became increasingly restless about the terms of the deal struck in 1901 with William Knox D'Arcy. He was aggravated further by other developments in the region. One was Britain's diplomatic recognition of neighbouring Iraq, a country which he saw as an artificial entity invented by the British.* A second concerned Bahrain.

From the Achaemenids in the third century BC to the rise of Islam in the seventh century AD, and then during the Safavid dynasty, Bahrain had been controlled by the Iranians. A majority of its population were Shi'a – as they still are. From the late nineteenth century, Bahrain became a British protectorate. In the early 1930s, Reza Khan sought to reassert Iran's sovereignty over Bahrain, only to be thwarted by the British.

In November 1932, partly from pique, but above all because APOC's profit-sharing agreement with Iran was so miserly, Reza Khan decided unilaterally to cancel APOC's concession altogether.

Britain, however, was not willing to give up the crucial strategic advantage it enjoyed with APOC. It took the matter to the League of Nations, dominated by the two European imperial powers, France and the UK. The league ordered direct negotiations between APOC

---

* He was correct about that: Iraq's borders were largely drawn up by the British Oriental Secretary Gertrude Bell.

and the Iranian government. In the end, Reza Khan had to retreat from his original decision to cancel the concession.

On the face of it, Khan nonetheless got a half-decent outcome. APOC's concession area was reduced by three-quarters, though it still covered 100,000 square miles. A fixed royalty per ton, and 20 per cent of the worldwide profits of APOC (now extending its activities into Iraq and the Gulf protectorates), was agreed. But for APOC it was not a bad deal either. It preserved their key areas of operation, and the concession, which was originally due to expire in 1961, was extended until 1993. There was also plenty of small print in the agreement that enabled APOC to manipulate the profit figures from which Iran's 20 per cent was calculated. The secret agreements between APOC and the British government for the Admiralty to buy oil at 'preferential' prices further depressed the posted profits of the company.

As the 1930s progressed, Iran made some social and economic progress. However, these advances were matched by an ever more draconian police state under the Shah, who saw enemies everywhere, including amongst many erstwhile allies, some of whom he had eliminated. The clerical establishment was cowed; down but certainly not out.

At the start of the Second World War, Iran declared its neutrality, as it had done (to no effect whatsoever) in the First World War. As we have seen, in the First World War the Germans had sought to exploit the hostility of the Iranian people to the undue influence of the United Kingdom and of Russia. By the late 1930s, German influence within Iran was even more extensive. German companies had played a significant part in Iran's economic reconstruction, including in the Trans-Iranian Railway. Trade arrangements favoured Germany and disadvantaged the UK. Yet again, the Germans had the fertile ground of anti-British feeling to exploit. The Nazis' propaganda machine made much of the common Aryan connections between Germany and Iran.

* * *

As well as their success with the Iranians, the Nazis had, in late August 1939, secured a major diplomatic and military advantage with the Nazi–Soviet Pact, by which each side agreed not to engage in war on the other. It was this which gave Germany the green light to invade Poland, provoking the declaration of war on it by the United Kingdom.

By early 1940, Britain had begun assembling a large force of the Indian Army to occupy Khuzestan and thus protect its oilfields and APOC's huge refinery at Abadan. Meanwhile, the British Minister in Tehran, Sir Reader Bullard,* was becoming increasingly alarmed by what he saw as the Shah's pro-Nazi tendencies. He reported these back to London. British suspicions were confirmed when the Shah appointed a Prime Minister well known for his pro-German tendencies.

The Times reported that there were German 'tourists' everywhere in Iran – 4,000, mainly on short-term visas. Two technicians at the Tehran radio station were known to be German secret service agents. As news of Axis victories and Allied defeats came in, the Shah took a bet on Germany winning the war. But Hitler made the single most disastrous strategic error of his leadership. On 22 June 1941, his forces invaded the Soviet Union, bringing the Nazi–Soviet Pact to an abrupt end, and making Russia and the UK allies once again.

Nine days later, Bullard demanded of the Iranian Prime Minister that four-fifths of the Germans in Iran be expelled because they were, under the noses of the Iranian government, plainly violating Iran's avowed strict neutrality. There were further joint démarches by the Soviet and British envoys, culminating in a formal note to the Iranians, reciting their knowledge of German activity and this time demanding the expulsion of all but a few Germans.

In response to these demands, the Shah simply prevaricated. He was unwilling to take any serious action that would disoblige Hitler. This would prove to be a mistake.

---

* Bullard (1885–1976) had an unusual background for a diplomat of his generation. The son of a docker, he gained a scholarship to attend Bancroft's School, Woodford, and Queen's College, Cambridge. He played a central role in the development of the UK's intelligence activities in Iran during the war.

CHAPTER 8

THE BRITISH (AND SOVIETS) TAKE OVER

*We still have in our memories the occupation of our country by you
and your allies during the world war and the imposition of famine on
our people, which caused the illness and death of thousands
of our vulnerable countrymen.*

*We have not forgotten how you planned to oust Reza Khan
and install his son, Mohammad Reza.*

Basij leaflet

On the wall of the dining room in the grand residence of the British Ambassador in Tehran there is a silver plaque recording the *placement* at a dinner held in honour of Winston Churchill on his sixty-ninth birthday, 30 November 1943. 'Marshal Stalin' and 'The President' (Roosevelt) sit either side of Churchill. Of the thirty-four present at the dinner, none was Iranian.

This was in the middle of the Tehran Conference, the first of the 'Big Three' Allied leaders' conferences held to determine the strategy for winning the war and the carve-up afterwards. It was at this conference that the US and the UK agreed to open a second front in the West to relieve the pressure on the Soviet Union.

It was relatively easy for the three Allied leaders to meet in Tehran. Britain and the Soviet Union occupied the whole country, and by this stage there were some thousands of American personnel in the country too. But the spectre of German influence in Iran hovered over the conference. The Soviets claimed to have thwarted a serious attempt by German agents to assassinate all three leaders. One consequence of this was that Roosevelt agreed to move into the Soviet Embassy rather than travel across town from the American Embassy. The British Embassy was conveniently next door to the Soviets'.

These days there is no collective memory in Britain that we, with the Soviets, ran Iran for almost five years. But the memory in Iran is fresh, and it is everywhere. This invasion was the seventh by one or both of these powers over a period of a century and a half.

* * *

The Shah's answer to the British–Soviet ultimatum to him in July 1941 was simply to play for time – a fatal error.

On 25 August 1941, Operation COUNTENANCE was put into operation. Russian forces invaded Iran from the north, British forces from the south. They did encounter some resistance from the Shah's army and navy, though that soon crumbled. The Shah still havered. An appeal by him to President Roosevelt to 'put an end to the acts of aggression' by the invading armies fell on deaf ears.

On 9 September 1941, British Foreign Secretary Anthony Eden reached for the standard tool to deal with a difficult Iranian leader. He told the Soviet Ambassador in London that 'perhaps the best solution of all would be if the Persian politicians were to invite us into Tehran in order to carry out a *coup d'état* to get rid of the Shah'.[1]

In fact, a coup was not needed. By now, the Shah had recognised the inevitable. On 16 September, he formally abdicated in favour of his eldest son, the 22-year-old Mohammad Reza Pahlavi. British and Soviet forces occupied Tehran the next day.

The question then was what to do with Reza Khan. He proposed that he should go into exile in India, and had remitted a large sum to an Indian bank for that purpose. He and his nineteen-strong party willingly embarked on a steamer sent to the Gulf port of Bandar Abbas, which sailed for Mumbai on 27 September.

But the British had a different idea. They had no intention of allowing Reza Khan into India, where he could easily have become a further focus for the intense Muslim agitation for independence that was already gripping the Raj. As the ship anchored off Mumbai, Khan was told that he was to be transferred to Mauritius. After a short stay there he was moved to South Africa, where he died on 26 July 1944, aged sixty-six.

The British diplomat Clarmont Skrine had been deputed to break the news to Reza Khan that he was not to be allowed to land in India, and to accompany him from Mumbai to Mauritius. In his memoir, Skrine comments that though Reza Khan's 'last act of his life's drama was a sad anti-climax, nothing can detract from the debt Iran owes him for releasing her national genius from the medieval bondage of the Qajar Shahs and setting her footsteps irrevocably upon the paths of modern progress'.[2]

Others will take a more nuanced view of Reza Khan's legacy. Had he not dallied with the Germans, had he shown greater skill and sensitivity with his reform programme, and had he not become quite so paranoid, he might have survived and now be celebrated as Iran's Atatürk. His failures, compounded by his son, laid the ground for the Islamic Revolution of 1979. But Skrine is correct in asserting that Reza Khan's key legacy was in ridding Iran of the 'bondage of the Qajar Shahs'. He carried out important reforms of Iran's economy, infrastructure and education system. He had helped create an educated middle class. He had, in the inter-war years, skilfully played off Britain and the Soviet Union, and had kept Iran independent. But all this had been accompanied by an increasingly brutal and dictatorial regime that traduced the fragile democratic institutions established in 1906.

* * *

As the Shah left Iran's shores in September 1941, never to return, the country descended into chaos.

This had been a one-man government. Into the vacuum created by his departure swept near anarchy. Tribal chiefs, cowed by Reza Khan, suddenly began to assert their autonomy. Inter-tribal skirmishing broke out. With the collapse of the Iranian armed forces, the writ of the state no longer held. Economic dislocation and public panics at rumours of food shortages ensued.

The invading armies made the situation worse. This was partly through poor conduct by both British Indian and Soviet troops, but principally arose simply because of their dominant presence. The Allies decided to float the Iranian currency from its unrealistic official rate. As the currency went down, so the Allies' buying power went up. Their troops' needs came first. Food and other essentials soared in price. At one stage, inflation reached 450 per cent. Those with stocks of grain and other foodstuffs in short supply hoarded them in the expectation of still higher prices. For the ordinary Iranian, the Allies' presence in their country, and the abdication of Reza Shah, did not mean liberation but serious hardship and in many cases outright starvation. There were bread riots in Tehran in 1942. Twenty people were killed, 700 wounded.[3] Martial law was declared.

For all this, the Soviets and the British were roundly blamed by the Iranians. Nor could the two powers deny their responsibility: the connection between cause and effect was too obvious to everyone.

The news for the Allies in late 1941 and through much of 1942 remained bleak. Nazi forces continued their advance into Russia. Rommel drove Britain's Eighth Army back across the desert to Alamein. The Japanese invaded British Malaya. Independence riots broke out across India. Many in Iran still harboured the hope that the Germans would win the war and finally free them from the yokes of Russia and the UK. Britain and the Soviet Union set up extensive intelligence and espionage networks, fearing that the Nazis would seek to sabotage critical infrastructure using those Iranians who were thoroughly disaffected by the Allies' presence. A large internment camp was established in the British zone, in Sultanabad, Arak.

To try to normalise the situation, Britain and the Soviet Union negotiated a tripartite treaty of alliance with Iran, signed with the Shah at the end of January 1942. This treaty guaranteed, in its text at least, Iran's sovereignty and territorial integrity. In a fig leaf convenient for all sides, it claimed that the two powers were not in occupation of Iran but there merely for strategic reasons. It required the Allies to evacuate from Iran within six months of the end of hostilities.

But the Soviets and the British *were* an occupying force. With uncanny echoes of the 1907 Anglo-Russian Agreement, Soviet forces had occupied the north, British forces occupied the south (including Khuzestan, where APOC operated), and both occupied the central area, including Tehran. There was no limit under the treaty on the number of Allied forces allowed into the country. In addition to British and Soviet forces, the numbers of US personnel (civilian and military) reached 30,000.

Although the proximate cause of the Allies' invasion of Iran was the Shah's refusal to expel all Germans in his territory, there was, once the Nazi invasion of the Soviet Union had begun, a strategic imperative to use Iran to transport crucial supplies from the Gulf and India to help the Soviets' existential battle against the Nazis, especially once the main fighting on Soviet soil shifted southwards. Those who claimed that the Allies had used Reza Khan's 'pro-German' sympathies as a pretext to invade were not completely wrong.

The Allies took complete control of Iran's road and railway system – and had carte blanche over its other critical infrastructure, including its oil pipelines and telephone, telegraph and radio systems. More than 4 million tonnes of equipment and goods, 150,000 vehicles and 3,500 aircraft were sent through Iran to relieve the Soviet Union, most from the Gulf, some from India.

* * *

In January 1943, at Stalingrad, and at huge cost, the Soviets forced the surrender of Field Marshal Paulus and 240,000 German troops. As that and other, more positive news of the war came through, the pro-German feeling in Iran began to evaporate. Feeling the wind, on 9 September 1943 Iran declared war on Germany, and became the thirty-second member of the embryonic United Nations.

Iran's now categorical assertion that it was on the same side was not followed by affection for the occupying forces. Shortages of food and other essentials continued. These would have been considerable even in a well-administered country. There was a world shortage of shipping, which disrupted food supplies and normal import–export trade. These external factors were compounded by the corrupt shambles that passed for the Iranian government.

Clarmont Skrine records how he tried to get a permit to import 1,500 tonnes of cane sugar from a reputable Indian firm to relieve the shortages in the east of the country, where he was working, and where the sugar price was running at six times the level in Quetta, on the western border of what is now Pakistan. The permit was obtained. But for fifteen months Iranian government officials prevented the shipment from passing the border whilst the sugar changed hands nine times, the price inexorably rose, and customs and other officials took their cut.

The Americans were the only Allied nation with the resources at the time materially to help Iran. They sent in Dr A. C. Millspaugh, a financial expert. He had worked in Iran before, from 1922 to 1927. Assisted by just fourteen other advisers, he had reorganised Iran's administration of the economy, placed its finances on a sound footing and, in doing so, ensured that Reza Khan had the money to carry out his great programme of reconstruction. For his success he was not honoured but ejected by Reza Khan, who complained that 'there isn't room in Persia for two Shahs at the same time'.

Millspaugh was now given full powers by the Majlis in 1943 as Administrator-General of Finance, and again tried to improve Iran's chaotic administration. He recorded that on his arrival, 'Rumours were going around of goods changing hands dozens of times without being offered for public sale, of fantastic profits, sudden incalculable riches, and the rapid turnover of real estate.'[4]

Despite, or perhaps because of, the absence of the domineering Reza Khan, Millspaugh's efforts were thwarted by the vested interests of landlords and others who controlled the economy. He lasted less than two years.

The abdication of Reza Khan did, however, lead to the gradual re-awakening of democratic politics in Iran. Elections to the fourteenth Majlis, which had been delayed for two years, were held in late 1943. Reza Khan had entrusted elections during his reign to local provincial governors under his command. If the 'wrong' candidate was elected on the first ballot, the poll was held again, with more efficient ballot-stuffing to secure the 'correct' result. The elections in 1943 were only a little better conducted, but they did result in the return of a number of candidates of the Tudeh Party (Party of the Masses), the direct successor to the previously banned Communist Party of Iran and, like its predecessor, strongly ventriloquised from Moscow.

In his memoirs, *Mission for my Country*, Mohammad Reza Shah claimed that during this period, officials of both the Soviet Union and the United Kingdom 'would actually prepare the lists of candidates for Parliament and would then instruct whoever was our Prime Minister to see that only their candidates were nominated and elected'.[5]

Sir Reader Bullard, British Minister in Tehran at this time, strongly refuted this allegation when it was made public in 1961. He could hardly have said anything else. At this distance, there is no way of checking from the publicly available records whether this happened or not. It is, however, an indication of the fact that suspicions that the country was always being manipulated from outside went right to the top in Iran. Given what we do know about Britain's, as well as Russia's, continued efforts to influence the course of Iranian politics, it would be a surprise if sometimes British officials had not at the very least tactfully suggested to sympathetic Prime Ministers what result they would like to see from the polls. For example, the official record does show that in June 1950 the British Ambassador informed the Shah that the appointment of General Razmara 'would please His Majesty's Government'.[6] He was appointed.

Britain's absolute imperative in Iran during the war had been to preserve access to APOC's refinery at Abadan and the oilfields in south-west Iran which supplied it. 'If this refinery is destroyed, we have not sufficient tanker tonnage to supply the wants of the Middle East and India, and our position in the Middle East would dry up for lack of oil,' the War Cabinet Joint Planning Staff advised in July 1941.[7]

Britain's efforts to secure its oil supplies from Iran during the war were positive. The absence of any successful German attack, and the presence of a large contingent of British (and British Indian) forces ensured that. But the apparent tranquillity in the oilfields and across Iran about our ownership of their oil was rapidly to change once hostilities were over.

CHAPTER 9

ABADAN – BRITAIN'S HUMILIATION

Some of the British staff had with them their dogs, tennis rackets, golf clubs – their yachts they had to leave behind, unsold.

ROHAN BUTLER, 'BRITISH POLICY IN THE
RELINQUISHMENT OF ABADAN IN 1951'[1]

On 9 September 1945, a week after Japan had formally surrendered, the Iranian government gave the occupying powers six months to evacuate all their forces in Iran, in accordance with the terms of the 1942 treaty.

The British and American forces had all left by the beginning of March 1946, within the six-month deadline. The Soviet Union, however, had other ideas. From the start of the occupation, the Soviet Army and its intelligence agencies had been assiduous in promoting the Tudeh Party. The ground was especially fertile in the north-west of the country, in the Azerbaijan province centred on the regional capital of Tabriz. This area had been in the vanguard of the Constitutional Revolution of 1906 and was the focus of heroic resistance to the attempts by Mohammad Ali Shah in 1908–09 to crush Iran's emerging democratic institutions. More significantly, the area had a separate ethnic identity and language – Azeri, a variant of Turkish.*

---

* This is the second-largest linguistic group in Iran, after Persian. Around 18 per cent of Iran's population speak Azeri. Persian, though the main official language of the state, is the first language to only around 60 per cent of the population.

Reza Khan had sought to 'Persianise' the whole of Iran by insisting on the compulsory study of Persian in schools, at the expense of Azeri. The Azeris also had well-founded grievances that their region had lost out in terms of infrastructure and development compared with other regions of Iran. With encouragement from Moscow, they drew up an ambitious programme for an independent Azerbaijan.

The Soviet Republic of the same name was just over the northern border of this province. Stalin had become preoccupied with the fragility of his country's oil supplies, with production in 1946 stalled at just 60 per cent of that seen in 1941. He claimed that 'saboteurs [from Iran] – even a man with a box of matches – might cause us serious damage'.[2] On the pretext of this concern for the security of their key oilfields around Baku, Stalin decided that his army would stay in northern Iran.

In November 1945, the Soviets helped the Tudeh Party to engineer a coup in Iranian Azerbaijan. Their partisans seized key government buildings, with the protection of the Red Army, and proclaimed an Autonomous Republic of Azerbaijan.

Like the Russian Tsars before them, the Soviets had long been jealous of Britain's massive oil concession in the south-west, and coveted a similar concession in Iranian Azerbaijan. The Soviets now demanded internal autonomy for Azerbaijan, and a Soviet–Iranian joint venture oil company, in which the Soviet Union would hold 51 per cent of the shares.

Pressure within the United Nations Security Council, to which the Shah referred the dispute, and skilful handling by Prime Minister Ahmad Qavam os-Salteneh (appointed in January 1946) resulted in an agreement with the Soviet Union that they would withdraw their troops from Iran. Iranian troops then marched into the province and, after a short but bloody conflict, restored the central authority of the state.

Qavam os-Saltaneh did make a provisional agreement to form a joint oil company with the Soviet Union, but this was subject to agreement by the Majlis.

Meanwhile, encouraged by the turbulence in Azerbaijan province, civil disorder broke out elsewhere in Iran. The Kurds, equally angered by the policy of 'Persianisation', demanded autonomy.

In the south-west, the Tudeh Party took their chance too. In July 1946, there were riots in Abadan and a general strike of workers at APOC's refinery. The Iranian employees of APOC had strong grounds for complaint. The whole of its operations were run on colonial lines. Abadan was a horrible place in which to work, with blasting temperatures above 40°C for five months in the summer and just a few days' rain over the whole of the year, usually torrential when it came.

The British staff (over 2,700) had the best housing and amenities, exclusive clubs and access to good water and ice. The contrast with the conditions of the Iranian workers could not have been starker. Of the 55,000 or so Iranians employed by APOC, 16,500 were casual labourers who were not included in the company's wage structure, nor enjoyed company facilities.[3] They had to live in appalling, squalid conditions, in shanty towns, without running water or electricity – as did many of the 'employed' Iranian workers.

For the UK, the imperative was to keep the oil supplies from Iran flowing. The British Labour government demanded of the Shah that he restore order in Abadan, stationed warships off the coast, and sent a brigade of troops from India to Basra to protect British and Indian lives in the oilfield area if the Shah failed to do so. In agreeing this policy, the British Cabinet also advocated 'a more sympathetic treatment' of Iranian labour by APOC – the first of many similar sensible demands, most of which fell on deaf ears.

Under pressure, the Shah did send troops to re-establish his authority. He was assisted in this effort by insurgencies organised by pro-British tribal chiefs in Fars and Khuzestan, the British Consuls in these provinces, and the usual lubrication.

This was the last occasion when Britain was able to call on the vast resources of the British Indian armed forces. India and Pakistan became independent nations in August 1947.

Elections to the fifteenth Majlis, in 1947, were rigged in the normal way, and by these means, Prime Minister Qavam os-Saltaneh secured a majority. But he could not prevent Mohammad Mossadegh being re-elected for Tehran.

* * *

At first blush, Mossadegh was an unlikely individual to lead a popular movement, his *Jebhe Melli* (National Front of Iran). Born in 1882, he came from a highly privileged background, as a Qajar aristocrat and major landowner whose father and wider family were revenue collectors – a position which Mossadegh himself inherited from his father at the age of fifteen. His higher education was in Europe: two years at the *Sciences Po* in Paris and then a PhD in law at a Swiss university.

There is, however, no rule that says that those from the upper classes are disabled from leading a mass movement. They tend to have a greater degree of self-confidence and the natural authority of the ruling class – along with an insider's understanding of how the regime against which they are working actually operates.

Mossadegh had first been elected to the Majlis in 1906, but at the age of twenty-four he had been unable to take his seat, as the minimum age for a member was at that time thirty. He was back in politics by the 1920s, first as minister in the dying days of the Qajar regime, and then in 1923 as a member of the Majlis. In 1925, Mossadegh was one of the few members of the Majlis to speak and vote against Reza Khan's proposals to abolish the Qajar dynasty and declare himself Shah of the new Pahlavi dynasty. He made a skilful speech protesting that Khan's plan was against the 1906 constitution, and correctly anticipated that the new Shah would dominate an autocratic regime in which the democratic ideals of 1906 would be subverted.

After Reza Khan's rise to power, Mossadegh was marginalised in Iranian politics. From 1928 to 1943, he lived on his estates, but he was unable to escape the brutality of Reza Khan's later years as Shah. In

1940, he was arrested on Reza Khan's orders, ostensibly on grounds of his alleged pro-German sympathies, but in reality because of the threat he posed to the Shah. Mossadegh was sent to a remote fortress in Birjand, near the Afghan border. He and his family anticipated that it would be only a matter of time before he was killed, with the usual official explanation that he had died of natural causes.

Indeed, Mossadegh could easily have died of natural causes, for he suffered from chronic ill health for most of his life, including stomach ulcers, insomnia, nervous tension and hysteria. Often he would collapse, weeping. He could faint to order, from time to time doing so in the Majlis to add additional drama to his oratory. He spent much of every day sitting in pyjamas on the bed in his private residence, from where he received visitors and conducted official business.

Mossadegh would almost certainly have gone the same way as other of Reza Khan's political prisoners, but for one of the great ironies of modern Iranian history. Five months later, his release, initially to house arrest and then under a general amnesty, was secured by the Crown Prince, Mohammad Reza Pahlavi. In time, Mossadegh was to become the new Shah's nemesis. The Shah was to comment acidly in his memoirs that he had released the man 'who later bankrupted the country and almost ended the dynasty established by my father'.[4]

The official secret Foreign Office history of this period described Mossadegh as 'anything but a statesman', an 'elderly xenophobe', and 'a clever political manipulator and unscrupulous demagogue'.[5] This says more about the failure of British officials to understand the phenomenon that was Mossadegh than accurately to describe the most significant Iranian non-clerical politician of the twentieth century.

The key to Mossadegh was not his alleged xenophobia but his overwhelming belief in Iran, its people and its future. He was a supreme nationalist, and a pretty secular one at that. What he objected to was the way in which Iran's interests had repeatedly been suborned to those of foreign states, particularly Russia and the United Kingdom. He was rich enough and principled enough not to have been tempted by the 'lubrication' of his views that had so often come the way of his contemporaries. He was an eccentric, completely bald, with a large nose and the ability to switch from laughter to rage in a trice. Most who dealt with him found him next to impossible to fathom.

Whether he was in general a xenophobe is beside the point. What is true is that he loathed Britain with a passion – what it stood for and what he believed it had done to his country. He had opposed Curzon's attempt to turn Iran into a British protectorate in all but name and had been suspicious of British involvement in the coup which began Reza Khan's rise to power. He profoundly resented the 1933 agreement with APOC which sealed for sixty years a meretricious deal which confirmed British control of the country's most important natural resource and gave the Iranian government less in royalties than the British government received in taxation, profits and cheap oil for the British Navy from the same source.* Mossadegh was pre-occupied almost to the exclusion of all else with the iniquities of the Anglo-Iranian Oil Company (AIOC) and the need to nationalise Iran's oil and remove foreign influence from his country.

* * *

The putative agreement with the Soviets for a joint Soviet–Iranian oil company that Prime Minister Qavam os-Saltaneh had made in 1946 required ratification by the Majlis, thanks to a resolution passed by that Parliament at Mossadegh's behest. When Qavam os-Saltaneh finally tabled his proposal, in late 1947, it was defeated by 102 votes to two.

As the 1940s progressed, pressures within Iran mounted inexorably, first for a better deal with AIOC and then for its outright nationalisation.

---

* For example, in 1947 the Iranian government received only £7 million in royalties under the 1933 concession, whilst the British government drew £15 million in taxation alone. To compound this injustice, Iran's share of the distributed profits on which its royalties were based were significantly reduced by the preferential, and secret, price the British Admiralty paid for its oil, which was less than 30 per cent of the market price. The Admiralty price was between £1 and £1.50 per ton, when the market price was between £3.50 and £4.50.

In these demands, the protagonists were further empowered both by a sense that Britain's authority was on the wane and by the consistently lamentable and myopic handling of its position by AIOC.

Britain had emerged from the war victorious but nearly bankrupt, heavily dependent upon the United States for financial support through the Anglo-American loan agreement of 1946. The balance of power between these two transatlantic 'partners' had irrevocably shifted during the course of the war in America's favour.

Between the wars, Britain and France had been successful in muscling the US out of involvement in the burgeoning oil industry in former Mesopotamia, which they controlled following the collapse of the Ottoman Empire. American oil majors had instead had to seek out oil in the Arabian Peninsula — first in Bahrain and then in Saudi Arabia, where oil in commercially exploitable quantities was struck in 1938 — making the US a major player in the oil politics of the Middle East and adding greatly to the complexities facing the AIOC following the war.

There were three problems which added to the post-war Labour government's difficulties in handling the emerging oil crisis in Iran. The first was that at home it was nationalising on a far greater scale than Iran had ever proposed. Foreign Secretary Ernest Bevin immediately saw contradiction staring his government in the face. 'What argument can I advance against anyone claiming the right to nationalise the resources of their country?' he asked in a letter to the Chancellor of the Exchequer and the Minister of Fuel and Power when the crisis with Iran first arose in 1946. 'We are doing the same thing here with our power in the shape of coal, electricity, railways, transport and steel.'[6]

It was a question impossible to answer satisfactorily. When, in 1951, Britain was in abortive negotiations with Iran, Prime Minister Mossadegh said that 'all [he] asked was that [the British] Government should let Persia enjoy the same benefits, social and economic, which the Labour Government had introduced in the United Kingdom'.

Bevin's successor as Foreign Secretary, Herbert Morrison, offered his answer to Bevin – and Mossadegh's – question, but it was hardly a convincing one. He argued that the difference was whilst Britain 'had nationalised a number of industries … this was always after proper discussion with all the interested parties. I have never heard of an act of nationalisation based on little more than a resolution hurriedly passed by a Parliament, except in communist countries.'[7]

Whilst it may have been technically correct, this casuistry cut no ice in Iran. All the sectors the Labour government had nationalised had been British-owned. We had had no experience of what it was like to have the key natural resource of our country controlled by a foreign power, for their profit not ours.

Bevin's argument that we were being inconsistent in our approach was, however, trumped by Britain's strategic imperative in maintaining its supplies of Iranian oil. At an interdepartmental meeting in March 1951, officials claimed that if there were no more oil from Iran, Britain would have to buy 22 million tons of oil products and 7 million tons of crude oil from elsewhere, at a cost of $250 million. The Admiralty added that the Royal Navy was securing 85 per cent of its requirements, 2 million tons per year, from Iran.[8]

The second problem facing the British government was the attitude and approach of those running the AIOC. Following Winston Churchill's virtual nationalisation of APOC in 1914, the British government had held a majority of the shares in the company. As already mentioned, there were two government-appointed directors on its board, with a formal veto over questions of 'foreign, naval or military policy'. Despite this, those running the company kept the British government at arm's length, expecting it to come to their aid whenever the company required whilst having no control whatever over the policies being pursued. Bevin complained furiously about this:

> It is virtually a private company with State capital and anything it does reacts upon the relationship between the British Government and Persia. [But] as Foreign Secretary I have no power or influence,

in spite of this great holding by the Government, to do anything at all. As far as I know, no other Department has.[9]

The AIOC was headed up by Sir William Fraser, its executive chairman. Christopher de Bellaigue, in his brilliant biography of Mossadegh, described Fraser as 'scabrous'.[10] Some of Fraser's own senior employees were even more pointed. Fraser and his board were 'helpless, niggling, without an idea between them, confused, hidebound, small-minded, blind', declared its labour adviser Sir Frederick Leggett to a senior Foreign Office official.[11] Another official said that Fraser 'still thinks that he can get away without conceding anything like what we may find the situation demands.'

The frustration with the antediluvian attitude of Fraser and his colleagues went to the very top. Anthony Eden, Foreign Secretary from October 1951, a Persian speaker who knew Iran well, complained that Fraser lived 'in cloud cuckoo land'.[12] Prime Minister Clement Attlee commented to his biographer that the AIOC had been 'a kind of imperial power, and they couldn't get out of the habit ... They brought a lot of trouble on themselves and us as a result.'[13] Worse, for us, Fraser was damned by President Truman, who said that he looked like 'a typical nineteenth-century exploiter'.[14]

Fraser employed a chief public relations officer, Mr A. H. T. Chisholm, who encapsulated everything that was wrong about the company. He had a 'monocle and an indolent air ... [which] lends colour to suspicions that AIOC is following a 19th century line', one distracted British official recorded.[15]

It was. The leadership of the AIOC failed at almost every turn to understand that times had changed. Their response to the clamour for nationalisation was to think they could ride out trouble. The concessions they did make were wrung from them, always too late.

The third problem facing the Labour government was the United States. The preoccupation of President Truman and his Secretary of State Dean Acheson was to contain the Soviet Union. They were impatient not only with the AIOC but also with the British government, whom they complained seemed to have less ability to bring the oil company it owned into line with its foreign policy than did the United States over its oil companies, all of which were in private hands.

Personalities played a significant part in the difficult relationship with the US. The key official in the State Department, George McGhee, Assistant Secretary of State for Near Eastern Affairs (and a former oil executive), and the American Ambassador to Tehran, Dr Henry Grady, were both of Irish extraction. An Iranian diplomat had made a point of drinking a toast to these two at a St Patrick's Day celebration at the American Embassy in Tehran, adding, 'There are many Irishmen in the United States who are critical of Britain.'

Whether it was because of their ethnic heritage or simply their considered judgement, both key players in the US system let the Iranians know that they took a different view from the UK of Iran's aspirations for control of its oil resources. Both caused exasperation in London. Foreign Secretary Herbert Morrison complained that it was 'almost as if American opinion did not approve of nationalisation excepting when it damaged British interests'.[16]

Bevin had proposed that a company owned 50–50 between the AIOC and the Iranian state be established. That suggestion was dismissed by the company. But the idea of a 50–50 share was now a reality abroad. American oil companies and Venezuela had already agreed to a 50–50 deal for supplies from the latter.

A Supplemental Oil Agreement was negotiated in July 1949 between Iran and the AIOC. Complex in its detail, this would have increased the royalty for Iran, though by exactly how much was obscure. Approval for the deal was talked out when it went before the Majlis in July 1949, and the Majlis itself was dissolved shortly afterwards.

Though they were seeking to operate a democratic system, members of the Majlis and ministers had to contend with another factor: their own personal survival. Violence was a factor in Iranian politics never far below the surface. In November 1949, the Shah's Court Minister, Mr Hazhir, was assassinated by a fanatical terrorist group, the *Fidayan-i-Islam* (Sacrificial Warriors of Islam), controlled by a powerful cleric, Ayatollah Abul-Qasim Kashani. Jailed by the British during the war for his alleged pro-Nazi sympathies, he shared with Mossadegh a hatred of the United Kingdom. He was to play a critical part in Mossadegh's rise to power — and in his demise.

By the end of the 1945–50 parliament, most of the senior members of the Labour Cabinet were exhausted, especially those who had been in Churchill's wartime coalition Cabinet, including Clement Attlee, Ernest Bevin and Herbert Morrison. At the general election of February 1950, Labour's majority of 146 was cut to five.

Bevin had been the towering figure in the government, and a key ally of Attlee, who deferred to him on most foreign policy issues. However, during 1950 he had been able to work in the Foreign Office for only a few weeks. Partly this was because he was absent on official visits abroad, but mainly it was because of illness. After the election, he was reappointed as Foreign Secretary but had to give up his position just two weeks later. The turn of the screw for him was that his successor was Herbert Morrison, for whom Bevin had nothing but scorn. He doubted Morrison's ability to manage the burdens of this high office and its paramount need for firm and consistent decisions. Indeed, the official record of this period is replete with examples of where 'Mr Morrison's tentative inclination towards a strong line was not projected into executive action'.[17]

Britain's handling of the Abadan crisis was further complicated by the Korean War, which had begun in July 1950 and would continue for three years. Britain joined with the US in fighting this war. This gave them greater leverage with the American administration, but also meant that there were fewer British troops available for other theatres, including, potentially, the Gulf and Iran.

In Iran, the drumbeat for nationalisation increased in intensity week by week and month by month. Mossadegh's party, the National

Front, had initially been a small minority in the Majlis. Despite that, its leader was able to secure the chairmanship of the Parliament's Oil Commission, which then worked up the aspiration for nationalisation in much more detail. The commission led the public campaign and helped stir up long-held feelings against foreign domination of Iran's economy and its polity.

The Shah's response to this mounting crisis was to try to move the debate on to other issues, and to change the composition of the Majlis. In January 1951, he told the British Ambassador in Tehran that if land reforms, income and luxury taxes proposed by Prime Minister General Razmara were not supported by the Majlis, it would be dissolved. He continued that, since 'free elections were impossible in the prevailing conditions, the election of public-spirited people would have to be arranged'.[18]

Razmara wanted to find a way through the oil nationalisation maze. He realised that unless this could be carried out by agreement with Britain and the AIOC, it was likely that Iran's revenues would suffer, since Iran had no means of selling its oil internationally except through foreign intermediaries. Once it became clear to him that the Supplemental Oil Agreement was a dead duck, he argued for a 50–50 profit-sharing deal, as Bevin had proposed. This was now becoming the international standard, and was about to happen just across the Persian Gulf, between the Kingdom of Saudi Arabia and Aramco, a conglomerate of huge US oil companies. So myopic was the leadership of the AIOC that their response to Razmara's proposal was to urge the US to keep the Aramco deal secret until the AIOC had agreed what they hoped were much less generous terms with the Iranians.

Though he was variously accused of being a 'British stooge' and an 'agent of American imperialism' by his opponents, Razmara in fact sought to secure reasonable relations with all three of the major powers with a vested interest in Iran. He initially took a relatively relaxed approach to the Tudeh Party.

But his efforts were not to be. On 4 March 1951, he had told the Majlis that Iran would not be capable of running its oil industry on its own, without the cooperation of the AIOC. On the morning of Wednesday 7 March 1951, Razmara was attending a memorial service at a Tehran mosque when he was shot dead. His assassin was a member of the *Fidayan-i-Islam*, the terrorist group controlled by Ayatollah Kashani.

Mossadegh was at this time working with Kashani, then Speaker of the Majlis. The Foreign Office history claimed that three days before the assassination, fifteen members of the *Fidayan-i-Islam* 'had conferred with Dr Mossadegh and M. Kashani. Both were reported to have stated categorically that the welfare of Persia depended on the disappearance of General Razmara.'[19] De Bellaigue says that whilst 'Mossadegh never admitted to knowing in advance about the attempt on Razmara's life … it is unlikely that he was unaware of so momentous a meeting [to agree the assassination] involving his closest allies'.[20]

Whether or not Mossadegh had had a direct hand in the Prime Minister's elimination, he certainly benefited from it. Opposition within the Majlis to oil nationalisation dissolved. A week after Razmara's murder, the Majlis unanimously passed a resolution for the state's ownership of AIOC. Politics moved from the Majlis to the street. Anti-British, pro-nationalisation demonstrations broke out across the country. In Abadan, a major strike of AIOC workers was called. The atmosphere in Abadan and the other key areas of AIOC's activity turned nasty. In mid-April, there was savage rioting against British residents, three of whom were lynched.

The British Ambassador lobbied the Shah hard for the appointment of Sayyid Ali to succeed General Razmara. Ali, it will be recalled, had been the political leader of the 1921 coup led militarily by Reza Khan, and had for three brief months in 1921 been Prime Minister, until his value to Khan had been exhausted and he had been exiled to Palestine.[*] But, as an indication of how the balance of forces was shifting against Britain, it was not the Anglophile Ali but an American protégé,

---

[*] Where he had considerable success as a farmer.

Hussein Ala, who was appointed Prime Minister. He had the added disadvantage for the UK of having 'some anti-British sentiments from having been bullied at Westminster School'.[21]

Ala was formally appointed on 11 March 1951, but he lasted just six weeks. On 28 April, the Majlis decided to invite Mossadegh to be his successor. He accepted.

Mossadegh's imperative was to make a reality of nationalisation. Everything was staked on that – including his life. A fear of assassination was never far from the minds of any Iranian public figure. Mossadegh had unleashed a tiger that he knew he could only barely control, and which could easily turn against him. Mossadegh's first act was to have his 'Nine-Point Law' passed by the Majlis to bring the oil industry under state control. It was given Royal Assent by the Shah on 2 May.

In the months from late April to September 1951, the British government replayed again and again the refrain of the Grand Old Duke of York. Plans were prepared in high secrecy in Whitehall for a military takeover of the AIOC's facilities in Abadan. One was appropriately called 'Buccaneer'; a second, 'Midget'. In these dying days of the Labour government, vacillation was the order of the day. Troops were put on three hours' notice, then stood down. There were serious arguments between government lawyers as to the legal basis for any invasion – for such it would be – of Iran's sovereign territory; and a resentful appreciation prevailed that, whether technically lawful or not, Britain would find itself isolated in the United Nations.

Morrison's colleagues were highly critical of what they saw as his unthinkingly belligerent attitude. Former Chancellor of the Exchequer Hugh Dalton commented that he was behaving like a latter-day Lord Palmerston, adding with vitriol that he suspected Morrison was overcompensating for the fact that he had been a conscientious objector in the First World War. So unimpressed was Attlee by Morrison that he effectively sidelined him, later saying that his appointment of Morrison as Foreign Secretary was his 'biggest mistake'.[22]

The Americans were consistent in counselling Britain against military action, a factor that weighed heavily with Attlee. He told his Cabinet that Britain 'could not afford to break with the United States on an issue of this kind'.[23] The US's fear, which the UK did not wholly share, was that military intervention by Britain from the south of Iran could provide an excuse for Stalin to move in Red Army troops from the north; given Russia's allies in the well-organised Tudeh Party, Iran could fall completely within the Soviet sphere of influence.

But if dealing with the United States was difficult enough, dealing with the AIOC was even more of a headache for British ministers. The obdurate head of the company, Sir William Fraser, had to be pushed, kicking and screaming, to agree to any half-decent proposals to put to the Iranians.

Even as late as September 1951, when the crisis was approaching its peak, Fraser was holding back key financial information from the company's majority shareholder, the British government. He refused the government's ministerial Iran negotiator, Major Richard Stokes, Lord Privy Seal, early sight of the company's balance sheet for 1950 – perhaps unsurprising given that the company had managed nearly to double its net profit (from £18.5 million to £34 million) in a single year after payment of UK taxation and royalties to the Iranian government.[24] Two weeks later, Stokes was to complain to the Prime Minister that Treasury figures comparing the amounts received by the British and Iranian governments between 1932 and 1950 had not been made available to him before he had gone to Tehran to try for a negotiated settlement with Mossadegh. He said that had he known about these figures he would have argued for a more than 50–50 split in favour of the Iranians.[25] In this eighteen-year period, the Iranians had received £103 million in total from the AIOC, whilst the British government had benefited by £194 million in taxation and dividends.

Stokes's mission to Tehran had taken place in August 1951. It had been immediately preceded by one by Averell Harriman, special representative of US Secretary of State Dean Acheson and President Truman.

Harriman's mission had served only to highlight fundamental differences in approach between the US and the UK, with the former repeatedly pressing the latter – and the AIOC – for a more constructive attitude to negotiations. Harriman took the view, shared by his principals in Washington, that though Mossadegh was irascible and had left himself little room to manoeuvre, it was better to see him kept in office than face the prospect of Iran becoming run by the Tudeh Party under Soviet control.

In these circumstances, Stokes's assignment in Tehran was doomed to fail from the start. After three weeks in the Iranian capital, he returned to the UK with nothing, increasingly exercised about the weak hand of cards with which he had been provided by his irresolute ministerial colleagues.

The British government had, earlier in the dispute, secured one advantage, by making an application to the International Court of Justice in The Hague for them to arbitrate on the dispute. The Iranians argued that the court lacked jurisdiction to hear the case. In its interim judgment in early July 1951, the court by a majority found broadly in favour of the UK, granting an interim injunction requiring that the *status quo ante* be maintained whilst negotiations between Iran and the UK were held. But the British government failed to make good use of this decision to garner international diplomatic support for its position.

In the midst of the crisis, on 19 September 1951, Prime Minister Clement Attlee announced, with little consultation with Cabinet colleagues (and none with Morrison), that a general election would be held on 25 October. Mossadegh had made a set of counter-proposals to the UK shortly before Attlee's election decision was made public. Though he had no prior knowledge of Attlee's decision, Mossadegh had picked up on speculation that a British general election might happen fairly soon, and with classic Iranian reasoning, had apparently concluded that he would have a better chance of a settlement once Labour had re-won its mandate.

The heat of the British general election campaign, including the dispersal of key figures around the country, and poor communications between them, made decision-making even more complicated.

Rather than playing for time, as the Americans and some in the British system had urged, Mossadegh's latest proposals were simply rejected – giving Mossadegh the excuse he needed to end Britain's involvement in Iran's oil industry. In the face of this move, the AIOC decided to withdraw all British personnel from Iran. A British cruiser, HMS *Mauritius*, had been stationed off the Iranian coast with the intention that it would spearhead military action to take and hold Abadan by force. Now it was used for the humiliating task of evacuating the last remaining AIOC staff. 'Some of the British staff had with them their dogs, tennis rackets, golf clubs,' the official Foreign Office history records, but, in a reminder of the high colonial life they were relinquishing, 'their yachts they had to leave behind, unsold'.

A few days before this final evacuation, the British government had made the extraordinary decision to take their case to the UN Security Council, deaf and blind to the fact that they were bound to lose, as their own Permanent Representative, Sir Gladwyn Jebb, had warned in advance. They had neither the Americans with them nor sufficient numbers of other members to win the vote. It is hard at this distance to work out what possessed ministers to agree to this course.

Mossadegh was never properly understood by most decision-makers in Whitehall, still less by the AIOC. Whatever his personal eccentricities, and no doubt maddening ability to be both obdurate and obtuse, he was a politician to his fingertips. He could see an opportunity when one presented itself. Britain's tabling of its resolution was, for him, heaven-sent. He decided to go to New York himself and present Iran's case to the Security Council in person. His visit was a *coup de théâtre*, and his speech a *coup de grâce* at the UK's expense. As de Bellaigue sets out, Mossadegh 'situated the Iranian struggle in the wider quest for human dignity'. European powers had respected the legitimate aspirations of the peoples of India, Pakistan and Indonesia. 'Iran demands that right.'[26]

Gladwyn Jebb did his best in reply, but, as he had warned in advance, Britain had placed itself in a hopeless position. It had already had to accept one dilution of its draft resolution after another. The final humiliation was to see the UK's resolution kicked into touch. Britain did not even know whether it was for or against this procedural motion to defer the vote *sine die*. It abstained.

Mossadegh had spoken in the perfect French he had learnt at university in France and Switzerland. There were none of the histrionics or fainting fits that had characterised some of his contributions to debates in the Majlis.

He had shrewdly calculated that if he could present a sober and forensic case, he could win the world. His reward was astonishingly favourable press coverage and an invitation to see President Truman in the Oval Office. This was followed by detailed negotiations about a way forward with George McGhee, the State Department official who had consistently ensured that the Truman administration never gave the British the blank cheque they sought.

Mossadegh's triumph in the Security Council had taken place on 15 October 1951, just ten days before Britain's general election. The Conservative opposition, led by Winston Churchill, had already made Labour's handling of the Abadan crisis an election issue. In the last Commons debate of the session, on 30 July, Churchill had accused Morrison of being no more than a 'caucus boss', who 'dwells below the level of events', adding (correctly) that foreign policy had fallen into disarray because of Bevin's illnesses.[27] Anthony Eden, who was to become Churchill's Foreign Secretary, charged that the British government had 'tried everything and followed through in nothing'.[28]

In the general election, Labour received its highest ever share of the vote.* However, it lost twenty seats. The Conservatives gained twenty-three, securing an overall majority of seventeen for Winston

---

* At 48.8 per cent, it has never been exceeded in any subsequent election – and it was greater even than Labour achieved in its landslide win in 1945. Labour was 220,000 votes ahead of the Conservatives.

Churchill. What precise difference the Abadan crisis played in Labour's defeat is impossible to tell. It certainly gained the party no votes. As events were to unfold, it was not good news for Mossadegh either.

*　　*　　*

As much as the 1956 Suez crisis, the tortuous Abadan saga should be studied by anyone with an interest in Britain's foreign policy in its post-imperial world.

Labour knew the days of empire were running out fast. Indeed, they had actively campaigned for colonial freedom for decades. As the demands for oil nationalisation in Iran had grown stronger, Bevin had swiftly realised that the British government was left making wholly threadbare arguments against exactly the same policy – nationalisation of energy – on which Labour had fought and won the 1945 election. Yet, beyond this, there was a much wider failure of analysis and policy. The leadership of the AIOC were outrageous, arrogant and ignorant at the same time. They should have been faced down by the government. After all, the one energy company Labour did not need to nationalise was the AIOC: it was already majority-owned by the British state, which had the power of veto over the AIOC's actions. Instead, in the acid comment of a senior Foreign Office official, the AIOC 'squeezed every pound they could out of Persia'.[29]

Alongside this failure, ministers and officials allowed themselves to be woefully ill-informed about the comparative shares the Iranian and British governments were taking in taxation and profit from the AIOC, and about the rising tide of agreements elsewhere between host governments and international oil majors to create joint ventures in the form of 50–50 partnerships.

Added to all this, there was the overwhelming reluctance of the UK to come to terms with the pre-eminence of the US in post-war foreign policy. The UK may have been on the victorious side in the war, but the only outright winner was the United States. It was – it still is – uncomfortable for Britain that the US had so much power. But it was a reality, and one that the UK failed to factor into its calculations when working out how to handle the Iranians. Mossadegh was able to exploit the obvious differences between the US and the UK to his full advantage.

To be sure, the US had its own political agenda and was flexing its mercantilist muscles to get the best deal it could for US businesses. But on Iran its analysis and prescription were not far from those of Ernest Bevin. If Bevin had had his way, and if he had not fallen ill, it might – just – have been possible to negotiate a deal with the Iranians which gave them a much bigger share of the profits of their oil, and which avoided the utter humiliation that Britain suffered in the debacle of its withdrawal from Abadan.

It was round one to Mossadegh.

CHAPTER 10

SPOOKS AND COUPS

We remember the clear and direct role your cunning actions played during the coup d'état *of 28 Mordad [19 August 1953].*

Basij leaflet

Britain's occupation of Iran in 1941 placed an urgent requirement on the UK to develop its intelligence network across the country. There was considerable anxiety about sabotage of the Allies' war effort in Iran, and disruption of the key supply system to the Soviet Union – along with a need, as the war progressed, to watch the Soviets as well.

The country's strategic position adjoining India, Russia and the Ottoman Empire, and its crucial oil supplies, had made it a place of interest for Britain's Secret Intelligence Service (SIS, otherwise known as MI6) from the First World War. The British Raj also maintained an extensive intelligence network in its near neighbourhood. It was officers from this service who originally ran the station in Bushehr, on the Iranian Gulf coast – well placed for coverage of APOC's oilfields and refinery at Abadan, and for central Arabia. In the mid-1930s, as the Second World War approached, much of the work was run from the SIS station in Baghdad, which had three agents dedicated to covering Iraqi and Iranian oil.[1] This station built up links with other friendly services, including the Poles, who it was said were 'very well installed' in Tehran.

Outside Tehran, Britain still had eleven diplomatic posts across the country,* which had long been valuable bases for intelligence work. Iran's rickety legal system, capricious governance and endemic corruption gave British officials plenty of opportunity to suborn well-placed individuals and to influence public opinion, including, later, by covert financing of some newspapers.

The SIS station in Tehran formally began its operation in April 1940, a year before the UK's invasion of Iran. During the period of the Nazi–Soviet Pact, the imperative was for information from the north of Iran, on Soviet activities. There was a real fear that Stalin's pact with the Nazis could extend to the Russians fighting with Germany.

Once the occupation had occurred, the Security Service (MI5), known regionally as the Security Intelligence Middle East (SIME), together with the Special Operations Executive (SOE) and sections of the Intelligence Corps, began work in Iran, under the Defence Security Office Persia (DSO Persia).[2]

SIS tended to concentrate on watching the Russians, whilst the DSO watched the Iranians and fugitive Germans. There was a high priority given to monitoring and moulding the internal politics of Iran. Once the occupation was over, the key responsibility for intelligence activities in Iran rested with SIS.

*   *   *

With its thousands of British and Indian staff, as well as tens of thousands of Iranian employees, the AIOC was an obvious source of agents and information. There was resistance from the AIOC's management to any of its staff being directly employed by SIS, on the understandable grounds that the repercussions for the company from the Iranians could be disastrous. On the other hand, said the AIOC, they were 'quite prepared to volunteer … any information of real inside importance, which may happen to come to their knowledge'.[3]

---

*   Their number had been reduced from twenty-three earlier in the century.

In practice, they not only did this but, especially as the Abadan crisis developed, also sought to influence opinion in Iran in every way they could. The official history of the Abadan crisis is remarkably reticent about Britain's, and the AIOC's, covert activities. Despite the high classification of this history, its author complained in his introduction that he had 'not been permitted to see all relevant papers in the Foreign Office'.[4] But occasional glimpses of the work of the intelligence network break through.

In early July 1951, the Iranians closed the AIOC's 'information offices' (used for intelligence gathering) in Tehran and Abadan. With a foretaste of what was to come when the US Embassy was invaded in November 1979, the Iranians removed as many documents as they could find – and published the juicy ones. Herbert Morrison, the Foreign Secretary, claimed that these had been distorted to be incriminating, and that many were forgeries. But the official history then continues: 'One, at any rate, of the company's documents, which was claimed by the Persians on insufficient grounds to establish bribery and espionage in Persia, was subsequently admitted by the Foreign Office to be genuine and to need "some explaining away".'[5]

The payment of agents is a necessary part of the stock in trade of all intelligence services. In some cases, such payments may amount to bribery. Since 1994, payments of this kind have by law to be authorised by the Foreign Secretary.[6] Before that, there was no statutory regulation of Britain's intelligence services. Indeed, the very existence of SIS was not officially admitted ('averred' was the euphemism used) until 1994. What controls existed for the first eighty-five years of its existence were purely internal.

When the Foreign Office's Information Policy Department had advised in May 1951 that it would be difficult to get pro-British material into the Tehran press short of bribery, Morrison had minuted in reply, 'Why not a bit of bribery?'[7]

The British Ambassador in Tehran had, two months earlier, telegraphed the Foreign Office to say, 'We are doing all we can to arrange that there shall not be a quorum' at the session of the Majlis the following day, which was scheduled to vote on the nationalisation resolution of the Oil Commission.[8] The implication was clear, though on this occasion insufficient members stayed away, and the Commission's recommendations were unanimously approved by ninety-five votes.

In June 1951, the official documents record that an unnamed 'experienced Englishman … was of the view that M. Makki [a key ally of Mossadegh] could and should be bribed to desert Mossadeq'.[9] The record is understandably silent as to whether this happened on this occasion, but there are claims that it did later.[10]

'Our action against Dr Mossadeq should be indirect and behind the scenes' wrote the British Ambassador in August 1951, adding that it was 'desirable that Dr Mossadeq should be removed from office as soon as possible'.[11]

Behind the scenes, at the heart of the seamier side of Britain's intelligence network in Iran, were the three Rashidian brothers, recruited by the Tehran station head, C. M. ('Monty') Woodhouse,* in the early 1950s as the Abadan crisis boiled over. They were for some time run by Robin Zaehner, a fluent Persian speaker who was officially an 'acting counsellor' in the Tehran Embassy. These brothers came from a wealthy Iranian family. They loved the UK, though the handsome monthly subvention they were paid of £10,000 (worth around £330,000 today) no doubt helped reassure them that Britain's feelings were reciprocated. The eldest brother, Seyfollah, was the intellect of the trio, a musician and conversationalist; Asadollah was the organiser, and a confidante of the Shah; Qodratollah, the businessman. They had connections everywhere that mattered, and used these to bribe and suborn politicians, officials, clerics, bazaar leaders and newspaper editors – anyone who had influence, and who could be turned. This work was unsavoury enough. But they also had access to a number of

---

* Woodhouse was later Conservative MP for Oxford, 1959–66 and 1970–74, and later Lord Terrington.

rough-neck Tehran gangs, including Shaban 'the Brainless' Jafari and plenty of others well trained in the *zur khaneh*.

*   *   *

Britain's humiliation at Mossadegh's hand was far from complete when the last of the AIOC's expatriate staff left Abadan in a hurry in October 1951.

Mossadegh had a long memory. On New Year's Day 1952, the Prime Minister decided to expel all of Britain's consular officers on the grounds of their interference in Iran's internal affairs – 'especially in 1920'. Along with this, he ordered the closure of the remaining eleven consular posts, because, with the end of British rule in India, these, it was claimed, were no longer needed. Three weeks later, Mossadegh refused *agrément* (consent) to the proposed new British Ambassador, the Hon. R. M. A. Hankey.* In response, the British government decided to downgrade our representation to chargé d'affaires level. When the outgoing Ambassador, Sir Francis Shepherd, went to pay his valedictory respects to Mossadegh, Shepherd wryly commented that at least Mossadegh had 'honoured the occasion by having put on his clothes'.[12]

Mossadegh had been implored on many occasions, especially by Henry Grady, the otherwise sympathetic US Ambassador, and by Averell Harriman, Truman's envoy to Tehran, to understand the economic consequences for Iran if they were to nationalise the AIOC without compensation for or cooperation from the oil company. They would lack technical staff to operate the rigs and the complex refinery in Abadan, and they would lack the ability on their own to sell the oil internationally.

Mossadegh dismissed these concerns, arguing that nationalisation was a moral right for his country and if there were short-term problems for the economy, his people would bear these with fortitude.

---

* This is an occasional habit of the Iranians. In 2002, they refused *agrément* to David (now Sir) Reddaway. See Chapter 16.

They had borne worse in the past. Neither for the first nor for the last time did an Iranian leader appeal to his nation's sense of victimhood, such a powerful part of the Iranian psyche, profoundly rooted in its national narrative and in the fundamental tenets of Shi'ism, in the martyrdom of Husayn at Karbala in 680 AD.

For a while, this approach worked for Mossadegh. The Iranians, as they had before and have since, showed extraordinary stoicism in the face of the material adversity that followed the nationalisation of AIOC. Mossadegh sought and received some financial assistance from President Truman in the spring of 1952.

In July 1952, an emboldened Mossadegh moved to consolidate his power by demanding of the Shah that he – the Prime Minister – and not the Shah should henceforth have direct control of the armed forces. The Shah refused this claim and Mossadegh resigned. On 17 July, the Majlis nominated, and the Shah confirmed, the appointment of Ahmad Qavam os-Saltaneh as Prime Minister. (Qavam was seventy-seven years old to Mossadegh's seventy.)

Instead of treading carefully, Qavam os-Saltaneh immediately made intemperate pledges to restore law and order to the country and to 'solve' the continuing oil crisis. There was outrage at the prospect of backsliding on oil nationalisation under Qavam os-Saltaneh, whose sympathies for the UK and the US were well known. Worse, many of his detractors, including Ayatollah Kashani, realising that they would be candidates for incarceration in the promised crackdown, decided to get their retaliation in first.

Factions which were in other respects diametrically opposed to each other joined hands in protest against a common enemy. These included Mossadegh's National Front, the communist Tudeh Party, the Islamist terrorist group *Fidayan-i-Islam*, radical clerics under Ayatollah Kashani, and *bazaaris*. A general strike was called. There were massive street demonstrations in Tehran and provincial capitals, with many killed when troops backed by tanks opened fire.

In the face of such intense disorder, Qavam os-Saltaneh resigned.

He had lasted just five days in office. The Shah retreated. Mossadegh was reappointed as Prime Minister, immensely strengthened by the Qavam os-Saltaneh debacle and by the concession wrung from a resentful Shah that he – the Prime Minister – should henceforth have control of Iran's armed forces.

Fate also intervened on Mossadegh's side. On the very day he was reappointed as Prime Minister – 21 July 1952 – the International Court of Justice in The Hague, which in its interim decision had come down in Britain's favour, decided in its final judgment in favour of Iran.

Mossadegh moved swiftly to consolidate his gains – too swiftly, and too far, as events over the following thirteen months were to show. The newly reinstated Prime Minister persuaded a reluctant Majlis to grant him full powers to rule by decree, initially for six months but extended in August 1952 to a full year.

Mossadegh had built his towering reputation in Iran in significant part as the supreme constitutionalist. He'd fought against the arbitrary exercise of power, a perennial characteristic of the Iranian system. Now he appeared to be doing exactly the same thing he'd rebelled against.

His arguments for assuming such centralised power were plausible enough. (They usually are.) The country was facing an economic siege. He wanted to make the nation self-sufficient. He set about a reform of the labour laws, the vast holdings of rich landowners (of whom he was one) and the finance system, and encouraged rural development – and he purged the armed forces of corrupt, disloyal and inefficient officers. In his view, these changes were too urgent to have to face the interminable procedures of the Majlis.

The problem for those who do decide to rule alone by decree is that they become isolated. Those who lose influence and power, including erstwhile allies, start complaining. A vicious circle develops by which the leader relies less on others' advice, more on their own. Paranoia grows. Civic rights, demonstrations, strikes are suppressed; the press controlled.

Mossadegh fell victim to all these perils – a tragic irony for one whose rise to power had so depended upon mass popular support and a vibrant, if rambunctious, press.

* * *

As predicted, there was an inherent difficulty in running what had been AIOC's facilities without well-trained British and Indian technicians, and in selling the oil without any international organisation with which to do so.

The AIOC had ensured that this task would be doubly difficult. As the company's staff left Abadan, they skilfully sabotaged much of its plant, covering their tracks as far as they were able. The world's largest oil refinery would appear to work satisfactorily, only for parts of it to 'inexplicably' break down.

Those technical problems were in the end resolvable. Selling oil was not. The AIOC (aided by the British government) persuaded the US oil majors and Royal Dutch Shell that they could be next for the Mossadegh treatment unless they came together to boycott Iranian oil. They did so. Third countries who did try to purchase from Iran faced legal actions on the grounds that the oil had been 'stolen' from the AIOC. Most prospective purchasers decided that it was not worth the risk. One tanker, the *Rose Mary*, was chartered to transport oil from Bandar Abbas for an Italian company. The Royal Navy intercepted the tanker and escorted it to the British protectorate of Aden, where, unsurprisingly, a British court held that the contents of the tanker were indeed stolen property.

There was one other factor that compounded Mossadegh's difficulties over oil sales, which he had simply never anticipated. When he began his campaign for nationalisation of the AIOC in the mid-1940s, Iran's oil was at a premium. He was convinced that it was a seller's market. Had that situation continued, the other participants in the international oil embargo might have been less resolute. But in the intervening period the wells in Saudi Arabia, Kuwait and elsewhere had started to produce massive amounts of oil. The market was easily able to absorb the loss of Iranian production.

Whilst Attlee was in power in Westminster, and Truman in Washington, Mossadegh could correctly calculate that he was unlikely to face substantial covert action by the UK and the US against his government. Truman had never been an enthusiast for Mossadegh. But his overriding concern, spelt out in the Truman Doctrine, was to prevent Iran from falling into the ambit of the Soviet Union. He had no time for the AIOC and its leaders trapped in their imperial mindset. He and his Secretary of State Dean Acheson knew that with surer footwork by the British government (not least to bring the AIOC to heel) a '50–50' deal could have been struck in the late 1940s before the extraordinary head of steam for outright nationalisation had become so strong. Truman thought that for all his eccentricities Mossadegh, and his National Front, could be a bulwark against the communist Tudeh Party rather than their fellow travellers. He also believed that military action of the kind that Morrison had considered could lead to Stalin moving into Iran from its north. He was opposed to any covert action against Mossadegh, fearing that it could lead to uncontrollable instability. Attlee, meanwhile, was heavily influenced by the White House's firm counsel against intervention.

However, Attlee had left office in October 1951, to be replaced by Churchill, and Truman would follow suit fifteen months later, in January 1953.

*　*　*

As he had made clear publicly, and in private meetings with his predecessor, Churchill's view of the Abadan crisis was altogether simpler than Attlee's or Truman's. Still lamenting the 'loss of the Indian Empire' (by the Labour government), he had said in the last debate of the parliament that Britain should use 'every means in our power' to prevent a total evacuation from Abadan, and that if necessary

Parliament should be recalled to consider the matter – i.e. military action.[13]

The evacuation from Abadan was a fait accompli by the time Churchill took office in late October 1951. But, undeterred, he and his Foreign Secretary, Anthony Eden, lost no time in seeking to persuade Truman and Acheson to take a tougher and more coordinated line with the UK against Mossadegh. Six years after the Allied victory in the Second World War, Churchill was able to use his unquestioned status as a great wartime leader to pressure Truman. The first fruits of this tactic came in March 1952, when the State Department refused an additional loan sought by the Iranians (though the US did continue with its $25 million of military aid for that year).

Shortly after Mossadegh had returned to power in late July 1952, Churchill proposed to Truman that they should send a joint message to the Iranian Prime Minister, with new proposals to resolve the oil dispute. Truman hesitated at first, worried that this would imply that the US and the UK were 'ganging up' on Iran. (It would, and it did.) To this, Churchill replied, 'I do not myself see why two good men asking only what is right and just should not gang up on a third who is doing wrong.' Truman gave in.

The joint message, sent at the end of August 1952, proposed that the International Court of Justice should be asked to arbitrate on compensation to AIOC for the nationalisation of their company; that there should be negotiations to resume the flow of oil; that the AIOC would pay for oil stored in Iran; that British restrictions on exports to Iran and its use of sterling (still a reserve currency) would be relaxed; and that the US government would grant the Iranians an immediate $10 million to assist with their budgetary problems.

The British chargé in Tehran commented that if these proposals had been offered the year before, they would have been greeted 'as a great victory'. However, 'Today Persian opinion is unanimous in rejecting the offer.'[14]

Mossadegh responded, unsurprisingly, by turning down the offer and tabling counter-proposals of his own. These were rejected by the US and the UK. Mossadegh thereupon decided to sever all diplomatic relations with the UK, on 22 October 1952, which had the especial advantage for him that this would disrupt the UK's intelligence work in Iran.

When Truman decided not to stand again at the November 1952 presidential election, he tried to recruit General Eisenhower as the Democrat candidate to succeed him. Eisenhower told him that he and his family were Republicans. He duly stood for the Republican Party and won by a landslide, carrying thirty-nine states to Adlai Stevenson's nine.

For Churchill and Eden, this was manna from heaven. At last they had a US administration that shared their views. Both men had been convinced for months that relations with Iran could only be restored if Mossadegh were removed. With the SIS controllers of their deep intelligence network forced to leave Iran when the British Embassy was closed, the UK's only hope of achieving regime change was with the active cooperation of the new Eisenhower administration.

Even before the election had been won, the US had sent a seasoned intelligence officer, Kermit Roosevelt Jr, to Tehran to assess the possibilities for a coup. Roosevelt was the grandson of US President Theodore Roosevelt, well connected with the Washington establishment, and had been director of operations for the CIA for the Middle East. On his way back from Tehran, he had meetings in London with SIS colleagues. This was followed by a trip to Washington by Monty Woodhouse, the SIS head of station until the UK Embassy in Tehran had been closed.

Eisenhower had appointed as his Secretary of State and head of the CIA two brothers, John Foster Dulles and Allen Dulles. In the early part of 1953, the two Dulles brothers agreed that a coup in Iran was necessary, and gained Eisenhower's consent. SIS was to be involved as its joint partner. However, such was the concern in Washington for the way in which the oil crisis had been handled by the UK that it was later made a formal part of the agreement with Britain that the coup could go ahead only if the British government provided, in advance, a written guarantee of 'its intention to reach an early oil settlement with a successor Iranian government in a spirit of goodwill and equity'.[15] This undertaking was duly provided.

The CIA/SIS operational headquarters for the coup were based in the then British colony of Cyprus – near enough to Tehran to be convenient, but far enough away to ensure complete security. The final operational plan was agreed in June 1953, with the added condition, insisted upon by the State Department, that US funds would be provided to the new Iranian government immediately after the coup, to sustain it until an oil settlement could be reached. The plan was formally agreed by Churchill and Eden on 1 July and by Eisenhower and the Dulles brothers on 11 July.

Very little about the planning and execution of the coup has been released from SIS's archive. The now-declassified secret internal history of the Abadan crisis, produced in 1962, devotes just two paragraphs to the coup, and never uses that word. Instead, the extraordinary events of August 1953 are presented almost as some act of divine intervention. The only direct reference to responsibility for the coup is a Delphic caveat which muses, in near-impenetrable prose, about 'whatever extent the downfall of the doctor [Mossadegh] was indeed promoted, as has been maintained [in press reports] by the American Central Intelligence Agency'.[16] On SIS's equal role in the planning and execution of the coup, and Churchill's prime role in initiating it, the document is wholly silent.

Serving Foreign Secretaries have no right to see any records from previous administrations. I saw none relating to the coup. However, by the time I took office in 2001, a huge amount of material had already been published about it, including an autobiography by SIS's head of station Monty Woodhouse,[17] an account by the CIA leader of the coup, Kermit Roosevelt,[18] and much more. Previously highly classified internal documents from the CIA were becoming available, which included chapter and verse on SIS's role.[19] Despite the continuing official British line of NCND (neither confirm nor deny) on this subject, I thought it would be wholly risible to parrot this line when everyone knew that our intelligence services had been involved. So, giving evidence to the House of Commons Foreign Affairs Select Committee in February 2006, I said that 'elements of British intelligence and the CIA stopped [forced] a perfectly democratic Prime Minister, Mossadegh, from office'.*

Amongst the official records made public was the CIA's clandestine internal history of the coup, written by one of its key participants, Donald Wilber, in 1954.[20] This includes the full text of the final 'London' plan for the coup.

The plan was straightforward enough, but shocking in its cold-blooded detail. The sum of $285,000 was estimated to be needed for the coup (oddly, split $147,500 from the US and $137,000 from SIS). In addition, there was $1 million in covert activity in support of their preferred replacement for Mossadegh, General Fazlollah Zahedi, as well as a specific authorisation to spend up to 1 million rials a week (about $11,000 then; around $110,000 today) 'in purchasing the co-operation of members of the Iranian Majlis'.[21] A further $5 million was allocated to help the new Prime Minister who would be replacing Mossadegh in the early days after he took office.

The Shah was seen as an essential component of the plan, since he would be required to issue orders – *firman* – dismissing Mossadegh, installing a more amenable Prime Minister and demanding the loyalty of the armed forces. The Shah, however, was notoriously indecisive. His self-confidence, never strong, had been shattered by his failure to sustain Mossadegh's dismissal in July 1952.

The plan identified the Shah's 'pathological fear of the "hidden UK hand"'.[22] He was worried that he too might be a victim of the coup. To counter this, and demonstrate that the leader of the British group was authorised to speak for the UK government, it was agreed that

---

* I am sure I said 'forced' but 'stopped' was how this was transcribed.

the Shah should choose a specific form of words from several options proposed by the group leader, which the British government would then broadcast back for the Shah to hear in successive dates in the Persian-language service of the BBC. The broadcasts took place. Despite this, it took a huge effort – by the Shah's twin sister, Princess Ashraf; by US General H. Norman Schwarzkopf, who knew the Shah; by a British agent close to the Shah; and by Roosevelt – to gain his agreement to sign the *firman*, ready for use when they were required.

The next question was who to put in Mossadegh's place. There were a number of candidates, but a consensus quickly emerged that Zahedi was the man. At first blush, this was odd, since Zahedi had been arrested by the British during the war for his part in a pro-German rebellion in Isfahan, for which he had been exiled. (Zahedi had been captured by the redoubtable Fitzroy Maclean, who executed a clever ruse to arrange a meeting with Zahedi – and then bundled him into a car at gunpoint.)*

Ever one to understand where his best interests might lie, Zahedi quickly became reconciled with the British.

Zahedi had managed to be appointed as Minister of War by Mossadegh in his first administration in 1951. However, he incurred Mossadegh's wrath when the Prime Minister learnt that he had had meetings both with British agents and with Ayatollah Kashani, a one-time ally of Mossadegh (and Speaker of the Majlis) who was now becoming his adversary. In October 1952, Mossadegh moved to have Zahedi arrested and tried for treason. Zahedi was a member of the Iranian Senate and therefore enjoyed parliamentary immunity. He took *bast* in the Majlis under Kashani's protection (and that of Kashani's thugs). The Majlis then dissolved the Senate (it had already reached its maximum term), which meant that Zahedi was liable to be arrested. He went into hiding.

* * *

---

* This was Operation PONGO, executed by Maclean and commandos from the Seaforth Highlanders.

The operational plan for the coup set out in detail that an 'increasingly intensified propaganda effort through the press, handbills, and the Tehran clergy' was to be conducted 'in a campaign designed to weaken the Mossadeq government in any way possible'. High-ranking officials in the US would then make public statements that would disabuse the Iranian public of the 'Mossadeq myth that the US supported his regime'.[23]

The propaganda was to 'hammer' the agreed themes that Mossadegh favoured the Tudeh Party and the Soviet Union (this was to be supported by 'black', i.e. fabricated, documents); that Mossadegh was an 'enemy of Islam' by his association with the Tudeh Party; that he was deliberately leading the country into economic collapse; and that he had been so corrupted by power that 'no trace is left of the fine man of earlier years'.[24]

A key assumption of the coup planners was that 'nearly all the important religious leaders with large followings' were opposed to Mossadegh. The most senior cleric in Iran was Grand Ayatollah Mohammad-Hossein Boroujerdi, based in Qom, the religious capital of Iran. The hope was that he would issue a *fatwa* against Mossadegh. But he had a quietist approach to politics and kept a low profile until the final acts of the drama. In contrast, many other clerics were heavily involved in politics, especially Kashani and 'his terrorist gang', who were assumed to be biddable by CIA/SIS agents.[25]

Whilst the Shah was vacillating as to whether or not to sign the *firman*, the psychological campaign against Mossadegh was approaching its climax. The 'controllable press was going all out' against him. The owner of one newspaper was granted a 'personal loan' of $45,000 to disrupt Mossadegh's premiership and to cause him trouble in the Parliament. Successful efforts were made to alarm religious leaders by issuing 'black' propaganda in the Tudeh Party's name. These leaders were threatened in print, by phone calls and, in some cases, by 'sham bombings' of their residences, with the Tudeh Party as the apparent culprit.

Destabilised by the campaign against him, Mossadegh then made what was perhaps the gravest error of his political career. His position had already been weakened by the economic crisis that was engulfing the country. Unemployment (including of thousands of former AIOC workers in Abadan) was rising.

In July 1953, Mossadegh was facing a motion of no confidence over the alleged torture of suspects involved in the assassination of the police chief of Tehran, General Mahmud Afshartus, an ally of the Prime Minister's. Mossadegh believed that he would lose this vote and that, with Kashani's support, Zahedi would be asked to replace him. To avoid this scenario, Mossadegh demanded of his supporters in the Majlis that they resign their seats. However, many of the Majlis members already 'purchased' by the intelligence agencies refused to resign, in a bid to thwart this effort. Mossadegh's response was to dissolve the Majlis. But this wheeze had a built-in trap. With no Majlis in session, the Shah could have appointed a successor without the necessity for Majlis approval.

To extricate himself from this trap, Mossadegh embarked on a course which – with a lot of help from the CIA and SIS – sealed his fate. He decided to call a referendum, to endorse his decision to upend the Majlis, to amend the election laws, and to allow him to rule by decree.

The opposition boycotted the process. Two million votes were cast in Mossadegh's favour, and just a few hundred against. Even by Iranian standards, the poll had patently been rigged. Mossadegh's victory was pyrrhic. He had unnerved his remaining loyal supporters, most of whom had advised him against this course. He had offered himself as a propaganda target not only to those many who had always opposed him but also to other powerful figures, like Kashani, who had previously worked with him. And, by ignoring the fundamental principles of the constitution, he had delivered himself to the Shah, who was now on rock-solid legal grounds to dismiss him and appoint a replacement.

The Shah's signature on the *firman* was not, in fact, forthcoming until 13 August, four weeks after Mossadegh's rigged referendum. Once the Shah had signed, execution of the coup – codenamed TPAJAX by the CIA, and Operation BOOT by SIS – could go into overdrive. But, as every battle commander knows, there are plans, and there is what actually happens.

Armed with the Shah's signed *firman*, the plotters were due to stage their coup on the night of Friday 14 August. There was then an inexplicable delay of twenty-four hours when the controllers lost contact with those intended to execute it.

Security was always a concern of the coup planners. By 15 August, their anxieties that there might be a leak became a reality. Mossadegh's chief of staff of the army, General Taghi Riahi, had learnt all the details of the plot by 5 p.m. that afternoon. There was sporadic action between forces loyal to Mossadegh and those loyal to the Shah. Colonel Nematollah Nasiri, given the task of delivering to Mossadegh the *firman* dismissing him, was arrested, along with many others. Those still at large, realising that the plot had failed, went to ground.

The ever-neurotic Shah was ensconced at his holiday home on the Caspian Sea when news reached him that the coup had been fatally compromised. He quickly left for Baghdad in his private plane. From there, he flew to Rome, anticipating that exile awaited him. Mossadegh, he thought, had won.

The driving force of the coup, Kermit Roosevelt, took a different view. He ignored a cable from Washington advising him to leave the country for his own safety, and calculated that he and his network of agents should make one final effort to topple Mossadegh. The *firman* was still valid and Roosevelt's most precious asset, Zahedi, was still in a CIA safe house.

The situation on the streets of Tehran was far from stable. Troops loyal to Mossadegh were stationed at key points and the royal palaces were sealed off. The city was awash with rumours and outlandish conspiracy theories.

One was that the coup had in fact been inspired by Mossadegh to give him an excuse to remove the Shah. Mossadegh himself gave this rumour credibility with those half-inclined to believe it when he issued a statement on Radio Tehran formally dissolving the Majlis (by constitution, the prerogative of the Shah). Foreign Minister Hossein Fatemi followed this up by making virulent anti-Shah statements. The Tudeh Party began preaching the virtues of a republic.

For a while, pro-Mossadegh forces had the upper hand on the streets. Fatemi went even further, accusing the Shah of being a traitor who should go to the gallows. A long list of alleged agents of the CIA and SIS was issued, with the suggestion that those already in custody would be hanged on 20 August.

For all his personal failings, the mystical idea of the Shah as the fount of all authority still held powerful sway with many in Iran. Some of those took to the streets, encouraged by those of the plotters still at liberty who decided they had nothing to lose by trying again. They were determined to free their arrested colleagues if they could.

On the evening of 17 August, spontaneous violence flared on the streets of Tehran. This took the CIA station in Tehran by surprise. Their official history comments that 'just what was the major motivating force is impossible to say', and speculated that four factors might have been at work. First, the flight of the Shah may have galvanised people into an 'irate pro-Shah force'. Second, the Tudeh may have overestimated its strength and alienated a lot of people by tearing down statues of the Shah and raising their own flags. Third, 'the Mossadeq government was at last beginning to feel very uneasy about its alliance [sic] with the Tudeh Party'. Lastly, the climax was 'now approaching of the … campaign of alleged Tudeh terrorism' – stoked by agents embedded into the Tudeh itself.

On 18 August, the Tudeh played into their opponents' hands with violent speeches and much criminal damage. On 19 August, the 'controllable' press carried facsimiles of the Shah's *firman*. A fake, if broadly accurate, interview with Zahedi was carried in two newspapers stressing that Zahedi's government was the only legal one. Thousands of broadsheets were issued with the *firman* and circulated across the city.

'On Wednesday morning at about nine, a group of weight lifters, tumblers, and wrestlers armed with iron bars and knives began marching ... shouting pro-Shah slogans,' reported Kenneth Love, the *New York Times*'s Tehran correspondent.[26] 'Two energetic sub-agents' were down in the bazaar and helped organise an excitable demonstration which decided to march on the Majlis, stopping on the way to burn down Fatemi's newspaper building. Another agent led a mob which sacked the offices of three Tudeh newspapers. The Rashidian brothers – 'full of glee' – now attempted to swing the security forces to the side of the demonstrators. Members of the disbanded Imperial Guards seized trucks and drove through the streets. A pro-coup colonel and a plotter appeared in the square outside the Majlis on a tank which the colonel had managed to 'borrow'.

Huge crowds gathered. The troops, under orders to disperse the crowds, simply fired over their heads and then joined the protests. Progressively key targets were taken over by pro-Shah forces: police and gendarmerie stations, the military police HQ (where those arrested four days before were being held), the telegraph office and Radio Tehran.

Thugs began attacking Mossadegh's private residence in Palace Street, from where he ran the government. There were pitched battles between his defenders and the attackers. His opponents brought up tanks. They began shelling the property and later sacked it. Mossadegh was forced to flee for his life over a neighbour's back wall. It was all over.

Mossadegh went into hiding. The next day, he was quickly found by the police and arrested. He spent weeks in prison whilst charges against him were prepared. He conducted his own defence at his trial, using the opportunity to defend his record in eloquent terms, and to damn his opponents. He knew that the verdict was a foregone conclusion. On 21 December 1953, the court formally announced that he had been found guilty. The Shah had let it be known that he wanted some clemency to be shown. Mossadegh was sentenced to three years' solitary confinement (in contrast to his Foreign Minister, Hossein Fatemi, who was executed). Once he had served his sentence,

Mossadegh was exiled to his estate in Ahmadabad, where he lived quietly until his death in March 1967, aged eighty-four.

Many of the Tehran clerics, a major political force since the tobacco revolt, had come out in favour of removing Mossadegh. They were led by Kashani. The quietist Grand Ayatollah Boroujerdi had not issued any formal *fatwa*, as the CIA and SIS had been hoping, but he, along with other senior members of the clerical establishment in Qom, as well as those closer to events in Tehran, had become increasingly concerned about the implications for them, and their faith, of the apparent alliance between Mossadegh and the Tudeh Party. When the latter started to campaign for a republic (which would have been a secular one on the Soviet model), their weight of opinion shifted to the Shah. When Mossadegh fell, Boroujerdi sent the Shah a message to say that he hoped that 'the return of your Majesty ... will put an end to [our temporal ills] and bring glory to Islam and welfare to Muslims'.[27]

The myth in the Islamic Republic today is that the clerics stood four-square with Mossadegh. They did the opposite. Their overriding concern, then as now, was to preserve their power and influence within Iran.

* * *

The Shah returned triumphantly from his temporary exile in Rome on Saturday 22 August. Zahedi was confirmed as Prime Minister, a position he held until April 1955.[*]

On his appointment as Prime Minister, Zahedi moved quickly to neuter all opposition. Martial law was imposed – which lasted until 1957. Supporters of Mossadegh's National Front in the armed forces and the bureaucracy were stripped of their posts. The Tudeh Party fared worse. Many of those who had not fled to the Soviet Union

---

[*] His power had become too much for the Shah, so he was sent to Rome and then Geneva as an Ambassador, never to return to Iran. His son, Ardeshir Zahedi, was to become Iranian Ambassador to the US between 1973 and the Islamic Revolution in 1979.

were imprisoned; the party's military and clandestine organisation was dismembered. The seventeenth Majlis was dissolved, to be replaced by the eighteenth, 'elected' in 1954.

On his way back to Washington, Kermit Roosevelt called in to London to see senior ministers and officials, including Prime Minister Winston Churchill.

Churchill was seventy-eight, almost eight years older than Mossadegh. He shared with the Iranian Prime Minister whose ousting he had instigated the eccentric habit of conducting much business from his bed. Roosevelt reported that Churchill 'appeared to be in bad shape physically' but was enthusiastic about the coup, and he believed that if its success could be maintained, 'it would be the finest operation since the end of the war'.

He commented that the AIOC had really 'fouled things up' in the previous few years, and he was determined that they should not be allowed to foul things up any further.[28]

It was imperative for both the US and the UK to get Iran's oil flowing again. Without its revenues, Iran would fall into bankruptcy and be prey to the very Soviet takeover that had so motivated Mossadegh's removal. There was no question of allowing the AIOC and its bone-headed leadership simply to begin where they had left off when cleared out of Abadan in October 1951. Its brand was so toxic that it had no supporters left in Iran, not even amongst the most strongly pro-Shah groups.

Instead, a plan was hatched for an international consortium to take over the production, sale and distribution of Iran's oil, under the aegis of the Iranian National Oil Corporation, who would own the country's oil resources and facilities. At long last it was *Iran's* oil. Sir William Fraser, AIOC's head, who had played such a lamentable role in 'fouling things up', was virtually ordered by the US and UK governments to propose this structure – one which he had so long resisted, with such calamitous consequences for his company and his staff.

By this stage, however, as Mossadegh had found to his cost,

production elsewhere across the Middle East had been ramped up to exceed the gap left by the embargo on Iranian oil imposed in late 1951. The other oil majors were therefore not keen on having to invest in Iran. They were in the end persuaded to do so, on the grounds that if the Soviets were able to take control of Iran they would flood the world market with Iranian oil. In return, the US government withdrew pending anti-trust actions against their oil majors.

The new deal was signed by the Shah in October 1954. Five US oil majors, Shell and a French oil company, CFP, were between them to have 60 per cent of the consortium. The AIOC took the remaining 40 per cent. By sheer persistence, Fraser was able to get the other members of the consortium to pay the AIOC the compensation it thought it was owed by Iran – $90 million up front, and a royalty on each barrel until another $500 million had been paid.[29] In the same year, the AIOC adopted the name of the former German-owned downstream distributor it had acquired during the First World War, becoming British Petroleum. The AIOC was no more, at least in name.

'Our operation had given us a wonderful and unexpected opportunity which might change the whole picture of the Middle East,' Churchill had added to Kermit Roosevelt from his bed.[30]

But just how 'wonderful' did this opportunity turn out to be?

Britain's humiliating ejection from Abadan in October 1951 had immediately been seized upon by Egyptian nationalists, campaigning for an end to the 1936 Anglo-Egyptian Treaty and to Britain's involvement in their country, which included the British Middle East HQ and its very large military base in the Canal Zone.

The dying Labour government had responded to this pressure by sending two further battalions of British troops to Egypt. On taking office, Eden upped the stakes. In January 1952, British tanks and troops stormed a police headquarters, killing forty. The next day, there was serious rioting in Cairo, with twenty killed and over 700 premises burned and looted, including Shepheard's Hotel, the symbolic centre of British rule. In July, a group of 'Free Officers', led by Gamal Abdel Nasser, staged a coup which forced King Farouk's abdication and exile.

Four years later, with Eden as Prime Minister, Britain suffered its greatest foreign policy debacle since the war: the Suez crisis.

After Nasser had nationalised the Suez Canal, Eden plotted with the French and Israeli governments in high secrecy to invade Egypt and remove Nasser's government by force. The invasion took place in late October 1956. It was, on the face of it, a military success. Politically, it was a total disaster. Pressure from Eisenhower, who had not been consulted and was in the closing days of his re-election campaign, forced Britain to withdraw. The defeat laid the ground for the 1967 Six Day War between Israel and Egypt, because of the lack of any peace settlement between these two countries.

The Abadan crisis and Mossadegh's removal in a coup financed and organised by foreign powers helped to fuel strong nationalist, anti-Western tendencies across the region, which can still be seen today. In the aftermath of Suez, Syria entered a pact with the Soviet Union, where military hardware and, later, a Soviet naval base at Tartus were exchanged for increasing Soviet influence in Syria. In Iraq, the pro-British King, Faisal II, was assassinated in 1958 in a coup which proclaimed Iraq as a republic, strongly anti-imperialist and with growing links with the Soviet Union. But it was above all in Iran itself where the long-term consequences of the 1953 coup became the opposite of that vision set out by Churchill from his sickbed.

As we will see, the coup did buy its instigators, the US and the UK, twenty-five years of Iranian cooperation with Western powers, and the Shah twenty-five years of power. It gave Western oil companies, especially BP, a quarter of a century of good profits, and fabulous opportunities for other British companies. Indeed, even in the mid-1970s the British Embassy was judging that Iran was 'one of the most promising markets in the world'.[31] But this 'success' came at a great and abiding cost.

'They that sow into the wind, shall reap the whirlwind,' counsels

Hosea in the Old Testament. The United States and the United Kingdom did sow into the wind. They reaped a whirlwind.

There is a direct line from the 1953 coup through the Islamic Revolution of 1979, through the 444-day siege of the US Embassy in Tehran, to today. Harry Truman and Clement Attlee were correct in their estimation, in Truman's words, that mishandling the Iran crisis would be 'a disaster to the free world'.[32] Attlee had told his Cabinet, when vetoing Morrison's plans for armed intervention, that

> Mossadegh had been able to form his government owing to the support of Persians, who were dissatisfied with [their] former rule by a corrupt clique. We could not safely assume that if we succeeded in upsetting the present government their successors would be less unsatisfactory, and we should risk identifying ourselves with support of an equally undemocratic regime.[33]

It can take centuries for democratic institutions to take root. In our case, it took the English Civil War, the execution of one monarch, the forced removal of a second, the 1688 Bill of Rights, three major Reform Bills in the nineteenth century and key reforms in the twentieth before our system could be described as stable and functioning.

In the United States, it took their civil war and the twentieth-century civil rights movement before they had anything like a free democracy for all their citizens – and in both cases without any interference by outside powers.

Iran, by contrast, had neither the time nor the freedom properly to develop its institutions. Near civil war followed the 1906 Constitutional Revolution. Most elections to the Majlis were rigged. After Reza Khan's coup in 1921, and still more after his installation as Shah, the Majlis was castrated, to become his creature. Then we and the Soviet Union ventriloquised the country for five years. Thus, it was only from 1946 that anything approaching democratic politics started to resume in Iran after a thirty-year gap.

It is testament to the resilience of the idea of democracy and the norms of the 1906 revolution that the system operated at all. Mossadegh was able to break through the 'corrupt clique'. The fact that the AIOC and the British establishment did not appreciate him is hardly the point. He became the standard bearer, the iconic figure of Iran's struggle against foreign powers over 150 years – and Britain, under Prime Minister Churchill, then instigated his removal. Although the coup could not have been effected without the active (and, indeed, the dominant) role played by the US, it would and could not have happened at all but for us. It was an English job – and we are still living with the consequences.

*   *   *

If Britain had had the imagination to make a deal with the Iranians in the late 1940s, without ejecting its elected government, Iranian politics would no doubt have continued on its rather chaotic way before probably settling down as its citizens saw what a stake they had in its democracy. If Britain and the US had not intervened as they did in 1953, Mossadegh might well still have lost office, to be replaced by some other political coalition. But there is little serious evidence that Iran would have become a Soviet satellite – to prevent which was the ostensible justification for the CIA–SIS coup.

This is because of the extraordinary strength and depth of the political influence and authority of the clerical class in Iran, and the strong alliance it had developed with the powerful *bazaaris*, who helped fund them. That alliance, it will be recalled, first came to the fore in the tobacco rebellion in the 1890s. Although Reza Khan sought with some success to neutralise it, he was never able to defeat it. Paradoxically, it played a leading part in the removal of Mossadegh himself on 19 August 1953, not out of any love for the US and the UK (whose hidden hand behind the coup was revealed only much later), but because they had been wound up to believe that Tudeh's support for

Mossadegh (itself transient) could lead to the declaration of a secular republic. Should that have ever come anywhere near fruition, the clerics and the *bazaaris* would have taken on the Tudeh, and in my view they would have won.

* * *

On his triumphal return to Tehran three days after the coup, the Shah gradually took complete control of government in Iran. He could enforce his will only by the use of extravagantly equipped armed forces, by empowering an all-pervasive secret police, and by effectively abolishing normal politics. Along with the 1906 Constitutional Revolution, the 1979 Islamic Revolution and the Iran–Iraq War, the coup against Mossadegh was one of the defining moments of twentieth-century Iranian history, and of itself explains the abiding suspicion, not to say paranoia, about foreign interference in Iran.

CHAPTER 11

THE SHAH IN HIS
ELEMENT

*To my Iranian friends, with the sincere wish that the progress
and prosperity which have marked the first half-century
of Pahlavi rule will long continue.*

SIR DENIS WRIGHT, BRITISH AMBASSADOR TO IRAN 1963–71,

DEDICATION IN *THE ENGLISH AMONGST THE PERSIANS*[1]

In his lament that he had saved Mossadegh's neck, Mohammad Reza
Shah complained that Mossadegh had 'almost ended the dynasty
founded by my father'.*

That dynasty was called Pahlavi, after an ancient Iranian written
language dating from the third century BC, around the time of the
Parthian dynasty (248 BC–224 AD). Reza Khan, the first of the Pahlavi
dynasty, which ruled from 1925 to 1979, could trace no roots back to
the Parthians, or even to the Qajars, whose dynasty he extinguished.
Rather, he was the ultimate *arriviste*. A private soldier, then a gunnery
sergeant, who had struck lucky, he chose the dynastic title of Pahlavi in
the hope of convincing his subjects of the provenance of his authority.

He at least was able to live up to being a king. Tall, imposing, with
a natural authority, he was both ruthless and decisive. In the sixteen

---

* See Chapter 9.

short years of his reign, until forced to abdicate by the British and the Soviets in 1941, he transformed Iran – for good or ill.

Apart from his growing paranoia, his son Mohammad Reza Shah shared few of his father's characteristics. Brought up in closeted luxury, the second and last Shah of the Pahlavi dynasty was weak and indecisive. He came to believe the fairy story that he was special, blue-blooded, possessed of an almost divine mission to transport Iran towards his vision of a Great Civilisation – and that, in the words he used when he returned to Iran after the 1953 coup, his people loved him. There was little awareness of the conditions in which most of his subjects lived, and which his father had suffered as a boy. As the years of his reign went by, so his appetite to spend the revenues of the country on himself and his immediate family increased.

This culminated in the most vulgar and extravagant state celebration that the world has ever seen – as *The Guinness Book of Records* confirmed. The occasion was to mark the '2,500th Year of Foundation of the Imperial State of Iran' by Cyrus the Great. It consisted of elaborate festivities over a five-day period in autumn 1971. The intention was to demonstrate to the Iranian people, and to the world, the antiquity of Iran's civilisation and the progress it had made under Mohammad Reza Shah and his father, Reza Khan (on both counts, in sharp contrast to Iran's Arab neighbours). The claim itself – of two and a half millennia of a continuous Iranian empire – required some serious historical amnesia, since from the Muslim Arab invasion in the seventh century through to the Safavids in the sixteenth Iran had been ruled mainly by outsiders.

The party took place in October 1971, in the ancient capital of the Achaemenid Empire in Persepolis. As Alice, our friends and I were to witness when we were its only visitors that day in October 2015, Persepolis is absolutely vast. Its terrace alone is 125,000 square metres. For the Shah's party, it was transformed into an enormous tented city. Monarchs and heads of government from across the world attended. The UK was represented by the Duke of Edinburgh and Princess Anne, the US by Vice-President Spiro Agnew. Six hundred guests sat down to a lavish, five-hour banquet, with the catering provided by Maxim's of Paris. The menu included roast peacocks stuffed with *foie gras*. The official estimate of the cost was $17 million; the true cost is likely to have been nearer $200 million.[2]

In the Shah's eyes, the celebration was a great success. For his Western backers, especially the US and the UK governments, anxious to keep him onside in the Cold War and to maintain access to the lucrative Iranian market for military and civilian exports, the ludicrous ostentation of the event aroused no public criticism, though this did not prevent there being much adverse comment in the Western press.

Ayatollah Ruhollah Khomeini, later to lead the Islamic Revolution in 1979 and become Iran's first Supreme Leader, was at this time exiled in Iraq. As we will see, in the early '60s he led a series of protests against some key reforms of the Shah. Having been arrested and released a number of times by the Shah's secret police, he was exiled in 1964, first to Turkey and then to Iraq (and in early 1978 to Paris). From the Shi'a shrine city of Najaf across Iran's western border, Khomeini damned the event as the 'Devil's Festival'.

There was no public criticism to speak of in Iran. By this stage of the Shah's reign, the country was effectively a police state, with a fully controlled press, and opposition forces intimidated into silence. But the Iranians are far from stupid. The contrast between the life of the Shah and his court on the one hand and their lives on the other was too stark. They could speculate on how such largesse might have been used to improve their lives. Many, especially clerics and their allies in the bazaars, were angry about how the Shah appeared deliberately to be downgrading the national religion of the country, Shi'ism, in favour of summoning up the spirit of Iran's pre-Islamic glories. This was an anxiety confirmed just a few years later, in 1976, when the Shah decreed that henceforth Iran was to abandon its Islamic solar calendar (which takes Year 1 as the date of the Prophet Muhammad's flight from Mecca, in 622 AD) for one which began with the accession of Cyrus the Great some 1,200 years earlier (around 600 BC).

Far from heralding decades of stability and prosperity for the Pahlavi dynasty, this celebration occurred just seven and a half years before the Shah was driven from office. The factors that caused his downfall were many and deep-rooted. But the Persepolis extravaganza certainly did not help the Shah's survival. This *folie de grandeur* came powerfully to symbolise the decadence and detachment of his regime.

*　*　*

Mohammad Reza Pahlavi was not yet twenty-two when his father was forced to abdicate in 1941 and he became Shah.

The following twelve years were a dismal time for him. For the first five, key decisions were made by the occupying powers, the UK and the Soviet Union. The next seven years were dominated by a rash of Iranian democracy, as the Majlis, with Mossadegh the dominant figure, sought to assert the Parliament's independence from the Shah, and the country's independence from the overweening influence of foreign powers.

That period ended, as we have seen, with a victory for two of those foreign powers, the US and the UK, and the crushing of the turbulent, at times chaotic, politics of Iran's emerging democracy.

After the new deal with the international oil companies, and the theoretical nationalisation of Iran's oil resources which accompanied this development, the Shah was assured of regular and growing revenue for his exchequer. In less than two decades, Iran's oil production increased five-fold, and its revenues twenty times.

The US was to add greatly to its initial emergency relief by a massive programme of aid for the general budget, as well as for specific projects in healthcare, education, dams, power grids and military hardware and training. That training extended not only to Iran's military services but also to its secret police, the 'Organization of National Intelligence and Security of the Nation', known universally by its Persian acronym, 'SAVAK'. SAVAK combined the functions of a secret police service, a domestic security service and an intelligence service. Early help on its formation was given by General Norman Schwarzkopf, who had previously trained Iran's gendarmerie, and who was one of those sent in by the CIA personally to persuade the Shah to sign the *firman* dismissing Mossadegh as Prime Minister. Very soon, both the CIA and Israel's external intelligence agency, Mossad, were giving detailed advice on SAVAK's structure and methods of operation. SAVAK became feared and despised in equal measure by Iranians. Its tentacles were everywhere – in a similar manner to the internal security agencies of the Soviet Union and its satellite states, like the KGB and the Stasi.

SAVAK used methods which were at least as unpleasant as those practised by the worst of Stalin's security agencies. It had virtually un-limited powers of arrest and detention, and no accountability beyond the Shah. It routinely used extreme methods of torture, and either non-judicial killings or executions after 'trials'. Whilst its actions were notorious in Iran and beyond, it aroused almost no criticism from foreign powers. The Soviet Union had no motive to complain. The US and the UK may have preened themselves on the high standards by which (up to a point) their domestic police and security services operated, but they turned a blind eye to SAVAK's excesses, judging that keeping the Shah on the West's side in the Cold War was the greater imperative.

The Shah did set about an extensive series of reforms, beginning with the country's antiquated system of land holdings and agriculture, and extending to literacy, industrialisation and the raising of living standards. These reforms were packaged by the Shah into what was described as his 'White Revolution' – an interesting attempt to pur-loin the notion of revolution, which had such positive connotations from the 1906 Constitutional Revolution, and the colour 'white' in contradistinction to the Red revolution which had occurred across Iran's border in the Soviet Union and which he was determined to avoid in Iran. The reforms from this White Revolution were largely implemented between 1961 and 1965.

Many, especially the urban middle classes, undoubtedly benefited in material terms from these reforms. They were able to enjoy their lives provided they kept well away from any political activity. Despite this, there was volcanic anger just under the surface, which occasionally erupted, albeit until the late 1970s in a way that the Shah was able to control.*

It was Ayatollah Ruhollah Khomeini who led by far the most serious challenge to the Shah's authority in the 1960s. Khomeini had been born in 1902 into a clerical and landowning family, which on its paternal side had originated in Kashmir. His childhood witnessed the violence and uncertainty of the age. His father was murdered when he was two; his mother died of cholera when he was sixteen. In 1921, he moved to Qom, which was to become the pre-eminent seat of Shi'a scholarship in Iran, close in esteem to Najaf. By study and application he rose quickly through the clerical ranks, in time becoming both a *marja* ('source of emulation') in Twelver Shi'a Islam and a *mujtahid* or *faqih* (an expert in Islamic law). He departed from the quietist view of Grand Ayatollah Boroujerdi (who, it will be recalled, had held back from active opposition to Mossadegh, in contrast to Kashani), and believed profoundly in the need for the clergy to be immersed in the political struggles of the time.

Khomeini has often been described as a fundamentalist by critics on the right of American politics, as if his view of Islam was some kind of copy of the genuinely fundamentalist creed of Sunni Wahhabis, from which Islamist terrorist groups like Al Qaeda and Daesh have drawn their theological justification. This tag of fundamentalism is to misunderstand both Khomeini's theology and his politics. He was a distinguished clerical thinker, ready to challenge those of his peers

---

* In 1958, the chief of counter-intelligence, Mohammad-Vali Gharani, was arrested and charged with planning a coup, allegedly with CIA assistance. Surprisingly, he was not executed and served only three years in prison for this offence. He even managed to ingratiate himself with the new Islamic Republic, serving for six weeks as chief of staff of the army. He was assassinated in 1979 by the Forqn Group, a Shi'a anti-clericalist Islamic group which also assassinated Morteza Motahari, a much more significant figure who was a close ally of Ayatollah Khomeini.

whom he thought had been trapped in Islamic texts. His political theory, though antithetical to Western political norms, was carefully thought through, contriving to balance, however imperfectly, the dominance of Shi'ism with some democratic institutions.

Khomeini was far from alone in trying to set out a new and distinctively Iranian polity for his country. One secular writer (albeit from a religious family) was Jalal Al-e Ahmad. In 1962, he published his most famous book, *Gharbzadegi* (*Westoxification*). This polemic lamented Iran's subjugation to the technological domination of a morally hollow and predatory West.[3] His intention, as Michael Axworthy has noted, was 'not to attack Western ideas as such ... but rather the uncritical way in which Western ideas had been accepted ... and taught in schools; producing people and a culture that were neither genuinely Iranian nor properly Western'. He compared the Iranian position under the Shah to a crow who saw one day how elegantly a partridge was walking. The crow tried to imitate the partridge and failed, but kept trying, with the result that he forgot how to walk like a crow but never succeeded in walking like a partridge.

After the revolution of 1979, *gharbzadegi* became a standard term of revolutionary politics.[4] Both the US and the UK were considered the prime corrupters of Iran, its culture, and its faith, with the US routinely called 'the Great Satan', and the UK 'the cunning fox'.

* * *

In 1962, the Shah sought public agreement in a referendum on six points of his White Revolution, including land reform, profit-sharing for workers, the privatisation of some state industries, female suffrage and a literacy corps by which young educated people would act as teachers in rural areas.

Mossadegh's National Front boycotted the referendum on the grounds that its proposals should have been drawn up by a properly elected government. Khomeini weighed in. Though Khomeini would later endorse female suffrage, and women's representation in the Majlis, in the 1979 constitution of the Islamic Republic, in the early '60s he was opposed to women's participation in public life. He complained that the land reforms were inconsistent with Islamic law (a line of reasoning which appealed to a section of the landowning classes) and widened his argument to damn the government for its arbitrary rule, rigged elections, endemic corruption and cronyism, and its growing relationship with Israel, to which it sold oil.

In March 1963, serious unrest broke out in Qom. Troops and SAVAK agents attacked the madrassa (religious school) where Khomeini was speaking. A number of students were killed. Khomeini was arrested, though released a few days later.

The trouble flared again in June, during the sombre time of Muharram, when the protests extended to Tehran and other major cities. Khomeini gained much support not only from clerics but from their allies in the bazaars and from the poor, whose interests, he charged, had been wholly neglected by the Shah. The deaths of those killed earlier in the year in Qom were compared to the martyrdom of Hussein. These latest uprisings were suppressed in an even more brutal manner. In early June, Khomeini was again arrested, provoking huge demonstrations in Tehran and elsewhere. Troops with tanks and machine guns moved in across the capital. Many were killed – estimates vary from 125 to 400 – with many more injured. Hundreds were detained.

From the Shah's viewpoint, the clampdown worked. 'Normality' was restored. Khomeini was held for two months and put under house arrest for eight. There was a high possibility that he might be executed (as were some of the south Tehran thugs who had joined in the protests). Although Khomeini was not especially popular with the more senior, and quietist, clerics in Qom, it was pleas from them that led the Shah to refrain from implementing the death penalty, principally from fear of further inflaming the populace. The clerics achieved this partly by the device of making Khomeini an Ayatollah, as there was something of a rule that Ayatollahs should not be executed.

Once released, Khomeini continued his attacks against the Shah's regime. He complained of the hidden hand of foreign powers, that the 'United States was worse than Britain, Britain worse than the US, and the Soviet Union worse than both'.[5] Khomeini was finally exiled after he had made a sharp attack on an agreement the Shah had reached with the US to give immunity from prosecution by Iranians to the large contingent of American military personnel in Iran. This was not only objectionable in itself but summoned up the folk memories of the 'capitulatory' regimes that had been imposed on Iran in the nineteenth century, by which first Russia and then the UK had insisted that all of its citizens (including Indians from the Raj) were exempt from any Iranian judicial process and would instead be dealt with by their 'consular courts'.

As noted above, Khomeini was initially deported to Turkey but quickly settled in Najaf in southern Iraq, somehow tolerated by Saddam Hussein until 1978, when, under pressure from the Shah, he was deported from Iraq to Paris.

Khomeini was accompanied to exile by his sons Ahmad and Mostafa, the latter a respected cleric in his own right. On 26 October 1977, two strangers visited Mostafa in his quarters in Najaf. The following morning, he was found dead. Although the official explanation was a heart attack, Mostafa's death, aged forty-seven, was widely attributed to SAVAK agents.

Khomeini and his supporters may have been socially conservative, pushing back against the relentless pressures of what they saw as decadent Western culture, but they were brilliant at using the new technologies of that culture in aid of their propaganda (just as their predecessors had done with the telegraph during the tobacco rebellion). In the 1960s, the cassette player was becoming ubiquitous. Tapes of Khomeini's speeches were smuggled into Iran, copied and recopied, and circulated to thousands.

For many years, this resistance to the Shah's rule remained underground. A combination of rising living standards and the reforms of the White Revolution gave the Shah a bedrock of consent for his regime. Where dissent surfaced, it was quickly suppressed by the Shah's security apparatus. Thus Iran enjoyed an apparent period of tranquillity and stability for the following fifteen years.

* * *

I can still recall the outrage in Britain in the early 1970s when the Middle East oil producers formed a cartel, the Organization of the Petroleum Exporting Countries (OPEC), doubled oil prices, then doubled them again. In 1969, the retail price of petrol (including taxes) was 7.3 pence per litre in the UK; by 1976, it had risen to 16.9 pence per litre.[6]

OPEC was doing no more than copying another, much older, cartel – the oil majors, which had kept oil prices paid to the producing countries as low as possible.

In the forefront of the campaign to rebalance the world oil economy, and to ensure that countries like his benefited more, was the Shah.

From the mid-1960s to the mid-1970s, GDP per head in Iran shot up, from around $3,000 per head to $6,300 in 1969, reaching a peak of just over $10,000 in 1976 (2017 constant prices).[7] There was further extensive investment in roads and railways, amongst other infrastructure, and in health and education. The improvement in personal living standards led, amongst many other changes, to a huge rise in car ownership.*

There was, however, no parallel investment in urban metros or underground lines, with the result that many large cities, above all Tehran, became grid-locked and heavily polluted, with a truly appalling road accident rate. Iran had, and still has, amongst the most dangerous roads in the world, with an annual death rate ten times that of the UK.[8]

---

* This was aided in part by a major investment by the now defunct UK Rootes Group in assembly factories in Iran producing a version of the Hillman Hunter.

Iran's traffic problems in the booming early 1970s were a metaphor for the systemic problems of the Iranian economy and society in properly absorbing the sudden and dramatic increase in income and wealth. Its sclerotic and corrupt system of public administration simply could not cope. A surging demand for imported goods led to the always-inadequate ports becoming clogged up. Desperate traders found that it was only through bribery that they could extract their goods from months of delay at the border. Many prospered, for a while – some became extremely rich – but such were the inherent inequalities that many others, in the rural areas or in the margins of Iran's ever-growing cities, suffered great poverty.

There are not many iron-clad laws in economics, but one is that too much money chasing too few goods is bound to lead to rampant inflation. Exactly that happened in Iran from about 1976. Shortages of essentials appeared, scapegoats were sought, *bazaaris* attacked for overcharging. Then the tap of ever-increasing oil revenues turned off, as OPEC enforced a Saudi-led reduction in production, and the screw was turned further on the people of Iran. GDP per head almost fell off a cliff. Within two years it was down from over $10,000 per head to under $8,000.

Before the economic storm hit Iran, the Shah had set about 'modernising' its politics. His experience in the 1940s and early 1950s had convinced him that his country was not ready for any Western-style democracy, in which there was a free market in ideas, with clean elections. The Majlis continued, but polls were routinely rigged.

Two parties had been allowed to operate. The strongest was the royalist Iran Novin Party, established in 1963. This group consistently gained over 70 per cent of the seats in the Majlis in its first decade of operation. The second was the Mardom Party, or People's Party, which won most of the remaining seats. Both parties aroused more cynicism than respect.

In 1975, the Shah, aware of the decrepitude of this artificial two-party system, decided to take a leaf from the Soviet and Chinese

Communist Parties and from neighbour Saddam Hussein in Iraq. He abolished the Novin and Mardom Parties and went for a single, all-embracing party, known as the Rastakhiz (Resurgence) Party.

In his excellent work *Revolutionary Iran*, Michael Axworthy makes the important observation that at this period Western-style democracy did not seem to be in very good shape. In Western Europe and North America there was recession and inflation, matched by labour disputes and political unrest. These countries, 'especially the UK', looked weak. The democratic systems we had bequeathed to Pakistan and India were in serious trouble too. Pakistan had already had two military governments. In 1975, the Indian Prime Minister had imposed a state of emergency, postponed elections and imprisoned hundreds of her opponents.[9]

Rastakhiz was supposed to be a party for all the people. Indeed, the Shah threatened that anyone who did not join Rastakhiz was to be either regarded as a member of the Tudeh Party, in which case he should be in jail, or treated as a traitor, in which case he should leave Iran for good.[10]

The new party was the occasion and excuse for further social control. The number of books published per year – always a useful (if not wholly reliable) proxy for political health – fell from 4,200 to 1,300. Writers were imprisoned. Amongst their other 'crimes' was that they had not sufficiently emphasised the achievements of the White Revolution. SAVAK went into libraries and bookshops to remove unsuitable texts. Hilariously, one they were assiduous in confiscating was the Shah's own work, *Mission for My Country*, published in 1961. In that book, the Shah had boasted that if he were a dictator 'rather than a constitutional monarch, then I might be tempted to sponsor a single dominant party' like Hitler and the communists. But as a constitutional monarch, he continued, 'I can afford to encourage large-scale party activity free of the straitjacket of one-party rule'.[11] Almost twenty years later, writing from exile as he surveyed the wreckage of his legacy, he said again, 'The establishment of truly democratic institutions seemed [to me] an absolute necessity in Iran as a safeguard against an oligarchy,' though he added that his Rastakhiz party was a 'mistake'.[12]

The Iranians had tasted democracy before, in the 1906 Constitutional Revolution, and in the 1940s and early 1950s. They had an acute notion of what they were missing, whilst they had to endure an economic downturn and the further serious drift to a police state. Moreover, the political discourse in Iran, religious as well as secular, had always strongly been informed by the Greek philosophers whose writings so inspired later generations. Khomeini himself was an avid student of the works of the tenth-century Persian polymath Avicenna (also known as Abu Ali Sina), who synthesised many of the Greek masters, including Plato.

The Shah should have had the sense, in the interests of survival if nothing else, to have taken his own advice so eloquently set out in his 1961 mission for Iran. Single-party rule was never going to work in Iran. Even in the most difficult times since 1979, and when human rights have been the most restricted, there has been a diversity of political parties, and a quite rumbustious debate.

Rastakhiz failed almost as soon as it had begun. It did not, perhaps because it could not, develop its own distinctive ideology, and was shackled from the start by a self-defeating edict which encouraged local participation but banned discussion of political choices. From exile, Khomeini condemned it as an affront to Iran's constitution, designed to undermine the country's devotion to Shi'ism. This and other criticisms led to the arrest of a number of senior clerics, all of whom were to play a prominent role in the revolution, including Ayatollahs Montazeri, Beheshti, and Rabbani-Shirazi, and a lesser-known cleric, Ali Khamenei – now Supreme Leader. Millions of ordinary Iranians simply ignored the new party, secure in the knowledge that not even SAVAK could jail them all.

Rastakhiz was in decay within two years and had collapsed altogether by 1978. Its legacy was the opposite of what the Shah had intended.

Its consequences were two-fold. First, it ended almost any prospect of normal democratic opposition. Secondly, in doing so, it stoked up that frustration and anger which the Shah had held below the surface, but which was shortly to erupt.

* * *

At the beginning of 1977, associations of writers, lawyers and journalists had led protests calling for a restoration of constitutional government. Trouble flared sporadically during the year, each time being broken up by SAVAK and its associated thugs. In early 1978, the Shah made what was probably his single biggest error. He allowed to be published in the newspaper *Ettela'at* an erroneous article under the headline 'Black and Red Imperialism'. It claimed that Khomeini was conspiring with communist and British agents against the Shah's government. It asserted that Khomeini was a foreigner (from his grandfather's birth in Kashmir), a homosexual and a poet. The latter was true. In some Islamic circles, poetry is *haram* (forbidden), but not in Khomeini's, and he did indeed study and write poetry (though some critics claim that he did this only to confirm his status as an Iranian).

The central allegations of this article, however, were palpably false. Its publication provoked outrage well beyond the clerical classes. The anger about it was so great that a specific reference to the article was included in the preamble to the Islamic Republic's constitution.* Many clerics, anxious about potential bloodshed, urged restraint, despite the provocation of the article. But thousands in Qom took to the streets. The police and SAVAK fired live rounds into the crowds. Several protesters were killed, provoking disturbances across the country.

The senior clerics decreed the traditional period of forty days' mourning. A forty-day rhythm then punctuated the disturbances.

---

* 'The publication of an outrageous article meant to malign the revered "ulama" and in particular Imam Khomeini on 15 Day, 1356 [7 January 1978] by the ruling regime accelerated the revolutionary movement and caused an outburst of popular outrage across the country.'

There was a huge demonstration in Tabriz, with police stations, the offices of the (nearly defunct) Rastakhiz and other official buildings attacked. The cycle continued in June, when the leading cleric Ayatollah Mohammad Kazem Shariatmadari called for restraint.

The Shah was now in a quandary. Did he try to pull the sting from the protests by making political concessions, or did he try further repression? In the event, he tried a bit of both – concessions here, repression there. He promised truly free elections (with the implicit admission about how they had been conducted in the past) and the reopening of an important seminary in Qom which he had closed. He apologised to Shariatmadari for an attack by SAVAK on his home, and removed the head of the SAVAK.

A new Prime Minister, Jafar Sharif-Emami, who had clerical connections, was appointed at the end of August, and the Shah announced that he was overturning his truly mad decision to have the calendar start with Cyrus the Great rather than the Prophet Muhammad.

By that Islamic calendar, 28 Mordad is a date every Iranian knows. It's 19 August to us – the anniversary of the 1953 coup. Equally implanted in the consciousness is Abadan, the site of the struggle for Iranian national sovereignty through the nationalisation of the oil industry in the late 1940s and early '50s.*

On 28 Mordad/19 August 1978, in Abadan, a terrible fire broke out in the Cinema Rex, located in a poor area of the town. The film, *Gavaznha* (*The Deer*), starring the well-known Iranian actor Behrouz Vossoughi, was controversial and because of its subliminal anti-government message had had difficulty passing the censors. It was a story about two men who have been friends since their school days. When one seeks out the other, he finds that he is a heavy drug user, involved in criminality, in an impoverished neighbourhood. Both perish when the police refuse the friend's request to allow him to persuade his drug addict pal to give himself up peacefully. Many regarded the film

---

* See Chapter 9.

as heavily critical of the Shah's White Revolution, which had driven unskilled rural labourers into a life of deprivation in the cities. Whoever had benefited from this 'revolution', it was not people like them.

During *Gavaznha's* screening, arsonists lit petrol and blocked the exits as the flames engulfed the building. According to the Shah himself, 477 people died in this outrage. As well as causing the kind of national grief that would occur in any society which had faced such an appalling atrocity, the Cinema Rex fire sparked national outrage on a much wider scale. The popular consensus moved strongly towards blaming the Shah and SAVAK for the incident, with claims that the fire had been seen as an efficient way of disposing of the anti-government elements who would have been watching the film. There was no evidence to support this allocation of responsibility, and at a time of relative quiet neither the Shah nor his agents in SAVAK had any motive for such a senseless act of mass murder. One newspaper, *Sobhe Emruz*, claimed, without any direct corroboration, that the fire may have been started by Islamist radicals. That simply stoked people up even more. Although many clerics were opposed to the cinema, people reasoned that no cleric would have gone so far as to murder hundreds of poor people, who were very much 'their people'. Various individuals were arrested for their alleged part. The Shah claimed that the real culprit fled to Iraq, where he was arrested and interrogated, but 'the affair was covered up by pusillanimous magistrates'.[13] In late 1980, a court convicted and executed five people for the crime. The leader claimed he was an unemployed drug addict. There is some evidence that an Islamist group may have been behind the fire.

Though it's almost certain that the Shah was not implicated in the fire, that was what people came to believe. Some observers of the months leading up to revolution believe that it was from this point onwards that many in the middle classes, even those who had done well from the White Revolution, began to abandon not just support for the Shah but any trust at all in him and his governmental apparatus.

* * *

New demonstrations broke out across the country. Martial law was imposed in some, but not all, cities outside the capital. There was a huge rally on 4 September. Senior clerics counselled the participants to ensure the protest was peaceful – and it was. So too was a further demonstration on 7 September.

Having made his political concessions, the Shah decided on more repression. That evening, he appointed General Gholam-Ali Oveissi as Military Governor of Tehran. Oveissi had played a central role in the ruthless suppression of the 1963 protests, which in the Shah's eyes had given his country fifteen years of tranquillity. Early the following morning, Oveissi announced the imposition of martial law in Tehran and a number of other cities.

These were the days before social media. Few had portable radios. It seems as though many of the thousands who assembled in Tehran that day were unaware that their treatment by the troops and SAVAK agents would be rougher than it had been in the days before. In the central Jaleh Square, as the crowd pressed forward, the troops opened live fire on the protesters. Scores fell; many more were injured. A French journalist reported that 3,000, then 4,000, had died. The BBC correspondent Andrew Whitley put the number at a 'couple of hundred'.

8 September quickly came to be known as Black Friday. It was the moment when the Shah's spell over his people was broken. As Michael Axworthy comments, 'The Shah lost the remainder of what in medieval Iran had been called *farr* – the aura of rightful kingship, associated with just rule and military success. [The Iranian people] did not want to hear any new suggestions from him, they just wanted him to go.'[14] After the revolution, the square was renamed *Maidan-e Shohada* (Square of the Martyrs).

The Shah's generals, and their SAVAK counterparts, knew how to repress demonstrations. What they found much more difficult to counter was the labour unrest which broke out across the country, especially within the oil industry, which was paralysed.

The strikes and protests continued. On 4 November 1978, crowds broke into the British Embassy compound at Ferdowsi, in downtown Tehran. In scenes reminiscent of the invasion of the Embassy in November 2011, the protesters set fire to many parts of the buildings, whilst the diplomatic staff retreated to the secure area at the top of the compound. In the 1978 attack, however, the police and the army intervened quickly and the crowds were quickly dispersed.

Oveissi continued his crackdown, with temporary success. But the liberalisation measures announced by the Shah's new Prime Minister, Jafar Sharif-Emami, had allowed opposition forces greater scope to organise publicly. Sharif-Emami lasted all of ten weeks. His replacement, General Gholam-Reza Azhari, appointed on 6 November, headed a military government. He lasted eight weeks, to be replaced by Shapour Bakhtiar, the last of the Shah's Prime Ministers.*

A new wave of violence began in Tehran on 23 December. Oil production plummeted. There were lengthy queues for petrol, and heavy gunfire in the city. Bakhtiar, seen as a neutral figure, had agreed to be appointed as Prime Minister only on condition that the Shah left the country. After a period of characteristic prevarication, he did so on 16 January 1979. The populace continued to demand his formal abdication. Khomeini promised to return to Iran, prompting Bakhtiar to close the airport. Demonstrators trying to get it reopened were gunned down.

Khomeini finally returned, triumphant, on 1 February, appointing Mehdi Bazargan as Prime Minister. Bazargan was a professor of engineering at Tehran University, the first head of Mossadegh's National Iranian Oil Corporation and a liberal, religious intellectual. For ten days there were two governments in Iran: the Shah's and the one Khomeini had appointed. There was a violent struggle for power between the Shah's Imperial Guard and revolutionary forces (including

---

* The Shah got through Prime Ministers swiftly. In the thirty-eight years from his accession in 1941 until his fall in 1979, he had thirty-three. (Britain had ten in the same period.) Only one of the Shah's premiers served a normal term – Amir-Abbas Hoveyda, who lasted twelve and a half years.

many leftist groups). Bakhtiar resigned on 8 February. On 10 and
11 February, anti-Shah fighters managed to take over military bases,
prisons and police stations across Iran. The Shah's power dissolved.
Khomeini was now in charge.

*   *   *

From the mid-1970s, many journalists and academics had charted the
decay of the Shah's regime. One British diplomat, Peter Westmacott,*
who had been responsible for Iranian internal affairs, wrote as he left
Tehran in 1978 that the intensity of opposition might increase, and
the 'Peacock Throne' might not be as stable as had been assumed.[15]
But virtually none others of those whose life's work was to observe,
analyse and report on the country – diplomats in the key Embassies in
Tehran from France, Germany, the Soviet Union, the United States,
the United Kingdom – spotted what was going on until it had almost
happened.

In October 1978, on advice from Britain's Ambassador in Tehran,
Sir Anthony Parsons, Foreign Secretary David Owen gave an interview on London Weekend Television in which he justified Britain's
continuing support for the Shah. Later, chastened by the fact that he
and his department had so misjudged the Iranians' mood, he asked
for a thorough historical analysis of British policy towards Iran in the
years leading up to the 1979 revolution. This report was conducted
by Nicholas (later Sir Nicholas) Browne, whose first posting from the
Foreign Office was as a Third Secretary in our Tehran Embassy, from
1971 to 1974. He was later chargé and Ambassador. A good linguist,
he 'spoke Farsi [Persian] like a nightingale', according to Mohammad
Khatami, who was President during Browne's tenure as Ambassador.
Browne took a year to complete his study.[16] His overall conclusion
was that – to paraphrase – the British system had been a victim of

---

*   Now Sir Peter Westmacott, later British Ambassador to Turkey, France and the USA.

what we now call confirmation bias. We had bet our shirt on the Shah succeeding in his mission, having huge interests at stake. These interests had clouded the collective judgement about what was really going on in the country. This error was compounded by the fact that for at least two decades before the revolution our diplomats had cut themselves off from contact with opposition figures, for fear of incurring the Shah's wrath. The other key diplomatic missions in Tehran fared no better. They all missed what was staring at them.

CHAPTER 12

KHOMEINI RETURNS

One definition of insanity is doing the same thing over and over again, getting the same results over and over again, yet expecting a different result every time from the one you got last time. If you accept that as a working definition of insanity, then [the US] policy toward Iran has been certifiably insane for nearly three decades.
THOMAS PICKERING, FORMER US AMBASSADOR TO JORDAN, ISRAEL AND THE UN.[1] (THIS DEFINITION OF INSANITY IS USUALLY ATTRIBUTED TO ALBERT EINSTEIN.)

The crowds were much bigger, the atmosphere more euphoric, than at any time in Iran's history. Such was the welcome given to Khomeini on his return from exile to Tehran on 1 February 1979.

Once back in Tehran, Khomeini moved swiftly to assert his authority. He was initially joined in this endeavour by other groups opposed to the Shah. Many of these were, however, secular in outlook, not theocratic. These included the pro-communist Tudeh Party and the Marxist Feda'i, along with deserters from the military, and the Mojahedin-e Khalq (MEK, or MKO). MEK had in the 1970s been actively involved in violence against the Shah's regime, and against US targets within Iran. It initially supported the revolution, but later became implacably opposed to the Islamic Republic. In 1981, it went into exile in Iraq, and, from its own dedicated base, became part of Saddam Hussein's war machine against Iran.

All these groups were, to begin with, involved in the revolutionary committees (*Komiteh*) which sought to replace the Shah's system of government. But by the autumn of 1979, as Khomeini consolidated his power, these groups, allied with the theocracy only by what they had been against – the Shah – and with objectives and ideologies miles away from the notion of an Islamic state, were increasingly isolated. Khomeini was contemptuous of atheistic Marxist-Leninism; the Tudeh were in time not just isolated but many of its members eliminated by execution, along with hundreds of others judged to be opponents of the new regime.

Revolutions are messy, chaotic affairs. There is no rule that asserts that once the old order has been overthrown, a new order will be established quickly and peacefully – or at all. Despite his understanding of the need to move swiftly, and ruthlessly, success for Khomeini was by no means assured in the early years of the revolution.

On 9 July 1980, Iranian General Oveissi and the Shah's last Prime Minister, Shapour Bakhtiar, both exiled in Paris, came close to effecting a *coup d'état* to be triggered from the Nojeh Air Base near Tehran. The plot was discovered and foiled only a few hours before it was due to happen.

Just under a year later, in June 1981, two bombs planted by the MEK at the headquarters of Khomeini's Islamic Republic Party killed over seventy of Khomeini's closest supporters, including the effective second-in-command of the country, Ayatollah Mohammad Beheshti, Chief Justice and chairman of the powerful Assembly of Experts. Photographs of these 'martyrs' cover one wall in the Majlis building – a constant reminder of the price many paid for their support for the revolution (though there were plenty more who paid a similar bloody price for their opposition to the form the revolution took).

In the same month, there was an assassination attempt on Ayatollah Ali Khamenei, at the time Khomeini's representative in the High Security Council. He was severely injured and has been left without the use of his right arm.

Then, on 30 August 1981, Mohammad-Ali Rajai, the President of the Islamic Republic, and the Prime Minister, Mohammad-Javad Bahonar, were both murdered, again by an MEK bomb. It was after Rajai's murder that Khamenei was elected as President of the Republic, becoming Supreme Leader on Khomeini's death in 1989.

A year before these assassinations, on 30 April 1980, dissident Arab Iranian terrorists holding Iraqi passports had seized the Iranian Embassy in London, taking the occupants hostage and making a series of demands including for the release of ninety-one prisoners being held in Iran. Negotiations over six days were abortive. When the body of one of the hostages, the press attaché Abbas Lavasani, was thrown out of the building onto the street, Margaret Thatcher gave orders for the Special Air Service (SAS) to go in.

The world watched as the SAS stormed the building. All the hostages still alive were rescued. One terrorist was captured; four were killed. The SAS's role gave it immense and favourable international coverage and bolstered Thatcher's reputation as a determined woman who did not give in to terrorism.

It was subsequently discovered that Iraq had trained the terrorists and provided them with weapons, as well as with their passports. The UK and Iran were later to agree that each host government would compensate the other for the damage to the Iranian Embassy during this siege and to the UK Embassy in November 1978.*

* * *

The key issue facing Khomeini in the early months of the revolution, alongside the imperatives of trying to return Iran's daily life and its economy to some sort of normality, was the drafting of a new constitution for the Islamic Republic.

The central feature of the constitution as it was finally agreed was

---

* See Chapter 11.

about the authority accorded to the Supreme Leader, standing in for the occulted twelfth imam. This provision, which is set out in Article 5,* is based upon the concept which Khomeini had developed in his writings of '*velayat-e faqih*'. The term '*velayat*' means the authority of a guardian or deputy, and '*faqih*', a jurist or expert in Islamic law who is a *mujtahid* (a senior member of the *ulema*, the clerical establishment).

The argument ran that legitimate government was the rule of God alone. When the Holy Prophet had been alive, he had governed; after him, it was his successors, the imams, who had. On the occultation of the last, the twelfth imam, the responsibility for governing had to fall on those who had a profound knowledge of Islamic law – the expert jurists. But best, Khomeini implied, was if this responsibility fell on one man, the most expert of all, the Supreme Leader.

The issue of whether there is a 'higher law' which can override those promulgated by humankind is one that has taxed jurists of many faiths down the centuries. A recent seminar in the Inner Temple considered just this question. One of the speakers reflected on the 'famous rebuke offered by Antigone to Creon in Sophocles' play, [in which] she says: "Your ordinance cannot overrule the unchangeable unwritten code of heaven," thereby implying the existence of a higher law by which our earthly laws are judged, and which can overrule the merely man-made law'.[2]

In our Judeo-Christian tradition, St Augustine, St Thomas Aquinas and Martin Luther all repeated Antigone's sentiments. English law itself has long recognised equity as prevailing over law. It does so by invoking principles of natural justice that are rooted in religious ideas – and which these days are enshrined in instruments like the European Convention on Human Rights and the UK's Human Rights Act.

Thus there was nothing in principle unusual, nor confined to

---

* Article 5: 'During the Occultation of the Wali al-Asr (may God hasten his reappearance), the *wilayah* and leadership of the Ummah devolve upon the just and pious *faqih*, who is fully aware of the circumstances of his age; courageous, resourceful, and possessed of administrative ability, he will assume the responsibilities of this office in accordance with Article 107.'

Islamic systems, in Khomeini's quest to see the idea of a 'higher law' prevail.

What was a major departure, not only from the Judeo-Christian tradition of law but also from the previous consensus of Shi'a jurists, was Khomeini's prescription. This was that in the (temporary) absence of a divine presence (the occulted twelfth imam), the responsibility to determine that higher law, and to override the decisions of an elected Parliament, should fall on the shoulders of one man: the Supreme Leader.

Because it was such a departure, Khomeini's prescription was, to begin with, heavily contested, not only by non-clerical revolutionary figures but also by many senior clerics. There had been some traces of Khomeini's ideas in earlier writings by Shi'a jurists during the Safavid period and by Sheikh Fazlollah Nouri during the Constitutional Revolution. Their sentiments influenced the clause inserted into the 1906 constitution which required that no legal enactment of the Majlis could be at variance with 'sacred principles of Islam' (until the reappearance of the twelfth imam), and that a committee of five devout theologians would be established to enforce this law.[3] But, as explained in Chapter 6, this committee never met. Khomeini was highly critical of the 1906 constitution, saying that, despite some Islamic window-dressing, it had been 'agents of Britain' who had thrust upon the Iranian people laws which were 'alien and borrowed'.[4]

Khomeini was opposed to any hereditary monarchy. But the monarchy had been a central feature of the 1906 constitution, and the idea had the support of a consensus of senior clerics in preceding decades. They had taken the lead successfully in opposing Reza Khan's plans for a republic. They had joined forces to help oust Mossadegh in 1953, because they had been scared by the prospect that he could pave the way for a secular, communist republic led by the Tudeh.

Ayatollah Mohammad Shariatmadari, who had been instrumental in 1964 in persuading the Shah not to execute Khomeini for his role in the 1963 uprisings, was one of the key figures who supported the structure of the 1906 constitution. He believed that the clerical establishment should play an important but not a decisive role in Iran's governance.

The first draft of the 1979 constitution, published in June, reflected this more nuanced view of the role of Islam within the new arrangements. There was to be a clerical council to ensure that any new laws were consistent with the tenets of Shi'ism, along similar lines to the clause inserted into the 1906 text, but, as Michael Axworthy notes, '*velayat-e faqih* was present neither in terms nor in spirit'.[5]

With minor amendments, Khomeini endorsed this text and was ready to see it come into force simply with a referendum to give it popular support. But the moderates, like the first President of the Islamic Republic, Sayyid Abol-Hasan Bani-Sadr,[*] and its first Prime Minister, Mehdi Bazargan,[†] then made a fundamental error, pushing their temporary advantage and becoming 'victims of their own principles'.[6] Instead of quitting when they were ahead, and agreeing that this first draft should be the one to be submitted to the referendum, they argued that the draft was defective because it contained few provisions to allow its amendment, and claimed that it should now be examined by a constituent assembly. The wily and evergreen Akbar Hashemi Rafsanjani, later Speaker of the Majlis, and President from 1989 to 1997, had apparently counselled Bani-Sadr, Bazargan and others against making the best the enemy of the good, claiming that any constituent assembly would end up dominated by radical clerics.

Rafsanjani's prediction proved entirely correct. Three-quarters of the new constituent Assembly of Experts were clerics. Under the guidance of its chairman, the conservative cleric Sayyid Mohammad

---

[*] Bani-Sadr was President from February 1980 until June 1981, when he was impeached. He fled to France, where at the time of writing he still lives, closely guarded by French police. Born in 1933, he is the oldest surviving President of the Islamic Republic.

[†] Bazargan was Prime Minister from February 1979 until November 1979, when he and his Cabinet resigned over their inability to end the hostage-taking at the US Embassy. He was a member of the Majlis until 1984. He was disqualified as a candidate in the 1985 presidential election. He died in 1995, aged eighty-seven.

Beheshti, the Assembly gradually moved to incorporate the principle of *velayat-e faqih* into the constitution. Although there was vocal opposition from figures like Shariatmadari and more liberal politicians, the key articles of the constitution to give the Supreme Leader supreme powers were passed with just a handful of votes against.

Bazargan and others attempted a rearguard action to defer the constitution, but it was all too late. Khomeini declared that the principle of *velayat-e faqih* had been ordained by God. The opposition effectively folded altogether when fate intervened in the form of the invasion of the US Embassy, which began on 4 November 1979, and lasted for 444 days, until the hostages were released in January 1981.

*   *   *

In October 1979, Bazargan had been in Algiers, with Khomeini's knowledge, to try to negotiate with President Carter's National Security Adviser, Zbigniew Brzezinski, about the restoration of normal relations with the US.

There was little understanding in Washington (despite the best efforts of some in the US Embassy in Tehran) about the need to deal directly with Khomeini, a man of God but hypersensitive about how he was treated by the outside world and never one to forget a grudge.

The Americans had three preoccupations. One, on which they might have been able to make common cause with Khomeini, was to thwart Soviet attempts to destabilise the region and gain support for the Tudeh, to which Khomeini was profoundly opposed. The other two were to ensure that Iranian oil kept flowing and that Iran continued to purchase large quantities of American arms. When, in August 1979, Iran cancelled $10 billion worth of arms purchases (because of a decline in its own oil revenues caused by the post-revolutionary turmoil in the country), all bets were off, as far as the United States were concerned. The US response was to place an embargo on spare parts.

Very soon after the 1979 revolution, there had been a brief invasion of the United States Embassy, but this ended almost as quickly as it had started. The US Embassy was, however, alive to the fact that the next protest might not end as swiftly. In July 1979, a senior US diplomat, Bruce Laingen, sent a classified cable from Tehran to Washington in which he warned that were the Shah 'to take up residence in the US in the immediate future ... [this] would continue ... to be seriously prejudicial to our interests and to the security of Americans in Iran'.

He went on: 'Any premature gesture toward the Shah ... could provide [an opportunity] for those revolutionary hotheads who would probably like nothing better ... than to take a crack at us.'[7]

The Shah had cancer, and his condition was deteriorating. There were a number of excellent hospitals in Mexico, where he was being treated by an American doctor. The Shah had thought about treatment in the UK, but Margaret Thatcher had had a message delivered to him that he would be refused entry to the country. She feared the consequences for British staff in our Tehran Embassy and was anxious about disruption to our trade with Iran if the Shah were allowed into Britain.

The ever-vacillating President Carter was at first reluctant to allow the Shah admission to the US. However, he came under pressure both from Henry Kissinger (whose support he needed to persuade a reluctant Congress to ratify the SALT II arms limitation treaty he had just signed with the Soviet Union) and from the Republican grandee David Rockefeller. Towards the end of October, Carter put aside the advice from his own Embassy in Tehran and agreed to allow the Shah into the US for treatment, on 'humanitarian grounds'. It was the next in that series of 'insane' decisions by the United States, not least because it was unnecessary, given the availability of good treatment elsewhere (and, in any event, not even US doctors could save him).

Many in Iran were enraged by Carter's decision and were convinced that it signalled a determination by the United States to restore the Pahlavi dynasty and snuff out the revolution. What had happened in

1953, they reasoned, was about to happen again.[*] Rumours abounded about the 'secret meeting' between the Americans and Mehdi Bazargan, the liberal Prime Minister.

On 4 November 1979, a large crowd of demonstrators passing the American Embassy climbed over the Embassy wall and took all the staff there hostage.[†] As Laingen had warned four months earlier, they did 'take a crack at us' – and what a crack it was.

Khomeini had been in the holy city of Qom at the time of the Embassy's invasion, and by all accounts had had nothing directly to do with it. But, once it had happened, he seized the opportunity the hostage crisis created. He was just as suspicious of the US's intentions and believed that if their Embassy were shut down, their ability to orchestrate a coup would be disabled. He publicly backed the hostage-takers and instituted what has become known as the 'clerical coup'. He had Bazargan resign, and began the establishment of the Basij, the youth militia of the IRGC.

All revolutionary leaders, however eminent, have to ride a tiger. Given everything he had been preaching about the 'Great Satan' of the United States, Khomeini had little option but to back the hostage-takers. Tactically, he was shrewd in the way he made use of the event to consolidate his position. But whether his handling of the whole hostage crisis was strategically wise is much more open to question. The hostages were badly treated. Some were held in solitary confinement for periods, some tortured. All this led to an almost indelible labelling in the US of Khomeini as a 'medieval fanatic', and it reinforced the international isolation in which the fledgling Islamic Republic was held.

Carter was already weakened by the uncertainty of his foreign policy. But it was his handling of the hostage crisis, including an abortive US military rescue attempt in April 1980 in which eight US

---

[*] Amongst many in Iran, this view persists. A 2018 headline in the conservative newspaper *Resalat* read, 'US Embassy takeover foiled American plotters'.

[†] Laingen himself and two other US diplomats were at the Iranian Foreign Affairs Ministry at the time. They were held there for a period. The US Ambassador was away at the time of the invasion.

military personnel were killed, which was the key factor in his failure to secure a second presidential term, losing to Republican Ronald Reagan on 4 November 1980.

There were inconclusive discussions between Iran and the US in the last days of the Carter administration, but Khomeini judged that it was better to negotiate with a winner than a loser, and secret negotiations with William Casey (soon to become Reagan's director of the CIA), brokered by the Algerians, began in earnest as soon as the election result was clear. On 20 January 1981, the fifty-two remaining hostages were finally released, carefully timed by both sides to coincide with Reagan's inauguration.

By then, Khomeini had been able to entrench the position of the Islamic Republic, and to secure a popular mandate for the revised constitution, with *velayat-e faqih*, the rule of the jurist, as its centrepiece – and Khomeini as Supreme Leader. But he had another, existential matter on his mind.

In September 1980, the Iraqi leader, Saddam Hussein, had begun the Iran–Iraq War, which was to last longer than any other conventional war of the century, costing millions of lives.

CHAPTER 13

THE IMPOSED WAR

We have not forgotten the support, financial and material aid you gave to Saddam, from armoured vehicles and assistance to Saddam, which caused bloodshed in our country.

BASIJ LEAFLET

There can be no understanding of contemporary Iran, the pursuit of its faith and its view of the world outside without an appreciation of the enormity of the Iran–Iraq War.

Intended by Saddam Hussein to secure the collapse of the Islamic Republic, and backed by the US for the same reason, it had the opposite effect. It solidified support for the Islamic Republic and provided the opportunity to extinguish the other revolutionary but less Islamic forces.

At the outbreak of hostilities, victory for Khomeini over all the other revolutionary factions within Iran was by no means assured. By the war's end, the narrative of the martyrdom of Husayn at Karbala in 680 AD and the 'martyrdom' of hundreds of thousands of Iranians during the war was woven into a single skein, in which the Shi'a faith and Iranian national identity became one.

Reinforcing this narrative was Iran's long-standing sense of exceptionalism, of a proud, singular nation, alone, repeatedly harried, bullied and invaded by outside forces, but surviving. If they needed any encouragement in this respect, the war demonstrated conclusively that Iran could only ever rely upon itself. Khamenei and Rouhani are both using exactly this narrative today to shore up popular resistance to President Trump's ever-tightening economic sanctions against Iran and belligerent threats of military action.

The Second World War finished over seventy years ago – three generations. The few surviving combatants from that conflict are now over ninety. Yet the experience continues to define our national identity, to write our national narrative.

By contrast, the Iran–Iraq War is recent. It finished just three decades ago. Many of the senior figures still active in Iranian politics today served in that war, including Supreme Leader Khamenei and President Rouhani. Tens of thousands of its casualties are still alive, many of whom continue to suffer from their injuries; some who fought as boys are not yet fifty. There is scarcely a family in Iran which was not directly touched by the war, who did not lose a loved one, or who cannot recall the horrors of the 'War of the Cities', when missiles rained down on Tehran and other key cities.

My aim in this chapter is not principally to provide a detailed narrative of the course of the conflict. Those are available in a number of good military histories of the war, of which by far the best is that by the French historian Pierre Razoux.[1] Rather, my purpose is to highlight the extent to which the United States, and almost all other nations of any significance, including the Soviet Union, sided with Iraq, in a perfidious and short-sided way. The only significant 'Western' power which did not was Israel. They were the only consistent supplier of arms to Iran, and coordinated some key military engagements with them. These are truths which neither the Israelis nor the Iranians trumpet these days. Just two Arab states supported Iran: Syria and Libya.

Although the UK was involved in the war to a degree, and did not depart from the US's position, it featured remarkably little in British consciousness during the 1980s. The latest biography of Lord Carrington, who was Foreign Secretary when the war broke out in 1980 until his resignation in April 1982 at the start of the Falklands War, has just one entry in its index for the Iran–Iraq War. 'This [1980] was the year … when the Iran–Iraq War started, with Britain and America supporting the Iraqis under Saddam Hussein in the hope that they could defeat the ambitions of the fundamentalist Iranian regime by proxy.'[2]

Carrington was succeeded by Francis Pym, who served for fourteen months until the June 1983 general election. Pym did speak about the Iran–Iraq War in a foreign affairs debate on the Middle East in June 1982, explaining that if he was speaking 'more briefly' on this conflict, it was not because he regarded it as less important than other issues in the region.[3] But beyond the standard platitudes urging both sides to accept mediation, his contribution was an exercise in hand-wringing, which was to characterise the British approach throughout the war.

From June 1983, for the remaining five years of the Iran–Iraq War, the British Foreign Secretary was Sir Geoffrey Howe. Remarkably, in the whole of his detailed and lengthy memoir (700-plus pages), there are just four references to Iran – three about the UN Security Council Resolution (No. 598) which paved the way to ending the war in 1988, and the Royal Navy's deployment in the Persian Gulf to protect British shipping from Iranian mines; the fourth about the *fatwa* on Salman Rushdie (see below, Chapter 14).[4] The references in the two published volumes of Charles Moore's major three-part biography of Margaret Thatcher are similarly scant.[5]

What this reticence underlines is the intense diplomatic isolation Iran faced in the decade following the 1979 Islamic Revolution. In the eyes of most governments in the West, and the Soviet Union, the Iranians had simply put themselves beyond the pale. Although Iran had a good cadre of intelligent and well-informed diplomats, little effort was made to modify the poor impression that decision-makers in foreign capitals had of the regime. Indeed, part of Khomeini's narrative to his own people was that the Iranians were the only ones in step.

The Chaplin affair was one more reason the British public and politicians had such a poor image of the Iranians.

Edward Chaplin was a British diplomat who spoke good Persian, as well as Arabic.* The UK's formal diplomatic relations with Iran had been downgraded after the invasion of the US Embassy in November 1979 and were handled by a British Interests section of the Swedish Embassy, which included some British staff. One of these was Chaplin. In January 1985, then aged thirty-three, he went out to Tehran as Head of Chancery. He was accompanied by his wife, Nicky, and his six-week-old daughter, Stephanie.

This was a tense time in the bilateral relationship, because of the accusations that the UK, amongst other Western countries, was helping the Iraqis. Iraqi air raids on Tehran were so bad that on two occasions Chaplin's wife and baby daughter were evacuated back to the UK.

By May 1987, Chaplin and his wife had two children – the youngest, a son, being just two months old. The Chaplins had been living in the main Ferdowsi compound of the UK Embassy, but had decided to move to one of the houses in the northern hills, in Gholhak, where the air was cleaner.

To make this move, Chaplin was driving his Embassy Range Rover with his wife and two small children, and another British diplomat and her baby, up the Modarres Expressway, the main road north from downtown Tehran.

A large Land Cruiser overtook Chaplin's vehicle and braked so suddenly that Chaplin could not avoid crashing into the back of it. As Chaplin got out to complain about this poor driving, three Revolutionary Guards in plain clothes leapt out of the vehicle and started dragging Chaplin towards their car. Nicky Chaplin, with her two-month-old baby in her arms, got out and started to remonstrate, tugging at the arms of one of the assailants.

By pure chance, the German Ambassador happened to be passing at the time, accompanied by a number of Iranian bodyguards. These questioned Chaplin's assailants and came back to tell Nicky that there

---

* Chaplin later served as British Ambassador to Jordan, Iraq and Italy, and as head of the Middle East and North Africa Department of the FCO.

was no point in arguing: this was not a random kidnapping but an organised arrest. The German Ambassador was at least able to raise the alarm.

One of the Revolutionary Guards got into the driver's seat of the British Embassy Range Rover and drove off with Nicky Chaplin and the other passengers at high speed. He abandoned the car shortly afterwards, leaving Nicky to find her own way to Gholhak.

Meanwhile, Chaplin himself had been hooded and handcuffed in the back of the Land Cruiser and was driven northwards. Over the course of the next twenty-four hours, Chaplin was held in three different places: in a villa in north Tehran, at a Basij establishment in the south, and at a local prison somewhere in central Tehran. Chaplin says that initially none of those holding him could offer any reason for his arrest. The original assailants disappeared rapidly.

Even the most serious situations in Iran often have an element of pure farce. Whilst being held at the first villa, one of the younger guards asked Chaplin in all seriousness if he (Chaplin, the prisoner) could help him get a UK visa.

At his last place of detention, Chaplin was interrogated, in the middle of the night, by a mullah, who asked him 'random questions' about Britain's role in Iran and the activities of the British Interests section, including whether staff in the Visa section wore Islamic dress.

The following day, a more conciliatory official arrived, inviting Chaplin to agree the text of a document which would allow his 'temporary release'. The document was 'irrelevant stuff about the workings of the Interests section'. As it did not incriminate Chaplin, he signed it.

Just over twenty-four hours after the hard stop and the kidnapping, Chaplin was once again hooded and handcuffed, put into the well of a car and eventually released in a back street which turned out to be near the Gholhak compound. He was fine apart from some bruising and a black ear from the initial struggle. He found his way to his much relieved wife and children.

Nicky Chaplin had been completely in the dark about the reasons for her husband's kidnapping, and his whereabouts. Strenuous efforts by the new head of the British Interests section, Christopher MacRae, revealed that the Iranian Ministry of Foreign Affairs (MFA) were equally in the dark – an indication of one of the verities of the Iranian 'system': that so much of the hard end of state power is completely beyond the influence of the elected government.

Fortunately for his peace of mind, Chaplin knew instinctively why he had been kidnapped. A few weeks before, an Iranian consular official in Manchester, Ahmad Ghassemi, had been arrested for shoplifting (two pairs of socks and a ladies' purse). He claimed diplomatic immunity, which he did not have save when carrying out his diplomatic duties. He was released but required to report to the police a week later. When he failed to show, the police went looking for him. There was a struggle as he was arrested, during which Ghassemi claimed that he had been beaten up by the Manchester police. In the event, all charges were dropped, but Ghassemi was expelled from the UK.

In retaliation, the Iranian MFA now ordered Chaplin and his family to leave Iran. When they got to Tehran Airport in compliance with this order, Revolutionary Guard officials told Chaplin that he was forbidden to leave Iran, as he was on a blacklist of those whose crimes were 'too serious to be expunged' – a further indication of how divided is the governance of Iran.[6] It took another twenty-four hours before Chaplin and his family were finally allowed to board their plane. They arrived at Heathrow amid a blaze of publicity: the British media were desperate for a different story from the UK general election campaign, which still had twelve days to run but whose result was already foregone.[*]

In the British government, there was some dispute about how far to go in retaliation for the outrageous treatment of Chaplin and his family. The Foreign Office were counselling caution, with its senior official, Sir Patrick Wright, noting in his diary (though not with great accuracy), 'We have to remember that Iran is our third largest trading

---

[*] Margaret Thatcher was to win this, her third election victory, with a majority of 102.

country in the world.'[7] Three days later, MacRae had reported that Iranian Foreign Minister Ali Akbar Velayati had returned to Tehran 'furious at the mess that Khomeini's people have got them into'.[8]

Thatcher was in favour of a total break in relations. She did not quite achieve this, but tit-for-tat expulsions were made by each side until just one diplomat was left in each capital. Eighteen months later, Foreign Secretary Geoffrey Howe agreed with Velayati to re-establish proper diplomatic relations. UK staff returned in January 1989, though their stay was soon to be thwarted by the next move to disrupt relations, this time by Khomeini himself.

* * *

There is no argument these days that Saddam was the aggressor in the Iran–Iraq War. On both sides the casualties were mainly Shi'a, for 80 per cent of Iraq's armed forces were themselves Shi'a (roughly reflecting the confessional balance in Iraq), whilst Iran's forces were almost wholly Shi'a. Saddam was a Sunni, but, more importantly, he was a Ba'athist (from the Arabic, meaning 'resurrection' or 'renaissance') – a secular ideology which sought a pan-Arabic hegemony through a vanguard one-party state. There had been a natural Arab–Persian rivalry between Saddam and the Shah, and this enmity was compounded by that between Sunni and Shi'a.

After the break-up of the Ottoman Empire at the end of the First World War, Britain had taken over Iraq as a protectorate. Iraq was granted independence in 1932, though the UK maintained military bases there until 1954. The UK then became the guarantor of security for the whole of the Persian Gulf until, in 1969, the Labour government withdrew its military commitments from East of Suez, including the Gulf. The United States decided to fill the vacuum which would otherwise have been left. Key to maintaining security was to raise the Shah's Iran to the status of the main regional power and anti-Soviet bulwark.

*　*　*

Iraq's long border with Iran includes the Shatt al-Arab waterway, which takes the river Tigris to the sea. Basra sits on this waterway, as does, downstream on an island, the Iranian city of Abadan, the first centre of the Iranian oil industry, with large refineries and storage areas.

There had long been disputes between Iran and Iraq over the exact border. These were 'resolved' in 1975 in the Algiers Accord, which put the border down the '*thalweg*' (the middle of the primary navigable channels of the estuary). Though Saddam signed up to this accord, he considered it to have been a humiliation for Iraq, a reflection of his weaker military power compared to Iran.

During the early months of 1980, there had been skirmishes between Iranian and Iraqi forces. A failed assassination attempt on the life of Saddam's Deputy Prime Minister, Tariq Aziz, in April was blamed on the Iranian regime. In Tehran, the rhetoric against Saddam was ratcheted up – including accusations that he was a 'US puppet' and an 'accomplice of Menachem Begin', the Israeli Prime Minister.[9] The revered Iraqi Shi'a leader Ayatollah Muhammad al-Sadr was executed on Saddam's orders. Saddam hoped that the turmoil and instability in Iran might lead to the internal overthrow of the Khomeini regime, but with the failure of the July 1980 coup that was no longer a feasible option.

By August 1980, Saddam had decided, on the excuse of Iranian provocations across his border, that Iran was weak enough – and so preoccupied with its internal crises – that he could launch a full-scale invasion into his neighbour. His first decision was to abrogate the Algiers Accord on the Shatt al-Arab waterway, on 17 September 1980. Five days later, on 22 September, Saddam invaded with an astonishing twenty-two divisions of ground forces, preceded by air attacks. The first assault involved 100,000 men, 1,600 tanks, 2,000 armoured vehicles and 4,000 trucks.

Iran had four times Iraq's population. During the Shah's reign, it had armed forces which were so much larger and better equipped than Iraq's as to deter any aggression across their western border, even from as megalomaniac a dictator as Saddam Hussein. Given Iran's inherent advantages, and despite its post-revolutionary turmoil, the Iranians were convinced that Saddam would never have gone to war unless he had been given the green light to do so by President Carter, outraged at the way in which the US hostages were being treated and by his own humiliation at the hand of the Iranian theocratic regime. Indeed, the Iranians dubbed this 'the imposed war' – imposed by the Great Satan, the United States.

The reality – at least at the start of the war – appears to have been much more prosaic. Saddam was no friend of the United States. Iraq's diplomatic ties with the US had been severed in 1967 following the Six Day War.* Saddam had a pathological hatred not just of Israel as a state but of Jewish people generally. He believed that it was in Iraq's interests to have close relations with the Soviet Union, both to secure major supplies of arms and to ensure that any American-led diplomatic assault on Iraq in the United Nations Security Council would be blocked by a Soviet veto. The Soviet Union reciprocated, even though they saw Saddam as a difficult and mercurial 'partner'.

Saddam had purchased no American – or British – arms. These went to Iran. His other supplier (in addition to the Soviet Union) was France, semi-detached from the Western NATO alliance at that time and only too happy to provide Iraq with nuclear technology (ostensibly for civil purposes) and with much investment in its oil industry.

Nonetheless, the assertions that the United States either pushed Saddam into war with Iran or consented to it have persisted. The journalist Dilip Hiro produced a bestselling book with these claims.[10] More recently, they appeared to have been confirmed by the release of a declassified document from the Reagan administration. In this memorandum, Reagan's Secretary of State, General Alexander Haig,

---

* A US Interests section was established in the Belgian Embassy in Baghdad in 1972. Full diplomatic relations were not restored until 1984.

reported to the President that both President Sadat of Egypt and Crown Prince Fahd of Saudi Arabia had confirmed 'that President Carter gave the Iraqis a green light to launch the war against Iran through Fahd'.[11]

There has, however, been no separate corroboration of what message President Carter may or may not have given Saddam via Prince Fahd. In his magisterial book on the Iran–Iraq War, the French author Pierre Razoux concludes that 'a meticulous analysis of the events, context, and statements by contemporary authorities … has left no doubt that the American government did not push Saddam Hussein to criminal behaviour [against Iran]'.[12]

Where the Iranians were correct, however, is that once the war had started, no one with any sway in the international community wanted Iran to win. It took the UN Security Council a whole week to debate the situation. When it did, it passed a milk-and-water resolution which simply called for both Iraq and Iran 'to refrain immediately from any further use of force',[13] pointedly failing to allocate what everyone knew to be Iraq's culpability for starting this act of aggression. Whatever had or had not been said by President Carter via General Haig, the Iranians profoundly believed that this was a war instigated by the US, using Saddam as their proxy.

*　　*　　*

The initial incursions by the Iraqis' vast invasion force did not succeed in its aim of reaching key Iranian cities like Kermanshah, in the central western part of the country, about 100 miles from the border, nor Ahvaz, on the Karun River, but they did succeed in taking a swathe of Iranian territory averaging around twenty miles wide from Khorramshahr and Abadan on the Shatt al-Arab in the south-west to well above Qasr-e Shirin, more than 400 miles to the north.

By the time winter set in, there was effectively stalemate. Despite continuing instability within the new Islamic Republic and intense

Cypress tree at Abarkuh (south-west Iran, Yazd province), a national monument estimated to be between 4,000 and 5,000 years old. It was here that a delegation of the Yazd Basij presented me with a detailed declaration explaining why I, as a British representative, was not welcome in Iran.

© ERIC LAFFORGUE/GAMMA-RAPHO/ GETTY IMAGES

Cyrus the Great (c. 600–530 BC), Persian Emperor and assumed author of the Cyrus cylinder, often referred to as the first bill of human rights.

Hafez (1315–1390), a lyricist from Shiraz and one of the most celebrated of all Iranian poets.

© HISTORIC COLLECTION/ALAMY STOCK PHOTO

Shah Ismail I, Shah of Iran from 1501 to 1524. He founded the Safavid dynasty in 1501 and made Shi'ism the religion of the state.

© GABINETTO FOTOGRAFICO DELLE GALLERIE DEGLI UFFIZI

Naqsh-e Jahan Square, Isfahan. Built by Shah Abbas between 1598 and 1629, when he moved the capital from Qazvin (north-west Iran) to Isfahan, it is the centre of one of the most beautiful cities in the world.
© BERNARD GAGNON/WIKIMEDIA COMMONS

William Knox D'Arcy (1849–1917), a British entrepreneur who obtained the first oil concession in Iran in 1901. The company he founded later became BP.
© GENERAL PHOTOGRAPHIC AGENCY/
HULTON ARCHIVE/GETTY IMAGES

Reza Shah Pahlavi, Shah of Iran from 1925 to 1941, who rose from a poor background to found the Pahlavi dynasty. He was replaced by his son, Mohammad Reza Pahlavi, on the insistence of Soviet and British invaders.
© KEYSTONE-FRANCE/GAMMA-KEYSTONE/GETTY IMAGES

TOP LEFT Prime Minister
Mossadegh with US President
Harry Truman, fresh from
his triumph at the UN in
worsting the UK, October 1951.
© EVERETT COLLECTION
HISTORICAL/ALAMY STOCK PHOTO

TOP RIGHT Royalist supporters
riding on a tank in August
1953, celebrating the success
of the Iranian coup.
© AFP/GETTY IMAGES

LEFT Abadan Oil Refinery,
Persian Gulf. Established in 1912
by the Anglo-Iranian Oil Company
(later BP), this was once one
of the world's largest refineries.
It was critical to the Allies' oil
supplies in both world wars.
© BETTMANN/GETTY IMAGES

LEFT Churchill's sixty-ninth
birthday celebrations at the British
residence, Tehran, November
1943. Left to right: Anthony
Eden, William Averell Harriman,
Winston Churchill, Marshal
Voroshilov and Joseph Stalin.
© FREMANTLE/ALAMY STOCK PHOTO

Mohammad Reza Shah's extravaganza to celebrate 2,500 years of Persian monarchy, Persepolis, 1971. The food was flown in by Maxim's of Paris.

© A. ABBAS/
MAGNUM PHOTOS

Ayatollah Ruhollah Khomeini, Supreme Leader of Iran from 1979 to 1989, returning to Tehran on 1 February 1979 after fourteen years in exile.

© BETTMANN/
GETTY IMAGES

Women protesting against the mandatory requirement to wear a hijab, 1979.

© HENGAMEH GOLESTAN,
COURTESY OF
ARCHAEOLOGY OF
THE FINAL DECADE

ABOVE American hostages on the first day of the US Embassy siege of 1979. The siege began on 4 November and lasted 444 days, ending on 20 January 1981 – the day of President Reagan's inauguration.

© BETTMANN/GETTY IMAGES

LEFT A child Basij soldier during the Iran–Iraq War, 1981. The Iranians made extensive use of child soldiers, some as young as twelve. Each one was given a gold plastic key to unlock paradise; tens of thousands were killed.

© ALFRED YAGHOBZADEH

ABOVE LEFT Sayyid Ali Khamenei, the most powerful man in Iran. He was President from 1981 to 1989 before becoming Supreme Leader in 1989. He lost the use of his right arm in an assassination attempt in June 1981.

© PETER PROBST/ALAMY STOCK PHOTO

ABOVE RIGHT Mohammad Khatami, President of Iran from 1997 to 2005. A cultured reformist, he is now a 'non-person' and the media are banned from giving him any coverage.

© ATTA KENARE/AFP/GETTY IMAGES

MIDDLE LEFT Kamal Kharrazi, Foreign Minister from 1997 to 2005, pictured with the author. Kharrazi is now head of a foreign policy think tank and is adviser to the Supreme Leader.

COURTESY OF JACK STRAW

BELOW LEFT Mahmoud Ahmadinejad, President of Iran from 2005 to 2013. A hardliner whose contested re-election in 2009 led to huge protests.

© ATTA KENARE/AFP/GETTY IMAGES

TOP Women protesting during the 2009 unrest following the presidential election.

© GETTY IMAGES NEWS/GETTY IMAGES

ABOVE The British Embassy in Tehran (main Ferdowsi compound) during the invasion by Basij, November 2011. Note the riot police standing by, allowing the demonstrators to enter.

© ATTA KENARE/AFP/GETTY IMAGES

LEFT Hassan Rouhani, President of Iran since 2013.

© KAVEH KAZEMI/GETTY IMAGES

Mohammad Javad Zarif, Foreign Minister since 2013, pictured with
the author during the British parliamentary delegation in January 2014.
COURTESY OF JACK STRAW

Protesters demonstrating against the author in Isfahan, October 2013, holding placards reading
'City martyr catering, English is not the enemy.' The English is a mistranslation of the Persian.

rivalries between the Revolutionary Guards (the *Sepah*), and the regular army (the *Artesh*), the Iranians had been far more effective than Saddam had ever calculated, for lower losses than the Iranian military commanders had anticipated.

Perhaps buoyed by this, the Iranians launched an ill-prepared counter-offensive in early January 1981. Its failure was one of the factors that led to the removal of the secular President Bani-Sadr in June 1981, and to the marginalisation of his supporters. So much materiel was lost by this offensive that the Iranians had to regroup and postpone any idea of a spring offensive. Unlike the Iraqis, who were able to rely on the bottomless pockets of their Gulf allies, the Iranians had to rely on themselves.

A new front was opened by the Iraqis in Kurdistan, with Saddam supplying one faction of the ever-fissiparous Kurds – the Democratic Party of Iranian Kurdistan – to enable them to stage an insurrection within Iran. There were uprisings in the province of Azerbaijan, whose capital, Tabriz, had long played a critical role in Iranian politics. All this placed a significant burden on Iran's ground forces, who would take some time before they were ready for any further major engagements.

Meanwhile, there were two connected air attacks, which serve to underline the degree to which the Israelis were assisting the Iranians. 'H3' was an Iraqi airfield, in the west of the country, so far from any Iranian air base that it was considered to be out of range. On this base were stored many Iraqi planes awaiting heavy maintenance, and those, like the new French Mirage-Fs, being made ready for active service. On 4 April 1981, using aerial photographs of the base supplied by the Israelis, the Iranian Air Force launched an audacious attack, destroying more than forty Iraqi planes, including half of all Iraq's bombers, with no Iranian losses at all.

Knocking out this base and so many of its planes was helpful to another air attack on Iraq, this one by the Israelis. The Iraqis had been building a large nuclear research reactor and other facilities at Osirak, with technology supplied by the French. Both the Iraqis and the French claimed that the reactor was solely for peaceful purposes and could not be used to build a nuclear weapon. Neither the Iranians nor the Israelis were convinced by these assurances.

There were early discussions between the Islamic Republic and Israel about coordinating action against Osirak. It was the Iranians who went first. They launched an attack on 30 September 1980, but this was unsuccessful and the plant was soon operational again.

The Iranians were, however, able to supply the Israelis with good aerial photography. Although Osirak was nearly 1,000 miles from Israel, meticulous planning and execution ensured that their second operation against this target was a success. The operation took place on 7 June 1981. The Israelis went in for some wonderfully imaginative feints. Over Jordanian air space, their pilots spoke in Saudi-accented Arabic, claiming that they were Saudi pilots who had gone off course; over Saudi Arabia, they used Jordanian call signs.

The Israelis' bombs completely destroyed Osirak's main reactor, its containment dome and its underground research laboratory – and so removed the potential threat of an Iraqi nuclear attack on either Israel or Iran.

There has been some debate since as to whether Osirak could have produced nuclear weapons if it had not been destroyed. No one can know for sure. However, the Israelis are the best informed by far of any Western nation about what is going on in their neighbourhood. They live there. Many of their citizens had only recently moved from Iraq and Iran. The operation against Osirak was heavily contested within the Israeli security cabinet before it was agreed. I think it improbable that the Israelis would have risked so much – though successful, the operation carried great danger for its pilots – unless they had had good evidence that Saddam would be able to manufacture a nuclear weapons system at that site.

Less conclusive, but suggestive nonetheless, is an answer that Tariq Aziz, Saddam's Deputy Prime Minister, gave to a visiting US congressional delegation. After boasting about the Iraqis' use of chemical weapons against the Iranians, Aziz said, 'If we had nuclear weapons, I'd guarantee you that we'd use them.'[14] The view of senior CIA officers was that but for the destruction of Osirak, Iraq would 'probably have a useable ... nuclear weapon by 1984–1985, or thereabouts'.[15]

At this distance, it might be thought that the reaction of the international community to Israel's efforts (with a little help from Iran) to wipe out the chance of Iraq manufacturing a nuclear weapon would have been one of gratitude. But not a bit of it. There was such a Manichaean preoccupation with the defeat of Iran that there was almost universal condemnation of Israel's actions. The *Los Angeles Times* described the attack as 'state-sponsored terrorism'. The UN Security Council passed a strongly worded resolution (No. 487) condemning the attack as a violation of the UN Charter. Even the US voted for this resolution, despite the explicit criticism of Israel.

The irony was that whatever Western powers and the Soviet Union were saying publicly in support of the Iraqi (and French) claim that the Osirak plant could be used solely for peaceful purposes, the removal of any threat of Iraq resorting to nuclear strikes against Iran now made it much easier for these powers overtly to support Iraq.

In late April 1982, the Iranians finally launched their major counterattack to retake their territory, including the key city of Khorramshahr. These and other initiatives shifted the balance of advantage firmly in favour of the Iranians – to Saddam's fury, who responded (as he often did) by executing some of the senior officers who had failed him, *pour encourager les autres*.

By July 1982, the UN Security Council, whose permanent members favoured Iraq, unanimously passed a resolution (No. 514) calling on both countries to cease their hostilities. Saddam, from a position of weakness, accepted the terms of the resolution. Supreme Leader Khomeini rejected it.

In January 1983, in the face of the unexpected victories the Iranians had secured, Saddam offered to go to Tehran to negotiate the terms of a ceasefire with Khomeini. Razoux claims that at this stage Khomeini 'was tempted to accept', but Speaker Rafsanjani and President Khamenei both insisted on rejecting Saddam's offer.[16] They demanded nothing less than Saddam's resignation from office, as well as what amounted to Iraq's surrender.

Given Saddam's total and ruthless dominance of his country and its security apparatus, and the glaring reality that his word could not be trusted, the view taken by Rafsanjani and Khamenei was not unreasonable. However, Khomeini was on this occasion the wiser counsel. In retrospect, Iran could and should have quit whilst it was obviously ahead. This would have spared the Iranians hundreds of thousands of casualties, the near bankruptcy of the country and the long stalemate which led, at best, to a draw when the war finally ended five and a half years later.

Thus the Iranians decided to plough on with the war. Thereafter, it was Khomeini who was the most obdurate in continuing the conflict, almost regardless of the casualties and of the increasing risk of defeat. In the years that followed, the Iranians (like the Iraqis) sustained the most terrible losses, never seen since the carnage of the First World War. By the end of 1983 alone, an estimated 120,000 Iranians and 60,000 Iraqis had been killed in battle.

One of the most terrible and abiding legacies of Khomeini's conduct of the war from this stage was his decision to recruit tens of thousands of young teenage boys into the Basij for use at the front. Many of these were as young as twelve. They were given cursory training and a few hand grenades or, if they were lucky, a rifle or a machine gun – along with a plastic key which they were told would open the door to paradise when they were 'martyred'. They were sent in waves to the front, where most perished as cannon fodder. Some, the most fanatical, were sent on suicide missions. No accurate data of the children killed in this way are available, but reliable estimates put the number at least at 80,000, with a similar number badly injured.[17]

*   *   *

After Iraq's failure in the first phase of the war, the Soviet Union, which had been on Iraq's side from the start, upgraded its support. This was in part a reaction to Khomeini's banning of the communist Tudeh Party, and the execution of many of its leading figures as Soviet spies. Such is the perfidy of war that it is claimed that the information about this spy network had come from the United Kingdom, who had been debriefing a Soviet defector, Vladimir Kuzichkin, a KGB agent in Baghdad, and had passed the intelligence to the Iranians via the US.[18]

The Soviets also regarded Iraq as a key market for its hard-currency arms supplies. These made up to 65 per cent of their total such exports in this period.

The Chinese, infinitely weaker than today, and with soured relations with Moscow, responded by agreeing to become a major supplier to Iran. To preserve appearances, most of their materiel was shipped through North Korea. The Chinese continued to meet various contractual obligations to supply Iraq as well.

The Iranians' unanticipated success in the first two years of the war, as well as the demolition of the Osirak facilities, so seriously worried the United States and allies that they shifted from a relatively relaxed encouragement of Iraq to much more active involvement on the Iraqi side.

The Saudis gave huge assistance to the Iraqis, building a pipeline to connect the oilfields of southern Iraq with its own network. It facilitated road transport of oil from Iraq, and bankrolled Saddam, with loans of billions of US dollars. So, to a lesser degree, did Kuwait, the Emirates, Bahrain and Qatar.

Compared to the Soviet Union, France and China, the supply of arms by the United States to Iraq was relatively modest. Razoux puts the approximate value of the Soviet Union's supplies at US$30–45 billion, France at $17 billion and China at $6 billion, with the US at just $250 million (and the UK at $60 million). Meanwhile, the United States' arms exports to Iran were $650 million (much of this through Israel), and the United Kingdom's $600 million.[19]

That said, there is no doubt which side the United States wished to win this bloody war, and that was Iraq. Their position is best summed up by the words of Charles Cogan, a career CIA officer who was chief of the Near East and South Asia Division of the CIA (covering Iran) from mid-1979 to mid-1984:

We had a score to settle with the Iranians. We had just floated through the hostage crisis, paralyzed, humiliated, and frustrated. Our thirst for revenge was unrequited. I think the Iranians never fully grasped the depravity of the hostage taking at the US embassy ... I don't think, to this day, the Iranians appreciate how despicable the world regarded, and still regards, the hostage taking in November 1979.[20]

David Newton, a US Foreign Service officer, added, 'By 1982 ... we began to see that the Iranians might win, and win big, and if they did, the US would be the big loser in the Middle East.'[21]

The US's efforts on Iraq's behalf became more intensive from the end of 1983. It was then that Donald Rumsfeld, President Reagan's special envoy for the Middle East, visited Baghdad to meet Saddam Hussein, with a view to normalising the United States' diplomatic relations with Iraq and to lay the ground for more extensive defence and intelligence cooperation. He went again in March 1983. The US Embassy was formally reopened in 1984.

*   *   *

The United States made three important contributions to Iraq's war effort, which unquestionably helped ensure that by the war's end in 1988 they had not been defeated by Iran, as surely they would have been but for the American support.

First, the US authorised the sale to Iraq of numerous types of dual-use technology, including chemicals which could be used in the manufacturing of pesticides or chemical weapons and live viruses and bacteria, such as anthrax and bubonic plague. Don Riegle, the chairman of a US Senate committee which examined what had happened, said, 'The executive branch of our government approved 771 different export licenses for sale of dual-use technology to Iraq. I think it's a devastating record.'[22]

Second, the US provided detailed satellite imagery of the Iranians' forces which enabled the Iraqis better to target their attacks, including with the devastating use of chemical weapons. As Bruce Riedel, career CIA officer, commented:

> On the question of targeting: if you give information to one side as to where the position of the enemy is, of course that's facilitating the accuracy with which they strike their target. The DIA [US Defence Intelligence Agency] was not telling the Iraqis, 'Put sarin here.' But did they know that that's what the Iraqis would do? Of course.[23]

Thomas Pickering, a US Foreign Service officer and former Ambassador to Jordan and Israel, added, 'There should have been a debate inside the upper levels of the [Reagan] administration ... There should have been enough recognition of US culpability in this chemical horror to provoke a debate about whether or not to provide the Iraqis with any intelligence, whatever the consequences may have been.'[24]

Third, and most disreputably, the US ran an active and knowing campaign of disinformation mendaciously to shift the blame for chemical weapons attacks, and some other terrible events, from the Iraqis to the Iranians.

After the unspeakable fatalities and injuries that chemical weapons had caused in the First World War, international law prohibiting their use was strengthened by the 1928 Geneva Protocol, in force at the time of the Iran–Iraq War.

There is some evidence that Iran had achieved the capacity to manufacture chemical weapons. Razoux claims that the Iranians used them on 9 and 12 April 1987 when they 'poured phosgene gas' into the third Iraqi Army Corps' sector, but causing only minimal losses.[25] Others, including the academic Joost Hiltermann, have claimed that there was no evidence at all that Iran ever used chemical weapons.[26]

The Iraqis showed no such restraint. They were utterly ruthless and indiscriminate in their use of these weapons. Saddam used them on Iranian troops, on Iranian civilians and, most notoriously, on his own people in the city of Halabja on 16 March 1988.

When information about the Iraqis' extensive use of chemical weapons first emerged, in 1984, the response of the US government, in concert with the Soviet Union, was to block a Security Council resolution denouncing the Iraqis' actions. This pattern of ensuring that, at worst, criticism of Iraq was minimised, but at best (from the US viewpoint), the blame could be shifted to Iran, accelerated as the war dragged on, and the US became ever more committed to ensuring that Iran did not win.

On 17 May 1987, the Iraqis mistakenly fired a missile at the USS *Stark*, a US Navy vessel stationed in the Gulf. Thirty-seven crew members were killed. Two days later, Saddam Hussein sent a personal message to President Reagan to apologise for the error. Nonetheless, the US essentially blamed Iran for the incident, claiming that Iran had created a dangerous situation in the Gulf, increasing the risk of errors of this kind.

On 27 June 1987, the Iraqis attacked Sardasht, in the Kurdish region of north-west Iran, with chemical weapons, killing some hundreds of people, mainly civilians. Everyone knew that it was the Iraqis, but there was no international censure of Iraq.

In a century punctuated by atrocities, what happened in Halabja in March 1988 ranks as one of the worst. It is now officially categorised as an act of genocide against the Kurdish people.

Halabja is a small town in the north-east of Iraq, of about 70,000 people. On 15 March 1988, the Iranians, with assistance from one of the Kurdish factions, the PUK, captured the town. They did not send many troops into the town itself, instead taking strategic positions around it.

The following day, well knowing how few Iranian troops were in the town and how many civilian Iraqi Kurds were still there, the Iraqis bombed the town with chemical weapons. Around 4,000 people died, and many more were injured.

As soon as the attack became known, the United States led an international campaign to blame the Iranians for it. A Security Council resolution on the atrocity was delayed for two months as governments around the world asked for the evidence that Iran had been responsible. To these questions, the State Department replied that they could not disclose the evidence. 'We now know why. It was fake' is the acerbic conclusion of the Middle East expert Joost Hiltermann. [27]

*   *   *

On 3 July 1988, the USS *Vincennes*, a large, modern, guided-missile cruiser, was on station in the Gulf. This followed a period of direct engagements by US naval forces against the Iranian Navy, to keep the Gulf open for international shipping. These actions had succeeded in destroying a very significant part of the Iranian fleet. The *Vincennes* was on high alert, trying to intercept some Iranian fast boats which had been harassing them.

An Iran Air Airbus A300 had taken off from Bandar Abbas on a scheduled passenger flight to Dubai. It was following the correct flight path for commercial aviation, and was still ascending. *Vincennes*'s radar picked this up. Confusion, error and fright in the *Vincennes* control room led the commander to decide that it must be a military aircraft about to attack them. He sent up missiles. The Airbus was immediately destroyed. All 290 people on board (274 passengers and sixteen crew) were killed. In a statement to Congress the next day, President Reagan claimed that the Airbus had been shot down by the *Vincennes* 'firing in self-defense at what it believed to be a hostile

Iranian military aircraft. We deeply regret the tragic loss of life that occurred.'[28] However, no apology was offered to the Iranians. Instead, there was the usual dissembling about how the Iranians had created the conditions in which things like this might happen. The captain of the *Vincennes* was later awarded the Legion of Merit by President George H. W. Bush.

* * *

In a Commons debate on the Middle East in June 1982, Labour's shadow Foreign Secretary, Denis Healey, complained that

> General [Ariel] Sharon [Israel's Minister of Defence] told us the other day that Israel had been supplying Iran with weapons during the Iran–Iraq War ... Necessity makes strange bedfellows. I would only say again that if Israel's role in the Middle East is to cement that sort of alliance, the less we have of it the better, and the better for Israel.[29]

There was, thus, no secret about the fact of Israel's support for Iran from early on in the war (if little of its detail was public); nor that Israel's position was unpopular in the West, as Healey's comment indicates. Given the enmity which currently exists between Iran and Israel, their approach back then seems extraordinary. So why did Israel strike out on its own, ignoring what its erstwhile allies, especially the US, thought of their policy?

Today, Israel appears to be secure, stable and prosperous, and enjoying the unqualified support of the United States for almost anything it chooses to do. But at the beginning of the 1980s, Israel's security was much more fragile. In the previous decade and a half it had been involved in two major wars with Arab states – the 1967 Six Day War and the 1973 Yom Kippur War. Though Israel had won the first and had staved off the Arabs' far more effective actions in the second, they were forever aware that they were a small nation of 4 million surrounded by much larger, hostile Arab states – with one such state, Iraq, possessed of huge oil resources and well-equipped military forces, developing nuclear weapons, and run by a dictator who hated them.

Under the Shah, Iran had developed close economic, political and military ties with Israel. Israeli and Iranian pilots trained together. Mossad advised SAVAK on how best to operate.

When the Islamic Revolution in Iran occurred in early 1979, the initial view in Israel was that they should simply wait and see what happened to the new regime. Like many others in the West, they were betting that it might collapse.

Eighteen months later, when Saddam launched his invasion of Iran, the Israelis were faced with a stark choice. They chose to support the Iranians.

Despite all the rebarbative rhetoric by Khomeini and his supporters against the 'Zionist entity', Israel's calculation was entirely rational. Tehran is almost 1,000 miles from Jerusalem, with Iraq and Jordan in between. Baghdad is only 550 miles away, with just Jordan between. The Israelis' view was that they faced much the greater and more immediate danger from Saddam. As well as his military capacity to attack Israel, he was harbouring the Palestine Liberation Organization (PLO) and other extremist Palestinian terrorist groups, which were committing a series of outrages against Israeli targets.

In addition, there was Saddam's attitude towards Jewish people. Although Baghdad had once had the largest Jewish population of any city, from 1948 Iraq had systematically employed antisemitic policies (with strong echoes of those used in 1930s Germany) to discriminate against its Jewish residents. As Saddam became more entrenched, so the hostility towards Iraq's Jewish population grew. By the end of the 1970s, almost all Iraqi Jews had left their home country for Israel, Europe or the US.

There had been no equivalent antisemitism in Iran. Under its 1906 constitution, Jewish citizens had one reserved place in the Majlis. This provision was repeated in the constitution of the Islamic Republic in 1979.[30] Khomeini issued reassurances that the traditional tolerance towards Iran's Jewish communities would continue. On the other hand, there was Khomeini's opposition to Zionism, and scepticism within the Israeli government that in practice Iran's Jewish communities – estimated at 75,000 at the start of the Iran–Iraq War – would be safe.

Two motives for the Israelis therefore coincided. They judged that if they provided arms to Iran, the war would be a more even contest and would drag on, weakening both their obvious adversary, Iraq, and a potential adversary, Iran. Along with this, they calculated that if they did provide such materiel, they should be able to come to an arrangement with Iran which would allow those Jewish Iranian citizens who wished to emigrate to Israel to do so without coming to any harm.

It was on this basis that Israel's Faustian pact with Iran was made. In consequence, the war did indeed drag on, and over its course about 55,000 Iranian Jews left the country safely. About 25,000 remain, permitted to practise their religion undisturbed (but not to proselytise 'Zionism').

Israel had one other motive. Its economy was in poor shape. If it could sell Iran a lot of arms, it could keep people in jobs and would have the funds to replace those arms with more modern ones.

Iran and Israel worked out their arms deals mainly through shady intermediaries. Israel also had an 'informal Ambassador' based in Tehran, Uri Lubrani.[31]

Under the Shah, Iran had purchased 225 F-4 Phantom fighter-bombers and 127 of the smaller F-5s from the United States. By the start of the war, it was estimated that only about a half of these were operational. Iran was desperate for spare parts for them – not least for tyres for the F-4. The tyres had a habit of blowing when the planes landed – made worse by the fact that Iran had many new, poorly trained pilots to replace those whose loyalty to the new regime had been in doubt. Amongst many other supplies from Israel were F-4 tyres.

Razoux estimates that in the first six years of the war, 'Israel made between one and two billion dollars from weapon and spare-part shipments to Iran, becoming the fourth biggest weapon supplier to Tehran'[32] (after China, North Korea and Libya).

Israel's alliance with Iran left it free to deal with what it believed to be its immediate threats from the PLO. In June 1982, Israel invaded southern Lebanon, after repeated incursions against them by the PLO, and the attempted assassination in London of the Israeli Ambassador to the UK (blamed on the PLO, even though it was, as Israel well knew at the time, the work of the Abu Nidal group, who were violently opposed to the PLO). Iran took no initial part in this conflict, though it was from this time that the elements of the large Shi'a community in Lebanon formed Hezbollah. Inspired by Khomeini, funded by Iran and trained by hundreds of IRGC men, Hezbollah quickly became the key militia, political party and social support organisation in south Lebanon. Its actions were fundamental in forcing the withdrawal of Israeli troops from Lebanon in 2000. There is an umbilical link between Hezbollah and Iran, which continues to fund and supply it with materiel. Its confessional connection goes back to the sixteenth century, when Iran was converted to Shi'ism by Shah Ismail I.

Israel's continuing supply of arms to Iran caused significant problems in their relationship with the US. 'Be nice to Iran; tilt toward Iran' was the message Yitzhak Rabin (Israeli Minister of Defence from 1984 to 1990, later Prime Minister) and agents from Mossad were giving to US officials, even though at the same time the Iranians were building up Hezbollah and assisting its efforts to drive the Israel Defense Force from Lebanon.[33] To quote Bruce Riedel, former CIA officer, 'The Israeli approach to Iran never changed throughout the decade of the 1980s. They were looking, and looking hard, for a strategic dialogue.'[34]

The Iranians and the Israelis were not the only ones capable of adopting two apparently contradictory positions. So too were the United States.

On 3 November 1986, the Lebanese news magazine *al-Shiraa* published details of secret US–Iran dealings over the previous six months.

The idea was to trade US arms to Iran, in return for Iran's help in obtaining the release of US hostages held in Lebanon by Hezbollah, who were backed by Iran.

President Reagan's initial response was to declare that the report in *al-Shiraa* was 'utterly false', but it was in fact Reagan himself who was being untruthful.* To make matters even worse for Reagan, some of the payments made by Iran to the US for the arms were then siphoned off illegally to support the Nicaraguan Contras, a right-wing rebel group opposed to the Sandinistas, who were governing with the support of both Cuba and the Soviet Union. Under US law, supplying arms to the Contras with US funds was illegal.†

Israel had brokered the US–Iran deal, and for the most part the arms were shipped through them. The Iranians were particularly anxious to secure anti-tank guided missiles (TOWs). Progress on deliveries was not smooth, however. They were punctuated by disputes between the Iranians, the US and the Israelis, particularly over the release of the hostages. In the end, the US obtained the release of three hostages (of a total of five), in return for 2,500 TOW missiles and the equivalent of 300 Hawk surface-to-air missiles.[35]

The Iran–Contra scandal caused mayhem in Washington. Reagan narrowly escaped impeachment. Many of his senior officials were not so lucky. Some had to resign; others had charges brought against them, though were subsequently pardoned by George H. W. Bush when he succeeded Reagan. It also emerged that some in the US military had been going in for a little private enterprise of their own. This included a skilful scam by a purser on the USS aircraft carrier *Kitty Hawk* who managed to purloin $7 million worth of Tomcat spare parts and have them shipped, via London, to Iran.[36]

On the surface, there was no similar turmoil in Iran. Those in

---

* Mrs Thatcher knew immediately that Reagan was not telling the truth. Through the UK's intelligence-sharing arrangement between GCHQ and the US's NSA, British analysts had clear prior evidence about the deals. See Charles Moore, *Margaret Thatcher: The Authorized Biography*, Vol. 2, op. cit., p. 605.
† Under the so-called Boland amendment.

direct charge of the war effort, particularly Khamenei and Rafsanjani, emerged from the scandal relatively unscathed. But the saga did have long-lasting consequences for the polity of Iran.

The Iranians were furious that their secret arrangement had come to light. The man who was identified as the source of the leaks to *al-Shiraa*, Mehdi Hashemi, had been arrested a few days before the story broke, on unrelated charges. He subsequently made a confession of guilt for the leaks and was executed the following year.

Hashemi's brother was the son-in-law of Ayatollah Hussein-Ali Montazeri, who had been a long-term ally of Khomeini. Montazeri had spent much time in the Shah's prisons, where he had been tortured. He had the appropriate clerical status as a *marja*. In 1985, he had been formally selected by the Assembly of Experts as Khomeini's heir apparent. But he was left-leaning. He favoured greater state intervention to help the poor – contrary to the interests of the conservative clerics and their allies amongst the *bazaaris*. Though he had been one of the few senior clerics to have actively supported the principle of *velayat-e faqih*, he later made clear his view that there had to be much better accountability by the Supreme Leader to the people than was provided in the constitution.

Montazeri was never a soft liberal. He had argued earlier for the export of the revolution and had defended suicide bombings. However, had Montazeri become the Supreme Leader on Khomeini's death in June 1989, the Islamic Republic would have survived, but its politics would have taken a very different and more benign course. There is even a chance that the bifurcation of the Iranian governmental system, which continues to hobble its effectiveness and legitimacy, might have been resolved, with the coercive powers of the state transferred to the elected government through amendments to the constitution. Iran would have been much the stronger as a result.

However, Montazeri's position as the chosen one to succeed Khomeini inevitably made him the subject of much criticism, and his family association with Hashemi proved to be the excuse his detractors were hoping for. After Hashemi's arrest, Montazeri was marginalised and later placed under house arrest.

* * *

A new Iraqi offensive in the early summer of 1988 put the Iranians on the back foot. Both Iran and Iraq had Soviet-built Scud missiles, but for every one the Iranians managed to fire at Iraq, the Iraqis managed three. By 1988, the Iranians were war-weary. Their economy was close to bankruptcy. Saddam's 'War of the Cities' was causing panic for many Iranians, especially those in Tehran. Those who could left the city.

The shooting down of Iran's Airbus by a US Navy missile, despite Reagan's protestations that this had been an error, had raised high anxieties in Tehran that the US might be moving to take an even more active role in the conflict. Already, Iran's navy had all but been destroyed by US action.

Meanwhile, the Iraqis had gained the upper hand on the battlefield. Huge Iraqi attacks in April 1988 helped Saddam to regain the Fao Peninsula, and in May and June, Iraq was able to regain all the territory it had previously lost. Saddam continued to make extensive use of chemical weapons.

In the second week of July, Saddam launched a further massive operation, of 140,000 troops supported by 1,000 tanks and 1,000 cannon, in the direction of the Iranian town of Dehloran, on the central front. It was a rout. Hundreds of Iranian armoured vehicles and artillery pieces were destroyed or abandoned in the retreat. Ten thousand Iranian soldiers were killed, and 5,000 captured.

A year earlier, on 20 July 1987, the UN Security Council had unanimously passed Resolution 598 calling for a ceasefire. On 17 July 1988, following Saddam's Dehloran offensive and after agonised discussions amongst the Iranian leadership, in which they recognised the impossibility of continuing the conflict, President Khamenei announced that Iran had unconditionally decided to accept Resolution 598.

On 20 July 1988, Khomeini made his famous speech in which he said that taking the decision to end the war 'was more painful and deadly to me than drinking a cup of poison ... It would have been more bearable to me to accept death and martyrdom, but I had to accept the enlightened opinion of all the military experts.'[37]

As is usual when a ceasefire is in the offing but has not been agreed, skirmishes, some serious, continued, most to Iraq's advantage, until 20 August, when the ceasefire finally took effect.

When it did, Saddam made a belligerent speech claiming that he had achieved a 'very great victory'. But he conceded navigation rights on the Shatt-al Arab waterway, and, as Pierre Razoux puts it, 'by doing so, he implicitly recognised the validity of the Algiers Accord, thereby putting an end to the absurd and atrociously bloody war he could have avoided'.[38]

*　　*　　*

No one can be certain whether Saddam would have made a different decision about starting the Iran–Iraq War if the United States had actively warned him off doing so, rather than initially giving him tacit approval and later providing much military and intelligence assistance. Saddam was certainly sufficiently arrogant to have begun the war without a nod from the United States. He might also have been able to rely on Soviet support, given the intensity of the Cold War at that time. The US and the Soviets were locked into a serious proxy war on Iran's eastern border in Afghanistan.

From a US perspective, it would have been difficult for any administration to stand back from some engagement against Iran. When Saddam invaded Iran in September 1980, the US hostages in its Tehran Embassy had already been held, in appalling conditions, for nearly eleven months, and would not be released until late January 1981. The hostage crisis alone put immense pressure on the Carter administration; as mentioned above, his inability to secure the release of the hostages was a key reason for his failure to win a second term.

To many in the outside world, what was happening in Iran continued to be seen almost entirely through the lens of the hostage crisis. The patent refusal of the Khomeini regime to follow the norms of international behaviour, without which normal diplomacy was unworkable, led to the dismissal of the new Islamic Republic as one run by a group of religious bigots with whom no serious discourse was possible.

Although the invasion of the US Embassy and the hostage-taking was unacceptable on any basis, the view of Thomas Pickering, the experienced US Ambassador quoted above, who said that over three decades the US policy towards Iran had been 'certifiably insane', though colourful, is not entirely wrong. The US would have been wise to have listened to Israel's counsel.

The war achieved the opposite of what the US had hoped. In Iran, the conflict solidified support for Khomeini's view of how a post-revolutionary nation should be run, and gave him the occasion for eliminating many of his rivals. In Iraq, Saddam's near victory in 1988 over the Iranians strengthened his megalomania and his ambition to become undisputed leader of the Arabs. Within three years, Saddam invaded Kuwait, on the grounds that it had been part of Iraq before the British took it over, and, more immediately, because Kuwait was insisting on repayment of the large loans it had provided to Iraq. As Thomas Pickering notes, 'Saddam was encouraged in his Kuwait adventure by our tolerance for just about everything he did.'[39]

On 20 March 2003, a US-led coalition, with heavy UK involvement, invaded Iraq. What had eluded the Iranians for eight years then occurred in less than four weeks: the downfall of Saddam Hussein.

CHAPTER 14

THE AFTERMATH: *THE SATANIC VERSES* AND VIOLENCE

Vote Bhikha, Vote Tory, Ban the Book
Slogan used by Conservative County Council candidate
Abdul Bhikha, who won the rock-solid Labour Bank Top
and Brookhouse Ward, Blackburn, for the Conservatives,
on calls to have Rushdie's book banned in May 1989

Ayatollah Khomeini came to Blackburn in 1989.
Figuratively, not literally – but you could feel his presence in parts of the town as if he were there in person.

In the ten years in which I had been the town's MP, I had never experienced anything like it. Khomeini's *fatwa* on Salman Rushdie for publishing his book *The Satanic Verses* had shot through Muslim communities around the world like a high-voltage bolt of electricity.

At the end of the 1980s, about a fifth of Blackburn's population were people of Muslim Asian heritage – half from the Indian state of Gujurat, half from Pakistan. I had close friendships with many from these communities. They had solidly voted Labour from the first.

At the heart of the Asian communities was the Brookhouse Community Centre – a converted three-decker Victorian school.

County council elections were due on 4 May 1989. We assumed that we would have no problem in holding the Bank Top and Brookhouse Ward on this occasion. We did not bargain for Khomeini's *fatwa*.

In early April 1989, I was called to a meeting at the Brookhouse Centre. I walked in and could tell that this was going to be difficult. About forty men were sat in a large circle; all Muslim, apart from a couple of councillors and town hall officials, a bemused police inspector and me.

What were we – the police inspector and I – going to do about the blasphemous Rushdie book, we were asked? We tried patiently to explain that there were no powers in the United Kingdom to ban books simply because some regarded their contents as offensive.

A fury suddenly possessed the meeting. The offending volume was kicked across the room, and back again. Impossible demands were made of me, as the senior politician present, to have the book banned forthwith. I tried again, reminding everyone that Mrs Thatcher's Conservative Party, not Labour, were in power in Westminster – but adding that even were we in government, we could not accede to their demands.

Most worrying was the fact that others in the room, who I knew to hold moderate views, seemed intimidated into silence by the sheer emotional force of those with the more extreme views. It was as if a spell had been cast. It was quite beyond argument. Rushdie was a British blasphemer. If we did nothing, we were complicit in his blasphemy.

When the votes for this ward were counted, our Conservative opponent Abdul Bhikha had won, on the immortal slogan of 'Vote Bhikha, Vote Tory, Ban the Book'.

*   *   *

The Satanic Verses was Rushdie's fifth novel. The title was taken from a legend about a few verses that had supposedly been spoken by the Prophet Muhammad as part of the Quran, and then withdrawn on the grounds that the devil had sent them to deceive Muhammad into thinking they came from God. The legend itself is hotly contested by Islamic scholars.

The book was first published in the UK in September 1988 and in the US in February 1989. It achieved immediate literary acclaim and won the Whitbread Award for the best novel of the year in November 1988.

Its publication sparked hostility straightaway in some Muslim countries; by the end of 1988, it had been banned in India, Bangladesh, Sudan, South Africa and Sri Lanka. But not in Iran. Initially, the book was imported into Iran and reviewed in the usual way. Michael Axworthy says that 'much as with the occupation of the US Embassy in 1979, Khomeini seems to have reacted initially with indifference ... [saying] that the book was not worth taking seriously'.[1]

Four months after its publication, Khomeini took a very different view. On St Valentine's Day, 14 February 1989, he issued his *fatwa* against the book: 'I would like to inform all the intrepid Muslims in the world that the author of the book *The Satanic Verses* ... as well as those publishers who were aware of its contents, have been sentenced to death.' A bounty of several million US dollars was put on Rushdie's head.[*]

News of the *fatwa* had an immediate effect internationally. There were widespread and often violent protests against the book, in many cases leading to fatalities or serious injuries. These continued for many years.

The British bookseller W. H. Smith reported that until the *fatwa* they had sold relatively few copies of the book, but once Khomeini had pronounced, the book 'flew off the shelves'. The same was true in the US and elsewhere. Khomeini had inadvertently made the book an international bestseller.

---

[*] There has been a recent claim in a BBC Two documentary that the *fatwa* had been requested by Kalim Siddiqui, director of the British Muslim Institute. This may explain Khomeini's apparent change of heart on the issue. *The Times*, 25 February 2019.

Evidently appreciating the appalling impact that Khomeini's *fatwa* was having on international perceptions of Iran, just when the country needed outside assistance with its post-war reconstruction, then President (now Supreme Leader) Ali Khamenei announced four days after the *fatwa* that if Rushdie were to issue an apology and disown the book, 'the people might forgive him'. Rushdie duly obliged, with a carefully worded statement which said that he profoundly regretted 'the distress the publication has occasioned to the sincere followers of Islam'. It was to no avail. Khomeini implicitly disavowed Khamenei's offer, and reiterated his death sentence on Rushdie. Rushdie had to be given intense police protection by the British government – which was continuing in place eight years later when I became Home Secretary, responsible for the level of protection offered to public figures vulnerable to terrorist violence.

In 1989, the British government had only just begun to restore normal diplomatic relations, which had been downgraded to almost zero following the kidnapping of Edward Chaplin two years earlier. Now, faced with an official threat of murder of one of its citizens by another state, Britain had little alternative but to break off diplomatic relations. The European Union withdrew all its Ambassadors for a period in solidarity.

Why did Khomeini issue his *fatwa* against Rushdie in such explicit, violent terms?

In the much more secular UK, parody or satire against Jesus Christ, or other prophets of the Old and New Testaments, can be and often is simply shrugged off as the price to be paid for freedom of speech. But blasphemy is still an offence in many European countries. The European Court of Human Rights has found that such anti-blasphemy laws are compatible with the Convention on Human Rights.

In England and Wales, blasphemy was a specific criminal offence at the time Rushdie published his book; the offence was not abolished until 2008. But the law referred only to the Christian religion, and specifically to the Church of England.* It was replaced by wider offences, which did cover Islam, of incitement to religious hatred.

For a great many Muslims, whether Sunni or Shi'a, their faith is much more personal and intense than that which is generally experienced these days in the Christian tradition. It has been said that for such Muslims, blasphemy is as objectionable as paedophilia is to people everywhere. This may help to explain why there were such strong reactions in many Muslim countries to the publication of *The Satanic Verses*. This was accompanied by the usual charge of double standards by the West, with many asking whether a book as defamatory as Rushdie's was of Islam would ever have found a mainstream publisher, still less literary acclaim, if it had been directed against Jesus or the Virgin Mary. It is a fair point.

It is, however, one thing to condemn a book's publication, or even have it banned; it is quite another for the full authority of the state to be used to condemn its author to death – and provide an incentive to do so, in the form of a large bounty.

Khomeini was never interested in the reaction to his views beyond the Shi'a *umma* – the faithful. He had long held the opinion that the world outside was hostile to the true Shi'a faith and to the intertwined interests of his nation. His experience during the Iran–Iraq War confirmed that belief. So the condemnation of him as 'that Mad Mullah', to quote a headline in the *Daily Mirror*,[2] simply washed over him.

What the *fatwa* did do was to excite true believers across the world, Sunni as well as Shi'a, and to re-establish Khomeini's place as the Supreme Leader of all Islam. It would have been particularly pleasing to him to have stolen a march on Saudi Arabia and its royal family, infected as he believed it was by the extreme apostasy of Wahhabism.

---

* 'Every publication is said to be blasphemous which contains any contemptuous, reviling, scurrilous or ludicrous matter relating to God, Jesus Christ or the Bible, or the formularies of the Church of England as by law established. It is not blasphemous to speak or publish opinions hostile to the Christian religion, or to deny the existence of God, if the publication is couched in decent and temperate language.' Stephen's Digest of Criminal Law, 9th edition (1950).

Khomeini's promulgation of the Rushdie *fatwa* was all of a piece with two other sets of decisions he took in the final months of his life, striking out against his frustration that he had led his country to near defeat.

The first of these was motivated, so far as one can judge, by revenge, a desire to institute what can only be described as a reign of terror. The MEK faction, which had begun during the Shah's period, working broadly in parallel with Khomeini's supporters, had long since become so opposed to the Islamic Republic that they had joined forces with Saddam – an act of abject treachery.

Khomeini had announced his acceptance of the ceasefire on 20 July 1988. Five days later, before it came into effect, the MEK launched a major attack on western Iran, and claimed that they would march on Tehran. They were easily repulsed by the Iranians, and large numbers of MEK fighters were killed. There were now some thousands of MEK supporters in Iranian prisons. There had been thousands more, but they had been executed already. It is reasonable to believe that those who were left in prison were regarded as lower-level MEK adherents. Some were young teenagers.

At the end of July 1988, Khomeini issued a decree ordering that all MEK prisoners 'who remain steadfast in their support [for MEK]' should be executed, along with many other political prisoners with no connections to MEK. Three religious judges were appointed to supervise the interrogations of these prisoners and determine guilt. But these 'judicial' proceedings were risible. However contrite, it was virtually impossible for any prisoner to expiate their 'guilt'. The long-established rule that all three judges on each panel had to be unanimous in their decision to impose the death sentence was abandoned.

This massacre of the MEK and other prisoners was conducted in strict secrecy. Details about it emerged only later. There are no reliable estimates of how many were executed in this way, but it is likely to have been around 5,000.

When Montazeri (who had taken part in hearings of this kind earlier in the war) heard about what was going on, he volubly protested to Khomeini. His objections had no effect, except to reinforce the Supreme Leader's view that on no account should Montazeri succeed him.

The second set of decisions Khomeini made was to have a lasting effect upon the politics of Iran to this day, and to the balance of power within its governmental system.

In early 1988, Khomeini refined the notion of *velayat-e faqih*, by the startling assertion that the needs of the Islamic state of Iran outweighed those of Islamic law. This was the consequence of what Khomeini described as *velayat-e motlaq*, or 'absolute guardianship'. It had parallels (though far from attractive ones) in other post-revolutionary situations, for example in the Soviet Union, where the high ideals of Marxist-Leninism and the freedom which this promised for the mass of the people were 'postponed' in the interests of the state. Who determined those interests were a small group, a 'vanguard', there to make decisions whilst the proletariat recovered from their 'false consciousness'.

An Expediency Council was established to resolve what had been crippling differences between the Majlis and the Council of Guardians. Under Article 112 of the constitution, the membership of this council is in the hands of the Supreme Leader. The revised constitution increased the political nature of the Supreme Leader, to see a relative decrease in his religious nature. This conveniently ensured that Khamenei could be a candidate for the position on Khomeini's death, despite his lack of clerical credentials to be a *marja*, as the constitution had previously required.

It was in its specific changes that the amendments to the constitution had their most critical effect. The Supreme Leader's powers were prescribed with great precision, reinforcing his direct authority over the armed forces, declarations of war and peace, the judiciary, state broadcasters, and over appointments to the Council of Guardians, which vetted election candidates and could veto legislation they considered to be un-Islamic.[3] The post of Prime Minister was abolished.

Other changes instituted by Khomeini also strengthened the

position of the Supreme Leader. These included determining who should lead Friday prayers at major mosques across the country, and greater control of many of Iran's '*bonyads*'. These long-standing institutions are semi-charitable (and often highly profitable) foundations. Those of the Shah were taken over by the Islamic Republic. Today, they control a significant proportion of Iran's economy and much of its social security provision. Their wealth, and the opportunity they have given those in the charmed (often clerical) circles around the Supreme Leader, have become a constant target of the sullen alienation of many ordinary people in Iran against the regime.

*　*　*

Ayatollah Khomeini was seen by his followers as the holiest of men ever to rule Iran, but he was also one with the most acute of political instincts.

Khomeini was, however, mortal. Mortals make misjudgements. His decision, from a position of great military dominance in early 1983, to continue the war until Saddam was defeated, was a great error. The war did not end in Iran's formal surrender. But no one, in Iran or elsewhere, was in any doubt that the ceasefire agreed in the summer of 1988 was a desperate act born out of a realisation of Iran's weakness on the battlefield and on the home front too.

When Khomeini spoke of having to drink from the cup of poison, he meant it. The personal humiliation for him was so grave that he could no longer walk. He never again spoke in public.[4] Nonetheless, he continued indelibly to stamp his authority on Iran until his death, aged eighty-six, on 3 June 1989. He remains the most powerful influence on Iranian politics to this day.

CHAPTER 15

THE REFORMERS
BREAK OUT

On 23 May 1997, Seyyed Mohammad Khatami was elected President
of the Islamic Republic of Iran – and Leader of the Opposition.
British diplomat with extensive service in Iran[1]

We have kept in our memories the ... support that your colonial regime
has provided terrorist groups against the Islamic Republic.
Basij leaflet

Akbar Hashemi Rafsanjani was one of the revolution's great sur-
vivors, active in Iranian politics for almost six decades, until his
death in January 2017 aged eighty-two. He gained his credentials as
an ally of Khomeini, including four and a half years in jail during the
Shah's regime, and managed to weave his way successfully through
the factions of revolutionary Iran.

Rafsanjani and President Ali Khamenei had worked in harmony
in the early stages of the Republic. As is often the case in high politics,
the further they advanced, the more their interests diverged. For much
of the war, Rafsanjani, as Speaker of the Majlis, was a more significant
figure than Khamenei. His pre-eminence was sealed when Khomeini
transferred command of the armed forces from Khamenei to Rafsanjani towards the end of the war.

Both Rafsanjani and Khamenei attended Khomeini as he lay dying.

Khomeini made both Ayatollah. Both were clerics, though neither had attained the emulation as *marja* to be a Grand Ayatollah, as had been expected for one succeeding to the position of Supreme Leader under the 1979 constitution.

Although Khomeini had indicated that his preference was that Khamenei should succeed him, the decision would not be his but that of the Assembly of Experts. It is impossible to say what would have happened if Rafsanjani had insisted that his qualifications and experience entitled him to be chosen as Supreme Leader. By all accounts, Rafsanjani did not pursue that course. Instead, he opted to be a candidate for the presidency, believing that in practice he would have greater power to secure the country's post-war reconstruction and to effect wider change than he would have as Supreme Leader.

Khamenei was duly elected by the Assembly of Experts on 4 June 1989, the morning after Khomeini's death. Because he lacked the qualifications of a *marja*, many senior clerics were – and remain – uncomfortable about Khamenei's lack of theological stature. Rafsanjani thought that this would hobble Khamenei's position as Supreme Leader, reinforcing his own as President.

But though he alone was the architect of *velayat-e faqih*, on which the Supreme Leader's powers was based, Khomeini had shown, especially in the early years of Islamic Republic, some deference to the democratic principles of the constitution. Those concessions faded later in the 1980s.

From the start there had been an inherent tension in the Republic's constitution, between the elected Parliament and President on the one hand and the unelected Council of Guardians on the other, with its powers to determine who could stand for election and to override decisions of the Majlis on the elastic grounds of 'incompatibility with Islam or the Constitution'. Khomeini had recognised this tension, but never satisfactorily resolved it, by his establishment of the Expediency Council to arbitrate disputes between the two bodies.

Khamenei had to start carefully, but as his record in the thirty years since his elevation as Supreme Leader has shown, he has exercised the temporal, rather than spiritual, powers of his office to the fullest extent, using his direct control over the state's security apparatus, including over the IRGC and the Basij, to undermine the democratic will of the people. It is he, and not Rafsanjani, who has had the last laugh.

* * *

In the presidential elections which took place in July 1989, Rafsanjani won an overwhelming landslide. Mehdi Karroubi, a cleric and successful lawyer on the reformist left, replaced Rafsanjani as Speaker of the Majlis, a post he held until 1992 and again from 2000 until 2004.

Rafsanjani served for two terms as President, from 1989 until 1997. During that period he was relatively successful in rebuilding Iran's economy and infrastructure and in continuing the extraordinary expansion of its education system, which has led today to almost total literacy and to a large and well-qualified middle class – though without the jobs needed to sustain their prosperity, or to guarantee their active loyalty to the regime.

Rafsanjani understood that if Iran was to have a secure future, it needed to normalise its relationships with the international community. As part of this effort, he wanted to rebuild diplomatic relations with the United Kingdom, so badly damaged by Khomeini's *fatwa* on Salman Rushdie. He could do nothing about the *fatwa* itself – it was too soon after its promulgation and Khomeini's death.

However, by 1990, as tensions mounted between Iraq and the West, it became mutually advantageous to both Iran and the UK to upgrade their relations. David Reddaway was appointed as the British chargé d'affaires, going out to Tehran in late summer 1990. Reddaway was one of the FCO's most experienced Iran experts. He spoke fluent Persian, had married an Iranian and had served in Tehran before, from 1977 to 1980, witnessing at first hand the collapse of the Pahlavi dynasty, the revolution and Khomeini's assumption of power. He stayed in Tehran as chargé until 1993.

As is too often the case for British diplomats in Iran, a considerable amount of Reddaway's time was spent trying to negotiate the release from an Iranian jail of a British citizen. This time it was Roger Cooper, a businessman who was being held in Tehran's notorious Evin prison, having been convicted of spying and sentenced to 'death, plus ten years' imprisonment'. In Britain, meanwhile, there was an Iranian student held on charges related to the fire-bombing of bookshops which had been stocking *The Satanic Verses*. The Iranians wanted a deal by which both detainees could be released and deported back to their own countries. Reddaway was facing the difficult task of explaining to the Iranians that in the UK ministers really were in no position to tell out courts what to do, when fate intervened.

A number of supporters of this Iranian suspect had travelled to Britain to give evidence on his behalf. Without the knowledge of the FCO, they were detained at Heathrow Airport. When the magistrate handling the preliminary proceedings in the case was told of this, he dismissed all the charges on the grounds that the suspect was being prevented from mounting a proper defence. The Iranians told Reddaway that they assumed this had all been part of an elegant British plan to secure Cooper's release. In fact, it was all a cock-up, but one with a happy ending. Cooper was indeed released – in total secrecy, as those making the arrangements were extremely anxious that others in the system might thwart the plan.

Rafsanjani was also able to open Iran up to foreign investment and loans, despite the instinctive hostility of many in the Majlis and elsewhere to incurring debts to overseas interests. This antipathy went right back to Iran's experience in the fading decades of the Qajar regime, as well as the more recent memory of Mohammad Shah's regime.

*   *   *

In August 1990, events in the region suddenly moved in Iran's favour. Saddam Hussein, the US and the Arab world's ally in their proxy war against Iran, overreached himself by deciding to invade one of the key states that had supported him during that war, Kuwait. Indeed, his invasion was in part a direct result of Kuwait's support in that war. Kuwait had loaned Iraq billions of dollars; now they wanted them back. Saddam disputed the terms, claiming that he had been acting for all his Arab brothers. But there were other deep-seated aggravations for Saddam to exploit. Historically, Kuwait had been part of the Basra province of the Ottoman Empire, and thus claimed by Iraq. When the borders in this area had been drawn by Britain in 1922, Kuwait had been made a separate nation (with British military protection until 1970), and Iraq had been left with only a narrow access to the sea, around Basra and the Shatt-al Arab waterway.

In November 1990, after repeated diplomatic efforts to end Saddam's aggression had failed, the UN Security Council passed Resolution 678, authorising international military action against Iraq if it failed to withdraw from Kuwait. A major US-led coalition was assembled, with the largest contributor (apart from the US) being the UK. The combat phase began in mid-January 1991 and lasted until the end of February, resulting in Saddam's withdrawal and defeat.

Ever flexible in his choice of allies, Saddam had sought to enrol Iran on his side, on the not-implausible grounds that his enemy's enemy should be his friend. But Rafsanjani was having none of this. He refused to assist Saddam in any way. When a large number of Iraqi warplanes landed in Iran for 'safe-keeping', Iran simply impounded them as a contribution to the reparations they were owed by Iraq.

At the end of the war, there were major uprisings by the Shi'a population in the south of Iraq. The US and its allies decided not to intervene, believing (correctly, as the experience post-2003 was to show) that to do otherwise would be to embroil the US in a civil war.

Iran, from its different perspective, could have judged that it would be in its interests to support this insurgency of their Shi'a brothers, because it might well have led to the partition of Iran, with a separate Shi'a state, which they hoped would be heavily dependent on Iran, in the south. But Rafsanjani decided not to get involved. Instead, he provided a safe haven for hundreds of thousands of Shi'a refugees who fled across the border into Iran. US Secretary of State James Baker publicly praised Iran for its efforts.

Rafsanjani's policy of 'positive neutrality' had helped the US and its allies, as he knew it would. He did not, however, receive the dividend from this that he was expecting – quite the reverse.

As the First Gulf War was reaching its climax, even more profound events had been taking place elsewhere. The fall of the Berlin Wall on 9 November 1989 marked the beginning of the end of the Soviet Union. One by one, the Soviet's client states in Eastern Europe cut through their shackles. Then the Soviet Union itself began to implode, as the 'autonomous' republics within the Union, from the Baltic States in the west, to Armenia, Georgia, and the others in the south, all began to secede. Whilst the formal end of the Soviet Union did not take place until December 1991, it was patent by early 1991 that we were rapidly moving from a bipolar to a unipolar world, with the United States as the pre-eminent power.

President George H. W. Bush and his Secretary of State, James Baker, had taken a tough line with Israel over the need for a settlement with the Palestinians. A major international conference was called in Madrid, in which the Israelis reluctantly agreed to participate, to shape a new future for the region. The Soviet Union co-chaired the conference, held in October 1991. All the significant countries in the area were invited, apart from one.

A consistent theme of Iranian foreign policy which wholly transcends the 1979 revolution is the desire for Iran to be respected internationally as one of the dominant powers of the region. Indeed, it is more than just a desire; rather, a craving. It is based on a deep-seated sense of Iranian nationalism, of pride in the antiquity of its civilisation, and of continued resentment that the country's strategic importance has not properly been recognised.

The one nation not invited to the 1991 Madrid Conference was Iran. (There was a similar slight over invitations to the 2012 and 2013 Geneva I and II conferences on Syria.) Up to this point, the Islamic Republic's position on Palestine had been broadly confined to words, not actions. Rafsanjani himself had earlier indicated that Iran would accept whatever the Palestinians themselves decided. But Rafsanjani and the whole of the Iranian regime changed their stance towards any Israeli–Palestine peace settlement in reaction to the insult they believed they had received from the United States and the wider international community. They moved from tacit acceptance of the peace process to active hostility, and thenceforward to support Palestinian rejectionist groups, including Hamas (despite the group's backing for Saddam in the Iran–Iraq War), in retaliation.

Although this response from the Iranians was comprehensible, it represented a major strategic error. With the immediate threat from Iraq having been removed by the US coalition's intervention, Iran quickly became the bogeyman of Israel – and was viewed as such by Israel's powerful supporters in the US Congress. Thus it has remained ever since.

It's also important to note that it was therefore the early '90s, when the struggle for power and influence in the Middle East began after the collapse of the Soviet Union and Saddam's defeat, that Israel and Iran seriously began to lock horns, and not the 1979 revolution.

'The Israeli shift [in 1992] was as intense as it was unexpected,' writes Trita Parsi.[2]

Although the Madrid Conference itself was inconclusive, it did push the peace process up the political agenda. In July 1992, Labor Party leader Yitzhak Rabin became Prime Minister after campaigning in the election on proposals to negotiate a settlement with the Palestinians. These negotiations began in strict secrecy in early 1993 in Oslo, facilitated by the Norwegian government. Their outcome, the Oslo Accords, then formed the basis of a formal agreement between Rabin, his Foreign Minister, Shimon Peres, and the chairman of the Palestine Liberation Organization, Yasser Arafat, signed on the White House lawn in September 1993, with US President Bill Clinton officiating.

Although Rabin had secured a mandate from his electorate for the negotiations, their outcome aroused huge opposition from the Israeli right, and even wider anxiety across the Israeli political spectrum. Rabin and Peres therefore had the unenviable task of convincing the Israeli public that Yasser Arafat and his PLO could be partners for peace, notwithstanding their long record of terrorism against Israel and its citizens. Like Peres, Rabin was brilliant at one-liners: 'You don't make peace with friends. You make it with very unsavoury enemies,' he proclaimed.

One way of achieving that goal was a kind of strategic body-swerve, to show that Israel now faced a much greater long-term threat not from the Palestinians but from Iran. Rabin could point to any number of anti-Israel speeches from Khamenei and Rafsanjani downwards, as well as to Iran's actions to undermine Arafat and the PLO. When Israel faced serious terrorism from the rejectionists, like Hamas and the Islamic Jihad, it was easy to blame Iran as the mastermind behind the attacks, even if their actual role was much less significant than that of the Palestinian groups themselves. Such an anti-Iran approach had the added merit that it would go down well in Arab states with which Israel was, with some success, seeking a rapprochement.

International recognition of Israel by some previously reluctant states followed, including India, China and Jordan. Diplomatic relations with Egypt had already been established under the Israeli–Egyptian peace treaty of 1979.

For Arafat, the Oslo settlement was a huge triumph, as it was in many ways for Rabin, though he was to pay with his life for his endeavours – he was murdered in November 1995 by a right-wing Israeli extremist at a rally in support of the Oslo Accords.

Iran, under Rafsanjani and Khamenei, saw it all very differently. Rafsanjani accused Arafat of having 'committed treason against the Palestinian people'. A small majority of the Majlis signed a statement of the need for 'the annihilation of Israel from the world map'. (These were in very similar terms to those used by President Ahmadinejad in a 2005 speech when he is alleged to have spoken about removing Israel 'from the map of the world'.)

The Iranians, far from their coveted position as a regional power, able to participate as equals in the future of their region, and to stabilise their own security, now faced humiliation – and the prospect of continued isolation, as the United States built up its alliances with Saudi Arabia and the rest of the Arab world.

*   *   *

Israel has long had amongst the best intelligence cover of Iran. In the summer of 1994, they concluded that they had sufficient evidence publicly to charge that Iran was in the process of developing a nuclear weapons system which could endanger the very existence of Israel in 'seven to fifteen years'.[3] This timeline was wholly implausible (as the Israelis knew); but on the fact that Iran was seeking to use the cover of its civil nuclear programme to develop a nuclear weapons system, along with missiles, the Israelis were almost certainly correct.

Nevertheless, there were those around the foreign policy establishment in the US who thought there were openings for a dialogue with Iran. Rafsanjani would have been only too pleased to have reciprocated. The Israeli view was that they had to stop this possibility at all costs. Their agent for doing so was the American Israel Public Affairs Committee (AIPAC).

It is hard for anyone in the UK – including active politicians – to appreciate the enormous strength of major lobby groups in the US. The absence of any effective upper limits on political spending, of any prohibitions on political advertising on radio and TV, and of effective protection from defamatory statements mean that some lobby groups can quite lawfully spend millions of dollars not just in support of particular lawmakers, or candidates they favour, but to undermine those of whom they disapprove. AIPAC is one such lobby group. Working with the Israeli government, they have shown themselves to be enormously skilful at securing majorities in Congress in favour of propositions sought by that government.

In 1994, Rabin and Peres ran a successful campaign, through AIPAC, to reinforce their new and hostile approach to Iran; first, to have the Clinton administration impose sanctions on Iran, and then, in 1996, to have this sanctions regime made law, in the Iran and Libya Sanctions Act. For Iran, its provisions are still in force.

* * *

The democratic elements of the Iranian constitution have many echoes of the Western constitutions from which they have been drawn. One such is the requirement in Article 114 that Presidents may serve for no more than two consecutive terms of four years. In early 1997, when Rafsanjani's second term was ending, there was speculation that he might, somehow, have the constitution altered to allow him to stand for a third consecutive term. In the event, this idea fell away. The search was then on for a candidate of the left, in the reformist camp, who could run against the hardliner already informally endorsed by Khamenei, Ali Akbar Nateq-Nouri, who had been Speaker of the Majlis since 1992. Mehdi Karroubi, Majlis Speaker between 1989 and 1992, and former Prime Minister Mir-Hossein Mousavi were both possibilities as candidates for the left. But the choice finally settled on Seyyed Mohammad Khatami.

Khatami is the most exceptional, and unusual, of politicians. Exceptional because of his impressive grasp of Western political philosophy and its influence on Iran; unusual because he always appeared to me to be too unworldly to be a politician ready to engage in the rough and tumble which is a fact of political life in all systems – and nowhere so intensely as in the Byzantine systems of the Iranian governmental machinery.

A sympathetic biographer of Khatami, Ghoncheh Tazmini, observes that

> Khatami's personality embodied the very changes he sought to implement in the Islamic Republic … [He] embraced democratic values, but … was also staunchly dedicated to the revolutionary ideas of the theocracy … A 'modernising mullah', Khatami embodied a unique contradiction in the region. He was both religious and enlightened: he was the son of a cleric and had a traditional upbringing; he was trained in Qom, the stronghold of Iran's conservative clergy. Yet, he was also influenced by some of the west's leading critical philosophers of enlightened rational thought, and he was inspired by the progressive economic and technological accomplishments of the west.[4]

There's an old joke in Iran that whilst in the West the results of elections are known within twenty-four hours of the polls closing, in Iran they are known three months before. Nateq-Nouri campaigned – if that's the word – as if he already had the presidency in the bag well before anyone had cast a vote.

On some occasions, this joke turns out to reflect reality – as it did in 2009. But not in 1997. Khatami had the measure of Nateq-Nouri. He had suffered at his hands.

Khatami had been Minister of Islamic Culture and Guidance – a key position in the government, responsible for propaganda, censorship and the licensing of newspapers – from 1982 to 1986, under President Khamenei, and from 1989 under President Rafsanjani. He had used his power in this ministry to ease restrictions on music, art, literature and film. In doing so, he earnt the enmity of the hardliners, ever nervous that too much freedom would undermine their own power and privileges. In 1992, when elections to the Majlis had produced a right-wing majority, Nateq-Nouri struck, forcing Khatami to resign. He spent the next five years as head of the National Library.

Nateq-Nouri assumed that with the active support of the IRGC, the Basij and state media, he was bound to win. However, appearing to have either Russia or the UK on your side is not persuasive with the Iranian electorate, given our joint malign influence on the country over so many decades. During the election campaign, Nateq-Nouri made an official visit to see President Yeltsin. It then emerged that one of the evergreen Larijani brothers had been intervening on his behalf. The Larijani family are amongst the most powerful in Iran. Ali is Speaker of the Majlis, whilst Sadeq was Chief Justice from 2009 until 7 March 2019. Another brother, Mohammad-Javad, had been a deputy Foreign Minister in the 1980s, and was then a senior MP. He made a secret trip to London for talks with the Foreign Office, in the course of which he had been disobliging about Khomeini. This conversation was leaked, discrediting Nateq-Nouri.

In contrast to Nateq-Nouri's wooden efforts, Khatami campaigned relentlessly around the country. On an 80 per cent turnout, he won by such a margin – 70 per cent of the popular vote – that even the hardest of the hardliners could see that they would have to put up with the result, at least for the time being.

Khatami's movement, known as the 2 Khordad, the date of the election in the Iranian calendar, comprised long-standing liberals and moderates, and others with a radical past, including some of the 1979 hostage-takers, like Abbas Abdi and Massoumeh Ebtekar.

In the very early period of his presidency, Khatami was helped by a virulent attack on Khamenei from Montazeri, in which he warned the Supreme Leader not to interfere with Khatami's reform programme, acidly commenting that Khamenei bore 'no resemblance to a *marja-e taqlid*' (the highest-ranking authority in Twelver Shi'ism).*

---

* Two major Ayatollahs holding this status after 1970 were Ayatollah Khomeini and Ayatollah Abu al-Qasim al-Khoei. Source: Oxford Centre for Islamic Studies Online.

Khatami's key domestic achievements in his early period as President included a serious liberalisation of the press, literature and, especially, the cinema. Iranian film flowered. There were other reforms too, including those to secure a greater emancipation of women.

Though they had been roundly beaten in a democratic election – or precisely because they had been – the hardliners in the IRGC, the Basij, the judiciary and security apparatus under the direct control of Khamenei lost little time in moving against Khatami. They couldn't directly touch Khatami himself, but allies of his were arrested and imprisoned, weakening the political advice and support available to him.

In November 1998 came one of the darkest events in Iran's post-war history. Dariush Forouhar, a politician with impeccable credentials as an opponent of the Shah (serving fifteen years in prison, thanks to the SAVAK), and his wife were found murdered in their flat. This was followed by the discovery a few weeks later of the murders of two writers. Details emerged of other deaths in suspicious circumstances over the previous three years. Once these killings became public, there were shock waves across the country; they became known as the 'Serial Murders' (or 'Chain Murders'). Suspicion focused on MOIS, the Ministry of Intelligence and Security, nominally part of Khatami's government, but completely outwith his control.

For once, Khatami took his courage in his hands, and he insisted to Khamenei that there be a full inquiry. This confirmed the culpability of MOIS, and for a time discredited them. But this side of the Iranian system rarely gives up. They were soon back in action. Thirteen Iranian Jews were arrested in Shiraz, on spurious charges that they were spies, assisting the 'Zionist entity' – Israel. International condemnation followed. My predecessor, Robin Cook, cancelled a planned visit to Tehran, which would have been the first by any British Foreign Secretary since 1979.

A febrile atmosphere developed. In July 1999, a moderate paper, *Salam*, was closed down by MOIS. Student demonstrations, first in Tehran, then in all the other large cities, broke out and attracted large numbers. The police, the Basij and their usual assorted thugs responded by carrying out savage attacks on students in their dormitories. The protests became more violent. This was part class war against middle-class students, part an effort at taking down Khatami's base.

Khamenei and the IRGC reached for the tired old saw that the agitation was all the work of counter-revolutionaries acting under the orders of 'foreign powers' (e.g. the US and the UK). The abject idea that some 'foreign power' could foment such protests provides a further illustration of a permanent characteristic of the hardliners: their paranoia, and their inherent insecurity.

Khatami was temporarily weakened by the reaction to the demonstrations, with the charge that he was in office but not in power. Nonetheless, neither the ardour for reform amongst the Iranian public nor its apparent faith in that segment of the governmental system that was democratic was diminished.

In the Majlis elections in February 2000, reformists gained a significant majority, despite the best efforts of the Council of Guardians to whittle that down by delaying ratification of the full results by some months. Of a total of 290 seats, reformists won 215. This was not least the result of reformist voters grasping the notion of tactical voting, and of the influence of the reformist press, which published lists of which candidates (out of very long lists) were most deserving of support. Remarkably, too, in this election, just a handful of clerics were returned – compared with over 150 in the 1980s Majlis.[5]

* * *

Khatami's efforts to introduce more liberal reforms within Iran were paralleled by a major shift in foreign policy, seeking to end Iran's diplomatic isolation and to build some bridges with Arab nations, EU member states and, if possible, the United States itself.

Khatami framed this effort by summoning the aid of Western philosophers, from Plato and Aristotle through Descartes, Kant, Marx,

Nietzsche, Hegel and Freud. He called for a 'Dialogue of the Civilisations', and argued that this had to be based on *Weltanschauung*[*], or belief in ethical, religious and political systems, and had to respect the 'divine traditions of Jewish, Christian and Muslim thinkers'. This dialogue was a brilliant rhetorical device for detaching Iran from the corrosive idea that it was always in conflict with the West. So successful was this strategy that the United Nations General Assembly decided to name the year 2001 as the 'Year of Dialogue Among Civilisations'.

Khatami had made another move early in his presidency to ease relations with the West, and especially with the UK. With Khamenei's acquiescence, Khatami's Foreign Minister, Kamal Kharrazi, negotiated with the UK's Foreign Secretary, Robin Cook, some careful words announced at the 1998 UN General Assembly. This amounted to a disavowal of the *fatwa* against Salman Rushdie, rather than its formal lifting, but was quite sufficient to allow the upgrading of our diplomatic representation to full ambassadorial status, and Sir Nicholas Browne, author of the report into the UK's failure to spot the 1979 revolution, became Ambassador in 1999.[†]

Robin was anxious to show that the UK, for its part, was serious about improved relations. As Home Secretary, I was about to take powers, in the Terrorism Act 2000, to ban international terrorist organisations, as well as Irish ones. At Robin's request, and on good evidence, I banned the MEK, along with twenty other terrorist groups, as soon as these powers came into force.

The Basij charge that the 'colonial regime' – the UK – has supported terrorist groups against the Islamic Republic is the opposite of the truth.[‡]

*   *   *

---

[*]   Khatami is fluent in German, as well as Arabic and English – he had spent two years as head of the Islamic Centre in Hamburg from 1980 to 1982.

[†]   Supreme Leader Khamenei tweeted on 14 February 2019 that the *fatwa* was irrevocable.

[‡]   The UK ban against MEK was later overturned in November 2007 by the independent Proscribed Organisations Appeal Commission.

Faced by the landslide of support for Khatami in the 2000 Majlis elections, Khamenei's reaction was to insist that the new parliament could not even discuss a restrictive press law passed by its predecessor and used to ban a number of reformist newspapers.

Khatami had developed proposals to trim the power of the Council of Guardians and ensure greater authority to the elected government. These, too, were blocked. Those around the Supreme Leader were desperate to hang onto their power.

The British diplomat's quip that in 1997 Khatami had been elected 'President of the Islamic Republic of Iran, and Leader of the Opposition', quoted at the beginning of this chapter, is an entirely accurate description of his role. On the first occasion that I met Khatami, I happened to say to him that it would help the perception of Iran in the outside world if it removed the slogans 'Death to Israel' plastered all over their missiles shown off at military parades. Khatami's response, with a shrug, was, 'You should hear what they say about *me*.'

CHAPTER 16

9/11 AND NUKES

For a secure and hopeful life ... [let] us build a coalition
for peace instead of war and hostility.
PRESIDENT SEYYED MOHAMMAD KHATAMI,
10 NOVEMBER 2001

Khatami's 'Dialogue of the Civilisations' was rudely interrupted before it had got underway by the attacks on those centres of Western power, Washington and New York City, on 11 September 2001. Directed by Al Qaeda, nineteen hijackers were involved: fifteen Saudis, two from the UAE and one each from Egypt and Lebanon. None was Iranian.

When news of the attacks spread, there was jubilation on some Arab streets. Saddam Hussein charged that the 'United States reaps the thorns that its leaders have planted in the world'.

In Iran, the reaction was very different. There were spontaneous, torchlight vigils on the streets of Tehran in solidarity with the victims. Left and right, Khamenei and Khatami, condemned the outrage.

There was, for once, an obvious confluence of interest between Iran and the US: Afghanistan. Al Qaeda's operational base for the 9/11 attacks was located there, where they enjoyed the protection of the Wahhabi Taliban regime. The Taliban were no friend of the Iranians. Part of its *raison d'être* was hostility to the Shi'a, whom they regarded as apostates. The Wahhabi Taliban controlled most, but not all, of

Afghanistan, and enjoyed strong support from Saudi Arabia and Pakistan, in a proxy war against the opposition Northern Alliance, led by the charismatic Ahmad Shah Massoud and backed by Iran and Russia.

In August 1988, Taliban forces had laid siege to the Iranian Consulate in Mazar-i-Sharif, killing ten Iranian diplomats (whom the Taliban claimed were spies) and an Iranian journalist. On 9 September 2001 – two days before 9/11 – Massoud was assassinated by Al Qaeda suicide bombers.

It was two weeks until the FBI formally confirmed that Al Qaeda was responsible for the 9/11 attacks. I had become Foreign Secretary (in place of Robin Cook) in early June 2001, three months before the attacks. When I called US Secretary of State Colin Powell on the day to express our solidarity with the US over the outrage, he told me that he knew immediately who had been behind the atrocities. Powell also knew that there was no chance of having the Taliban government cooperate with the US to yield up the AQ terrorist bases with impunity from the vast area of Afghanistan that the Taliban controlled. Powell had a team work through the night on a military coalition to take out AQ and the Taliban.

Up to this point, the US had adopted an ambiguous approach to the Taliban's takeover of Afghanistan. Many of the Taliban had developed their fighting skills in the 1980s in cooperation with the US and Pakistan, when mujahidin opponents of the Kabul communist government and of Soviet troops were provided with training and equipment by the CIA. That was later to include, from September 1986, the provision of US Raytheon Stinger ground-to-air missiles, which proved decisive against the Soviets.

The US did not like the way the Taliban were governing, but their view before 9/11 was that provided the Taliban carried out their horrors within Afghanistan, this benighted country could be left to its fate. This had the added advantage for the US of diverting Iran's attention to its eastern border.

9/11 changed nearly everything. Suddenly, the imperative was to remove AQ and its Taliban protectors. Powell, and many others within the US administration, understood that to achieve this quickly and at minimum cost in terms of coalition lives it would be hugely helpful to have assistance from the Iranians. The Iranians had an intimate knowledge of the country and excellent intelligence cover of it. They spoke the local language of Dari, 'Afghan Persian', the first tongue of many Afghans (though not of the Pashtun, who speak Pashto, the other official language).

When Khatami, with Khamenei's support, issued his statement of condemnation of the 9/11 atrocity, and condolences for the victims, he was not just expressing what every decent person in the world felt – though he is a thoroughly decent man. He was sending out an olive branch to the US that the Iranians were ready to help.

Robin Cook had on two occasions planned to visit Tehran, but had to cancel both trips because of complications with the Iranians. (It's a rare day when there are not complications.) Before 9/11, a visit to Tehran was on my to-do list; immediately afterwards it shot to the top.

The US had some back-channels with the Iranians, the most important of which was in Geneva, where the US career ambassador Ryan Crocker, who had served in Iran before the revolution (and was fluent in Persian and Arabic), held secret negotiations with senior Iranian officials. (He served as US Ambassador to Afghanistan between 2011 and 2012.)

In the absence of their own functioning Embassy in Tehran, the US were able to supplement that work with advice from the UK Embassy. Nicholas Browne, our Ambassador, was a brilliant diplomat and a fluent Persian speaker and knew virtually everyone in the system. So too his deputy, Neil Crompton. They and their colleagues worked extremely hard to reinforce a security and intelligence relationship for the US-led coalition to invade Afghanistan, which was in the early stages of being assembled.

I got to Tehran on 24 September 2001. It was the first visit of any British Foreign Secretary since the revolution in 1979. My task was to strengthen our relationship with Iran and to try to make it operational. In doing so, I was inadvertently helped by the most ridiculous, synthetic storm, which had blown up in Israel over a boilerplate article from me for the Iranian press, published that morning. The draft had entirely been written by officials, without any guidance or direction from me. The piece commended Iran's response to 9/11 and talked of the 25,000 people of Muslim faith in my Blackburn constituency. It noted that the vast majority of Muslims throughout the world had been outraged by the attacks on New York and Washington. It continued, 'Equally I understand that one of the factors which helps breed terrorism is the anger which many people feel at events over the years in Palestine.' Prosaic, and indisputable, it seemed to me. I had seen the draft in the car on the way to the airport, signed it off with tiny changes, and thought no more about it – until the Israelis, who must get their Iranian papers early, went into overdrive to protest.

Israeli Prime Minister Ariel Sharon expressed 'anger, outrage, and disappointment'; an Israeli Cabinet minister called it 'obscene' and 'pornographic', and a Foreign Ministry spokesman insultingly claimed that the FCO was 'pro-Palestinian' because of the large number of Muslim constituents in Blackburn. (I am pro-Israel, and pro-Palestine – there's no contradiction.) What happened when I got to Israel is a separate story, not for this narrative.[1]

In Tehran, I met with President Khatami, other senior officials, and Kamal Kharrazi, his Foreign Minister, with whom I was to develop a close relationship, and whom I regard as a friend.

It was also in Tehran that I was to have the first meeting of many with Dr Abdullah Abdullah, then 'Foreign Minister' of the Northern Alliance's United Front, and Foreign Minister of Afghanistan itself after Kabul's liberation some weeks later. This meeting was held in the ornate dining room of the British residence. Neil Crompton and I can still recall Abdullah Abdullah eyeing this room in some amazement at its opulence and tranquillity.

The collaboration the US had sought from Iran was forthcoming.

The Iranians provided much valuable intelligence, volunteered to perform search-and-rescue operations for downed US pilots, and served as a go-between with the Northern Alliance. In turn, the US provided information to identify, and kill, AQ leaders who had fled to Iran.

The Taliban were presented with an ultimatum by President George W. Bush, which they contemptuously rejected. Covert insertion of special forces began on 26 September, and full-scale military action on 7 October. One month later, on 12 November, the capital, Kabul, began to fall to coalition forces and the Northern Alliance. The Taliban were finally dislodged from their key stronghold in Kandahar at the end of the month.

In parallel with the military action, urgent discussions were taking place over the political future of Afghanistan, with the US and Iran in the lead. The outcome, in late December 2001, was the UN Bonn Conference, hosted by Germany. I attended on behalf of the UK. One of the most important contributions the Iranians made, behind the scenes, was to press for clear language in the draft on the development of a democratic constitution for Afghanistan. In the horse-trading in the margins of the conference about how many ministries each faction should have, Mohammad Javad Zarif (soon to be Iran's Ambassador to the UN, and, under President Rouhani, its Foreign Minister) managed to resolve a deadlock with the Northern Alliance, persuading them to take fewer ministries than they had bid for.[2]

All was apparently set fair for the improvement in relations between Iran, the US and, by extension, the UK.

*   *   *

There were, however, many in the Israeli government, and amongst their neo-con friends within the Bush administration, who were distinctly uneasy about any cooperation with Iran. Their belief was (as it remains) that Iran is a monolithic and dictatorial theocracy sometimes sedulously disguised by the apparent rationality of its elected officials like Khatami, Rouhani and Zarif, but never to be trusted, and dealt with only on a long spoon. They had not been able to influence much in the immediate aftermath of 9/11 – the necessity of cooperating with Iran over the invasion trumped their concerns – but they began to reassert their position through the agency of the draft of President Bush's State of the Union speech, his first since his inauguration in January 2001.

In the weeks following 9/11, the US had received 'credible reporting [i.e. intelligence] that terrorists would again attack the United States, perhaps with radiological or nuclear weapons', wrote Condoleezza Rice, Bush's National Security Adviser at the time.

> The President sought in the 2002 State of the Union to place all of this into context and to make clear that the United States could defend itself only by taking on the proliferation challenge. In that regard he [then] uttered one of the most often cited and, frankly, overdramatized phrases of his time in office. After describing the North Korean, Iranian, and Iraqi regimes and their link to terrorism and weapons of mass destruction, the President said: 'States like these, and their terrorist allies, constitute an axis of evil.'[3]

Rice says in her memoirs that both she and President Bush were 'stunned' by the focus on these three words, 'axis of evil', in the media coverage of the speech. The phrase had been 'inserted by a speech-writer' and no flags about it had been raised when the draft had been cleared in State and the Pentagon. How and why it crept into the draft, and stayed there, remains something of a mystery – as was confirmed when I interviewed one of the speechwriters concerned, David Frum, for a BBC Radio 4 documentary in 2015.[4] Frum had expected his draft to be amended and rewritten by those further up the food chain – but it was not.

It was not only Condoleezza Rice and President Bush who were left stunned: Bush's speech dropped like a bomb on Tehran. The old guard were delighted and went into overdrive to initiate a sinister crackdown on writers and intellectuals. For President Khatami and his allies, the speech was a kick in the teeth for the risks they had taken in reaching out to the US and in providing all the cooperation they had given over the previous four months.

Nonetheless, the reformists initially fought back. In the Majlis, 172 reformist MPs signed a statement that domestic repression diverted 'affairs to a path desired by all the opponents of the Islamic Republic, including those in the USA'.

But overall it was clearly the hardliners who reaped a long-term dividend from the Bush speech. President Bush's apparent threat of military action against Tehran served to change the domestic debate in Iran, radicalising borderline 'conservative moderates' who had not completely dismissed the possibility of a dialogue with the US government. Khatami represented an opportunity that an American government might have converted to their own interests but instead turned their back on.

Khatami had won a second term in the summer of 2001, again by an overwhelming majority, securing nearly 80 per cent of the vote. The turnout was down a bit on 1997, but was still a respectable 68 per cent – better than in many UK general elections. If Khatami had been able to achieve his aim of bringing Iran out of the cold, re-establishing half-decent relations with the US and showing the Iranian people the dividends, then it is unlikely that the hardliner Mahmoud Ahmadinejad could have been elected in 2005, and nor could his rigged re-election in 2009 have occurred.

The question is: how far did the 'axis of evil' speech itself stymie Khatami's reformist ambitions? Some date the beating back of the moderates in the system precisely to the State of the Union speech – 29 January 2002. British diplomats involved with Iran take differing views. One experienced British diplomat serving in Tehran at the time believes that by January 2002 Khatami 'had already passed his sell-by date'.[5] The hardliners around Khamenei had gradually strengthened their control well before January 2002 and were getting ready to ensure that another 'mistake' like Khatami could not happen in the presidential elections due in 2005. Against this, another experienced Iran hand says that Bush's speech did have an adverse effect: 'It reinforced negative trends in public perceptions and debate, confirming stereotypes and making cooperation harder.'

It is impossible categorically to answer this 'what-if' question as to how US–Iranian relations might have improved in the absence of the 'axis of evil' speech. Not much, but somewhat, is my answer, given what was about to emerge about Iran's nuclear programme. Certainly, it did not help the reformers – and the damage it did was the more gratuitous because that phrase had found its way into the speech almost inadvertently.

* * *

'I was stunned to learn that there was no independent Iran desk in the [US] Department of State,' writes Rice about what she found when she began as Secretary of State in early 2005. 'It turned out that the department thought in terms of "relations" with countries. Since we had no "relations" with Iran, it didn't warrant its own desk. Amazing. We created an Iran desk, and later an outpost in Dubai to follow Iranian affairs from a place with geographic proximity to Tehran.'[6]

In Afghanistan, an International Stabilisation Force had been established by the UN, with an extensive US presence and large contingent from the UK along with many other nations. It is one of the many ironies of this period of US-led foreign policy that thanks to the US's military might (with help from others, the UK included) Iran had been rid of the threatening, sectarian Taliban government in its eastern neighbour. The Iranians, despite their anger about being lumped in with Iraq and North Korea in that speech, continued to be pretty constructive partners.

It was in the interests of all sides in Iran that a non-Taliban government, friendly towards (and in part dependent upon) Iran, should be sustained. Many of the discussions about this were handled on the British side by David Reddaway. He, it will be recalled, had been our chargé in Tehran between 1990 and 1993. When Sir Nick Browne had to leave Tehran as our Ambassador prematurely on grounds of ill health in late 2001, David was proposed as his replacement.

Under international rules, the host government has to agree to give *agrément* (approval). This is normally routine. David was the outstanding candidate for the job, given his seven years' experience in Iran, and his fluent Persian. The Iranian government delayed their approval, hoping, I think, that we'd withdraw his name. There were repeated discussions between Kharrazi and me, as well as protracted negotiations with the Ministry of Foreign Affairs and the President's office, both of which were happy for the appointment to go ahead – but the issue was not in their hands. The hardline press in Tehran carried stories that David was a 'Zionist spy', and had been 'too active' in the past. As it happens, David is not Jewish, though that would have been an outrageous reason for refusing him, and neither was he a spy. However, when the matter went up to the Supreme Leader, he personally vetoed the appointment, on the grounds that David had been publicly labelled as a spy (by the hardline newspapers under his influence).

Anxious not to lose David's expertise, Tony Blair made him the UK's Special Representative on Afghanistan, and during 2002 he had a series of mainly positive meetings with the Iranian Ambassador and other diplomats in Kabul to secure better coordination on Afghan policy. They did not mind in the least having discussions with someone who knew Iran well.

Any diplomatic quiet for which the Iranians were hoping was, however, rudely shattered when in August 2002 the National Council of Resistance of Iran (NCRI), the political wing of the terrorist organisation MEK, published claims that Iran was building two nuclear facilities which they had not disclosed to the International Atomic

Energy Agency (IAEA) as they were required to do as a signatory to the Nuclear Non-Proliferation Treaty (NPT). It is likely that the intelligence behind the claims came in part from the Israeli intelligence agency Mossad.

The two sites were a uranium enrichment plant at Natanz and a heavy-water plant at Arak. The initial reaction of the Iranian government was a semantic dance about whether disclosure was required under the NPT. They finally told the IAEA about them in February 2003, just a few weeks before the US-led invasion of Iraq.

Iran's civil nuclear programme had begun under the Shah in 1957 as part of President Eisenhower's 'Atoms for Peace' programme. On a state visit to the UK in May 1959, one of the trips the Shah made was to the Harwell Atomic Energy Research Establishment.

He later wrote in his memoir:

We planned the rapid installation of four electro-thermal nuclear power stations: Iran 1 and 2, built by the Germans near Bushehr, and Iran 3 and 4, to be built by the French on the River Karun not far from Ahvas. The first two were to come into service in 1980 and 1981, and the other two at the end of 1983 and 1984.[7]

It is also tolerably certain that the Shah was developing a nuclear weapons programme. A 1974 CIA proliferation assessment stated, 'If [the Shah] is alive in the mid-1980s ... and if other countries [particularly India] have proceeded with [nuclear] weapons development we have no doubt Iran will follow suit.'[8]

In 1967, the Tehran Nuclear Research Center (TNRC) was established, run by the Atomic Energy Organization of Iran. The TNRC was equipped with a US-supplied, five-megawatt nuclear research reactor, which was fuelled by highly enriched uranium – the production of which has been a dominant issue of the nuclear negotiations with Iran over the past decade and a half. Later, Siemens were contracted to build two large (1,200 MW) reactors at Bushehr, and a French company (Framatone) to build two pressurised water reactors (of 950 MW each) at Darkhovin, near Ahvaz.

The 1979 revolution brought an abrupt end to all the joint ventures with Western companies. Iran sought assistance from China, but that was abandoned after US pressure. An agreement was made, however, with a Russian nuclear company for it to take over the construction of the Bushehr nuclear power station. This was finally completed in 2011 – over thirty years after its planned completion date.

Under the NPT, the world is divided into 'nuclear-weapon states' and 'non-nuclear weapon states'. In the first group are the five permanent members of the UN Security Council, each of which had nuclear weapons system when the treaty was agreed. All other signatories, including Iran, are in the second category and are prohibited from developing or using nuclear weapons. The four other countries which have nuclear weapons – India, Pakistan, North Korea and Israel – are not signatories.

Under the NPT, non-nuclear weapon states in principle have a clear right to manufacture and to enrich uranium. Article IV of the treaty states, 'Nothing in this Treaty shall be interpreted as affecting the inalienable right of all the Parties to the Treaty to develop research, production and use of nuclear energy for peaceful purposes without discrimination and in conformity with Articles I and II of this Treaty.'

By the time Iran made a formal disclosure to the IAEA about its previously undeclared nuclear facilities, in February 2003, the international community was preoccupied with the prospect of a US-led invasion of Iraq.

Huge military forces were being assembled in the region: 46,000 service personnel from the UK alone were involved. There were high-stakes efforts at the UN in New York to resolve the crisis by diplomatic means, including five ministerial-level meetings of the Security Council between mid-January and early March. Sadly, these endeavours failed. After Saddam had rejected a coalition ultimatum, military action commenced on 20 March 2003.

Saddam had the largest and strongest standing Arab army. All the endless contingencies for which we had planned – for a long war, for the use by Saddam of chemical and biological weapons, for house-to-house guerrilla fighting – quickly dissolved. After twenty-one days, the great Iraqi Army collapsed. Baghdad fell on 9 April 2003. Three weeks later, President Bush declared the formal end of major combat operations. The Americans and their allies had achieved in a few weeks that which had eluded the Iranians in eight gruelling years of their war with Iraq.

The Iranians had been ambiguous about the possibility of a US-led coalition to remove Saddam. They were regularly briefed by our Embassy about preparations for military action. At one point in the planning stage, after Turkey had said that it would not allow US-led invasion forces through its territory, some Iranian officials flew a kite with our diplomats about the possibility of Iran allowing over-flights by UK (but not US) planes from bases in Uzbekistan, though this idea was not pursued.

The Iranians loathed Saddam for the immense human toll of the 'imposed' war against them; for his terrible treatment of their faith compatriots, the Shi'a communities in Iraq; for the damage he had inflicted on their economy; and for the dominance which for a time he had exercised over the Arab street. On the other hand, they knew that Saddam had been hugely weakened by the serious defeat he had suffered in the First Gulf War. They thought that containment was the best way of handling him – a view shared by the US until 9/11. They were uncomfortable about having large contingents of US forces both to their east, in Afghanistan, and now to their west, in Iraq.

Further west in the region, the ease with which the US could move in and change regimes was concentrating the mind of Colonel Gaddafi, leader of Libya. By the end of 2003, having been presented with a secret démarche by the US and UK, Gaddafi agreed to the international inspection and dismantling of his hitherto covert nuclear facilities.

The Iranians – or rather some of those in the government – appear to have decided that their best, and potentially safest, approach was to offer to the US a comprehensive set of proposals on all the issues in contention with the US.

In the academic literature, this is known as the 'Grand Bargain' offer. Unfortunately, if the potential scope of the proposals was grand, the manner in which they were conveyed to Washington was anything but. They were sent by fax to the general State Department number by the Swiss Ambassador to Tehran. Because of the way in which the proposals were delivered, the doubts about their provenance, and the absence of any follow-through by the Iranians, the proposals failed properly to register with senior principals in the Bush administration, and they simply fell away.

Seyed Hossein Mousavian was head of the Foreign Relations Committee of Iran's National Security Council from 1997 to 2005. In his comprehensive account of Iran's nuclear negotiations, he says that in late April and early May 2003 a detailed 'non-paper' was prepared through discussions between Sadegh Kharrazi, the Iranian Ambassador to France and nephew of Foreign Minister Kamal Kharrazi, and the Swiss Ambassador to Tehran, Tim Guldimann. Guldimann was considered one of Switzerland's more energetic diplomats. The Swiss had looked after US interests in Iran ever since their diplomatic relations had been broken off in 1979. A 'non-paper' is diplomatic jargon for proposals which are made without formal commitment.

Although the non-paper produced no result, it is worth summarising its content, since it gives an indication of what the Iranian system at the time might have been willing to contemplate as the price for normal relations with the West – and what it might still be willing to trade. By some accounts, the proposals were agreed not only by Khatami, which was to be expected, but also by Khamenei. Sadegh Kharrazi is married to Khamenei's daughter.

Under the non-paper, the US was to accept a 'mutual dialogue' and to agree to put on the agenda a halt to 'hostile US behaviour', a rectification of Iran's status in the eyes of the US away from an 'axis of evil' and its inclusion of a list of terrorist states; the end of all sanctions against Iran; a democratic and representative government in Iraq, showing respect for Iran's interests and its religious links in Najaf and Karbala; reparations for the Iran–Iraq War; full access to peaceful nuclear technology; and pursuit of all anti-Iranian terrorist organisations, especially the MEK.

In return, Iran was ready to ensure 'full transparency' of its nuclear programmes, and the adoption of intrusive inspection protocols; decisive action against terrorist groups, especially AQ operating within its territory; the exchange of information about them; and coordination of Iranian activity in Iraq.

The most arresting of the proposals were in respect of Iran's activities in its near neighbourhood – long the source of much of the US's hostility towards Iran. The Iranians' non-paper promised that Iran would cease any material support for Palestinian opposition groups (e.g. Hamas, Islamic Jihad and others) in Iranian territory and put pressure on these groups to stop violent action against civilians 'within the borders of 1967' – i.e. the internationally agreed borders of Israel. They would take action on Hezbollah so that it became a 'mere political organisation' within Lebanon, and they would accept the Arab League Beirut Declaration, the plan of Crown Prince Abdullah of Saudi Arabia for a two-state solution to the Israel–Palestine conflict.[9]

Mousavian says that this offer was an 'incredible opportunity' which the United States dismissed. The writers Trita Parsi and Michael Axworthy offer a similar narrative about what happened next. They say that Secretary of State Colin Powell and National Security Adviser Condoleezza Rice took the proposal to President Bush and 'argued for a positive response' but were thwarted by Vice-President Dick Cheney and Defense Secretary Donald Rumsfeld.[10]

The problem with these accounts is that they do not accord with the clear recollections of both Condoleezza Rice and Colin Powell, nor with that of British diplomats serving in Tehran, and nor with the US archives. When I approached Rice late in 2018, she went to some trouble to have the purported 'Grand Bargain' paper located in the archives. Rice also checked with Steve Hadley, who was Deputy National Security Adviser at the time. She wrote:

> The 'fax' came through the Swiss Embassy and just landed at the State Department. It wasn't addressed to anyone in particular. After significant efforts to locate the 'parentage' of the fax, the Deputies concluded that it was in fact an entreaty from a Swiss diplomat acting on his own and proposing what he thought would be acceptable to the Iranians.
> The Iranians never owned it so there was nothing to pursue.
> This explains the mystery around this non-proposal that has been touted as a Grand Bargain.

Rice added, 'There never was a Grand Bargain offer. I would have known if there had been such an offer, and Colin [Powell] would have told the President. But this didn't happen.'[11]

Colin Powell's independent recollection is the same as that of Condoleezza Rice. He wrote:

> I am very familiar with this issue, as is Rich Armitage [his deputy] and my old team. This unsigned document showed up via the Swiss. We had been burned in the past over mysterious Iranian documents. When the 'Grand Bargain' story hit the press we consulted with the State Department Middle East guys and we all have the same memory that we did not give it much credibility or act on it. Condi and her White House associates came to the same conclusion independently. Nobody was overruled. Dick Cheney may have been worried about State's position but [in the circumstances] … he didn't need to be.[12]

By this stage, I had developed a very close relationship with Colin

Powell. We talked on a secure line most days, including about Iran. If something as significant as serious proposals for a 'Grand Bargain' with Iran had been on Powell's desk, he would have mentioned this to me. In the extensive record of my calls with him, there is not one word about this.

In truth, therefore, these proposals appear to be more of a trial balloon than of a formal offer of a 'Grand Bargain' backed by the full authority of the Iranian Republic.

The Iranians have a cadre of very professional and experienced diplomats, including ones with an intimate understanding of the US system. They would have known that if they had wanted such a radical set of proposals to have been considered at the highest level in Washington, and with a positive response, they would have to lay the ground very carefully, and confidentially. Why did senior Iranian diplomats not link up with their US counterparts in the many capitals where both countries have Embassies, or, for example, have used the British Ambassador in Tehran to set the process in motion?

Just as there would have been high anxiety in Tehran about such a set of proposals being prematurely leaked, with all the consequences of charges of treachery by the hardliners, so these Iranian diplomats would have been aware that premature leaking could have gravely embarrassed the Bush administration, both with Congress and in its relations with Israel.

The impression one is left with is that either this was a uniquely amateurish effort by the Swiss Ambassador and a single (albeit well-connected) Iranian diplomat, or there was never the full and active support of the key Iranian leaders, including Khamenei, which would have been necessary to get talks off the ground. In the event, in Rice's words, 'the Iranians never owned it, so there was nothing to pursue'.

It would have been transformational for Iran if the Iranian government had been fully behind the 'Grand Bargain' fax and had pursued its proposals with the care and tenacity which is a hallmark of their diplomacy. I do not believe that the US government would have refused to engage. Why would they? What they had to offer President Bush, according to the fax, was nothing less than a fresh start, with complete transparency about their nuclear programme; an end to their association with Palestinian rejectionist terrorist groups; an acceptance of the two-state solution to bring an end to the Israel–Palestine conflict; and, if not a recognition of Israel, an acknowledgement of its existence. Achieving all that, if that were the offer, would have been a major diplomatic coup for the Bush administration. Against that, the deal the US and UK struck with Libya in late 2003 would have paled in comparison.

A 'Grand Bargain' would also have saved us all a lot of trouble. The reality, however, was that the process of negotiations with the Iranians on the nuclear dossier alone took twelve years to produce a result, in the Joint Comprehensive Plan of Action (JCPOA) agreed in July 2015 between Iran and the major world powers in the P5+1.* That effort began in the summer of 2003.

---

* The Permanent Five of the UN Security Council (the US, Russia, China, France, the UK), and Germany.

CHAPTER 17

'CHOCOLATES, JACK, CHOCOLATES'

*We still have a grudge and spite against the insults from people
such as you against the officials of our country during the
nuclear negotiations at Sadabad Palace.*

BASIJ LEAFLET, REFERRING TO E3 NEGOTIATIONS
IN OCTOBER 2003

The revelations by the National Council of Resistance of Iran, the MEK's political front, which had publicised Iran's undisclosed nuclear facilities, and Iran's belated declaration about those facilities just before the invasion of Iraq led to mounting international difficulties for Tehran. Dr Mohamed ElBaradei, the IAEA's Director-General, and his team had conducted a thorough investigation into Iran's failure to meet its obligations under the NPT. His eight-page report in early June 2003 set out these failures in detail, expressing concern about the possible diversion of Iran's civil programme for military purposes and the existence of many technical ambiguities.

There was some interesting left-field information coming in. A European diplomat in Tehran had bumped into a former Soviet rocket scientist in the street whom he had known in Moscow. Further enquiries suggested that a number of such scientists whose employment prospects had come to an abrupt end with the chaos following the Soviet Union's collapse had decamped to work for the Iranian government. The Israelis were briefing diplomats in Tel Aviv that they had 'ample evidence' of a military nuclear programme being run by Iran.

My fourth visit to Tehran, at the end of June 2003, was dominated by the nuclear dossier. I met with President Khatami and Foreign Minister Kamal Kharrazi, but the key discussions were with Dr Hassan Rouhani, then the secretary of Iran's National Security Council, the man with the greatest influence on the issue outside the Supreme Leader's immediate circle.

We made a little progress. Dr Rouhani was more Delphic than usual, especially on the need for intrusive inspections under an Additional Protocol, and for Iran to suspend its uranium enrichment activities. Rouhani's vagueness was because the Iranian system had yet to agree a clear line. Dr Ali Akbar Velayati, the Supreme Leader's diplomatic adviser (another evergreen Iranian official, former Foreign Minister), had compared the Additional Protocol to the 1828 Treaty of Turkmenchay, which, as we have seen, is part of Iran's folk memory of a great betrayal by foreign powers.[1]

My own concern was that Iran's opaqueness and obduracy would simply feed those in Washington who were relishing the possibility of a serious confrontation with Iran, possibly with military action.

* * *

The debate about whether or not to take military action against Iraq had led to a split down the middle of the European Union, with the UK, Spain, Italy and most of the East European countries (who would formally join the EU in 2004) on the side of the US, and the others, led by France and Germany, in strident opposition.

The diplomatic drama that was acted out in the early months of 2003 in the UN Security Council pitted the US and the UK against France and Germany (the latter by chance holding one of the non-permanent seats on the council). This led to some electrifying spats, with French Foreign Minister Dominique de Villepin and German Foreign Minister Joschka Fischer on one side and me on the other. Despite this, personal relations between the three of us managed to remain not just cordial but friendly.

As soon as the NCRI claims had been made public in 2002, our Embassy had proposed that there should be discussions with the French about a way forward. Joschka Fischer had suggested to me in early March 2003 that we – the EU – needed a process for dealing with Iran. These ideas came together in the late spring of 2003 when Fischer, de Villepin and I agreed that at all costs we should avoid Iran becoming the subject for the next split in the EU, and the next theatre for a US-led war. We decided instead that our three countries, the key powers in the EU, should work together to get Iran off the hook on which they had impaled themselves. If we were successful, it would help make a reality of the idea of a 'European foreign policy' which had so eluded the EU in the past.

Iran, after its apparent brush-off by the US from its ill-prepared two-page 'Grand Bargain' fax, was in the market for discussions. In late May, Kamal Kharrazi had sent me a paper on the 'peaceful nuclear activities' of the Islamic Republic. Our Ambassador to the IAEA in Vienna, Peter Jenkins, was reporting that a senior Iranian official had talked to him about negotiations on an Additional Protocol.

There was to be no two-page 'non-paper' fax from us, sent through an intermediary country. Instead, there were detailed discussions by senior officials from the 'E3' (as we quickly became known) in July and early August 2003 on the terms of a joint letter from the three of us to the government of Iran, and Iranian Foreign Minister Kamal Kharrazi's draft reply.

The letter went through endless iterations. Alice and I had left for a holiday in a hideaway in France as soon as Parliament rose. A fax in-stalled by the Foreign Office groaned with one draft after another. Our heads of government took a close interest in what we were proposing. Though the US would not formally be part of the negotiations, we did our best to keep them on board, since we knew, as did the Iranians, that progress would only be possible with the tacit consent of the US administration.

I talked frequently to Colin Powell about the detailed steps we were taking. Though there were times when he expressed concern that we (the E3) might be leaning too heavily in Iran's favour, his overall view was that since the US were not going to invade Iran, it was important to have an engagement with them. He repeatedly told me that President Bush had made clear to him that Iran was 'not on the list' for military action.

The letter from us was delivered in its final form by our three Ambassadors in Tehran, including the UK Ambassador Sir Richard Dalton, to the Iranian government on 6 August. The letter sought to open a formal dialogue with Iran. Included in this would be full cooperation by Iran with the IAEA; that Iran should sign up to an Additional Protocol providing for intrusive inspections; and a cessation by Iran of its capability to produce fissile material. In return, we were ready to recognise Iran's right to generate nuclear power and to gain access to modern nuclear technology.

Meanwhile, the Iranians were getting very twitchy about what might happen in the IAEA's board of governors. Some in the US administration were pressing that Iran's failure to provide a full and timely disclosure of its nuclear facilities should be referred to the Security Council, where Iran would suffer some humiliation, and which could have decided on the imposition of UN sanctions.

The September meeting of the board did agree a tough resolution on Iran – so tough that its Ambassador, Ali Akbar Salehi, decided to walk out. A deadline of 31 October for Iran to sign up to the Additional Protocol was given. Iran's discomfort was the worse because the resolution was supported by Russia and China as well as by the West.

'A great crisis engulfed the country,' Mousavian writes.[2] Iran's economy was hit, with a flight of capital estimated at $1 billion. The crisis was made worse for Iran by the fact, obvious to outsiders, that the system was in turmoil about which strategy it should adopt. Hard-liners thought that Iran should stand and fight. Wiser counsel, led by Hassan Rouhani, believed that the only way out was for Iran to negotiate with the E3. De Villepin, Fischer and I had told the Iranians often enough, as we would continue to do, that we were their 'human shield' – from sanctions, and from the possibility of US military action. We were ready to play our part to resolve the crisis peacefully, but the Iranians had to do so too.

Rouhani's view prevailed. The E3 ministers were invited to Tehran for negotiations on 21 October, but many issues about the format of our meetings and the agenda had to be pinned down before we agreed to this date. On more than one occasion I had to reassure Powell that we were not going to let the Iranians pick us off one by one.

The meeting in Tehran was one of the most extraordinary of the many diplomatic sessions in which I was involved in my five years as Foreign Secretary. I had wanted to leave London before lunch, to ensure that I arrived in Tehran and got a decent night's sleep, given what was likely to follow. However, Tony Blair had fallen ill with an irregular heartbeat, so I had to take his place to give a detailed statement to the Commons on what had happened at a meeting of the European Council we had attended at the end of the previous week. I did not get away from central London until 4.30 p.m. With the time difference, this meant that I did not arrive in Tehran until the small hours.

I snatched a little sleep. When I got up, I offered some advice about the plumbing in the residence. (Three of my uncles were plumbers – I used to work for them in the school holidays.) Then it was off to a breakfast meeting at the German Embassy to prepare for the day.

Much of the draft communiqué had already been agreed by our officials. What was left was the really tricky issue: whether Iran should suspend or cease its uranium enrichment activities.

The main Iranian government buildings are in downtown Tehran, in the southern, usually polluted, valley. The middle classes live in the healthier north, in the hills leading to the Alborz mountain range.

Our meeting took place in north Tehran, in the Sadabad Palace, surrounded by fine gardens – though we were in a large rectangular room with no natural light.

The key issues were batted across the table, with the Iranians hoping that the textual gymnastics for which they are world-famous might produce a crack in the united front we were presenting. The plan was that once we had reached agreement, we would all go to report to President Khatami. This had been pencilled in for 10.30 a.m. 10.30 came and went, and there was still no agreement, when Rouhani suddenly announced, 'It's time for us to go and see the President.'

The three of us looked at each other. 'But there's nothing to go and see him about,' I said. 'Our planes are at the airport,' said Dominique. 'And we are perfectly happy to go and get on them,' added Joschka. We suggested an adjournment and got out of our seats.

There was consternation writ large on the faces of the Iranian side. This had not been in the script. They started working their phones to the President and to the Supreme Leader's office.[3] The three of us went into the gardens for a breather. Finally, the negotiations resumed. This time they were workmanlike. We were able to agree the Tehran Declaration. Iran undertook to sign an Additional Protocol and until that was finalised to operate as if they had done so, by allowing intrusive inspections. Enrichment and reprocessing activities would meanwhile be suspended. In return, we recognised Iran's right to civil nuclear power and agreed that Iran would gain access to modern technology once satisfactory assurances were received.

It was off to see the President.

There was a narrow road leading from the Sadabad Palace, which was blocked by members of the Basij. De Villepin got out of his car to remonstrate with the demonstrators. I was about to do so when my two protection officers ordered me to stay in the car. I did as I was told.

Quite how the Yazd Basij who demonstrated against me in 2015 got the idea that we had insulted officials of their country, as they claimed in the declaration with which they presented me, I do not know. The three of us were impeccably polite and respectful throughout. But the Basij demonstration against us, and what their counterparts in Yazd wrote twelve years later, is a good indication of the intensity of feelings in some quarters about Iran's nuclear programme, though the Basij are viewed as the 'enemy within' by most ordinary Iranians, not least because of their brutal role in suppressing the 2009 protests.* We knew that the protests were not principally targeted at us but at President Khatami and his reformist government.

The press conference which followed our meeting with President Khatami was huge, even by Iranian standards, and much of the questioning hostile. One attempt after another was made to open up some disagreement between Joschka, Dominique and me. All failed. There was confidence and trust of the highest order between us. We were aware of the prize if we did pull off a deal. Many in the Iranian system understood that the more they could constructively negotiate with us, the less likely it would be that the US could assemble a coalition to refer Iran to the Security Council.

We showed that was the case when Iran was back on the agenda of the IAEA board in November. Precisely because of the progress we had made in Tehran, we were able to persuade the US that there should be no report to the Security Council and no charge that Iran was in 'non-compliance' of its obligations.

But suspicions about Iran's true intentions took off again in the New Year of 2004 when it emerged that Iran had still not made full disclosures about what it had been doing. Documents obtained from the Libyans following their decision in December 2003 to come in from the cold and give total access to IAEA inspectors showed that Iran had purchased drawings of the much more advanced P-2 centrifuge, and that parts, and drawings which could be used to develop a bomb, had been sold for $3 million cash to the Iranians by a Sri Lankan arms

---

* See below, Chapter 19.

dealer who obtained the materiel from Pakistan. The IAEA had also obtained information about Iran's experiments with polonium, which had not been mentioned in Iran's declaration to the IAEA in October. (Polonium can be used to manufacture the explosive charges of nuclear weapons.) To add to the potential distrust, there was a dispute with Iran about the amount of plutonium it had produced.

Mousavian claims that at meetings with the Director-General of the IAEA, Iran's lead negotiator, Dr Rouhani, had felt completely blindsided by others in the Iranian system, since he knew nothing about these hitherto undisclosed Iranian nuclear activities. This claim could be credible, and consistent with the Byzantine and sometimes poisonous internal politics of Iran's elite; equally, internal arguments are sometimes dressed up to fool the outside world. In any event, the E3 decided to bite its tongue in the hope of achieving a longer-term settlement of the nuclear issue with Iran.

Further protracted negotiations followed, culminating in ministerial-level discussions in Brussels at the end of February. We reached agreement, including on the neuralgic issue of an extension of Iran's suspension of its enrichment activities. We had a lot of difficulty in heading off the United States administration, some of whose members were implacably opposed to the work of the E3 – as well they might have been, since it was we who were thwarting those in the US administration, egged on by the Israeli lobby, who were determined to have Iran referred to the Security Council.

The Brussels Agreement was followed by a resolution of the June 2004 IAEA board which was critical of Iran, whereupon the E3 ministers and the IAEA were formally told that Iran would no longer respect what had been decided in Brussels. The agreement had got caught up in the axles of the regime's decision-making system. The Supreme Leader, forever suspicious of the West, without seriously distinguishing between those of us trying to help Iran and those not, had pulled the plug.

Part of our difficulty was that there were in principle some easy wins which would have strengthened the hands of the reformists around Khatami and Rouhani, but we could only provide these with US cooperation. One of these easy wins included spare parts for Rolls-Royce engines installed on a number of Iran's civilian fleet. Rolls were happy to provide the parts, but only if the US were content, given the huge amount of business they did with the Americans. Colin Powell was very sympathetic. I gave him more and more information – down to the serial numbers of the parts required – but even this did not satisfy those in the US who were determined to block what we were seeking to do.

Amongst the US blockers was Defense Secretary Donald Rumsfeld, who said in his memoirs that he considered the whole E3 process a 'disaster'.[4] Not long after this, in July 2004, I was singled out by John Bolton, then an Under-Secretary in the State Department (now National Security Adviser to President Trump), who briefed the London *Times* that I was known in Washington as 'Jack of Tehran'.

Bolton himself had always opposed the E3 process. He told an FCO official of his 'anger' that we had written the letter that started the negotiations, and that Colin Powell had tried to dissuade me, a claim which fits with neither my recollection nor the record of my calls with Powell. In sharp contrast, Bolton's boss, President Bush, described the work of the E3 Foreign Ministers in Tehran in October 2003 as a 'fine job', and he was to repeat that commendation in 2005.[5]

Though we were sympathetic to the internal problems faced by Khatami, Rouhani and Kharrazi, there had to be a limit to how accommodating we could or should be. The about-turn by the Iranians to go back on what they had agreed in Brussels led to a decision of the IAEA board in September 2004 which expressed 'deep concern' over Iran's decision to resume enrichment and its failure to sign up to the Additional Protocol. More worrying for the Iranians, it meant that international patience was running out, and it could not be long before the thing they most feared – referral to the Security Council – actually happened.

The hardliners in Tehran made it worse. Their proposal to use a 'triple-urgency' procedure in the Majlis to force through a vote to withdraw altogether from the NPT simply fed the propaganda of the neo-cons in Washington, and of the Israeli government, that a nuclear-armed Iran was a close prospect unless severe action, possibly including military strikes, was taken. So too did a decision by the hardliners to convert 27 tonnes of yellow cake (a uranium compound made from ore) to UF6 (uranium hexafluoride), which was technically premature and 'politically motivated'.[6] Khamenei was as usual playing a double game – using Rouhani to push for concessions whilst increasing Iran's nuclear activity to raise the stakes.

We needed Iran's assistance to move them from the dangerous position in which they had placed themselves. The September meeting of the IAEA governors passed a critical resolution which brought Iran a step closer to being referred to the Security Council, with a thinly disguised threat that this would happen at the November meeting if no progress could be made.

Meanwhile, the 2004 US presidential election, in which President Bush was seeking a second term, was nearing its conclusion. The rhetoric was being ramped up, with briefings to suggest that if Bush were re-elected he would be much more hawkish, with the possibility of military intervention against Iran moved higher on the agenda.

On 2 November 2004, Bush won his second term, defeating John Kerry by a convincing margin. Two days later, whilst accompanying the Queen on a state visit to Germany, I was interviewed on the BBC's *Today* programme. Asked a direct question as to whether the UK would support military action, I said this was 'inconceivable ... I don't see any circumstances in which military action would be justified against Iran, full stop.'[7] This caused some raised eyebrows in Washington and teeth-sucking in Downing Street. My view was that it was hopeless for the UK to parrot the standard formula that 'all options are on the table' when everyone knew, after our experience in Iraq, that there was absolutely no prospect of a majority in Parliament in favour of military action against Iran, so why suffer the opprobrium of keeping this on the agenda? It was also my judgement (borne out by events) that Bush was wise enough never to launch an attack on Iran. I've no idea what difference the *Today* interview made to the Iranian negotiators, but at least the hardliners were denied the card of claiming that negotiations with the E3 were useless because the UK was preparing for a war on Iran.

On 15 November 2004, after three weeks of intensive negotiation, the Paris Agreement was signed. The text recognised Iran's rights to a civil nuclear programme under the NPT and noted, 'To build further confidence, Iran has decided on a voluntary basis to continue and extend its suspension including all enrichment related and reprocessing activities.' The suspension would continue pending negotiations on long-term arrangements. The E3 agreed that once suspension had been verified, negotiations on a trade and cooperation agreement would resume; it would 'actively support' Iran opening accession negotiations with the World Trade Organization (WTO); and it would back an invitation for Iran to join an Expert Group on the nuclear fuel cycle.[8]

But there was another glitch. Khamenei's reaction was to veto the deal, because of his long-standing suspicions of the West's intentions, reinforced by the fact that he had (and has) little direct contact with the outside world since he became Supreme Leader in 1989.[*]

This intransigence left President Khatami, Dr Rouhani and the negotiating team 'shocked, stranded and stumped'.[9] Yet again, the extraordinary constitutional arrangements of the Islamic Republic were going to force them to snatch defeat from the jaws of victory. It took a lot of pressure from Rafsanjani, Khatami and Rouhani before Khamenei acquiesced in the agreement. If that had not happened, Iran would have been referred to the Security Council by the IAEA at its next meeting.

We had been able to achieve some movement on the US side,

---

[*] In thirty years as Supreme Leader, Khamenei has never been abroad. He made a few overseas trips earlier in the 1980s as President.

too, thanks to Condoleezza Rice, newly installed as US Secretary of State. On a visit to Europe in February, President Bush had expressed support for the E3 process. (Later, that support was upgraded into a decision formally to join the grouping, which they did in May 2006. With Russia and China as well, it became known as the 'P5+1'.)

We knew that the US's first preference was a complete and permanent prohibition on enrichment by Iran, but there was gradually an acknowledgement by them that the terms of the NPT did give the Iranians, like any other state, the right to the full nuclear cycle, including enrichment, provided this was not for military purposes and Iran complied with its obligations under the NPT.

Negotiations on the 'long-term arrangements' began in earnest in early 2005. They came to a head at a ministerial meeting in Geneva on 25 May. The E3 went further than it had ever done before, with a package of measures which promised full support for Iran's nuclear programme for peaceful purposes, including the provision of power plants by Western countries; the removal of obstacles to dual-use technology; the removal of restrictions on the export of civil aircraft to Iran; and much else besides. Iran at last would be able to get hold of those desperately needed spare parts for its ageing civil aircraft fleet.

'Chocolates, Jack, chocolates' was Iranian Foreign Minister Kamal Kharrazi's dismissal of this package. It was no great surprise to me. If we'd been able to offer this deal a year before, it would almost certainly have been welcomed and agreed by the Iranian government.* What had changed, however, was that Khamenei had changed his mind. He had reverted to type.

It was now too late. The nuclear issue was caught up in the poisonous 2005 Iranian presidential election campaign. Three days before the Geneva meeting, the Guardian Council (the twelve-member clerical body) had announced its approved list of candidates for the presidential election, for which the first round of voting was due on

---

* This is reminiscent of what happened in the protracted negotiations with the Iranians over oil nationalisation – see Chapter 9.

17 June. As the world was quickly to find out, Khamenei was seizing his chance fully to dictate Iran's nuclear policy, ending the 'inconvenience' of a reformist government trying to argue with him, even though he always had the final say.

Khamenei had agreed everything that the Khatami government had offered the E3 in the nuclear negotiations. But he was showing increasing reluctance to continue to do so, sometimes knowingly blindsiding Rouhani and his team. One interesting illumination of Khamenei's motives came through in early May 2005, from which we understood that it was Khamenei himself who had ordered an immediate resumption of enrichment just before a late April meeting of the E3. However, this was not – on this interpretation – because Khamenei wished to develop a nuclear weapons programme. He wasn't interested in that, it was said. Iran had been offered that, for money, in the early 1990s by Russia and North Korea, but Khamenei had turned the offers down. Rather, Khamenei's interests were political – to give him and his allies another decade in power. Iran's nuclear energy programme was at the time popular with the Iranian people, a matter of national pride; taking a tough line with the international community enhanced that popularity – and enabled the hardliners to open up clear dividing lines with the reformers.[10] That was why his acolytes were now accusing the elected Khatami government and its senior negotiators of 'treason' and 'cowardice' for the Tehran and Paris Agreements, notwithstanding Khamenei's consent to them.

There were seven candidates on the ballot paper for the presidential election:* three reformists – Mehdi Karroubi (former Speaker of the Majlis), Mohsen Mehralizadeh (a Vice-President in Khatami's government) and Mostafa Moeen (a minister under Rafsanjani and Khatami); and three conservatives – Mohammad Bagher Ghalibaf (former police chief of Tehran, with impeccable IRGC credentials), Ali Larijani (head of broadcasting) and Mahmoud Ahmadinejad.

---

* An eighth, Mohsen Rezaei, a conservative, was approved but withdrew.

Somewhere in the middle was Akbar Hashemi Rafsanjani, former President (1989–97) and Speaker of the Majlis.

Rafsanjani was the front-runner. A poll conducted in March 2005 (when other candidates later vetoed by the Guardian Council were still in the running) gave Rafsanjani 28 per cent, and the eventual winner, Ahmadinejad, less than 2 per cent. International 'experts' were confident that Rafsanjani would win.

Unlike all the other contenders, Ahmadinejad was an outsider, from a modest, devout family. He had served in the Basij and in the IRGC, but not at a senior level. He got his PhD in transport engineering, later a source of some snobbish mockery. He worked his way up the system, becoming Governor of the Ardabil province from 1993 until 1997, when Khatami removed him – something he did not forget.

Two years before the 2005 presidential election, the hardliners had begun their electoral fightback. In 2003, the conservatives won many local elections, including the municipal council of Tehran. Ahmadinejad was appointed Mayor. A year later, the hardliners – known as the 'Principalists' – won 196 of the 290 seats in the Majlis. The Guardian Council had gone into overdrive to weed out as many credible reformist candidates as they could. The turnout, at 51 per cent, was the lowest of any previous Majlis election. There was plenty of evidence of irregularities, but these were easily dismissed by the hardliners as sour grapes.

In some ways, the 2005 election was an echo of the 1997 presidential election. Then, it will be recalled, it was the hardline establishment candidate Nateq-Nouri who had been so confident of his victory that he had scarcely deigned to campaign. Now it was Rafsanjani, the rich and powerful cleric, who was complacent, leaving most of the campaigning to his supporters.

In sharp contrast (and as Khatami had done in 1997), Ahmadinejad was very active, especially outside Tehran, where he was little known. He stressed his humble origins, dressed down and drove himself in a cheap car. As the campaign progressed, the hardliners coalesced around him. Ghalibaf, originally their favoured candidate, had dropped a number of gaffes and was suspected of financial irregularities. He was abandoned, with Khamenei letting it be known to the IRGC and the Basij that its members should back Ahmadinejad.

In the first round of voting on 17 June 2005, Rafsanjani received 21.1 per cent, Ahmadinejad 19.3 per cent. Karroubi wasn't far behind on 17.2 per cent. He and the other losers dropped out. In the second round of voting the following week, on 24 June 2005, something weird happened – miraculous or fraudulent depending on your point of view. Ghalibaf and Larijani had received less than 20 per cent of the first-round votes between them. Their votes were bound to go to Ahmadinejad, but that still only brought him up to 40 per cent. Yet, when the results of the second round were officially announced, Ahmadinejad was on 62 per cent, to Rafsanjani's 36 per cent. This had to mean that a large number of voters for the reformist candidates in the first round – Karroubi, Moeen and Mehralizadeh – all of whom were well to the left of Rafsanjani, had a rush of blood to their heads and transferred their support to the most right-wing candidate on the ballot paper; or that an equal number of reformist voters had suddenly decided to stay home for the second round, to be replaced by hardline supporters who had not bothered to vote on the first round but who did so in the second round. Both explanations defy everything we know about voter behaviour, including in Iran.

But, as with the Majlis elections the year before, the conservatives weren't bothered about complaints of ballot tampering. They had won big. For the first time in the history of the Islamic Republic, every key institution was in the hands of the so-called Principalists, the hardliners: the Supreme Leader, the Majlis, the judiciary, the executive, the defence and security apparatus. The lot.

Life was about to be rather different for Iranian people, and for us on the outside. Despite the final authority vested in the Supreme Leader by Iran's constitution, Khamenei had been constrained on foreign and domestic policy during the presidencies of Rafsanjani and Khatami. He was now off the leash.

CHAPTER 18

THE HALO OF LIGHT

Oh mighty Lord, I pray to you to hasten the emergence of your last repository, the promised one, that perfect and pure human being, the one that will fill this world with justice and peace. Oh Lord, include us among his companions, followers and those who serve his just cause.

PRESIDENT AHMADINEJAD, FIRST SPEECH TO THE UNITED
NATIONS GENERAL ASSEMBLY, SEPTEMBER 2005

It was those two early nineteenth-century treaties, again; the ones by which Iran lost huge swathes of territory to the Russians, never to recover them; doleful, perpetual symbols of Iran's humiliations at the hands of great powers.

For newly installed President Ahmadinejad, the Tehran and Paris Agreements of 2003 and 2005 were worse even than Turkmenchay or Golistan, as he told a meeting of the Assembly of Experts.[1]

Ahmadinejad declared a 'year zero' on all that had gone before during the sixteen years of the two previous peacetime Presidents. The negotiating teams under Rouhani had sold out to the West; Iran's nuclear programme was non-negotiable; threats that Iran could be referred to the UN Security Council for its failures to meet its obligations under the NPT were just bluff; and in the unlikely event that sanctions were imposed, that would only make Iran more self-sufficient, and therefore stronger.

One of Ahmadinejad's first foreign policy decisions was to withdraw from the November 2004 Paris Agreement and to resume activities at the Isfahan uranium conversion facility.* His calculation appears to have been that this act of bravado would force the E3 back to the negotiations with lower demands than we had been making, especially for an indefinite suspension of enrichment. His theorists asserted that Iran's new 'aggressiveness' would compel the United States to come to terms with the realities of Iran's power in the region.

Over the summer, there was a flurry of diplomatic effort to try to shift the new Iranian government from the politically suicidal position on which they were impaling themselves. The ever-patient UN Secretary-General Kofi Annan called me in mid-August and suggested that he preside at a meeting during the UN General Assembly (UNGA) ministerial week in mid-September between Ahmadinejad and the E3 Foreign Ministers.† We agreed without hesitation. The Iranians are sticklers for protocol. As mere Foreign Ministers, we would never have been admitted alone into the presence of Iran's head of state and government (HOSG); as Kofi was of equivalent HOSG rank, it would be fine.

The meeting duly took place in Kofi's office, high in the UN building in New York. Ahmadinejad reminded me of Ken Livingstone, vintage early 1980s, fashion wise. (Ken had made scruffiness into a political statement.) The new President sat uncomfortably next to his chief nuclear negotiator, Ali Larijani, at the opposite end of the sartorial – and class – spectrum. Larijani was immaculate, wearing a carefully pressed Ralph Lauren polo shirt. Their clothes said it all. The unkempt outsider; the suave, polished insider's insider. We were all very polite, but the meeting produced no positive outcomes. The gulf in understanding, still more in common ground, was too great.

At meetings at UNGA with the President's new Foreign Minister, Manouchehr Mottaki, we sought to persuade him that his boss should

---

* Technically this was made in the last days of the Khatami presidency, as there's a two-month transition period after the presidential elections in Iran.
† The French Foreign Minister was Philippe Douste-Blazy. In May 2005, he had replaced Michel Barnier, who had taken over from Dominique de Villepin a year before. Joschka Fischer was replaced as German Foreign Minister by Frank-Walter Steinmeier in November 2005.

use his speech to the General Assembly to present a new and softer image to the world, without compromising his beliefs.

Mottaki said that he understood our points and later showed me a draft of his President's speech. It was terrible. I suggested where some changes might be made.

I was not holding my breath that my advice would be accepted. Ahmadinejad did not disappoint his hardline supporters at home – nor his hardline opponents in Washington and Tel Aviv. He failed everyone else.

He was on a different planet from the rest of us.

It's worth pausing a moment to explain why.

Ahmadinejad's most important clerical mentor was Ayatollah Mesbah Yazdi. Yazdi is a follower of Mohammad-Baqer Majlesi, who was appointed Sheikh al-Islam (chief religious leader) by Shah Sultan Husayn in 1687. Majlesi wrote over a hundred books and shifted one important strand of Shi'a thinking away from rational philosophy to superstition, focused on the occulted twelfth imam. He made Shi'a thinking available to the masses. The Shi'a scholars who were invited by the Safavids to settle in Iran came mainly from Bahrain and from the Jabal Amel in the mountainous region of south Lebanon. They wrote in Arabic. It was Majlesi who translated many of the key Islamic texts into Persian and wrote his own in his native language. His was 'an ideology [which] sought to assure the absolute rule of the Shahs whilst keeping the people docile and subdued by maintaining them immersed in superstitious beliefs'.[2]

This school of thought is contested in post-revolutionary Iran. A leading critic, Ayatollah Yusuf Sane'i, has argued that 'the spreading of superstition is a pre-meditated project that certain people use in a goal-orientated manner'. Superstitious ideas were contrary to Islam, he said; Khomeini had battled them to his dying days.[3]

But Yazdi is a true believer in Majlesism and had instructed Ahmadinejad of its merits – for him. A few days after Ahmadinejad's installation in 2005, Yazdi claimed:

Once the President is ... confirmed by the [Supreme] Leader and becomes his agent, he will be exposed to the rays emanating from this source of light [Khamenei]. When the President receives his edict from the Guardian Jurist [Supreme Leader], obedience to him [the President] is the same as ... obedience to God.[4]

* * *

To return to UNGA.

Ahmadinejad began his speech by an appeal to spirituality: 'Today, humanity is once again joined in celebrating monotheism and belief in the Creator as the originator of existence.' He ended with the supplication at the head of this chapter:

Oh mighty Lord, I pray to you to hasten the emergence of your last repository, the promised one, that perfect and pure human being, the one that will fill this world with justice and peace. Oh Lord, include us among his companions, followers and those who serve his just cause.[5]

Most of us listening in the General Assembly were not entirely clear as to whom Ahmadinejad was referring. To his true believers back home, it was as clear as light – he was talking of the return of the occulted twelfth imam. One Tehran commentator said, 'Some [in Iran] gloated at the idea that by calling on the international community to recognise the Twelfth Imam, Ahmadinejad was in effect countering the Western bogy or "straw text of human rights", the pride of reformists and ex-President Khatami, with the true Shi'a heritage of messianic Mahdiism.'[6]

The bulk of the speech was a denunciation of 'the Zionist occupation regime' (Israel) and understandable complaints about the West's role supporting Saddam during the Iran–Iraq War and mujahidin in Afghanistan, together with statements of what Iran would and would not accept in negotiations with the E3. It was not designed to persuade, and it fulfilled its objective. It was poorly received across the international community.

But Ahmadinejad's perception of his speech was entirely different, not to say paranormal. He explained, in a meeting that autumn with a leading conservative cleric, Ayatollah Javadi-Amoli, that from the moment he had begun his speech to its final words, he had been enveloped in a 'halo of light'. This, he claimed, had affected every single delegate in the vast General Assembly hall; a hand was holding each one of us motionless; all eyes were on the President; so transfixed were we that we were incapable of blinking.

Ahmadinejad's speech lasted just under half an hour. I blinked. I winced. I worried. Some of us, I guess most of us, represented nations which had a huge well of affection and respect for Iran and its people. Ahmadinejad had a world view which might be discordant to many, but it was still one capable of rational explanation, and by the end of his speech he might have found that understanding of what he stood for had greatly been enhanced.

One charge of Ahmadinejad was that the Islamic Revolution 'had toppled a regime which had been put in place by a coup'. Notwithstanding what was later to happen in 1953, the victim of that coup, Mossadegh, had earlier gone to the United Nations Security Council in 1951 to put his case; against all the odds, his had been a spectacular triumph. Why couldn't Ahmadinejad have done the same?

Though Ahmadinejad was later embarrassed by his 'halo of light' claim (difficult explicitly to deny since his meeting with Amoli had been filmed), it was all of a piece with his appeal. Ali Rahnema, author of an important work about the influence of superstition in Iranian politics, wrote that Ahmadinejad was presented to 'common folk as the trusted instrument of the Hidden [Twelfth] Imam charged with carrying out his will' whilst preparing the ground for the Imam's imminent return. Hagiographic works about the new President portrayed him as the commander of the Hidden Imam's army, leading the IRGC, the Basij and the security apparatus as members of that army.[7]

Eccentric as all this may be to contemporary Western eyes, there was clear political calculation in what Ahmadinejad was doing. Superstition can play a part in all religions, since there is a point at which faith has to supersede reason, and that can easily be extended to provide a supernatural explanation for both the good luck and the ill luck that can be suffered whilst on this earth. 'The rich man in his castle, The poor man at his gate, God made them high or lowly, And ordered their estate' goes the third verse of Cecil Frances Alexander's High Victorian hymn, justifying as God-given the profound inequalities of mid-Victorian society. (She wrote those words in 1848, the same year as Karl Marx published his *Communist Manifesto*. A few years earlier, he had charged that 'Religion is the sigh of the oppressed creature … It is the opium of the people.')[8]

What is unusual about Ahmadinejad, which marks him out from many of his Principalist colleagues as well as those from a different tradition, including both Khomeini and Khatami, is the degree to which he, and those behind him like Yazdi, claimed that his political agenda was exclusively a divine mission; that those who disagreed with him (especially from the left) were verging on apostasy; and later, when his temporal policies ran into difficulties, that this could be attributed to divine intervention. In the end, as we shall see, Ahmadinejad's curious amalgam of pastiche Shi'ism and naked nationalism was to detach him even from the bulk of conservative clerics.

Five days after Ahmadinejad addressed the General Assembly, he received the international community's first response to his 'aggressive' new foreign policy. By an overwhelming majority, the IAEA's board of governors declared Iran's failures to comply with its obligations under the NPT to be 'within the competence of the Security Council'. Only Venezuela opposed. Twenty-two countries voted in favour, including India; twelve, Iran's natural allies like Algeria, Pakistan and Nigeria as well as China and Russia, sat on their hands and abstained. It was a harbinger of much worse to come, but an inevitable consequence of Ahmadinejad's – and Khamenei's – decision to lead with their chins.

Ahmadinejad compounded his problems with a speech expressing the hope that the 'Zionist entity' would be annihilated. The most resonant phrase in his remarks was that Israel 'should be wiped off the map'. There was controversy as to whether or not this was an accurate translation from the Persian, but that is beside the point, since during his presidency Ahmadinejad repeatedly called in violent terms for Israel to be abolished. He then descended into a moral abyss, with a conference of Holocaust deniers held in Tehran in December 2006. (Amongst those attending was a former head of the Ku Klux Klan.) Iran lost any benefit of the doubt in the court of world opinion.

*　*　*

Condoleezza Rice had already started to bring the United States on board as an active partner in the Iran negotiations, though it took until May 2006 before she was able to persuade President Bush that she could conditionally sit across the table from the Iranians with her P5+1 colleagues.[9]

In late January 2006, I hosted a dinner for the six Foreign Ministers from the Permanent Five of the Security Council and Germany. The dinner went on into the small hours, with much jostling, particularly between Condi and Sergei Lavrov, the long-serving and consummate Foreign Minister of Russia. At around 1.30 a.m. we finally reached agreement. There would be a two-track approach to Iran: they would be offered negotiations, with a threat of UN sanctions if they refused a deal.

Over the next four months, Iran was presented with a package of measures including loans and technology to meet its energy needs, and a clear recognition of Iran's right to develop nuclear energy for peaceful purposes, in exchange for negotiations and Iran's suspension of its enrichment programme, which, provocatively, it had restarted. Any sensible Iranian government would have jumped at the deal. But the package, and all further iterations, was rejected.

By the end of July 2006, international patience with Iran had run out. The Security Council passed Resolution 1696. Just one member – Qatar – voted against; all others were in favour, including non-aligned nations like Tanzania, Congo and Ghana, along with Russia and China. It was a monumental defeat for the Ahmadinejad/Khamenei school of diplomacy. Two years before, such a resolution was just a gleam in the eye of the neo-cons in Washington, not least because of the 'human shield' which the E3 were providing Iran in return for difficult but productive negotiations. Now the Iranians had brought on themselves what they most feared – international isolation, and a mandatory resolution under Chapter VII of the UN Charter. The resolution made Iran's suspension of all enrichment-related and reprocessing activities obligatory.

The Iranians could with some justification complain about the double standards of the international community, since the passage of Resolution 1696 coincided with a major military operation by Israel into Lebanon, with hundreds killed and thousands of Lebanese displaced. But the brutal truth was that Iran's actions had left them without allies.

Ahmadinejad's response to this resolution was to raise the stakes still further, by announcing that the heavy-water facility at Arak had been put into operation and then that it would double the number of centrifuges in operation.

By the end of December 2006, Iran was back in the Security Council. This time every member voted in favour of Resolution 1737, Qatar included. The resolution was tough. It repeated the requirement that Iran suspend all its enrichment-related activities; banned the supply of nuclear technology to Iran; imposed asset freezes on Iran's Atomic Energy Organization; and introduced travel bans on key individuals involved in its nuclear and missile programmes.

Various offers were made to Iran to restart negotiations. Javier Solana, the foreign policy chief of the European Union, an experienced international diplomat, tried with immense patience to persuade

Larijani of a way forward. Ahmadinejad's response was further bravado and intransigence. He announced that Iran had 'thrown away the
brakes and reverse gear of the nuclear train'.

* * *

From the beginning of the US-led invasion of Iraq in 2003, British
warships had been patrolling the north-west end of the Gulf, close
to the Shatt al-Arab waterway, the boundary between Iran and Iraq.
They were acting under Security Council authority to prevent the
smuggling of arms into Iraq.

In June 2004, eight British military personnel in three small inflatable craft were seized by the Iranian navy, who alleged that they were
in Iranian waters. After conversations between Kamal Kharrazi and
me, they were released unharmed three days later. The position of
our boats was put down to a 'misunderstanding', though we had no
evidence that they had been in Iranian waters.

On 23 March 2007, as the Security Council was discussing its next
resolution on Iran, the same happened again, but this time the consequences could have been much worse, since the Ahmadinejad government was so obdurate and counter-suggestible. A troop of fifteen
British Marines and naval personnel (including one woman) in two
inflatable craft, from HMS *Cornwall*, were checking a dhow for con-
traband when they were seized by members of the IRGC. They were
taken to Tehran. When it was pointed out to the Iranian government
that the coordinates given to our diplomats by the Iranians themselves
showed that the boats were not in Iranian waters, the Iranians said
that their own figures had been wrong. It took thirteen days of tortuous negotiations by our Ambassador in Tehran, Geoffrey (now Sir
Geoffrey) Adams, and the FCO minister in London, Lord Triesman,
before a decision was made for their release. Ahmadinejad announced
that 'on the occasion of the birthday of the Prophet Muhammad', the
UK personnel were being pardoned as a 'gift to the British people'.

On 24 March, the day after the British military personnel had been arrested, the Security Council unanimously passed its third and toughest yet resolution, No. 1747, with wider banking and asset bans, freezes on loans and prohibitions on the supply of arms. A sixty-day grace period was given to Iran to comply. Ahmadinejad's response to this ruling was to announce, just two weeks later, that Iran was producing nuclear fuel on an 'industrial scale'.

Seyed Hossein Mousavian, a key member of Rouhani's negotiating team, was quick to spell out publicly how and why Ahmadinejad's foreign policy was leading Iran down a blind alley. Within weeks, Ahmadinejad had Mousavian arrested on espionage charges. Seven of the thirteen charges against him alleged that he had been in direct contact with members of the British intelligence agencies and had handed over secret Iranian documents to them. The charges were fabrications. In ten days of interrogation in Tehran's notorious Evin prison, Mousavian refused to oblige with the 'confession' for which his interrogators were desperate in the absence of any other evidence against him. He was released on bail. A year later, he was acquitted of all charges of espionage, but one of the three judges involved found him guilty on other grounds of jeopardising national security by his opposition to the President's policies and sentenced him to a two-year suspended prison term.*

Mousavian was closely affiliated with powerful figures like Rafsanjani, Khatami, Rouhani and Ali Akbar Nateq-Nouri, who had been the right-wing, establishment candidate against Khatami. The charges served their purpose in helping to silence critics of the President.

Nonetheless, Ahmadinejad could not disguise the fissures which, by the early summer of 2007, were opening within the hardliners' camp. The chief commander of the IRGC, General Yahya Rahim Safavi, was dismissed, following his criticism of 'war-mongering' by Ahmadinejad.

---

* In 2009, Mousavian moved to the USA to take up a position at Princetown University, where he has remained.

Condoleezza Rice had sought to use Sergei Lavrov's offices to pass a message from President Bush to Khamenei that the United States wanted to negotiate a way through.[10] As chief nuclear negotiator, Larijani would have been key to any rapprochement. Ahmadinejad's answer came in October 2007 when his official spokesman announced that Ali Larijani had 'resigned', on 'personal grounds'. This explanation convinced no one.

By March 2008, the UN Security Council was ready with a fourth, still stronger, mandatory resolution, No. 1803. Passed on 3 March with just Indonesia abstaining, this resolution replicated air, land and maritime sanctions similar to those imposed on Iraq in the 1990s.

A new Majlis, the eighth since the revolution, was elected in April 2008. Larijani was made Speaker. Thanks to the elimination of 90 per cent of the most effective reformist candidates by the Guardian Council,* the conservatives maintained their hold on the Majlis, but a significant proportion of these members were uncomfortable about Ahmadinejad's style and suspicious of what *The Economist* described as his 'folksy and superstitious brand of ostentatious piety and his favouritism to men of military rather than clerical backgrounds'.[11] It was an augury of worse to come for Ahmadinejad in his second term.

Undaunted, Ahmadinejad became convinced that Iran's diplomatic isolation could be resolved if Iran itself were elected as one of the non-permanent members of the Security Council, and that, as the only Muslim country in Asia competing for a seat, election was all but assured. Japan received 158 votes, Iran thirty-two.

Ahmadinejad was back at UNGA in mid-September 2008 for his fourth address. It was part millenarian homily, part gratuitous attack on the 'criminal and occupationist Zionists'. This was no more persuasive than his previous outings. Five days later, yet another Security Council resolution, No. 1835, was passed against Iran, with even Indonesia voting in its favour.

---

* In all, 1,700 candidates were barred from standing by the Guardian Council, on the grounds that they were not sufficiently loyal to the revolution.

This resolution, like its predecessors, specifically endorsed the 'twin-track' approach of the P5+1, combining incentives to Iran if they complied with its international obligations with the prospect of more sanctions to come if they did not. For the international negotiators involved, there was every merit in this approach, since it offered Iran a ladder on which it could, if it wished, climb down. But British diplomats in Tehran at the time were struck by how differently the Iranians viewed this strategy. To them, offering gifts with one hand and threats with the other smacked of the hypocrisy that had typified Western attitudes towards them, especially those of the British, for centuries. The Iranians simply dug in.

Resolution 1835 was the last one with which the Bush administration were involved. In early November 2008, the Democrat candidate Barack Obama won the US presidency by a landslide. When he took office in January 2009, one of his first foreign policy decisions was to try to begin on a new page with Iran. In a video message in late March, timed for the Iranian New Year, Nowruz, he said:

> For nearly three decades, relations between our nations have been strained … We have serious differences that have grown over time. My administration is now committed to diplomacy that addresses the full range of issues before us, and to pursuing constructive ties among the United States, Iran and the international community. This process will not be advanced by threats. We seek instead engagement that is honest and grounded in mutual respect. You, too, have a choice.

However, Ahmadinejad, with the unleashed Khamenei behind him, were incapable, not to say terrified, of departing from the cul-de-sac into which they had inserted themselves. They were quick to make their choice. But it was not the one Obama had counselled. It was terrible and bloody.

CHAPTER 19

THE SEDITION OF '88

We remember during the Sedition of '88 [the Green Movement
protests of 2009] the way you supported the heads of sedition,
expensive turmoil, and the troublemakers.

BASIJ LEAFLET

Iran has amongst the world's largest reserves of oil and gas. It is both
a blessing and a curse for Iran, since its prosperity is so dependent
on how much oil, and at what price, it can sell on the international
markets. In 2009, 80 per cent of Iran's exports and 60 per cent of its
government revenues were from oil.

The oil price was around $50 per barrel when Ahmadinejad took
over in 2005. It rose steadily during the first three years of his presidency to $91 in 2008 before falling back to $53 in 2009. Despite
continuing structural inefficiencies within the Iranian economy, corruption and the effect of sanctions, and thanks principally to buoyant
oil revenues, the Iranian economy grew at a respectable 5 per cent
during Ahmadinejad's first term.

The 2008 world financial crisis adversely affected Iran, not least
through the fall in the price of oil. By the time of the presidential
election on 12 June 2009, inflation was running at around 25 per cent
and unemployment officially at 12.5 per cent, though the real level was
likely to have been higher.

Ahmadinejad had continued the expansion of the education

system, invested in new technologies and increased support for those on low incomes – 'his' people. He was a populist. Throughout his term of office, he worked assiduously to support his base – the poorer, more marginalised in Iranian society, and the more devout – and to define himself against the urban middle classes, who had so strongly supported his predecessor, President Khatami. His crude nationalism, of 'sticking it' to the US and the international community generally, had a strong appeal with some Iranians, but this was also a period of rampant corruption in Iran, with particular favouritism shown by Ahmadinejad to his cronies in the IRGC and the Basij.

Four hundred and seventy-six men and women applied to the Guardian Council for approval to stand in the 2009 election. Four men were approved. From the right, Ahmadinejad and Mohsen Rezaei, former commander of the IRGC and secretary of the Expediency Council; from the left, Mehdi Karroubi, former Speaker of the Majlis, and Mir-Hossein Mousavi, who had served as Prime Minister from 1981 to 1989, when the post was abolished by the 1989 constitutional changes. Khatami had earlier indicated that he might run, but in the event he decided to throw his weight behind Mousavi, who quickly established himself as the front-runner against Ahmadinejad.

The campaign was unusually open for Iranian elections – the first in Iran where there were television debates between the candidates – and acrimonious. In one bizarre comment, Ahmadinejad said:

No one has the right to insult the President, and they did it. And this is a crime. The person who insulted the President should be punished, and the punishment is jail ... Such insults and accusations against the government are a return to Hitler's methods, to repeat lies and accusations ... until everyone believes those lies.[1]

Polls in Iran are unreliable. The ones for this election gave widely differing results. One, taken a month before polling (paid for by the Rockefeller Brothers Fund, with a reputation for greater reliability), suggested that Ahmadinejad was ahead by a margin of two to one – 34 per cent to Mousavi's 14 per cent.[2]

Over the course of the campaign, and by relentlessly challenging Ahmadinejad in the televised debates, Mousavi was plainly in the lead. The writer Afshon Ostovar commented, 'When voting began on June 12, only four weeks into a short campaign season, Mousavi was arguably Iran's most popular personality and seemed poised to be its next President.'[3] One late opinion poll, taken by the hardline Tabnak website, had Ahmadinejad on 26 per cent, Mousavi on 38 per cent.[4]

But if poll results in Iran are unreliable, so are election results themselves. Like the Shahs who went before, the deep state of the Islamic Republic is so inherently insecure that it has never been willing to establish truly independent institutions to conduct and to monitor its elections. A reform was introduced after the 2009 elections to establish an Electoral Commission, though its relationship to the Ministry of the Interior, which conducts the electoral process, is unclear. There is, for example, nothing in Iran like the fiercely independent and effective Electoral Commission in India. The consequence is that there is little, if any, faith in the integrity of the system, and widespread cynicism about the results it produces. It could be that Ahmadinejad would have won a completely fair election. We shall never know. What we do know is that when the results were announced the next day, giving Ahmadinejad 63 per cent to 34 per cent for Mousavi (and a claimed 85 per cent turnout), there were spontaneous demonstrations across the country, with not only Mousavi and Karroubi but also Rezaei alleging systematic irregularities.

A defector from the Basij told a Channel 4 journalist that they had received instructions through their chain of command that Khamenei had decided that Ahmadinejad should win the election. Michael Axworthy observed, 'The regime's handling of the results deepened suspicions to the point at which the election looked increasingly like a coup carried out by the ruling group to keep Ahmadinejad in office.'[5] This indeed appears to have been the case. A confidential letter from

Hojjat al-Islam Ali Saidi, the Supreme Leader's representative to the IRGC, had stated that Khamenei had been 'clear' that Ahmadinejad 'should be re-elected'.[6]

The demonstrations grew in size and strength over the coming days. They were the largest mass protests in Iran since the revolution in 1979, and the most threatening to the regime. When the Guardian Council formally certified the results on 29 June, there were further demonstrations in Tehran and many other cities, despite a ban on protests which the government had imposed.

Khamenei preached that the election result had been a result of 'divine assessment' and trotted out the threadbare lines that the protests were all the work of foreign infiltrators. To emphasise this claim, nine locally engaged Iranians employed at the British Embassy and two at the French Embassy were arrested and put on trial on a variety of charges which included 'causing panic to the public'. They had a very uncomfortable time but were in the end released.[*]

The protests, which became known as the Green Movement or Green Revolution, continued until 11 February 2010, the thirty-first anniversary of the end of the 1979 revolution. Thousands were arrested. Many were injured by the security forces and by thugs from the Basij, who were let loose. Official figures claim that thirty-two were killed; protesters say the number was seventy-two.

The most powerful condemnation came from Grand Ayatollah Hossein-Ali Montazeri. It will be recalled that he was for years Khomeini's chosen successor, before he was sidelined for protesting the arbitrary use of executions at the end of the Iran–Iraq War. In a blistering attack, he said that the government had used the 2009 elections in

the worst way possible. Declaring results that no one in their right mind can believe, and despite all the evidence of crafted results, and to counter people's protestations, in front of the eyes of the

---

[*] Most, though not all, countries in the world employ locally engaged staff in their Embassies. They are not used on sensitive issues, nor do they have access to all parts of the Embassies.

same nation who carried the weight of a revolution and eight years of war, in front of the eyes of local and foreign reporters, attacked the children of the people with astonishing violence. And now they are attempting a purge, arresting intellectuals, political opponents and scientists.[7]

As the Yazd Basij leaflet issued against me on our 'holiday' makes clear, the hardliners continue publicly to peddle the line that the 'Sedition of '88' (2009 is 1388 on the Iranian calendar) was all the work of outsiders, including people like me. The paranoia inherent in the upper reaches of the regime is illustrated by a claim by Iran's Minister of the Interior that over the course of the election the US and the West had paid $17 million to instigate the overthrow of the Islamic Republic. Ayatollah Ahmad Jannati, chairman of the Guardian Council and one of Ahmadinejad's most fervent supporters, upped that figure, claiming that the US, through Saudi Arabia, had given £1 billion to protest leaders, with the promise of £50 billion if regime change were successful.[8] Israel has even been blamed for a lack of rain in Iran.[9]

When the protests broke out in June 2009, there was conflicting advice offered to President Obama. Did he respond vigorously and proclaim his support for the Iranian people against the heavy hand of its regime, or did he stay quiet, hoping that his silence would deny the regime at least one propaganda tool? He chose the latter course, despite the inevitable criticism this attracted from the Republicans, who claimed that Obama was more interested in engaging with the regime than in standing up to it. 'It was a difficult, clear-eyed call,' writes the then US Secretary of State Hillary Clinton, in her memoirs, 'the right thing for the protesters and for democracy, nothing more.'[10]

However, Clinton says that in retrospect, 'I'm not sure our restraint was the right choice. It did not stop the regime from ruthlessly crushing the Green Movement.'[11] With my own benefits of hindsight, Clinton was, I think, correct in this assessment. Obama's silence was a response. The regime blamed the US and the West in any event – as the Basij made clear in their declaration against me. Many Iranians today feel that Obama's failure to react to Khamenei's ruthlessness left them high and dry. With Obama's support there would have been no guarantee that the outcome in 2009 would have been any better, but it could not have been worse.

Obama had reinforced his public Nowruz message in March with a private letter sent to Khamenei in May. It was Obama's olive branches that discombobulated the regime the most. 'You cannot talk about friendship and at the same time hatch plots … to harm the Islamic Republic' was Khamenei's public reply to Obama's letter. A US President bearing gifts was not in their playbook. They knew how to deal with sanctions. Indeed, although the US sanctions, in place for many years, and the more recent, incrementally strengthened, sanctions by the Security Council (and by the EU) did unquestionably hit ordinary Iranians, for those in control they were an opportunity to enrich themselves. This was through, for example, the IRGC's involvement in sanction-busting, and the favouritism shown in the allocation of government contracts to those who supported the regime.

* * *

If Obama had had the political space to persevere with his proposals for direct talks with the Iranians, it is possible, just, that some positive result may have emerged – or, at the very least, that he might have been able to open up divisions within the regime. Such a prospect was, however, ruled out by emerging intelligence about the construction by the Iranians of a secret enrichment facility deep into the mountains at Fordow, near Qom.

The Iranians' reasons for its secrecy, and the construction of this facility, deep underground, might have been entirely innocent. But when the facts emerged, they did nothing to enhance Iran's international reputation and only added to the suspicions of Iran's real intentions with its nuclear programme, as did their hasty notification to the IAEA about the facility once its fact had in any case been made public.

The Fordow facility had been kept secret not only from the outside world but from many within the inner counsels of its government, according to Mousavian. Most Iranian diplomats had not had the first idea about Fordow until Obama went public about it. Prime Minister Gordon Brown said that 'the level of deception by the Iranian government … will shock and anger the whole international community, and it will harden our resolve'.[12]

The Fordow revelations completely changed the metrics of Iran's international engagement. It exasperated Russia, who had been on their own dual track, cajoling and encouraging Iran, and doing its best from time to time to protect them from worse in the Security Council.

* * *

On 12 January 2010, a prominent Iranian nuclear scientist, Massoud Ali-Mohammadi, was assassinated when a booby-trapped motorbike was placed near his car. Some in the Green Movement said that Ali-Mohammadi had been a prominent reformist critic of the regime; his funeral was turned into a political rally. Two years later, Majid Jamali Fashi was convicted of his killing and executed. A confession by Fashi was read out at his trial which implicated the Israeli intelligence agency Mossad. *Time* magazine claimed that Israeli sources had confirmed that the confession was accurate.[13] Another Iranian nuclear scientist, Majid Shahriari, was murdered on 29 November 2010 by skilled assassins on motorbikes who attached a suction bomb to Shahriari's car whilst he was driving to work – again, likely a Mossad operation. Altogether, six nuclear scientists have been murdered in a similar way in the past decade.

At the margin, Iran had been helped by the approach of Mohamed ElBaradei, Director-General of the IAEA from 1997. He had worked hard to get alongside the Iranians. I always found him even-handed and easy to work with. But he had been under increasing criticism from the US for allegedly soft-pedalling on Iran.

When, in early 2009, ElBaradei announced that he was not seeking a further term of office, the US ran an intensive campaign to put a more 'reliable' Director-General in his place. After six rounds of voting in the IAEA board of governors, the US's preferred candidate, a senior Japanese diplomat, Yukiya Amano, won the contest, beating South Africa's Abdul Minty in the final round. Amano took office in December 2009. It was bad news for the Iranians. Amano was much tougher than his predecessor, and much closer to the US. His first report was a catalogue of Iran's failures to meet its obligations under the NPT, and the series of Security Council resolutions that had already been passed since Ahmadinejad had set out on his 'aggressive' foreign policy path.

The leaders of Turkey and Brazil, Prime Minister Erdoğan and President Lula, had tried to get Iran off the hook with a deal which, amongst other things, would have put 1,200 kg of low enriched uranium under 'escrow' in Turkey, in return for no further sanctions on Iran. Turkey and Brazil were non-permanent members of the Security Council at the time. If there had been a greater natural level of confidence between Iran and the international community, the structure of this deal might have been built on to create a wider consensus. But, at the time, confidence had dropped near to zero.

By June 2010, Iran was back in the Security Council, facing by far the toughest resolution yet, on top of the six already passed against it during Ahmadinejad's presidency. The new resolution, No. 1929, was agreed with just two against, Brazil and Turkey, and one abstention, Lebanon. It targeted arms sales and the IRGC and included extensive prohibitions on the provision of financial services, including insurance and banking, without which international trade is well-nigh impossible. This resolution, supported by China and Russia, prompted a US Act providing unilateral sanctions against Iran's energy and economy, and parallel, though slightly narrower, EU sanctions. Taken together, these sanctions were a major blow to Iran's financial trans-actions worldwide, and to its economy. Multinational companies, from Toyota, Siemens and Honeywell to Lukoil, major banks and the principal oil companies, either withdrew from Iran altogether or significantly downgraded their exposure.

Ahmadinejad's initial response was predictably belligerent. He claimed that Iran would only come back to negotiate with the P5+1 if Brazil and Turkey were included, and if all participants made clear their position about Israel's nuclear arsenal.

Despite, or maybe because of, his apparent success in the 2009 election, Ahmadinejad was in a weaker position after the election than he had been before. The economy was faltering, sanctions were biting badly on ordinary Iranians, and his incontinent rhetoric was causing discomfort from within the regime. A shift in Iran's negotiating position began to be evident from 2011. It was enough to keep the P5+1 process alive, albeit on a backburner. But the whole regime was so locked into their positions that any serious movement would have to wait for some major change within Iran. No one could predict when or whether that would happen.

*　　*　　*

The old quip that Iran is the only country in the world which still believes that the UK is a superpower continues its currency not least because both the US and the Israeli Embassies have been closed ever since the 1979 revolution. In their absence, and given the prominence of the UK's two large diplomatic compounds, our Embassy buildings are the next best target for those wanting to vent their spleen against Western imperialism and the 'Zionist entity'.

The conservative-dominated Majlis was already more twitchy than usual about the 'cunning fox' of the UK. The new chief of the Secret Intelligence Service (MI6), Sir John Sawers, had made the first ever speech by a serving head of the agency in October 2010.

Sawers knew the Iran dossier very well – he had been the senior official involved when I was Foreign Secretary, and he had then moved to New York as Britain's Ambassador to the UN. In his speech, Sawers referred to the work of the Western intelligence agencies in uncovering the secret facility at Fordow, and continued, 'We need intelligence-led operations to make it more difficult for countries like Iran to develop nuclear weapons ... [and to] identify ways to slow down their access to vital materials and technology.'[14] Ever-suspicious Iranians took this to be some kind of confession by Sawers of UK complicity in the assassinations of Iran's nuclear scientists. It was not, but no official denials were going to make any difference to what hardliners in Tehran chose to believe.

Simon Gass,* who had arrived in Tehran as the UK's Ambassador shortly before the 2009 elections, had relinquished his post in March 2011, leaving Jane Marriott as chargé.† An experienced diplomat, Dominick Chilcott,‡ been appointed as our new Ambassador to succeed Gass. When *agrément* was sought for him from the Iranian government, the FCO were told in July that the Iranian government would refuse and were asked for another candidate. The reasons were unknowable: the Iranians could not have any objection to Chilcott personally; he had never been posted to Iran before, nor was he a 'spy'. Foreign Secretary William Hague dug in. There was only one nomination; carry on refusing and their Ambassador in London would be sent home. After some weeks, consent was forthcoming. But the difficulties did not end there. On two occasions the Iranians told Chilcott to postpone his journey to Tehran, on the grounds that the political conditions were 'not suitable' for his arrival. Chilcott made it at the third attempt and arrived on 23 October.

On 23 November, Ahmadinejad had denounced EU countries as puppets of the US and said that he was surprised at their decision to

---

* Now Sir Simon Gass, Commandant of the Royal College of Defence Studies.
† Now British High Commissioner to Kenya.
‡ Now Sir Dominick Chilcott, UK Ambassador to Turkey.

isolate Iran's Central Bank as part of their sanctions. By chance, the UK was the first member state to pass domestic regulations imposing these EU sanctions on the Central Bank.

On 28 November, the Majlis 'erupted', in Mousavian's words, 'into a fresh frenzy towards its old imperial foe', as members of the Majlis, chanting 'Death to England', voted to expel Chilcott.[15] It was nothing personal, of course. Chilcott had been in place for just a month and is the least likely diplomat I know to offend gratuitously.

Iranian Foreign Ministry officials thought that there might be a way through. They did not want to downgrade our representation (which would inevitably result in reciprocal action in London); significantly, neither did Ahmadinejad. At a meeting on the morning of 29 November, MFA officials indicated that there was a legal route by which the decision of the Majlis could be delayed for up to fifteen days whilst 'something was sorted out'.

There's scarcely a dividing line between a spontaneous and a semi-official hardliners' demonstration in Tehran. When Embassy staff saw that a very large scaffold platform for TV crews had been erected in front of the main compound in Ferdowsi, they knew that the demonstration planned for that afternoon was likely to be large, and actively supported by some in the ever-fissiparous Iranian system. The Embassy had already received six phone calls threatening to 'chase [us] out of town and burn down the Embassy'.

The date – 29 November 2011 – was the first anniversary of the nuclear scientist Majid Shahriari's assassination, which was to add to the level of emotion.

A long-serving member of the Embassy staff says that they were all used to demonstrations.

They usually ran through the same pattern. Everyone who had been paid to be there would be bussed in by about 2 p.m. Crowds of demonstrators would be whipped into a frenzy from 2.10 p.m. to 2.40 p.m. Someone would then set fire to a US flag and maybe the

Union Jack. There would be the ritual chants of 'Marg ba Amreeka; Marg ba Israel; Marg ba Engleysa' (Death to America/Israel/England), then everyone would go home.

Three days after Chilcott had arrived, a lone demonstrator had got onto a roof in the compound and had thrown Molotov cocktails into the grounds below, but no damage had been caused. Even at the height of the 'Sedition of '88', after the disputed 2009 elections, demonstrators had in the end dispersed, and there was never a siege of our Embassy in 1979 as there had been of the American's. But in early 2009, after another Security Council sanctions resolution had passed, demonstrators had got over the wall of the Gholhak residential compound, rampaged through the estate and forced one family to take refuge in their bathroom whilst the intruders ransacked the house.

The police knew all about the planned demonstration. Riot squads had been brought in but, unlike in previous demonstrations, had not been deployed. Instead, some were left sitting in their vans, 'awaiting orders', whilst others at the main gate stood aside to allow the demonstrators unimpeded access.

At earlier demonstrations, the crowds had been overwhelmingly male. This one kicked off with a crowd of about seventy chador-clad women, who were harangued by a speaker on a flat-bed truck, brought up specially for the occasion.

The number of demonstrators 'suddenly exploded', reported an eyewitness. The chador-clad women melted away. 'No space for them in this Iranian game of violence and machismo.' Three intruders scaled the compound's walls, one quickly scampering to the flagpole to remove the Union Jack. The Embassy's alarm was triggered. At 140dB, that's much louder than a live rock concert. Since no one could get to the gatehouse to switch the alarm off, it stayed on for hours, adding to the tension.

Many more men stormed the walls. The crowd got into the guardhouse and worked out how to operate the 'open gate' switch. They surged into the compound, unchecked by the riot police.

Unlike the residence, a grand neoclassical building in the centre of the compound, the operational centre of the Embassy is a modern building close to the main gates. This has a consular section on its ground floor, and three heavily fortified upper floors of the Chancery section, where the principal diplomatic work is carried out.

The demonstrators were not able to break into these upper floors. Instead, they started a fire in the consular section. All the British officials were on the third floor of this building. It took a while for them to notice the smoke billowing up from the ground floor. It was the worst moment for Chilcott and his colleagues (and the Chilcotts' dog), who were left pondering whether they would be able to escape in any safety. Two staff members tried to tackle the blaze with fire extinguishers but had to abandon this attempt when the smoke grew too severe.

The crowd ran amok through the carefully tended gardens, breaking into all the buildings they could. They smashed their way in through the doors and windows of the residence, ripped up valuable government art collection paintings and swept all the ornaments and antiques off the tables and sideboards, as well as smashing every piece of official crystal glassware onto the kitchen floor. In the Ambassador's private quarters, they tore open many crates of baggage which the Chilcotts had not yet unpacked, helping themselves to jewellery, clothing and whatever else took their fancy – and daubed 'Down with the English' on the walls.

In the functional Visa section, they trashed everything in sight. (When I saw this section two years later, it was still in the same state and reminded me of the damage I'd witnessed as Home Secretary when drug-fuelled burglars had broken into offices and had lost all self-control.)

The mob had then moved into the Embassy Club, where they stole all the alcohol; not a single bottle was emptied or broken (an interesting commentary on these devout Basij and their like). The pool table was smashed; one of the staff has never forgotten the fate of the green spot ball, which had a huge chunk taken out of it, an indication of the rage these young men had stoked up inside them.

Unforgivably, the rioters also broke into the private houses of some of the staff, stealing many personal items and trashing what they did not take. 'It was carnage,' reported one member of staff, as they surveyed their sitting room. Mirrors smashed, every drawer turned out, wardrobes ransacked, electronics taken – and their cello found in pieces in a gutter.

Two Iranian intelligence officers in plain clothes arrived to survey the scene. They had an 'air of controlled panic' about them, according to one on the scene. Who knows whether they were part of the same security organisation who had organised the demonstration in the first place, and were now panicking that they had lost control? That's what happens when crowds become intoxicated with their own power.

Despite the terrifying experience the staff at the Ferdowsi compound had suffered, none had been molested by the rioters. Up the hills in north Tehran, at the Gholhak residential compound, the situation was significantly worse. Families lived there, with the British School located within the compound.

The Tehran police had confidently informed the Embassy that no demonstration was expected there. They were wrong; misinformed or deliberately misleading. Simultaneously with the assault on Ferdowsi, a riot had begun at Gholhak. Quick-thinking staff had closed the main gate in such a way that it could not be opened, but a number of rioters got over the walls. They broke into the 'safe rooms' into which some of the staff and their partners had retreated, rounding everyone up to be taken into 'care' by the authorities. Some staff had been beaten when resisting capture. Two of the compound's guards, and, improbably, their captors, managed to keep a 'baying mini-mob' at some distance, but still 'within terrifying earshot'.

The Ambassador's wife, Jane Chilcott, was one of only two staff who was in neither compound at the time of the invasion. She was at a lunch with some Iranian friends, who themselves had had some advance information that the demonstration was likely to be a big one. She had to watch the invasion streamed live on her hosts' computer. She was able to get messages through to her four children in the UK to reassure them (without burdening them with the frightening reality) that their parents were still alive, but she could not make contact with her husband or anyone else in the compound for the next six hours. When would this be over, she worried? Would it be that day, with no one hurt; would these thugs 'do a Chaplin' and kidnap her husband; would it be a siege like the 444-day American Embassy one; or worse?

There were repeated representations made by phone to the Ministry of Foreign Affairs. Their officials are on the whole decent people, but almost as detached from the deep state as foreign diplomats, and, in situations like this, not much more use than a postbox. They promised to do everything they could to have the situation brought under control. Even the President's office made clear that they, and their boss, did not approve of this blatant breach of the Vienna Convention on the safety of diplomatic staff and the inviolability of Embassies; but still the mob raged. What did the view of the President matter when far more powerful people within the system were egging them on? The rioters, Basij, were permitted by the Tehran security apparatus to range freely around the compounds for seven hours, running parades in and out of the compound to assert their control.

The officials who were being smoked out in the Chancery Building had managed to evacuate that building without too much trouble and had taken refuge in a corner of the (now wrecked) Embassy Club.

All the staff in the Ferdowsi compound were finally assembled to leave, with the assistance of staff from the French Embassy. But they were held up, in the words of one of the staff, 'to await the arrival of the police chief of Tehran', which gave the Iranian intelligence agencies on site the time to search and remove interesting items like mobiles, laptops and hard disks, which could later be examined to find out with which Iranians the Embassy had been in contact. When the police chief finally arrived, Chilcott told him that the invasion had not been the spontaneous act of an angry mob: the state had had a hand in it. The police chief then said that our staff were free to leave and went to report to the waiting media, disingenuously to say that he had spoken to our Ambassador, and 'everything is fine'.

The instinct of our senior staff in Tehran was that, if possible, they should stay. They were reluctant to see the hardliners being given a double victory of both the invasion and the closure of our Embassy, which is what they had most sought. Back in London, however, Foreign Secretary William Hague decided that he had no alternative but to pull out all the staff, to close our Embassy and to require the Iranians to do likewise. He stopped short of severing all diplomatic relations. In the Commons, the official Labour opposition supported the government, as I did from the back benches.[16]

These decisions are very difficult. I do not know what exactly I would have done if I had been Foreign Secretary at the time. The overwhelming imperative has to be for the safety of the staff and their families. I would certainly have considered whether it would have been possible to maintain a skeleton staff of volunteers, to see whether the situation was going to stabilise – and not to award the hardliners the prize they had been seeking – a near total downgrading of our relations. But in the end, given the egregious conduct of the deep state, part of which organised this invasion, and which could have stopped it in a trice, I might well have come to the same decision as William Hague.

For the staff, the ordeal was not quite over. When the party got to Tehran's main airport, Iranian officials told some of the staff that they could not board the plane because their paperwork was 'not properly in order'. Of course it wasn't, but that was hardly the fault of the staff. Many of their passports had been stolen by the rioters, or they were in sections of the Embassy to which access was no longer possible. They had to be given temporary travel documents by the French. Some of these staff were ones who had been most traumatised by their experience, still in their smoke-scented, grimy shirts and suits of the day before. They all started to worry that they were going to be used as bargaining tools or trophies by the regime.

The senior British official at the airport told the authorities that none of the party would leave unless they were all allowed to do so. In an inspired move, they asked London to persuade the carrier not to take off until all of the Embassy's party had been allowed to board. The carrier, a prominent Middle East airline, readily agreed. This concentrated the minds of the Iranians, who relented.

Jane Chilcott was able to leave on this plane. Dominick Chilcott and a small group of UK staff stayed behind to clear up the Embassy and put it into cold storage, to await a possible future in which relations with Iran could be returned to normal.

Senior staff going to posts abroad may spend months preparing to do so. Chilcott had spent three months before taking up his post learning Persian. He'd moved out there with his wife, and Pumpkin their dog. Thanks to the Basij and their allies in the Majlis, he served as Ambassador for just thirty-one days.

Serious offences of assault, kidnapping, arson, theft and criminal damage were committed by the rioters. There was extensive video footage which could have been used in evidence – not least from the television crews on the officially installed scaffold platforms outside the Embassy's perimeter. Iranian justice can be peremptory when the authorities wish it. According to reports at the time, however, only twelve people were arrested in connection with the attacks. Just one was convicted and sentenced.

Iran is a singular country in many impressive ways. But its record for ignoring one of the fundamental tenets of diplomacy – that the host country has an absolute responsibility to protect diplomatic compounds and to guarantee the safety of their staff and families – is one of the worst in the world. Diplomatic relations are self-evidently important for countries which are allies. They are essential for countries which are adversaries. Four years after this invasion, on 2 January

2016, mobs invaded the Saudi Embassy in Tehran, setting it on fire; its Consulate in Mashad was ransacked.

The rioters were angry about the execution of a leading Shi'a cleric, Sheikh Nimr al-Nimr, based in Saudi Arabia. The Saudis claimed that he was a terrorist, though the evidence against him was thin, and most – including many British parliamentarians – considered that al-Nimr's only offence was that he was a thorn in the Saudis' side.

On this occasion the police and fire services were a little quicker to react, clearing the Embassy of rioters, though not before the buildings had been badly damaged by the fire. Around a hundred were arrested, though it appears that none were punished, despite overwhelming CCTV evidence.

In contrast to the 2011 invasion, even the Supreme Leader felt bound to condemn the attack as a 'very wrong and bad incident'. The truth, however, is that with their extensive internal intelligence networks and well-staffed police, the authorities could and should have deployed sufficient personnel from the start to prevent the incursion. They showed in their response to the 2009 protests that when they want to, they can suppress huge demonstrations of hundreds of thousands. The fact that they chose not to do so with either the 2011 invasion of our Embassy or the 2016 invasion of the Saudis' speaks volumes about the fact that it was elements of the deep state itself that organised these invasions.

The invasion of the Saudi Embassy was a costly move economically for Iran. In 2018, the Iranian Tourism Board announced that tourism from the Gulf states had declined by 85 per cent since the 2016 attack.* This cost Iran nearly $2 billion.

At a conference in Tehran which I attended in early 2018, I suggested, in very gentle terms, that following these two breaches of the Vienna Convention it would help Iran's international reputation and its friends abroad (me included) if they were to make it an absolute

---

* In the thirteen months prior to the attack, Gulf tourists numbered 1,776,012; in the thirteen months following, this figure dropped to 262, 077.

imperative to protect diplomatic staff and property in Iran. This led to a sustained riff from the official spokesman there, comparing the 2011 invasion to the terrorist attack on Iran's London Embassy in 1980. But there was no moral equivalence between the two, as the spokesman well knew. The British state's only role in the 1980 attack was to secure the release of the hostages (mainly Iranian diplomats) with the minimum of casualties. The Iranian state's role in the invasion of the British Embassy compounds was to organise it, and to have riot police sitting on their hands whilst the Basij rampaged for hours. Unless Iran changes this aspect of its behaviour and does what every other country in the world does, to guarantee the safety of foreign diplomats and their compounds, it cannot be expected to be treated like a normal state.

* * *

In January 2012, the EU imposed an oil embargo on Iran, to take effect from July.

As Ahmadinejad's second term progressed, he gradually lost the support of Khamenei, the hardliners in the deep state, and many in the clerical establishment.

Ahmadinejad's maverick, pastiche Shi'ism had long been viewed with suspicion by the more serious clerics. His promise (made to a Foreign Minister of a non-aligned state) that there 'were signs' that the twelfth imam would reappear 'within two years' were seen as no more than superstitious nonsense.[17] It was reported that he left an empty chair at Cabinet meetings for the twelfth imam. He unnerved the clerics, too, by swerving between apparent religious devotion and naked nationalism, on one occasion donning clothes in the manner of Cyrus the Great. His proposal that women should be allowed to attend football matches (in segregated stands) was knocked back by the clerical establishment.

The 2012 Majlis elections were said to be a contest amongst the hardliners, between Khamenei's supporters and Ahmadinejad's. The reformists refused actively to campaign, in protest against the continued detention of Mousavi and Karroubi, the two leftish candidates in the 2009 presidential election. Unsurprisingly, it was the Supreme Leader's list which won the most seats.

Thereafter, Ahmadinejad had an uncomfortable time with the Majlis and with the Supreme Leader's office. Allegations of cronyism and corruption mounted against him. He was summoned to the Majlis – the first time this had happened to a President – to explain his economic policies, his views on the compulsory wearing of headscarves by Iranian women, and his relations with the Supreme Leader. Ahmadinejad's fall from grace was nearly complete when in 2017 he was refused permission to stand as a presidential candidate by the hardliners of the Guardian Council, though he continues to serve on the Expediency Council, which arbitrates between the Guardian Council and the Majlis.*

The nuclear negotiations at this stage were in the deep freeze. The sanctions imposed by Security Council Resolution 1929 in June 2010 and the associated US and EU sanctions were having a serious effect on Iran's oil revenues and its domestic economy. Quarterly reports to the IAEA board of governors by its Director-General showed a continued expansion of Iran's nuclear programme. The last IAEA report of the Ahmadinejad presidency, in February 2013, gave details of the 2,700 centrifuges by then operating at the previously secret site at Fordow and noted that the Iranian government continued to refuse access to its military site at Parchin, where satellite imagery suggested the construction of a large containment vessel for 'hydrodynamic experiments' which could be used for the development of nuclear weapons.

Even Khamenei and his advisers realised that something would have to change. Just what would be a surprise to him, as well as to the world.

---

* Some of Ahmadinejad's close compatriots have suffered a worse fate. His former chief of staff Esfandiar Rahim-Mashaei has been sentenced to six years in prison on national security charges, and his former Vice-President for External Affairs Hamid Baghai to fifteen years.

CHAPTER 20

THE GUY IN YOUR
EARPIECE

*What you just said is false. You yourself know it is false ... The guy [in]
your earpiece is telling you differently ... He doesn't know, but you do.*

*I want to say something else. Your channel has entrenched these [false]
claims. [They have] remained in your mind and that of the guy speaking
into your earpiece.*

DR HASSAN ROUHANI, UPBRAIDING HIS INTERVIEWER,
HASSAN ABEDINI, ON THE IRANIAN PUBLIC TV CHANNEL
DURING THE 2013 PRESIDENTIAL ELECTION[1]

'When the 2013 election was called, Rouhani had less than 5
per cent in the opinion polls,' the President's chief of staff,
Mohammad Nahavandian, told a four-strong British parliamentary
delegation in early January 2014. Consisting of Conservative MP Ben
Wallace, Conservative peer and former Chancellor of the Exchequer
Lord (Norman) Lamont, and backbench Labour MPs Jeremy Corbyn
and me, this was the first such delegation for years; an indication of
Rouhani's determination to end the isolation into which Iran had
been trapped in the dismal Ahmadinejad years.

Six hundred and eighty candidates had applied to the Guardian Council to stand as candidates in the election, held on 14 June.
Any women amongst the applicants were automatically eliminated.

Although women can vote and be elected to the Majlis, a questionable interpretation of the relevant article in the constitution has allowed the Guardian Council (all men) to ensure that no woman has ever been a candidate for the presidency.

Ahmadinejad could not stand in this election: a sitting President is prohibited from a third consecutive term. Rafsanjani, whose previous terms as President had ended sixteen years earlier, in 1997, was not caught by these provisions; instead, his application as a candidate was rejected by the Guardian Council.

Eight candidates were allowed to stand; three dropped out. The five remaining included three conservatives: Mohammad Bagher Ghalibaf (Mayor of Tehran from 2005, former IRGC commander and the front-runner for the right wing in the 2005 election until his campaign nose-dived); Saeed Jalili (chief nuclear negotiator from 2007, secretary of the Expediency Council and founder of the hardline website Baztab); Ali Akbar Velayati (former Foreign Minister and diplomatic adviser to the Supreme Leader); an independent, Mohammad Gharaz, and Hassan Rouhani.

Rouhani was born in 1948. He trained as a cleric at the Qom seminary; took a law degree at the University of Tehran and then spent some years at the Glasgow Caledonian University to complete a PhD there in 1999. During the Iran–Iraq War, Rouhani was secretary of the Supreme Defence Council (1982–88) and combined that with membership of the Majlis, on which he served for twenty years, from 1980 to 2000.

As in France, there are few restrictions on 'double-hatting' (holding more than one official position at the same time) in Iran. Rouhani was made secretary of the Supreme National Security Council (SNSC) from 1989, a job he kept until Ahmadinejad's election in 2005. He was then placed on the SNSC as Khamenei's representative.

There were intense internal arguments within the Iranian system in early 2003 as it tried to decide its response to the disclosures of its previously secret nuclear activities (see Chapter 16). These difficulties were in part resolved by the appointment in early October 2003 of Rouhani as Iran's chief nuclear negotiator.

Rouhani is quintessentially an insider. He has an encyclopaedic knowledge of how the system works and is a very canny operator, much more feline than Khatami. Though he had always been associated with the centre-reformist camp, he kept his head down pretty successfully during the Ahmadinejad years.

This may have been one reason why the Guardian Council let his candidacy through. Another reason may have been a realisation that the regime itself could have been in peril if an election as flawed as that of 2009 was again allowed to take place.

The election campaign began on 24 May. Those in the Guardian Council who had placed Rouhani on the list as a makeweight would have been reassured by the (never very reliable) opinion polls ten days later. These gave Rouhani just 8.1 per cent of the vote, with Ghalibaf way out in front on an apparently unassailable 39.0 per cent.[2]

Iran is full of surprises, as we have seen.

The deep state in Iran is paranoid about the internet, for the freedom it can provide for individual expression and because it is dominated by the United States. In Iran, the internet is subject to heavy censorship. There are blocks on most social media sites – at times of unrest, on all of them. But Iranians are a resourceful people and the young very tech-savvy, and a great deal of internet traffic does get through. Rouhani was able to use social media in his campaign with considerable success.

The control of the Guardian Council over who can be on the ballot paper in any election in Iran (including for municipal councils) means that its system does not meet one of the basic tenets of any properly democratic system – that citizens are free to decide for themselves whether to stand for election. In practice, it is only insiders, whether conservatives or reformists, who make it onto the ballot. But once through that high hurdle of the Guardian Council's vetting, the campaigns themselves enjoy some level of freedom, within limits, and, these days, equal access to air-time on Iran's public TV and radio channels.

In the 2013 election, candidates had nearly six hours of interviews and took part in two lengthy debates. The interviews were live. Rouhani was like a man released from decades of self-imposed constraint. He went for broke and turned the election in his favour. In one celebrated encounter, quoted at the start of this chapter, he mocked his suave, establishment interviewer for listening too much to the 'guy in his earpiece' rather than thinking for himself. Rouhani knew all about how the state broadcast system worked – he had been the head of the Republic's Broadcasting Council some decades before. In the interview, Rouhani stoutly defended his record as chief of Iran's nuclear team, rejecting accusations that the Sadabad negotiations held in Tehran in October 2003 had resulted in the whole programme being shut down. He also spelt out to electors that Iran faced some serious choices, implicitly acknowledging the damage that sanctions were inflicting on Iran's economy:

> When a centrifuge is supposed to keep spinning while the entire country remains stagnant, meaning that we launch the single Natanz nuclear facility but hundreds of our factories face problems, stop operating or work at a 20 per cent capacity due to a lack of parts, raw materials and sanctions ... that [I] do not approve of.

He explained in his interviews what he was intending to do to extract Iran from the morass that was Ahmadinejad's legacy.

> Regrettably, the Security Council has discredited itself by allowing the United States to impose this counter-productive Israeli agenda. If elected, I will reverse this trend by restoring international confidence ... Nuclear weapons have no role in Iran's national security doctrine, and therefore Iran has nothing to conceal. But in order to move towards the resolution of Iran's nuclear dossier, we need to

build both domestic consensus and global convergence and under-standing through dialogue.

* * *

By the first week in June, Rouhani's support in the opinion polls had shot up to 27 per cent, passing Ghalibaf's on the way down. In the last published polls before the election, Rouhani was on 38 per cent, Ghalibaf on 25 per cent.

In the election itself, on a high turnout of 73 per cent, Rouhani's declared share of the vote was 51 per cent, with Ghalibaf on 17 per cent and the other four candidates trailing behind. With over half the votes cast, Rouhani was the winner without the need for a run-off ballot. Some have claimed that Rouhani had in truth received many more votes than the official result. There has been a persistent story that as the numbers in the first round came through, senior officials went to Khamenei and asked whether they wanted him to re-arrange the numbers so there was a second round. Khamenei reportedly replied that as he had been castigated for rigging the 2009 result, he was not going to authorise this again.

Rouhani's was, in any event, an extraordinary victory. Analysis of his vote showed that he had managed to gain majority support even in religious strongholds like Mashad and Qom, and suggested that he had received a high level of support from the middle classes and from younger voters. His victory was widely seen as unfinished business from the flawed 2009 election and the 'Green Revolution' which was so savagely crushed in its aftermath.

Key amongst Rouhani's Cabinet appointments were that of Javad Zarif as Foreign Minister and Ali Akbar Salehi to head Iran's nuclear programme. Both had PhDs from American universities – Zarif in international law from the University of Denver, and Salehi in nucle-ar physics from MIT. Altogether, Rouhani's first Cabinet had more American PhDs in it than did President Obama's.

Rouhani's principal appeal – apart from the contrast he offered with Ahmadinejad – was his commitment to improve living standards, which had been badly affected by continued and ever-tightened sanctions. A 'resolution of Iran's nuclear dossier', as Rouhani had put it during his election campaign, could therefore have the twin consequences of ending Iran's diplomatic isolation and helping its economy.

Ali Akbar Salehi, Rouhani's head of the nuclear programme, had taken over as Foreign Minister of Iran in early 2011. Although Ahmadinejad was still President, Salehi's appointment seems to have presaged a decision by Khamenei that it was time to see whether there was a way out from the six Chapter VII Security Council resolutions Ahmadinejad had managed to provoke amongst an otherwise divided international community. Key to this would be the attitude of President Obama, who had tried hard early on in his presidency to begin a rapprochement with the Iranians, only to have that thwarted by the reactionaries in the Islamic Republic.

*   *   *

The northern tip of Oman overlooks the narrow throat of the Straits of Hormuz, with Iran on the other side. Iran has a population of 80 million; Oman less than 5 million. Thus, Sultan Qaboos, ruler of Oman, has long maintained good relations with Iran, as well as with the other states in the Gulf. In mid-2011, a key emissary of Sultan Qaboos, Salem al-Ismaily, reached out to John Kerry, then chairman of the US Foreign Relations Committee. It's worth pausing here to reflect on the role of the US Senate in foreign relations. This is much more than the kind of accountability that, for example, the Foreign Affairs Committee of the House of Commons exercises over British foreign policy. In the US, the Senate's Foreign Relations Committee is an active player in the US's overseas relations. No treaty signed by the President can come into force unless it is ratified by a two-thirds majority;* all Ambassadorial nominees and scores of senior positions in the US State Department require Senate approval.

Al-Ismaily had been very helpful to the US in obtaining the release of three American hikers who had inadvertently wandered into Iranian territory and had been detained as 'spies'. Al-Ismaily made clear to Kerry that he was acting as an intermediary for Khamenei, who had transferred oversight of Iran's nuclear programme to the new Foreign Minister Salehi specifically to take it away from the direct control of the hardliners in the system.

However, a fundamental problem in the way of any agreement was the issue of uranium enrichment. The Iranians, as we have seen, had always argued that they had a clear right to enrichment under the terms of the NPT. In my view this had always been indisputable on any reading of the NPT, provided the Iranians met their other obligations under this treaty. There were, after all, thirteen other member nations of the NPT enriching uranium at the time.

This had also become the explicit position of the other five members of the P5+1, including the UK. However, the US were holding back, saying no to any enrichment by the Iranians for fear that any access to the nuclear fuel cycle was a clear route to an Iranian nuclear weapon.

The argument of the other five members of the P5+1 was a powerful one. Without a recognition of Iran's right to enrichment, Iran would simply refuse to negotiate. In the absence of any international agreement, it would continue to expand its nuclear programme – including enrichment. Javad Zarif had pointed out to the UK parliamentary delegation in early 2014, 'When, Jack, you were last involved in the active nuclear negotiations [in 2006], Iran had 200 centrifuges running; it now has 18,000.'

As Kerry wrote in his memoirs, 'The aggressive sanctions regime we

---

* Article II of the US constitution. However, the President can in some cases circumvent this by reaching international agreements (not formally treaties) which can come into force unless two-thirds of the Senate vote against. Obama was to use this procedure with the JCPOA – see below.

and our international partners were pursuing was having a dramatic effect on Iran's economy, without question, but it was simultaneously strengthening the Iranians' resolve to accelerate their nuclear programme. Time was running out. We were essentially at the threshold of a nuclear-armed Iran.'[3]

In private, President Bush had, towards the end of his presidency, come to the view that the US would need to shift its position towards that of the rest of the P5+1, but Ahmadinejad's posture made impossible any serious negotiations at that time. Kerry came to the same view, and, as he came to learn, so did President Obama.[4]

* * *

Obama won a second term in November 2012. Kerry was appointed as US Secretary of State in January 2013, replacing Hillary Clinton. Negotiations were put on hold until the outcome of Iran's June 2013 presidential election became known, but once Rouhani had been elected and his Foreign Minister Javad Zarif was in post, Kerry reopened the back-channel to the Iranians which had been operating for the past two years via the Omanis. He appointed one of the most experienced and distinguished US diplomats, Bill Burns, to run these talks.

Zarif is one of the most impressive of Iran's impressive cadre of diplomats. His years in the US studying for his PhD and then five years in New York as Iran's Permanent Representative to the United Nations during Khatami's presidency meant that he is completely fluent in English and understands how the US governmental system works.

The other lucky happenchance was in the personality of the EU's Commissioner for Foreign Relations, the British Labour peer Cathy Ashton. Cathy had served as Leader of the House of Lords in Gordon Brown's government for fifteen months in 2007–08, followed by a year as the EU's Trade Commissioner, before taking over the EU's foreign policy brief. By this stage, the EU had become a full partner in the P5+1 team. Unlike many politicians, she has no enlarged ego which has continually to be massaged; no airs and graces. She just gets on with her job, always on top of her brief and able to command the confidence of those across the table – in this case, the Iranians. She played a key part in the negotiations. So too did UK Foreign Secretary William Hague, ably assisted by British diplomats, led by the FCO's political director, Sir Simon Gass, who had been British Ambassador in Iran between 2009 and 2011.

Detailed discussions with the Iranians took place throughout the autumn of 2013 and through to the New Year. The outcome was an interim deal – the Joint Plan of Action – which was agreed on 20 January 2014. Under this plan, Iran froze production of its highly enriched uranium, stopped installing centrifuges and halted work on the heavy-water reactor at Arak. In return, tranches were released of $4.2 billion of Iran's own money which had, under sanctions, been frozen in banks around the world.

The next stage, of a full deal, was going to be the most difficult.

In the UK, there has long been bipartisan agreement on the approach that should be taken towards Iran. Labour had support from the Conservatives when we were in office. That was reciprocated by Labour when David Cameron and William Hague took over in 2010. Not so in the United States, with the Republican Party (and parts of the Democrats) umbilically linked to Israel's Prime Minister Bibi Netanyahu. Although many in Israel's security establishment, in the Israeli Defence Force and its intelligence agencies, did support what Kerry and Obama were seeking to do, and considered the wild talk of Netanyahu's allies for military strikes on Iran to be just that, Netanyahu was implacably opposed to any deal with the Iranians, on the grounds that it would simply pave the way to an Iranian nuclear bomb.

With exquisitely awful timing and content, Khamenei made the situation much worse for the Obama administration with a speech in early July 2014 in which he spoke of Iran's desire not to cut back enrichment but to bring thousands of centrifuges online. Zarif claimed to Kerry that he had been blindsided by this speech – almost certainly true, given the compartmentalised way the Iranian government operates and the suspicions of the deep state about its diplomats.

The original plan had been to finalise a deal by the end of July. With Khamenei's intervention, that became impossible; a new deadline of the end of November 2014 was agreed, then another of 31 March 2015.

Meanwhile, in the 2014 midterm elections in the US, the Republicans had trounced the Democrats, increasing their majority in the House and taking control of the Senate for the first time since 2006.

One of the Republicans' first moves was to invite Netanyahu to address a joint session of Congress, without any consultation with the White House or Kerry in advance – which, as Kerry noted, represented 'a total departure from protocol and tradition'.[5]

Netanyahu's speech was entirely predictable. He slammed the negotiations and sent a warning to US lawmakers not to approve any deal with the Iranians. The American Israel Public Affairs Committee would be watching.

This speech was followed by an extraordinary letter sent by the Republican Senator Tom Cotton direct to the Iranian government, presciently warning that any deal struck with the Obama administration would be undone as soon as Obama was out of office.

Thankfully, these noises off served only to strengthen Kerry's determination to reach a deal, and to make sure that it would be tough enough to survive the inevitable mauling it would receive on Capitol Hill. Congress was about to pass legislation requiring that any deal would be nugatory if the Senate voted by two-thirds against it.

A detailed framework was reached in early April 2015. Precisely because its publication was well received in the West, it enraged the hardliners in Iran that their negotiators were selling out Iran's national interests.

In all diplomatic negotiations of any seriousness, national interests will set the parameters, but whether the talks succeed or fail also depends crucially on whether there is trust across the table, whether the personal chemistry helps or hinders. Thankfully, that between Zarif and Kerry, and with Cathy Ashton, was good. It was just as well, given the endgame of this drama. There were eighteen days of non-stop talks in Vienna before finally, on 14 July 2015, the text was agreed. New Foreign Secretary Philip Hammond signed on the UK's behalf.

But the agreement was still not over the line. There were weeks of discussion on the Hill to persuade more than the necessary third of senators to allow it through. British Ambassador to the US Sir Peter Westmacott led the team of P5+1 Ambassadors to explain to dozens of senators and over a hundred members of the House why the deal was worth having and why AIPAC's widely circulated talking points were wrong. Thanks to their efforts, and of course to John Kerry's, in the end forty-two senators voted for the deal. Under Senator Corker's law, President Obama could now bring it into effect.

The agreement itself was not to come into force until 'Implementation Day' – once the IAEA had certified that Iran had complied with a number of steps to roll back its nuclear programme, and the US, the EU and the UN had suspended their nuclear-related sanctions. This was thought likely to run well into 2016. In fact, the Iranians got their ducks in a row much earlier, partly to have the deal bolted down before the Majlis elections in February.

Everything with Iran is a transaction. Whilst waiting for Implementation Day, and to help that along, the US and Iran made two side deals. First, they agreed on a prisoner swap: four US citizens jailed in Iran on spurious charges, in exchange for some Iranians held in US prisons on nonviolent charges. Second, the US agreed to settle a long-outstanding claim from Iran for the return of cash paid by the Shah's regime for US arms which were never delivered because of the Islamic Revolution in 1979. The claim, made to a court in The Hague, was for $10 billion. Kerry's officials were able to get this down to $1.7 billion. A synthetic 'scandal' erupted – care of AIPAC – over the fact that this sum had to be paid in foreign currency; but this was inevitable, given that US sanctions, so dear to AIPAC's heart, prevented the international banking system from processing transactions in US dollars with Iran.[*]

* * *

The Joint Comprehensive Plan of Action – JCPOA in the West, or the BARJAM in Persian – runs to scores of closely typed pages, with five detailed appendices. Its essence is straightforward. The agreement was made international law, under Security Council Resolution 2231, passed on 20 July 2015. Under this, all the previous resolutions passed from 2006 imposing UN sanctions against Iran were to be terminated on Implementation Day. The EU agreed to lift all its sanctions and to open up cooperation with Iran on trade, technology, finance and energy. Many of the US's sanctions pre-dated the nuclear dispute with Iran and could not in practice be lifted because there was no majority in Congress to do so. But the US did commit itself, by executive action, to lift its so-called secondary sanctions. These give the US wide extraterritorial jurisdiction over any transaction in US dollars (as so many international transactions are denominated) and over any third-country entity which is doing business with Iran but also has business in the US.

In return, Iran agreed that for the lifetime of the deal it would adhere to the Additional Protocol to allow the IAEA to conduct intrusive inspections of all its nuclear sites; restrict its stockpile of enriched uranium from 7,000 kg to 300 kg – too little to make a nuclear bomb; cut its operational first-generation centrifuges from 19,000 to 6,000; refrain from operating any of its 1,000 advanced centrifuges; make only low enriched uranium (too low to make a bomb); destroy its only plutonium reactor; and agree that there would be an additional 130 IAEA inspectors living and working in Iran on the supervision of their nuclear sites. Most of the deal's provisions run for fifteen years; some

---

[*] The Iranians have a similar claim, for about £400 million, against the UK for cash paid for Chieftain tanks which were never delivered. See below, page 320.

for ten. If Iran is shown to be in breach of the deal, 'snapback' provisions can enable sanctions immediately to be reimposed by a majority vote, without the possibility of China or Russia exercising a veto.

In his memoirs, Kerry comments that 'the limitations we put in place bought us important time and offered the best chance for peace, even as we maintained security and all our military options. To me, that's a damn good deal, and it made the United States, Israel, the region and the world safer.'[6]

I wholeheartedly agree. As one of those who started the process of nuclear negotiations with Iran back in 2003, I believe what the Foreign Ministers and officials were able to achieve is extraordinary. The sadness is that it took twelve years to reach this deal; if the US had been able to come on board at an earlier stage, we almost certainly could have made a similar agreement in 2004 – when Iran had only 200 centrifuges operating, not 19,000.

The greater sadness is that US President Trump decided in 2018 to withdraw his country altogether from the arrangement.

* * *

The trip I made in early 2014 with my three parliamentary colleagues was one stage of a process set in train by Rouhani to reopen relations with the United Kingdom, following their suspension in the wake of the November 2011 invasions of our compounds.

We were greeted on that trip by an unexpected frankness in the discussions we had with senior ministers, members of the Majlis and diplomats. Zarif told us that sanctions against Iran had been 'crippling', but added that they were, however, 'welcomed by many' in Iran, because for some they were both 'corrupting and enriching'.

In a separate debate with international relations experts, one drew our attention to the fact that '600 Porsches have been sold in six months', but there was a grave 'shortage of medicines [because of sanctions] with people crying in the pharmacies'. Another at this debate made the acute point that in both the US and Iran a '"reward structure" had developed which favoured hostility to the other ... Those in the Majlis who call for better relations with the US end up paying a price for this.'

But we heard other voices too. Alaeddin Boroujerdi, a Principalist and chairman of the Majlis Foreign Policy and Security Committee, had been one of those in the Majlis calling in 2011 for our newly installed Ambassador, Dominick Chilcott, to be sent home. He began our discussion by reminding us that 'when the twelfth imam reappears [from his occultation] he would be accompanied by Jesus Christ', and emphasised the reserved seats in the Majlis for the Christian, Jewish and Zoroastrian communities of Iran.

Boroujerdi went on to speculate on why Iranians were 'more bitter' towards the United Kingdom than they were to Russia, given that both countries had exercised great influence on the Shahs' regimes. Part of his answer was that he had never seen any recognition by British officials of the UK's malign attitude towards his country. When the Shah was in power there were thousands of US 'consultants' in Iran, and some from the UK. 'We did not have any dignity then. Now we do.'

* * *

The supply of British Chieftain tanks – hundreds of them – was one of the issues raised with us. Just when was the UK going to pay the millions it owed Iran for Chieftain tanks ordered by the Shah and never delivered, we were asked.

Altogether 1,750 such tanks were to be sent to Iran, but only 185 of these were delivered before the Shah fell, and Britain cancelled the remainder of the order. The Iranians had, however, paid in advance for all 1,750 tanks, and now they wanted the balance back – about £400 million. The Iranians were also understandably concerned about 'double-dealing' by the UK; some of the tanks undelivered to Iran had subsequently been sold to Saddam Hussein and were used against Iran in the 1980–88 war.

I recall seeing some papers about this when I was Foreign Secretary, but I have not been able to retrieve them when researching this book. My recollection is that the submissions simply reported that protracted arbitration was taking place about the precise sum the British government owed. In hindsight, I wish I had been able better to grip this issue. Paying up would have been relatively straightforward, since there were no nuclear-related sanctions in place until 2006. When the matter was brought to our notice in the 2010 parliament, a number of us in the All-Party Group on Iran sought to persuade the British government to do the decent thing and pay. We had – and have – no legal defence to the Iranians' claim, which has been the subject of endless litigation in the British courts and in international arbitration.

One of my parliamentary colleagues on our 2014 trip to Tehran, Conservative MP Ben Wallace, told the House of Commons that the British government's approach was 'not only a sorry story, but un-British … The process that I will describe has been marred by double dealing and obfuscation.'[7] He was right.

One particularly 'un-British' aspect of Britain's handling of the issue was what happened when three senior Iranian officials travelled to the UK in January 2013 to assist in arriving at a settlement. These three had provided accurate details of the purpose of their trip to London and had been given valid UK visas by the British Consulate-General in Istanbul. When they arrived at Heathrow, they were told that their visas had been revoked that very day. They were detained in an asylum detention centre, their passports were confiscated and they were peremptorily deported two days later. The explanation offered by the Home Office was that since the invasion of our Embassy in Tehran in November 2011 it had been policy not to allow any Iranian officials to visit the UK. But this was wholly unconvincing, given that the officials had made a full disclosure of their reasons for travel on their visa applications. The officials also claimed that they had been treated 'very badly' whilst in detention, though there was no independent corroboration of these allegations. In a letter to me, Foreign Secretary William Hague later expressed regret over what had happened.

It was poor behaviour by the British officials involved. Incidents of this kind simply feed the narrative in Iran that the UK is perfidious. They serve no practical purpose whatever, particularly when Britain's overall record on human rights and the respect for foreign diplomats is so much better than Iran's.

The debt is still unpaid. Although there is now an understanding within the British government that it will have to be paid, the re-imposition of secondary sanctions on the international banking system by President Trump makes the transfer of these millions to Iran inherently more difficult.

* * *

Crab-wise, relations between the UK and Iran were slowly restored to normal. Non-resident chargés were appointed. Ours was Ajay Sharma, who had been deputy head of our mission in Iran in 2007 and 2008 and is now British Ambassador in Qatar.

On 23 August 2015, Philip Hammond made the first trip to Tehran of any British Foreign Secretary since my last official one in October 2003, and formally reopened our Embassy, coincidentally with the reopening of the Iranians' London Embassy. This was followed by the appointment of full Ambassadors a year later. Our first was Nicholas Hopton, followed now by Rob Macaire. The Iranians appointed one of their senior diplomats, Hamid Baidinejad, as their Ambassador. He had previously been a key member of Iran's nuclear negotiating team for the JCPOA.

David Reddaway, whose appointment, it will be recalled, as British Ambassador to Tehran in 2002 had been blocked by Khamenei on the entirely spurious grounds that he was a 'spy' (and the more likely grounds that he spoke excellent Persian and had married an Iranian), commented to me how significant it was that, despite the obvious rubbing points in our relationship with Iran, 'both we and the Iranians always want to get back to normality'.

The Majlis election, by which time Rouhani was anxious to have the JCPOA in operation, took place on 26 February 2016. There had been the usual filtering out of candidates by the Guardian Council; 5,200 people, mainly reformists, were refused permission to stand. In the event, the reformists were able to secure the largest block of seats, at 121, though this was short of the 146 needed for an absolute majority. The Principalists managed eighty-three, and another 'moderate conservative' block had eleven. Not quite the clear victory for which Rouhani was hoping, but, even so, the result gave him a more amenable parliament than its predecessor, elected in 2012 when Ahmadinejad was President.

Rouhani faced his second election as President in June 2017. His principal opponent was the hardliner Ebrahim Raisi. Raisi was one of those named by Ayatollah Montazeri as responsible for the judicial killings of hundreds of low-level MEK supporters, leftists and others, which had been ordered by Khomeini in 1988. He has served in many judicial positions and is head of the wealthy *bonyad* (charitable trust) the Astan Quds Razavi.* The deep state originally tried to block live interviews in this election but had to relent under pressure. There was widespread use of the Telegram messaging service. Rouhani won by a landslide, achieving 58 per cent of the vote against Raisi's 38 per cent.

* * *

Household budgets for Iranians peaked at $14,800 in real terms in 2007, the year that the first tranche of nuclear-related sanctions was coming into force. They declined in every year thereafter until the JCPOA began to take effect. The average household lost about 15 per

---

* In late February 2019, Raisi was appointed by Khamenei to be the Chief Justice of Iran.

cent of its purchasing power in this period; the middle classes (on higher incomes) around 20 per cent. The Iranian economy as a whole went into a deep recession in 2012 (the year when the toughest sanctions were imposed), and also saw negative GDP growth in 2013 and 2015. However, the high price of oil early in the decade enabled Iran to increase its foreign exchange reserves to $144 billion (up from $5.28 billion in 1999).[8]

In 2016, Iranians did start to see some positive results from the JCPOA. Living standards began to rise modestly. The IMF reported that Iran's GDP had grown by 12.5 per cent in the first year following the deal. Oil exports had been cut to around 1.1 million barrels per day by 2013. By early 2018, they were running at almost 2.5 million barrels a day.

Iran's GDP per head on a 'purchasing power parity' (PPP) basis was around $20,000 per capita, roughly the same level as Bulgaria and Mexico but significantly below Turkey (on $27,000 per capita) and less than half that of Saudi Arabia (on $55,000 per head). In terms of its overall GDP, Iran is the eighteenth largest economy on a PPP basis and 25th–30th on a nominal basis.* Official unemployment runs at around 11 per cent. Iran's population, at 81 million, makes it the eighteenth most populous country in the world.[9] Its population has doubled in the forty years since the 1979 revolution, with half under thirty-five. (By way of comparison, the UK's population grew by 13 per cent from 1980; 42 per cent of its population is under thirty-five.)

Traditionally, Iran's main trading partners have been its near neighbours (Iraq, Afghanistan, the UAE, Turkey) and India, China and South Korea. Amongst European nations, Germany, France and Italy have been the main exporters, with the UK lagging some way behind.

Sanctions had a severe impact on exports from EU countries during the early part of this decade, in many cases dropping by more than

---

* Sources: IMF, World Bank, CIA Factbook. PPP takes into account the relative cost of local goods, services and inflation rates of the country, rather than using international market exchange rates which may distort the real differences in per capita income.

half. Ironically, the only Western country which recorded an increase in exports to Iran was the United States, albeit from a very low base. They rose from around $13 million in 2009 to around $100 million in 2013. The US looks after its own; long-standing exemptions from sanctions are in areas where the US is strong – pharmaceuticals, medical equipment, food and agricultural products.

The Iranian currency, the rial, was standing at around 9,000 to one US dollar in 2009. Its decline since then has been catastrophic. By mid-2013, the rate had fallen to 25,000 rials to a dollar. It almost stabilised at around 30,000 when the JCPOA came into force.

Anticipating these falls, those with savings have sought to convert them into hard currency, mainly the US dollar. It was reported that some $30 billion of capital left Iran in the first quarter of 2018, mostly to neighbouring countries and to the Caucasus. In early 2019, the Iranian government tried to restrict the foreign exchange market, banning exchange offices from selling hard currency, and introducing limits on the amount of cash that can be held, in a bid to rescue the rial.

A rapidly deteriorating exchange rate pushes up the price of imported goods and the rate of inflation. The vast disparities between the official and the open market exchange rates have enabled those within the system to make significant profits. There have been many opportunities too for smuggling, with strong reports that the IRGC has played a key role (presumably excused on the basis that breaking the effect of sanctions is in the national interest). Despite the political antipathy between the UAE and Iran, Dubai has been a key centre both for official trade with Iran and from which smuggling operations can be organised. The iPhones in their thousands and the scores of new Porsches on the streets of Tehran had to have come from somewhere.

*   *   *

There were just twelve months between Implementation Day for the JCPOA in January 2016 and President Trump's inauguration in

January 2017. In that period, as we have seen, there were some limited improvements in living standards and the economy as a whole as a result of the lifting of sanctions. But the effect was considerably less than Iranians had expected. This was principally due to the continued reluctance of the international banking system to facilitate trade and investment with Iran, for fear that they could still run foul of the US Department of Justice, which had previously exacted billions in fines on some non-US banks for alleged breaches of Iranian sanctions.

After the Islamic Revolution, there was a significant improvement in the level of inequality in Iran. Measured by the widely used Gini coefficient, inequality dropped from .46 to .39 between 1979 and 1985, but this was in a situation where overall living standards also dropped, because of the revolution and the war. This measure dropped again between 2006 and 2012 to reach .37. It has since risen to above .40. All these numbers are high (by way of comparison, the Gini coefficient for the UK is .34.)* In a period when household incomes had already been squeezed, and when the real levels of unemployment and under-employment, especially amongst the young, were likely higher than the official figures, Iranians noticed the rise in inequality, in unfairness in the distribution of incomes, and they did not like it.

At the end of December 2017, apparently spontaneous demonstrations protesting against hardship – the regime's economic policies in general and a hike in food prices in particular – broke out, not in Tehran but in Mashad, in the north-east. Mashad is the second largest city in Iran. It has the holiest shrine in the country and is considered conservative in habit. If these demonstrations had begun in Tehran, it might have been possible for the regime to blame 'middle-class students' for the trouble. But no such explanation was credible for the disturbances in Mashad. Some journalists suggested that the protests

---

* The Gini coefficient measuring inequality varies between 0 and 1. If, in the group measured, income was shared exactly equally, the score would be 0; in a group where all the wealth was held by one member of the group, the score would be 1.

may have initially been organised by hardline opponents of Rouhani (of which there are many in Mashad) to embarrass him.[10]

Aided by social media, the protests quickly spread to virtually every city of any size in the country. Protesters were heard chanting 'Death to the dictator; death to Khamenei'; some of these chants included Rouhani as well. Amongst other slogans, onlookers heard cries of 'No to Gaza, no to Lebanon, my life is only for Iran', 'Leave Syria alone, think about us' and 'Our enemy is right here, they [the regime] lie telling us it's America'. From an initial concentration on economic woes, the protesters targeted Iran's involvement elsewhere in the Middle East, angry at the sums spent in Syria and Yemen when ordinary Iranians felt so much hardship.

Whilst Rouhani pleaded for some understanding of the protesters, the deep state in Iran reacted in an entirely predictable way: suppression. Almost all social media sites were blocked. The IRGC and the Basij were brought in to 'assist' the local police. Twenty-one protesters and two members of the security forces were killed. Thousands were arrested: one estimate by a human rights lawyer put the figure at 3,700; the state asserted that the real number was many fewer. But with such an opaque judicial system it is impossible accurately to know.

I was in Tehran to attend a security conference held over 7–10 January 2018, a few days after the disturbances had ended, but they were still the biggest domestic political issue. What was striking to both Norman Lamont, my travelling companion, and to me was that there was unexpectedly open discussion about the causes of the protests, even on state television.

Conservative Iranian politician and economist Ahmad Tavakkoli, a cousin of the ubiquitous Larijani brothers, blamed the protests on economic conditions experienced by the poor, which he said were the responsibility of the Rouhani administration, the policies of the International Monetary Fund, and problems experienced by depositors due to non-regulation of financial institutions.[11] The reformist academic Sadegh Zibakalam blamed the protests on the lost hopes of young educated unemployed Iranians, who he said felt betrayed given the Rouhani administration's earlier promises of change.

As ever, Khamenei's reaction was to accuse 'the enemies' of the Islamic Republic for the unrest, saying, 'In the events of the past few days, the enemies of Iran are deploying every means at their disposal including money, arms and political and intelligence support to coordinate making troubles for the Islamic establishment.'[12] He offered no evidence in support. He then suspended the teaching of English in primary schools, a limp if illuminating indication of how Jalal Al-e Ahmad's teachings about *gharbzadegi* – 'Westoxification' – continue to obsess the more out-of-touch of the regime.*

* * *

Donald Trump was a little cautious about his intentions with the JCPOA early in his campaign for President. 'It's very hard to say, "We're ripping it up,"' he said during an NBC interview in August 2015, adding, 'I would police that contract so tough that they don't have a chance. As bad as the contract is, I will be so tough on that contract.'[13]

But by the time the Republican primaries were in full swing in New Year 2016, Trump's attitude to the deal had hardened to implacable opposition. '[My] number one priority is to dismantle the disastrous deal with Iran,' he told an AIPAC audience in March,[14] referring to the risk of Iran making a nuclear bomb, to its missile programme and to its military involvement elsewhere in the Middle East.

For the first sixteen months of his presidency, Trump stalled on whether to withdraw altogether from the JCPOA. Under the complicated legislation that Obama and Kerry had had to agree with the Republican-controlled Congress to stop them blocking the JCPOA from its inception, the US nuclear-related sanctions were not formally

---

* See Chapter 11 above.

repealed; instead, the President was given the power to issue periodic 'waivers' from the sanctions, provided that the IAEA was certifying that Iran was keeping to its obligations under the deal. Faced with the IAEA doing exactly that, and pressure from his original, more moderate advisers, including Rex Tillerson, his first Secretary of State, Trump continued to sign the waivers. But in March 2018 Tillerson was fired, by tweet, to be replaced by Mike Pompeo. More ominously for the Iranians and the future of the JCPOA, John Bolton replaced General H. R. McMaster as National Security Adviser in the White House.

Bolton has form on Iran. He has echoed Israel's threats of military action against Tehran – and has had a close association with the MEK, the Iranian opposition and terrorist group which was banned as a foreign terrorist organisation in the US as well as the UK.* Indeed, Bolton campaigned for the MEK to be removed from the banned list and has taken large fees for appearing on platforms in its support, according to reports of information he was required to file on taking a government position.† He has repeatedly called for regime change in Iran. There are plenty of much better Iranian diaspora groups abroad campaigning for major reforms in Iran. They steer clear of the MEK. It is odd that Bolton has chosen not to.

With his new senior team in place, in early May 2018 Trump announced that the United States was pulling out of all its obligations under the JCPOA and would reinstate all the US sanctions which had been waived whilst it was still in force in the US. He said that the JCPOA was 'a horrible one-sided deal that should have never, ever been made' and added, 'It didn't bring calm, it didn't bring peace, and it never will.'[15]

---

* The US's ban ended in 2012.

† In May 2018, Joanne Stocker, a journalist and researcher studying the MEK, told Richard Engel of MSNBC that she estimated Bolton was paid 'on the low end, $180,000'. Bolton's office refused to comment on the matter. According to the 5 USC app. § 101-required 'US Public Financial Disclosure Report' (2018) for Bolton, released by Al-Monitor, he received a $40,000 speaking fee for 'Global Events – European Iranian Events' on 1 June 2017, the same day he made a speech for the MEK in a gathering in Paris, France.

Non-oil sanctions were reimposed in August 2018; sanctions against the oil trade in November 2018. The effects on the Iranian economy have been serious.

Trump's decision was wholly unilateral. However, such is the worldwide reach of the US's so-called secondary sanctions, by which any individual or entity doing business with Iran risks severe sanction in the US, that the result of his decision was immediately to cause a further collapse in the Iranian currency (see below, Chapter 22), and an effective freeze on investments in Iran by Western corporations. As one example, British Airways had reinstated its direct flights to and from Tehran in August 2016 following the normalisation of relations with the UK and amid rising business interest from British companies about opportunities in Iran after the JCPOA came into force. But in 2018 BA suspended its flights indefinitely. Business travel from Britain had collapsed so much that the flights were no longer deemed commercially viable.

All the other signatories to the JCPOA made clear that they were determined to stick with the deal. Commendably, this group includes the British government, who have never wavered in their approach. It has taken some courage. In her time as Prime Minister, Theresa May, along with her Foreign Secretaries, Boris Johnson and Jeremy Hunt, and the Chancellor, Philip Hammond (who signed the JCPOA when Foreign Secretary), deserve considerable credit for resisting strong pressure from the US administration to join them. Although there were a number of occasions under previous Presidents when British governments, Labour and Conservative, have agreed to differ from the US, I can think of no recent example where such a wide gulf in foreign policy has opened up across the Atlantic.

Indeed, France, Germany, the UK and the European Union have gone further, to try to keep the JCPOA alive. First, they passed a blocking statute to allow EU businesses to recover damages from the extraterritorial US sanctions and nullify the effect in the EU of any foreign court rulings based on them. It forbids EU persons from complying with those sanctions unless exceptionally authorised to do so by the Commission in cases where non-compliance would seriously damage their interests or the interests of the Union.

Secondly, in early 2019, France, Germany and the UK brought into operation a 'special-purpose vehicle' designed to bypass US banking restrictions and facilitate trade with Iran.

In a speech on an MEK platform in June 2017, Bolton said:

The outcome of the president's policy review should be to determine that the Ayatollah Khomeini's 1979 revolution will not last until its 40th birthday ... The declared policy of the United States should be the overthrow of the mullahs' regime in Tehran ... The behaviour and the objectives of the regime are not going to change and, therefore, the only solution is to change the regime itself ... And that's why, before 2019, we here will celebrate in Tehran![16]

Bolton never made it to Tehran as he had promised he would. The fortieth anniversary of the Islamic Revolution on 11 February 2019 came and went. The 'mullahs' regime' remains intact, though it is more fragile than it appears. How long it is able to survive, and what could happen next, is the focus of the remaining chapters of this book.

CHAPTER 21

THE DEEP STATE AND
IRAN'S SECURITY

The [Supreme] Leader is essential to the IRGC's place in Iran's system,
and the IRGC is the foundation of the Leader's power.
AFSHON OSTOVAR, VANGUARD OF THE IMAM[1]

Our strategy is the elimination of Israel from the world's political geog-
raphy; and it appears that given the evil deeds Israel is undertaking, it
is bringing itself closer to that reality … We declare that if Israel does
something to start a new war, that war will clearly be the one which leads
to its elimination, and the occupied territories will be taken back, and the
Israelis won't even have a cemetery in Palestine to bury their dead.
GENERAL HOSSEIN SALAMI, IRGC CHIEF, JANUARY 2019[2]

In the three months between my submission of the manuscript of
this book and its despatch to the printers, much has changed in
Iran, all of it for the worst from the viewpoint of ordinary Iranians.

President Trump used the first months of 2019 to tighten, and
tighten again, US extraterritorial sanctions on Iran. When oil sanctions were reimposed in November 2018, the US issued waivers to
eight main buyers of Iranian crude oil – China, India, Japan, South
Korea, Taiwan, Turkey, Italy and Greece – to give them time to find
alternative sources of supply. India is particularly dependent on oil
imports from Iran, and China is a major customer. In April 2019, the

US announced that from 2 May these waivers would end. 'Our policy is to completely zero out purchases of Iranian oil – period,' commented the US Special Representative for Iran, Brian Hook.[3]

The result has been a catastrophic reduction in Iran's oil exports. In May 2019, they were estimated to have plunged to 400,000 barrels per day (bpd), half the level of the month before, and less than one-sixth of their 2.5 million bpd peak in April 2018, just before President Trump's sanctions began to bite. Iran's oil exports were now below even the level to which they had dropped in 2012 after the EU had imposed further sanctions in addition to those of the US.

In mid-April 2019, the US designated the whole of the IRGC as a Foreign Terrorist Organisation (FTO), the first time the US has imposed this sanction on an organ of a foreign government. The effect of the designation will make it even more hazardous for companies, including those which do not trade in US dollars nor have any other connections with the US, to do business with Iranian entities. The IRGC's financial and business interests are wide and deep, and not all are obvious to outsiders. The risk for these businesses is of criminal as well as civil actions in the US – enough to deter most businesspeople from opening negotiations. There are already some signs of companies in Iran cutting their ties with the IRGC. The designation may have serious implications for some Chinese companies who have not been too choosy about their business partners in Iran.

In retaliation, Iran designated the US Central Military Command (CENTOM), whose area of responsibility includes the Middle East, as a 'supporter of terrorism'. However, given Iran's profound economic weakness, this will have no practical effect whatever.

There have been some efforts by third countries to bypass US sanctions. There are reports that India plans to begin negotiations with Iran to pay for its oil in Indian rupees. China has protested against the sanctions, saying that its trade with Iran is perfectly legal.[4] It could seek to use companies which have no connection with the US to conduct its oil trade with Iran, but whether it chooses to do so will in part depend on how it believes such an approach will affect the continuing US–China trade dispute.

As we saw in the previous chapter, the E3 – the UK, France and Germany – have taken determined steps to establish an alternative trading institution known as INSTEX to bypass US sanctions. This would in essence be a facilitator of bartering deals (known as a net-ting organisation) and would still need access to third-party banks. INSTEX has a high-level board (chaired by the UK's most senior diplomat) and distinguished German banker Per Fischer as its chief executive. It has already done a great deal of preparatory work and is aiming to begin with trades in humanitarian goods like food, phar-maceuticals and some consumer products. Iran has reciprocated with its own special-purpose vehicles. However, to date it has not facili-tated any trades. The US has threatened sanctions on anyone trading through INSTEX with Iran,[5] though some British officials are scepti-cal about these threats and say that they receive conflicting messages from the US, some of which tacitly recognise the obvious truth that keeping Iran within the JCPOA is a far more reliable way of delaying for years any development of nuclear weapons than if they pull out of the agreement.

The overall consequence of the Trump sanctions has been a further serious deterioration in living standards and life chances for most Iranians. However, much as the regime seeks to use the Trump meas-ures as the reason for all Iran's ills, the Iranian people know that the underlying causes have been domestic. The serious and spontaneous protests against the regime in December 2017 and January 2018 took place when Iran was still enjoying the benefits of the JCPOA.

It is worth recapping on what has happened to Iran's currency in recent years, to which I referred in Chapter 20. Between 2003 and 2009, the rial was relatively stable, falling slowly from 8,200 rials to the US dollar in 2003 to 9,000 by 2009. In those days, the official rate and the open business rate were the same. Since then, these rates have diverged, but both have plummeted. The official rate fell to 25,800 in

2014 and now stands at 42,000 – a more than four-fold deterioration in ten years. The open business rate has fared even worse – it fell first to 32,400 in 2014, then slumped to 138,000 in May 2019, an astonishing fifteen-fold decrease. If this had happened in the UK, a pound in 2009 would now be worth just ten pence against the US dollar.[*]

In a situation where Iran cannot sell much of its oil, foreign currency is in short supply and imports are expensive, even where they can be sourced. The import of dozens of goods, including cars, fridges, powdered milk, cameras and musical instruments, has been banned, but some economists say that these measures are not likely in reality to mean much, since the official ban would be offset by smuggling, organised by state organs.

Despite President Trump's unilateral decision in May 2017 to pull out of the JCPOA, the Iranians wisely decided to continue to observe all their obligations under the agreement, as the IAEA has repeatedly confirmed in its regular reports. However, the US decision to end all waivers from May 2019 led the Iranians to recalibrate their approach to the agreement. This was partly because of the understandable need for them to be seen to do something in the face of US provocation. 'The Iranians felt they were being pushed over a cliff and needed to respond' was how one Iran watcher put it. There has also been strident public criticism of the delay in making INSTEX operational, with Khamenei and other Iranian officials publicly complaining of 'bad decisions' made by the Europeans and their alleged lack of commitment to the obligations on them – of opening up markets – within the JCPOA[6] (though in private Iranian officials acknowledge that the European powers have in fact been doing everything they can to make INSTEX operational).

The result of Iran's reconsideration was announced by Rouhani in early May 2019 on behalf of Iran's Supreme National Security Council, which he chairs. In a televised speech, Rouhani gave the remaining five powers still observing the JCPOA, and particularly

---

[*] By comparison, the UK pound stood at $1.43 on 6 March 2009 and at $1.26 on 31 May 2019.

France, Germany and the UK, sixty days – until 8 July – to 'meet their commitments, especially in the banking and oil sectors'. If the five powers were unable to do so in this period, then Iran gave notice that it would lift the restrictions on the level of uranium enrichment and the modernisation of the Arak heavy-water reactor.

The Iranians justified their decision by relying on text in the JCPOA itself, under which 'Iran has stated' that if the US were to impose sanctions, these would be grounds for Iran to 'cease performing its commitments' under the agreement.[7]

Iran has made some headway, within the caps agreed by all sides under the JCPOA, slightly to increase its stockpiles of heavy water and enriched uranium. However, if Iran does ramp up production after 8 July, any breaches of these caps will be reported by the IAEA to its board of governors. This is because the section in the agreement on which Iran relies is not one to which the other signatories are bound, and Iran knew that when the text was agreed. If there had been consent to Iran's position, the text would have said that 'all parties recognise Iran's right', rather than 'Iran has stated'.

Iran may be willing to take this risk, as a hedging exercise to ensure that it still has the potential to move forward on a nuclear weapons capability if the need arises.

Iran's moves to date have been careful, but this has not been reflected by many in the system, particularly in the IRGC, who have made aggressive statements against the US and its allies. To a degree, this rhetoric has been matched by the Trump administration. But one former UK diplomat says that we need to bear in mind that Trump's approach is the opposite of Theodore Roosevelt, who famously said, 'Speak softly and carry a big stick.' In contrast, Trump speaks loudly and carries a small stick.

Trump is a deal-maker. His original offer of talks with Iran was constrained by pre-conditions which no Iranian government could ever accept. The White House now say that he is willing to talk without pre-conditions. However, given the high level of suspicion (paranoia amongst some) in the Iranian system about the US, any possibility of such discussions ending satisfactorily would require the most careful preparation, in secret and through trusted intermediaries (as Obama and Kerry undertook through Oman).

The chances of that are slim. The bigger risk is of miscalculation by one or both sides. Already, tensions in the Gulf have been rising, with claims by the US (vehemently denied by Iran) that Iran was responsible for attacks on four empty tankers; these tensions have not been eased by a significant increase in US assets in the area. Decision-making in the Trump system is notoriously chaotic. The Iranian system is a little more ordered. Up until now, Iran's calculations have been thought through. But the very heterogeneity of what passes for Iran's state institutions, for example by elements in the IRGC, could lead inadvertently to miscalculations and an escalation they did not want. Iran has already ramped up its use of its proxies in the region to increase attacks on US allies. If it went further, Iran would have to expect retaliation from Israel, Saudi Arabia or the US.

* * *

Let me now return to my wider conclusions. In this penultimate chapter, I want to look at Iran's security forces, how they are controlled, what is their current defence strategy – and whether this helps or hinders Iran's development.

At the heart of Iran's deep state is the Islamic Revolutionary Guard Corps (known in Iran as the *Sepah-e Pasdaran*), and its subsidiary, the Basij, with whom my wife, our friends and I had our unpleasant experiences in October 2015.

The IRGC has around 130,000 personnel. The Basij has an estimated 90,000 full-timers and 300,000 reservists and can call on some millions of members. These bodies are distinct from the regular armed forces (the *Artesh*) in Iran, which number around 400,000 (of whom about 220,000 are conscripts).

The role of the *Artesh* as laid down in the constitution is similar to that in any other country: 'The Army of the Islamic Republic of Iran is responsible for protecting the independence and territorial integrity of the country and the order of the Islamic Republic.'[8]

In contrast, the IRGC are described by Article 150 of the constitution as 'the guardians of the revolution and of its achievements'. Khomeini's original vision for the IRGC was limited – he argued that the military should be above politics – but his vision for the Iranian revolution was unbounded: he wanted to see it exported beyond Iran's borders, and had some ambiguous words inserted into the constitution on that aim.*

The notion, not to say the fantasy, that Iran could export its revolution worldwide dissolved with Iran's weakness and isolation at the end of the Iran–Iraq War. However, Khamenei has ensured that in the immediate neighbourhood Iran will do all it can to extend its influence, as it has in Syria, in Iraq, in Yemen and in Lebanon. Khamenei has also extended the IRGC's role into almost every aspect of Iranian life. It has a symbiotic association with a key political grouping in Iran: the Alliance of Builders of Islamic Iran. It has wide powers of arrest and detention (as does the Basij). As in its suppression of the 2009 Green Revolution, and again with the disturbances in the 2018 New Year, it can be ruthless and effective in putting down any popular uprising against the elite's control.

'No one ever leaves the IRGC,' one British diplomat told me. 'Its senior officers are a freemasonry, an Ivy League network.'

The IRGC has extensive business interests in construction, manufacturing and much else. It owns a major telecom company and has stakes in Iran's motor industry, in its oil and gas undertakings and in a large shipbuilding and repair company. With control of many ports and land entries to Iran, it has been able to 'supervise' sanction-busting

---

* Article 154: 'While it completely abstains from any kind of intervention in the internal affairs of other nations, it supports the struggles of the oppressed for their rights against the oppressors anywhere in the world.'

and smuggling on an industrial scale, enriching its members in the process.

The central and critical question in the international community's dealings with Iran is, as we have seen, whether or not it has a role for nuclear weapons in its defence strategy. Back in 2007, the US, in its National Intelligence Estimate, said, 'We judge with high confidence that in fall 2003 Tehran halted its nuclear weapons programme.'[9] In December 2015, the IAEA issued a report concluding:

> The Agency assesses that a range of activities relevant to the development of a nuclear explosive device were conducted in Iran prior to the end of 2003 as a coordinated effort, and some activities took place after 2003. The Agency also assesses that these activities did not advance beyond feasibility and scientific studies, and the acquisition of certain relevant technical competences and capabilities. The Agency has no credible indications of activities in Iran relevant to the development of a nuclear explosive device after 2009.[10]

Has Iran had a nuclear weapons programme? Does it still have one?

Without access to the highest levels of the Iranian regime, it is impossible conclusively to answer these questions. We know that Khomeini disapproved of nuclear technology in general – civil or military – and regarded the Shah's programmes as wasteful and unnecessary. All work on the Bushehr plant was stopped in 1980.

Four years later, Iran was in the middle of the most horrific war in its history. Its early victories – on which they should have based a peace – had long since dissolved into a terrible war of attrition. The Iranians faced the increasing use of chemical weapons by Saddam, notwithstanding that they had themselves commendably eschewed such weapons. Had it not been for the Israeli attack (with some Iranian help) on Osirak in 1981, Saddam might have developed a nuclear weapon. Iraq's Foreign Minister Tariq Aziz said that if they'd had one, they would have used it against the Iranians.

Any rational policy-maker in Tehran in the mid-'80s, pondering the fate of so many young men in the trenches, might well have concluded that developing such a weapon system was essential if Iran was ever to be able to deter any belligerent neighbour, or a superpower behind them. Deterrence, after all, is the justification for the UK, amongst others, keeping its nuclear capability.

It appears that this kind of consideration did lead Khomeini to changing his original decision in the mid-'80s. By the time Rafsanjani became President, there had for certain been a resumption of Iran's civil nuclear programme, and, it seems highly probable, a resumption of its weapon programme too.

There is no categorical evidence, no 'smoking gun' that Iran is now using its civil nuclear programme for military purposes. US intelligence chiefs, for example, played down any nuclear threat from Iran in evidence they gave to Congress in late January 2019 – much to the ire of President Trump.[*]

However, Iran's problem with the international community is that its behaviour since the existence of its undisclosed facilities became public in 2002 has been opaque and contradictory. At times, especially during Ahmadinejad's presidency between 2005 and 2013, it has been downright obstructive. We have also to bear in mind the Shi'a concept of *taqiya*, which allows dissembling for a greater good.

It would be an act of folly for Iran now to develop a nuclear weapons system. For a country with huge demands on its resources even in the best of times, it would be cripplingly expensive and would exacerbate the unrest that is already patent within Iran about the cost of its foreign interventions in Syria, Yemen and elsewhere in the region. It would make Iran more isolated and lose it key allies including Russia, China and friends in Europe. Saudi Arabia or Egypt might start the development of their own nuclear weapons systems in reaction to

---

[*] 'The intelligence agencies said Iran continues to work with other parties to the nuclear deal it reached with the U.S. and other Western nations. In doing so, they said, it has at least temporarily lessened the nuclear threat.' US Defense News, 30 January 2019.

Iran's programme. An Iranian nuclear capability would lead to the US being even more active in its deployment of these weapons in the Gulf and its bases in the Middle East.

I have no evidence contrary to the views of the IAEA and US intelligence experts to suggest that Iran is currently deceiving the hundreds of IAEA inspectors in the country and that it is actively working on a nuclear weapons programme. However, the working assumption must be that Iran wants to keep its options open. If the programme had only ever been about the generation of electricity and the production of medical isotopes for X-ray machines, there would have been none of the need for secrecy which has been a feature of its programmes. And beyond its potential as a base for nuclear weapon production, there is one other factor which cannot be ignored in handling this issue: Iran's national pride. The regime has invested large sums in the programme and feel they have a right to pursue it. But, as with so much regime policy, many of my Iranian friends tell me that this approach is widely contested by the Iranian public. They are strongly nationalistic too, but many believe that the regime has wasted vast sums on the nuclear programme which could and should be better used to improve the lives of the people, and that the regime's pursuit of the programme is ultimately ideological, not grounded in Iranian nationalism.[*]

During the twelve years of nuclear negotiations, Khamenei went along with his Presidents, Khatami and Rouhani, and signed off on the outcome, the JCPOA. He had the final say. However, his instincts are plainly against such negotiations, as shown by his tolerance of Ahmadinejad's rebarbative approach to the international community, and in the profound resentment and suspicion he continually displays to the West as a whole.

This is what Khamenei said in a speech at the time of the fortieth anniversary of the revolution:

---

[*] For example, see the comments of Sadegh Zibakalam, an Iranian academic in Tehran.

My advice is to not trust the Europeans either ... From two or three years ago, when there were those nuclear talks, I constantly said in private meetings with officials, but also in public, I don't trust them. Don't trust them. Don't trust their words, their promises, their signatures, their smiles ... Well, now the officials who were negotiating in those days are saying the United States is untrustworthy ... Today, I'm saying this about Europe. They're untrustworthy. I'm not saying you shouldn't have contacts with them ... The issue is that you have to look upon them with pessimism.[11]

It has to be a working assumption that Iran could at some stage restart its nuclear weapons programme. For this reason, it is imperative that the European powers endeavour to keep Iran within the JCPOA. The agreement does not guarantee that Iran will never produce a nuclear weapon. It does, however, delay that prospect for many years, and make concealment by the regime more difficult.

If Iran withdrew from the deal, even if it stayed within the NPT, intrusive inspections of its nuclear programme would cease. Trump's decision to withdraw the US from the JCPOA was reckless. If other signatories had followed suit, the world would already be a more dangerous place. That which Trump and Bibi Netanyahu claim they most want to avoid – Iran developing nuclear weapons – would have become more likely. They might also ponder that there are those in the deep state in Iran who hate the JCPOA just as much as they do. These opponents are in the IRGC, amongst reactionary clerics. Interesting bedfellows for the President of the US and the current Prime Minister of Israel.

One of the complaints of the Iranians is that they are subject to double standards. Pakistan, India and Israel all have nuclear weapons and the international community does nothing about this. This grievance is understandable, but making the complaint serves no purpose beyond a debating point. The fact that these three states (and North Korea) are outside the NPT is an argument for ensuring that no other states develop nuclear weapons systems, not the reverse.

The Israelis steadfastly refuse officially to confirm their nuclear weapons capability, though on one occasion an Israeli minister in a private conversation inadvertently admitted this to me. It's for Israel to explain why they have a nuclear arsenal, but it is worth pointing out that though the Israelis have the best-trained and best-equipped armed forces in the Middle East, it is a small state of 8 million people (of whom just 6.5 million are of the Jewish religion). For good reasons, given its history, it feels very vulnerable to the hostile forces in its neighbourhood. And Israel has not promised the 'elimination of Iran from the world's political geography' as General Salami and many others in the deep state in Iran have done for Israel.

Central to Iran's difficulties with the West, making it an easy target for its enemies, and at times creating excruciating difficulties for its friends, is its obsession with Israel. The Iranian regime's line on Israel goes much further than that of other countries in the Arab and broader Muslim world. There have been official attempts by some of these states to play a more productive role in the Israeli–Palestinian conflict; the 2002 Saudi-backed Arab Peace Initiative is one example. Meanwhile, Iran has focused on funding Islamist terrorist groups that are responsible for the vast majority of attacks on Israel. Even Qatar, which has supported Hamas, is now playing a more productive role in Gaza.

The regime refers pejoratively to Israel as the 'Zionist entity', in a lame linguistic attempt to deny Israel's right to exist as an independent nation within the United Nations. Ahmadinejad's dreadful statement that Israel should 'be wiped off the map' may, as I discussed in Chapter 18, have been based upon a mistranslation of his exact words, but he and other conservatives continued to argue that Israel should be abolished. There are myriad examples of such speeches. In the heading for this chapter, I chose one of the most recent, made by General Hossein Salami, IRGC chief. The hardliners run this hostility towards Israel into a wider antisemitic trope, routinely talking about 'world arrogance and international Zionism'.[12]

To all this, one has to add the constantly played slogans of 'Death to America, Death to Israel', allied with the burning of American and Israeli (and British) flags. Even Khamenei has spotted that some of these slogans may not be the most persuasive for Iran to adopt. In the same speech in which he warned his audience not to trust the Europeans, he explained that '"Death to America" means "Death to Trump and John Bolton and Pompeo" ... We have no problem with the American people.' What Khamenei and those around him fail to understand is that such a 'clarification' does not help the perception of Iran in the eyes of the international community. Indeed, the 'clarification' makes his position worse, since he has moved the incantation of 'Death to America' beyond a worthless and impersonal chant to a specific call for the murder of the leaders of another country.

There are plenty of people across the world who have profound objections to the policies that Israeli governments have pursued in recent decades, in their extension of illegal settlements onto Palestinian land in East Jerusalem and the West Bank, and their inhumane and unnecessary mistreatment of Palestinians. I am one of them. There's a large minority of Israelis who have the same views. What we know of the 'deal of the century' being worked up by President Trump's son-in-law Jared Kushner for Palestine would be a disaster for the Palestinians and 'would pull the rug from under Palestinian leaders who have remained steadfast and faithful to the two-state idea at great personal and political cost', according to one commentator in a leading Israeli newspaper. It will play into the hands of the most extreme violent groups, like Islamic Jihad. 'Palestinians are losing faith fast with the foundational idea of peace through negotiations.'[13]

But the error Iran makes is to conflate disagreements with the current policy of the Israeli government (and the US) with a commitment to eliminate Israel altogether. In doing so, for no practical purpose, this undermines the influence Iran could have in securing justice for the Palestinians. Khomeini used to speak about Israel in unflattering terms, but it has been Khamenei who has become obsessed with

Israel, making it a greater focal point for the regime. It's a policy which is driven entirely by ideology, not national interest; it is deep-rooted and antisemitic.

Particularly since the end of the Iran–Iraq War, and Khamenei's becoming Supreme Leader, Iran has diverted substantial resources to achieve their goal of seeing an end to Israel. One key aim of the IRGC's Quds Force is the liberation of Palestine and destruction of Israel.[14] The name tells its own story: 'Quds' in Persian means 'Jerusalem'.

Since 1998, the force has been led by Major-General Qassem Soleimani, who has become a very public figure in Iran.

Soleimani reports directly to Khamenei. It is he and the Supreme Leader who determine Iran's foreign and defence stance in its neighbourhood, not the elected government (except through the participation of Rouhani and some other senior ministers in Iran's National Security Council). 'Soleimani is arguably the most powerful and unconstrained actor in the Middle East today,' observes US General Stanley McChrystal, adding, 'Iran's resistance toward the United States' involvement in the Middle East is a direct result of US involvement in the Iran–Iraq War, during which Soleimani's worldview developed.'[15]

The key relationship in the region of Soleimani's Quds Force is with Hezbollah (literally 'Party of Allah') in Lebanon. It was Israel's invasion of Lebanon in 1982 that left the Shi'a population in south Lebanon very exposed and led directly to the formation of Hezbollah, which is heavily financed, trained and advised by the Iranians. There are also strong confessional links with this Shi'a community going back to the Safavid era.

Iran gave this active support to the resistance against Israel's occupation of south Lebanon at the same time that Israel and Iran were cooperating over the supply of arms and materiel to the Iranian armed forces and over the emigration of Iranian Jews who wished to move to Israel during the 1980–88 war.

There was, thus, something of an accommodation between these two countries. However, as set out in Chapter 15, following what

Rafsanjani saw as Iran's unwarranted exclusion from the Madrid Conference in 1991, Iran has adopted an increasingly disruptive, not to say nihilist, approach to peace in the Middle East. It has deliberately sought to undermine the more moderate elements amongst the Palestinians, particularly Fatah and the Palestinian Authority, by arming not just Hezbollah but also Sunni extremists in Hamas and Islamic Jihad, operating within the Occupied Territories. It is provocatively constructing military bases in Syria close to Israel's border, it paints 'Death to Israel' on its ballistic missiles in Hebrew and Persian, and it has created a 'countdown timer' that shows the hours and minutes left until the destruction of the 'Zionist regime'.[16]

Overall, the Islamic Republic's stance on Israel is not just unacceptable; it is self-destructive. It unnecessarily makes Iran's isolation much worse; it cannot be justified even by Iran's friends; and it plays into the hands of its adversaries. It would be strongly in Iran's interests for it to change its stance and listen to its own people, many of whom can see the regime's policy and rhetoric for the very dangerous nonsense it is.

We can debate for ever the perfidy of the United Kingdom a century ago in making three incompatible promises in the Balfour Declaration, the McMahon letters and the Sykes–Picot Agreement during the First World War,[*] and its less-than-glorious role in abandoning its mandate for Palestine after the Second World War. But the State of Israel was agreed by the United Nations in 1949;[†] its existence is a

---

[*] The McMahon letters (1915–16) were correspondence between Lt Col Sir Henry McMahon, British High Commissioner to Egypt, and Hussein bin Ali, Sharif of Mecca. In return for the latter's support in driving the Turks from their Arab possessions, the Arabs were promised independence for what is now Saudi Arabia, Israel, Jordan and Iraq, up to an area to the west of Damascus (roughly west Syria and Lebanon). These promises were completely inconsistent with the terms of the secret 1916 Sykes–Picot Agreement, by which all the former Ottoman Arab provinces, apart from Saudi Arabia, were to be carved up between the UK and France. Both undertakings were in conflict with the public Balfour Declaration made by the then Foreign Secretary in 1917 to the Zionist Federation promising UK support for a 'national home for Jewish people' in Palestine, without prejudice to the civil and religious rights of existing non-Jewish communities in Palestine.

[†] UN Security Council Resolution 69 proposing to the General Assembly that Israel be admitted as a member of the UN was agreed, with one against (Egypt) and one abstention (the UK), on 4 March 1949. The General Assembly resolved to admit Israel on 11 May 1949, by UN General Assembly Resolution 273. The UK again abstained. The Soviet Union voted for both resolutions.

fact. That won't change in this century or the next. I have never seen a single text from the Iranians explaining how this reality could be altered.

Moreover, the almost total diplomatic isolation in its region which Israel suffered for the first four decades of its existence is now dissolving, as Arab (and other Muslim) states gradually come to terms with Israel's existence. Egypt, Jordan and Turkey all have formal relations with Israel. In late 2018, Oman, an important pivot between the Gulf Arab states and Iran, hosted Israeli Prime Minister Bibi Netanyahu. Saudi Arabia is inching towards some kind of recognition of Israel. Encouraged and cajoled by the United States, one of the key drivers of this growing closeness between other Middle Eastern states is the fear in their minds of Iran.

After the decades of enmity between Iran and Israel, no one could expect Iran to do a complete volte-face and recognise Israel. Rather it should start to acknowledge the fact of the State of Israel in its foreign policy doctrine and in its rhetoric and, maybe, remind its own people that, alone of any Western nations (and Russia), Israel cooperated with Iran, rather well, during the 1980–88 'imposed war'. Iran could have lost that war altogether without Israel's arms supplies.

Beyond the self-defeating rhetoric about the elimination of Israel as a state, Iran does have a wider security policy, which is designed to preserve Iran's independence under the Islamic Republic. Compared to its potential adversaries, Iran's armed forces are not strong. Javad Zarif, Iran's Foreign Minister, commented recently, 'Our military budget per capita is the lowest among regional countries, except for Egypt, which gets foreign aid and does not include arms expenditures in its budget … Saudi Arabia has spent $69 billion on weapons. The Islamic Republic's total military expenditures are below $16 billion.' Zarif continued in this speech to ask, 'So what has made us the most powerful country in the region?' His answer: 'It is the people.'[17]

In any conventional warfare, Iran's air and naval forces would be little match for those of Saudi Arabia, Israel and the United States. Instead, as a recent assessment by RUSI suggests,

> The Iranian government perceives the US and Israel as the most serious threat to that objective, and has therefore established a strong deterrence posture founded on increasingly accurate rocket and ballistic missile technology, based in Iran and in Lebanon, which in the event of war will be used to strike US bases and economic infrastructure in the Gulf, and Israeli towns and critical national infrastructure. Meanwhile, Iranian-backed units in Iraq and the Navy of the Islamic Revolutionary Guard Corps would strike US forces in Iraq and the Strait of Hormuz respectively to deny space to US forces, slow the build-up of US units, and inflict casualties.
>
> The Iranian government has high confidence that, following the experience of Iraq and Afghanistan, a comprehensive ground invasion of Iran is unlikely. Instead the expectation is for adversaries to launch an extensive air campaign, to occupy key installations and terrain, and to attempt to cause an internal uprising against the government. The Iranian government believes it can withstand an internal rising, and thereby protract the conflict, inflicting casualties on its adversaries in a regional deep battle to force a settlement.[18]

It is Iran's relative weakness which in their eyes requires them to engage in asymmetric warfare on the scale they do, to use its Quds Force and proxies in their neighbourhood as a form of forward defence. The Iranians speak from time to time about the need for a security agreement across the region. That would, however, require a significant change in Iran's approach, as well as reciprocity by the US's allies, Saudi Arabia in particular. It's a distant prospect. However, the government in Tehran, sensible to the needs and opinions of its people, wanting to end Iran's self-imposed isolation, could take unilateral steps in its own interests, to reset its defence and security doctrine to concentrate on the measures required to protect Iran's territorial integrity, and abandon its focus on the hopeless aim of eliminating Israel. But that depends in turn on whether Iran is capable of domestic political reform to wrest control of all its coercive forces from the unaccountable deep state to an elected government.

CONCLUSION

IRAN'S FUTURE

I believe that Islam, the revolution, and regime will not be destroyed by foreign enemies, but this could happen at the hands of friends ... including the hardliners, who by pursuing the wrong path will separate the people from the revolution ... The majority of the people do not support the hardliners, but the hardliners can separate the majority of people from [the regime] ... No danger from foreign enemies can threaten us ... But we will face domestic dangers from divisive, profiteering and hardline individuals.

GRAND AYATOLLAH NASER MAKAREM-SHIRAZI,
QOM, 13 FEBRUARY 2019

*We in the government have no control over the judiciary ...
The President does not have any control over the judiciary.*
JAVAD ZARIF, IRANIAN FOREIGN MINISTER, MUNICH
SECURITY CONFERENCE, FEBRUARY 2019, INTERVIEW
WITH LYSE DOUCET OF THE BBC

In order to live in Tehran you have to lie. Morals don't come into it: lying in Tehran is about survival ... Lying for survival in Iranian culture goes back a long way ... a practice known as taqiya *... Some of the most pious, righteous Tehranis are the most gifted and cunning in the art of deception ... Tiny children are instructed to deny that daddy has any booze at home; teenagers passionately vow their virginity;*

shopkeepers allow customers to surreptitiously eat, drink and smoke in their back rooms during the fasting months and young men self-flagellate at the religious festival of Ashura, purporting that each lash is for Imam Hossein, when really it is a macho show to entice pretty girls, who in turn claim that they are there only for God.

But here is the rub: Iranians are obsessed about being true to themselves.
RAMITA NAVAI, *CITY OF LIES*[1]

Iran is a most curious country. Its people, with few exceptions, are delightful. They are possessed of the greatest of gifts, of imagination, inventiveness, a great sense of their literature and culture, a passion for poetry. Yet they are trapped in their history. The story of Iran today is about the struggle taking place within its society, as some want to break free from its history and others want to use that history to keep their power.

A key aim of this book has been to show how Iran's history has shaped Iran's present, and why Iranians have such powerful feelings about Britain's role. Of course, every country in the world is defined by its history. What is different about Iran is the way its history weighs it down, how it is used by part of the governing elite to justify repression and intolerance into Iran's future.

As I hope I have shown, Iranians have good reasons for feeling sensitive about the way they have been treated by other, more powerful, nations in the past, including by the British. There's no collective memory in the UK about our actions towards Iran over the whole of the nineteenth and most of the twentieth century, including during the Iran–Iraq War, which ended only three decades ago. There is in Iran. But there's a wide spectrum of opinion in the country about where Iran should go next, how Iranians should live their lives.

We were witnesses – victims, if you like – of that breadth of opinion on our 'holiday' in Iran in October 2015. To be given police protection against criminals or terrorists is one thing; that happens across the world. To be given police protection against other parts of the same state is quite another. I can think of no other country in the world where that occurs, save Iran.

'I had a bodyguard from the normal police,' one of our former diplomats who had served in Iran told me, 'protecting me from their own side! My impression of the Iranian regime was its absolute unpredictability; with the multiplicity of different state institutions, it feels terribly insecure.'

In the narrative of the American right, and some of the Iranian diaspora in the West, there is no difference between the elected and appointed elements of the Iranian state. They are one homogenous whole. The elected officials are under the thumb of the theocracy, the judiciary, and its coercive force, the IRGC and the Basij; worse, the likes of Rouhani and Zarif are sedulous, credible spokesmen (and they are all men) apologising and covering up for the repression that takes place under their noses.

This is not a view I share.

A striking feature of the Iranian system is its heterogeneity. Parts of the system are almost literally out of control. It's thus that we can have the hardline President of Iran impotent in the face of an embarrassing invasion of the foreign Embassy, with the intelligence agents who might well have been behind the original idea of an unpleasant demonstration against the British having 'panic in their eyes' when matters get out of hand.

When elections have been allowed to take place in Iran with relative freedom, the results have led to clear differences in the policy of successive Iranian governments. Khatami's successful proposition in 2001 to the United Nations General Assembly for a 'dialogue of civilisations', and Ahmadinejad's address to the General Assembly just four years later of belligerent venom about the 'Zionist entity', sandwiched between messianic promises of the second coming of the occulted twelfth imam, came from men on different planets. The difference was not only rhetorical.

Elected officials do not have the final say over much domestic and foreign policy, but they do have some power of initiative, the power to try to set the agenda, and to challenge Khamenei and his cohorts not to block them. Sometimes they win; more they often lose.

Khatami tried hard for a nuclear deal.

Ahmadinejad wilfully wrecked any chance of a deal; worse, he so undermined Iran's national interests that he achieved what I never thought was possible: abandonment by Iran's allies, unanimity in the UN Security Council to pass ever-tighter resolutions against Iran. It took Rouhani's election in 2013 for there to be any prospect of Iran extracting itself from the pit into which Ahmadinejad had propelled his country. Two years later, the JCPOA was agreed. If, in late 2016, a Democrat had been elected to the White House, the deal would have stuck.

A further irony of Trump's attitude is that it is greatly strengthening China's influence over Iran, with its 'Belt and Road' initiative to create a Chinese hegemony over most of Asia to its west. China also has a natural affinity for Iran because of its ancient culture. Iranians to whom I have spoken are deeply uncomfortable about China's growing role. They are resigned to it, however, so long as the US continues to be so hostile and actively seeks to undermine Europe's efforts in support of the JCPOA and the economic benefits its full implementation could bring.

Equally, it's important not to allow the current policy of the US government to divert attention from the fact that in large part Iran's economic and social difficulties have been created by the regime itself, by its diversion of substantial resources into foreign adventures in its neighbourhood, by its endemic corruption, and by its refusal to allow Iranians the freedom they crave to live their lives as they wish.

In Khatami's first term, there was some liberalisation of the media. The Iranian film industry flowered; the free press grew. Predictably, because the deep state is so threatened by fresh ideas, constraints were soon reimposed.

Rouhani, though less liberal than Khatami, has tried to introduce other reforms. These include changes to Iran's banking and financial systems to bring them into line with international norms. But the difficulty Rouhani has had in securing these measures of financial reform is a small illustration of a fundamental problem about the way in which Iran works. There are four linked Bills. All have passed the Majlis. In any normal system, subject to any presidential veto, these Bills would become law. Even where a President is able to veto legislation, normal constitutions provide the legislature with an override. (In the US, it is by a two-thirds vote.) Not so in Iran. Two of the Bills are currently blocked in the Expediency Council, at Khamenei's behest.

The Iranian Parliament, the Majlis, is called in the constitution the 'Iranian Consultative Assembly'. It is subordinate to the Guardian Council: 'The Islamic Consultative Assembly does not hold any legal credibility without the Guardian Council.'* This council is the creature of the Supreme Leader,† and the agency by which the Leader day by day sets the parameters for the role of the republican institutions of the state. As we have seen, it determines who can run in any election, routinely sifts out thousands of mainly reformist candidates, and vetoes legislation on the grounds either that it is contrary to the constitution or that it is incompatible 'with the commands of Islam';[2] in this latter case, only the six clerics have a vote. Where there is a disagreement between the Majlis and the Guardian Council, the matter goes to the Expediency Council to be resolved. This body is entirely appointed by the Supreme Leader.

There is at times a greater degree of pluralism in the Iranian system, and a wider choice offered to electors, than may be expected; even so, the intermediation of the Guardian Council is wholly incompatible with a properly functioning democracy. It's no wonder that President

---

* Article 93. The only exception is in respect of the power of the Majlis to approve six members of the Guardian Council.
† The Guardian Council is composed of twelve members: six clerics, appointed by the Supreme Leader, and six lawyers, appointed by the head of the judiciary (himself appointed by the Supreme Leader), but subject to approval by the Majlis.

Rouhani reportedly told reformist figures at an Iftar* party in May 2019: 'The government has no authority in foreign politics, doesn't know where/when it is allowed or not to negotiate; cultural policies, IRIB state TV, mosques and cyberspace aren't under government control,' according to journalist Fereshteh Sadeghi.[3]

The singular feature of the Iranian system is the position of Khamenei, the Supreme Leader. Every one of the coercive powers of the state – the police, the judiciary, the intelligence agencies, the army, the Basij and the IRGC – is vested in him. Elected ministers have no role. Thus, two loyal servants of the revolution, and candidates in the 2009 election – Mousavi and Karroubi – have been under house arrest since 2011; some reactionary MPs have even called for their execution.[4] Their 'crimes'? Campaigning for a more liberal Iran. Former President Khatami has been declared a kind of 'non-person'. He cannot travel abroad, and the Tehran prosecutor has prohibited the media from reporting his words or publishing his photograph because of his support for Mousavi and Karroubi.

When he was first elected, Rouhani indicated that he would help secure Mousavi's and Karroubi's release. Six years later, they remain under arrest. Rouhani can plead with Khamenei, and those running the judiciary, for clemency. In response, Khamenei and the deep state can ignore such pleas, as they routinely do.

It's the same story with a dual British-Iranian national, Mrs Nazanin Zaghari-Ratcliffe, who has been detained in Iranian jails since April 2016 and sentenced to five years' imprisonment for allegedly plotting against the regime. She was on a family visit at the time.

British ministers and diplomats have tried hard to secure Mrs Zaghari-Ratcliffe's release, but they can talk only to officials within the elected Rouhani government. As Foreign Minister Javad Zarif explained in the quotation at the head of this chapter, 'We in the government have no control over the judiciary.'

---

* 'Iftar' – breaking of the fast at sundown during Ramadan.

All properly functioning democracies have a judicial system which is at arm's length from the executive. But, at the same time, these systems all derive their powers from an elected legislature, and elected ministers have reserve powers to intervene. In the UK, where the judiciary is at the far end of the spectrum of independence, the Attorney-General can intervene to stop a prosecution, and the Lord Chancellor to grant a pardon (as I did on a number of occasions). Here, as in other democracies, the police, the armed forces and the intelligence agencies are all subject to active supervision by our elected Parliament and ministers. Such control is wholly absent in Iran. The rule of law there is a flexible, fungible concept, and not that different from how the system operated under the Shahs.

In consequence, the real President of the Islamic Republic is not Rouhani, who can serve for only two consecutive terms, but Khamenei, effectively President for life. As we have seen, he formally derives his authority from his status as the guardian of the occulted twelfth imam, awaiting his return. But with the passage of time that theological justification has worn thin. He has never been a jurist of the highest order. Much more than Khomeini ever did, he has simply behaved like any other working politician – but one with more power than anyone else, above all through his direct control of the IRGC, the Basij and the courts.

* * *

On the surface, in Tehran and other cities of Iran, all may appear calm, orderly and devout. Women all wear their headscarves, as required by law; the devout turn up in their thousands to religious ceremonies, as they did in their tens of thousands to rallies to celebrate the fortieth anniversary of the Islamic Revolution (though if they are state employees, they are required to attend).

Just below the surface, Iran is far from calm. The regime is going one way; the majority of the population the other. Iran is full of paradoxes, a mass of contradictions; some Iranians say that they have to live their lives by masking its reality from the deep state, shrouding it in lies.

Walk round Tehran or any big city and for sure most women will routinely be wearing their headscarves. But observe more closely. The headscarves on many women, middle-aged as well as young, are pushed back as far as possible, in insolent defiance to the old men who lay down how women should dress.* The women's eyes and faces are heavily made-up. Under a loose coat they may be wearing the tightest of tight jeans.

Iranian women have amongst the highest use of cosmetics in the world, per head of population. As Misagh Parsa, an Iranian-American commentator, points out, 'Makeup professionals estimated that Iranian women bought one tube of mascara every month, in contrast with one in every four months purchased by French women. In a population that ranked seventeenth in the world, Iran's consumption of makeup was seventh.'[5]

All this might appear as something of a game, like teenage school-girls in the UK constantly challenging their school's uniform policy by raising the hems of their skirts. But in Iran this defiance can have serious consequences. It can bring these women into conflict with the official 'Morality Police', a police force to ensure compliance with the rules. In three months in 2014, for example, 220,000 women were taken to a police station to sign statements promising the proper use of the headscarf, and 8,269 women were detained for this offence, according to the Ministry of the Interior.[6]

TV and radio in Iran are strictly controlled. Though there is some plurality in the print media, with hardline and moderate newspapers, there's much self-censorship to avoid the peremptory closure of titles. A reformist paper was shut down in February 2019 by the regime for using the title 'Unwanted guest' on a front cover that showed a picture of Khamenei with the Syrian President Bashar Assad.[7] The

---

* There have been repeated protests by some women, refusing to wear their headscarves at all.

state devotes significant resources to filtering the internet and at times blocking social media sites like Facebook and Twitter – not that this has stopped the Supreme Leader himself from occasionally using his own Twitter account. Foreign television channels, including BBC Persian, are periodically jammed.

Despite the risks they may run, millions of Iranians use their ingenuity to get round this censorship. More open access to the internet is secured through virtual private networks (VPNs); fly over any city or town and see the roofs festooned with (illegal) satellite dishes. BBC Persian plays cat and mouse by switching satellites. One way or another, 11 million or so watch BBC Persian, and millions more watch a wide range of other foreign TV channels, many from Turkey. The state claimed that they had confiscated 270,000 satellite dishes in 2015.[8] But foreign broadcasters still enjoy large audiences. The deep state is losing the battle to stop people from watching or listening to what they want.

There is, however, one group in Iran who do not have to go to these lengths to evade the rigid codes of the Islamic Republic. These are families of the elite which runs the country. They are known, sarcastically, as the 'aghazadeh', or 'noble born'. One of the charges against the rule of the Shahs was that the country was run by a thousand families who enriched themselves at the expense of the poor. Khomeini insisted that all should lead modest lives, 'in huts not palaces', that he was leader of the 'dispossessed' (mostazafin) of the world. Now, however, the thousand families close to the royal households have been replaced by those families close to the power centres of the Islamic Republic. There are incessant reports of these families openly flaunting their wealth and their luxurious lifestyles – whilst living standards for the majority go downhill fast.

The examples are endless, not least because these 'aghazadeh' have little shame about posting photographs of themselves on Instagram. Thus, the son of retired General Saeed Tolouei of the IRGC is shown posing with a pet tiger, driving a Cadillac and throwing a lavish party for his two-year-old daughter.[9]

Even Khomeini's family itself has shown no respect for the memory of the Grand Ayatollah. During a recent visit to London, Khomeini's great-granddaughter Yasaman Eshraghi published on Instagram a picture of herself with a $3,800 Dolce & Gabbana handbag, alongside an expensive BMW. Khomeini's great-grandson Ahmad Khomeini, a 21-year-old cleric, was shown in a photograph at an equestrian club wearing fashionable imported gear, standing next to a young woman in a riding helmet. The post caused outrage, but this did little to stem the lifestyles of this elite.[10]

Other 'sons of notables' display their contempt for the average Iranian even more openly. The *Arab Weekly* carried a report that Mohammad-Reza Sobhani, the son of a former Iranian Ambassador to Venezuela,

> systematically uploads photos of himself enjoying champagne at the pool, occasionally with naked women in the background. Other photos show him driving a Bugatti and lighting his cigarettes with dollar bills. In a video on Instagram, he urged people not to be so nosy about his lavish lifestyle: 'Instead of envying me, go make some money. If you can't make money and you can't make a living, die. Full Stop!'[11]

No one in Iran believes that all this wealth could have been acquired lawfully; the salaries of Iranian officials, whether diplomats or in the IRGC, are wholly insufficient for that. Rather, these illustrations are an indication not just of the pervasive financial corruption of the system but of its moral corruption, which is eating away at the legitimacy of the regime from the inside.

The abuse by the elite is not confined to conservatives but extends to reformers as well; one more reason why the alienation of the ordinary public from the whole of the elite is so strong, and cynicism about them so powerful.

* * *

'Nothing would be what it is, because everything would be what it isn't,' wrote Lewis Carroll in *Alice's Adventures in Wonderland*. It is a bit like that in Iran. Take sex and alcohol. The rigid codes on women's dress in public, the ban on them attending soccer games, the requirement that they must have their husband's or father's permission to go abroad, are justified on the grounds of necessity – of preserving 'the modesty of women' (as well as having the obvious function of male domination). But the furtive touching and the odd surreptitious assignation which one can sometimes observe in public is simply the tip of the iceberg. What actually goes on in private is brought out in forensic detail in Ramita Navai's fascinating book *City of Lies: Love, Sex, Death and the Search for Truth in Tehran*, an extract from which is quoted at the head of this chapter. Iranians appear to be one thing in public but are quite another in private, because the rules of the regime are not those which so many in Iran wish to follow. The tension in Iran is not just between the individual and the state, but between the generations. There's a hilarious account in Christopher de Bellaigue's *In the Rose Garden of the Martyrs*, in which the author discusses the attitude of lust and sex amongst young seminarians in the holy city of Qom with a man in a tea house.[12]

Islamic law in Iran has, too, a curiosity which goes a little way to acknowledging the reality of relationships between men and women. This is 'sigheh', temporary marriage: legal, short-term marriage contracts which can last for anything from a couple of hours to many decades. In one report of this arrangement, a mullah in a park gets talking to a young (foreign) woman who wants to live with her Iranian boyfriend. The mullah 'whipped out a notepad and asked how long we wanted the marriage to be and how much money [the boyfriend] would settle on me. And then he signed it ... and that was that.'[13]

As mentioned earlier, alcohol is officially banned in Iran – but it is so widely available that it is now recognised more as a public health issue than as a criminal one. According to *The Economist*, the Iranians' use of alcohol ranked third amongst majority Muslim countries as early as 2003–05, exceeded on a per capita basis only by Lebanon and Turkey, where its sale and consumption is legal.[14]

The Basij who ransacked the British compounds in 2011 smashed most things they could – ornaments, paintings, furniture – but stole the liquor without breaking its bottles. They would have had a reason for doing so.

There are plenty of ways of making palatable alcohol, from non-alcoholic beer through grape juice to the distillation of spirits. The ever-ingenious Iranians have it all worked out.

This split world, of public face and private face, is but one indication that Iran is not a country at peace with itself. Beyond what people do in their private homes, there is a constant anxiety for many Iranians of falling foul of the 'authorities'. But who exactly are they, and what might they do?

It's not just the reformers who can and do end up in jail. When he was President, Ahmadinejad would never have dreamt that the worm might turn and two of his most senior colleagues would now be incarcerated – by some of the same people who were previously cheering him on. It cannot make for a peaceful night's sleep.

* * *

A British diplomat with years of experience of serving in Iran, as well as elsewhere in the region, told me, 'Iran is the most secular country in the Middle East.' There's a reason for this – the pull of Iranian culture, with both its strong secular elements and its still-surviving Zoroastrian traditions, like Nowruz. There's been a worrying decline for the elite in the numbers attending mosques regularly. 'People laugh at all the nonsense the mullahs are telling them,' says Darioush Bayandor, a former Iranian diplomat.[15]

Most ominous of all for the elite's future, in my view, is the large number of educated Iranians who leave the country each year. *The Economist* suggested that this was at a rate of 150,000 per annum.[16] Whether it is running at this level or some thousands fewer, it's palpable how many highly qualified Iranians there are in a wide diaspora across the world, who could in better times be making a very important contribution to Iran's development.

'Tehran today reminds me of Prague or Budapest in the 1980s,' one British diplomat who had served both in the Eastern Bloc and in Iran told me. 'There's an uneasiness; the conversations behind cupped hands; and the appreciation that something is going to have to give.'

The question is, what will give first?

The hardline elite in Iran today suffer from intense insecurity, personal and institutional. To take our own experience: what was so threatening for the IRGC and the Basij about having my wife, our friends and me take a holiday – no more – amongst delightful Iranians, and their astonishing history, that they had to set about disrupting our holiday so badly that we had to leave? How does that help the respect for these institutions amongst ordinary Iranians, or the reputation of Iran more widely? (And I have sufficient affection for Iran that I'd be pleased to go back. It will be interesting to see whether I can.)

But the evidence of the hardliners' insecurity runs much deeper. It was exhibited in the suppression of the 2009 Green Movement; in the way that since the New Year of 2018 the authorities have been putting down protests and strikes; in their jailing of dual nationals like Mrs Zaghari-Ratcliffe; in the continued detention of a former Prime Minister and Speaker of the Majlis, Mousavi and Karroubi; and their silencing of former President Khatami for speaking out against repression.

Central to the elite's difficulties is that they have bought into the mythology of *velayat-e faqih*, the guardianship of the jurist. The form this notion took in the Islamic Republic's constitution, of the secular guardianship of the whole of the state and its people, was literally invented by Khomeini. Though the idea could be traced back to Plato (whom Khomeini studied), it has no serious provenance in Shi'a texts. It was contested at the time of the revolution by many other jurists and has been consistently rejected by the greatest of Shi'a jurists alive today, Grand Ayatollah Sistani, based in Najaf. At least Khomeini had some idea of its limits. Khamenei has widened and widened the concept as justification for the coercive institutions of the state, particularly since 2009.

The elite of the regime know they do not carry popular legitimacy. If they did, they would not be frightened by the prospect of a governmental system where there were free elections, and which controlled the whole of the state's operations, as is normal.

Supreme Leader Ali Khamenei is seventy-nine at the time of writing. He is not in good health. He may try to hang on to power through his eighties and into his nineties, as Robert Mugabe did in Zimbabwe. There have even been suggestions that he would like his second son, Mojtaba, to succeed him. But it is probable that in the next few years he will relinquish his post; many others of his generation, those who in their thirties and forties were active in the revolution and have been in control ever since, are now passing.

Whenever Khamenei ceases to be Supreme Leader, those around him, and those dependent on the Supreme Leader's authority, particularly the IRGC, will strive hard to retain the enormous power they have, and the wealth which has gone with that power. What mocks the record of the Islamic Republic as much as anything else is that for all the rhetoric about the needs of ordinary Iranians, Iran has significantly greater levels of inequality than the United Kingdom – and our record is nothing of which to be proud.

For the future, we could see a continuation of more of the same; if there were serious unrest, always bubbling below the surface, there could be the institution of a military dictatorship cloaked by the ideology of *velayat-e faqih*. Were serious protests to occur, the reaction of the international community would be very important. The lesson of 2009 is that the regime will blame the US and the UK regardless of whether these two governments are silent or not; so better to be vocal in support of the Iranian people.

Alternatively, we could see Iran start down the road towards more open and democratic institutions. Some within the country have already been brave enough to call for such change. Reformist Islamic Iran Participation Front senior member Mostafa Tajzadeh (previously jailed for dissidence) has proposed that the post of President be merged with that of the Supreme Leader, who would then have to be elected to that office and would be allowed to serve no more than two terms.[17]

Iran is a proud country and intensely nationalistic. It cries out for respect and recognition in the international community. For all the increasing secularity of much of its population, its Shi'ism is deeply rooted in its sense of what being an Iranian means.

Whilst Iran's future is unclear, there is one thing of which I am certain.

What happens to Iran internally will in significant part be influenced by how Iran is treated by the outside world. This is more true for Iran than for any other country I know, for the reasons I have spelt out. The more that the reformists can point to the benefits to Iran of cooperating with the world outside, the more empowered they will be, and the less and less convincing will be the hardliners' position to their own people.

There is a dynamic in play in Iran today that is profoundly unsettling to the regime. That was underlined by the leading reformist cleric Grand Ayatollah Naser Makarem-Shirazi, in the passage quoted at the head of this chapter, when he said that 'no danger from foreign enemies can threaten us ... but we will face domestic dangers from divisive, profiteering and hardline individuals'. Or, to put it another way, the English job is no longer. It's now an internal one. These days, more often than '*kar kareh ingilisee hast*' (it's always an English job), the complaint is '*kar kareh khodeshoon hast*' (it's always an internal [regime] job).

The international community can help or hinder that dynamic, not by the covert methods it resorted to in the past, with such disastrous consequences, but by understanding and honouring Iran and its people, working to end its isolation, and speaking out against the continuing excesses of the regime.

APPENDIX

BASIJ LEAFLET IN ENGLISH AND PERSIAN

In the name of God

On behalf of the revolutionary youth of Daralababadeh, Yazd, to the former Foreign Minister of Britain Mr Jack Straw!

We have heard that for the past several days you have stepped foot in Daralababadeh, Yazd, as part of your travels and holidays. Although it is in our tradition as Iranians to 'welcome' guests and we have a hospitable culture that we abide by, this 'welcome' gesture does not apply to you! To be honest with you, we are not at all happy with your presence in our town. Not only are we not happy, we're negative and suspicious! We don't have a good feeling about you walking on the soil of Daralababadeh of Iran.

These days our town and our country is wearing black and is mourning the Seyed of the Martyrs (PBUH) [Imam Hussain, peace be upon him], and in the hosseiniyes [mosques] of Iran people are deeply mourning for Imam Hussain in a special and heartfelt way. During these days the blood of the young Shi'a is boiling because of the injustices caused to the Prophet's (PBUH) family and several times a day they cry 'Harb laman harabokom', therefore we are annoyed and hurt by the fact that someone like you is on holiday enjoying yourself.

Mr Straw!

The people of Iran do not have good memories about you and the British regime. Our historical memory remembers scenes that were bad and exploitative of British presence in Iran.

You know better than us about the crimes and the ample plots that were orchestrated by your country against the people of this holy land.

We have not forgotten the 'Paris Treaty' and separation of Afghanistan from Iran!

The cunning contracts of Darcy, Talbot, Reuters, Reji etc. are still fresh in our history.

We have not forgotten how you spun the Constitutional Revolution of Iran and in doing so you produced a dictator who listens to your orders.

We have not forgotten that for years you had your tentacles engaged in Iran's natural resources, in particular stealing and looting Iran's oil.

We still have in our memories the occupation of our country by you and your allies during the world war, and the imposition of famine on our people, which caused the illness and death of thousands of our vulnerable countrymen.

We have not forgotten how you planned to oust Reza Khan and install his son, Mohammad Reza.

We remember the clear and direct role your cunning actions played during the *coup d'état* of 28 Mordad [19 August 1953].

We have not forgotten the support, financial and material aid you gave to Saddam, from armored vehicles and assistance to Saddam, which caused bloodshed in our country.

We still have in our memories the various methods of support that your colonial regime has provided terrorist groups against the Islamic Republic.

We have kept in our memories the English government's participation in the cruel and cowardly sanctions against the people of Iran.

We still hold a grudge and spite against the insults from people such as you against the officials of our country during the nuclear negotiations at Sadadabad Palace.

We remember during the Sedition of '88 [Green Movement protests of 2009], the way in which you supported the heads of the sedition, expensive turmoil and the troublemakers.

Mr Straw!

Although the listed crimes and seditions of the British regime will be familiar to you and for us is painful, we thought we'd say them so that you know we are not forgetful people and we know you very well. It's because of these dark historical plots that Iranians have given Britain the nickname of 'the old colonial fox' and will never have a good feeling about the presence and appearance of the English in their country.

Since we heard about your presence in Yazd, we are concerned about the plans that are being made [against Iran by the English]. Jack Straw comes to Iran and then travels to Yazd?! In his presence what sedition is planning to occur, and we think this way because the negative and hateful sedition of Britain is ingrained in our psyche.

These days us youths of Hosseineh Iran are mourners for the grand Seyed of the Martyrs (PBUH), and we revise the lessons and his historical prophecy to Shia followers. Every day and night within ourselves we cry 'Hayhaat mena zela' ['We won't bow down to cruelty'].

The spiritual children of Imam Khamenei have their hawk eyes open towards the plots and conspiracies of America and England and the occupying Zionist regime. Don't think that our current political situation in Iran following the nuclear agreement has opened a space for the presence of you and your allies.

Soldiers of Khamenei these days will follow their Supreme Leader's revolutionary patience and will close the open spaces in Imam Khomeini's revolution through their cultural and political jihad.

Know that in our gut we have held our spite and grudges against the enemies of the Islamic revolution until we find the right moment to release revenge upon them and be sure that on that day, even the old cunning fox wont be able to escape these grudges.

Students group of Yazd University
The Students of Yazd's Basij
The Group of Ansaareh Velayat of Daralabadeh Yazd
The Group of Shahid Mujahed Seyed Abbas Mousavi
The Cultural Institute of the school of Eshgh
The Culutral Insititute of Borouj Daralabadeh
The Cultural and Societal Institution of 9 Day Daralabadeh
Cultural School of Imam Mahdi
The Institute of Hazrateh Monjee
The Institute of Seema Khorsheed
The Institution Raheh Ayandeh
The Group Ansar Amir Al Momenin
The Group of Fatehmeh's Children
The Club of Andisheh Motahar
The Cultural Islamic Institute Yazd

بسم الله الرحمن الرحیم

از طرف جمعی از جوانان انقلابی دارالعباده یزد به وزیر اسبق امورخارجه بریتانیا؛

آقای جک استراو!

شنیده‌ایم چندروزی است برای تفریح و گردشگری به دارالعباده یزد قدم گذاشته‌اید. البته که رسم ما ایرانی‌ها این است که حضور مهمان را خیرمقدم و «خوش‌آمد» گفته و آداب مهمان‌نوازی را به جا می‌آوریم؛ اما زبان ما به «خوش‌آمدگویی» به شما نمی‌چرخد! راستش را بخواهید ما از حضور شما در شهرمان اصلاً خوشحال نیستیم. نه که خوشحال نباشیم، بدبین و مشکوکیم! از اینکه روی خاک دارالعباده ایران قدم می‌زنید احساس خوبی نداریم.

این روزها شهر و کشور ما سیاه پوش عزای سیدالشهداء(ع) است و حسینیه ایران خاص‌تر و ویژه‌تر در تب و تاب مظلومیت و شهادت امام حسین(ع) به عزاداری مشغول است. اینکه در چنین روزهایی که خون بچه شیعه‌ها از ظلم و ستم رفته بر خاندان پیامبر(ص) به جوش است و روزی چند بار «حرب لمن حاربکم» بر زبان‌شان می‌گذرد، کسی مثل شما در این شهر به تفریح و قدم‌زنی مشغول است، بیشتر آزارمان می‌دهد.

آقای استراو!

مردم ایران خاطرات خوبی از شما و حکومت بریتانیا در ذهن ندارند. حافظه تاریخی ما صحنه‌های بد و آزاردهنده‌ای از حضور انگلیسی‌ها در ایران به یاد می‌آورد!

خودتان بهتر می‌دانید که چه جنایات و توطئه‌های فراوانی به دست کشور شما علیه مردم این سرزمین مقدس رفته است.

ما «پیمان پاریس» و جدا کردن افغانستان از ایران را یادمان نرفته است!

قراردادهای حیله‌گرانه دارسی، تالبوت، رویترز، رژی و... هنوز در تاریخ ما مانده است!

یادمان نرفته چطور انقلاب مشروطه ایران را به انحراف کشاندید و از دل آن دیکتاتوری گوش به فرمان خود در آوردید!

سال‌ها چنبره بر منابع طبیعی و به خصوص دزدی و غارت نفت ایران را هم فراموش نکرده‌ایم!

اشغال کشورمان به دست شما و همدستان‌تان در جنگ جهانی و تحمیل قحطی به مردم و بیماری و مرگ و میر هزاران نفر از هم‌وطنان مظلوم‌مان را در ذهن داریم!

نقشه شوم حکومت شما برای فرار رضاخان از ایران و روی کار آوردن پسرش، محمدرضا هم فراموش نکرده‌ایم!

نقش آشکار و مستقیم اسلاف حیله‌گر شما در کودتای سیاه ۲۸ مرداد را خوب به یاد داریم!

حمایت‌ها و کمک‌های مالی و معنوی شما از ماشین جنگی صدام و یاری او در به خاک و خون کشاندن سرزمین‌مان را از یاد نبرده‌ایم!

پناه دادن به نویسنده مرتد و موهن به قرآن و اسلام نیز در کارنامه ننگین بریتانیا ثبت است!

انواع و اقسام حمایت‌های حکومت استعمارگر شما از گروهک‌های تروریستی و معاند با جمهوری اسلامی در خاطره ما هست!

۱

مشارکت دولت انگلیس در تحریم‌های ظالمانه و ناجوانمردانه علیه مردم ایران را در حافظه‌مان نگه داشته‌ایم!

از توهین گستاخانه شخص شما به مسئولان کشورمان در جریان مذاکرات هسته‌ای سال‌ها پیش در کاخ سعدآباد، هنوز بغض و کینه داریم!

یادمان هست در جریان فتنه سال ۸۸ چگونه از سران فتنه و اغتشاش‌گران و اراذل و اوباش حمایت کردید!

آقای استراو!

اگرچه لیست کردن جنایات و فتنه‌گری‌های حکومت بریتانیا برای شما تکراری است و برای ما دردآور، اما گفتیم که بدانید ما فراموش‌کار نیستیم و شما را خوب می‌شناسیم. به خاطر همین سیاهه توطئه‌های تاریخی است که ایرانی‌ها لقب «روباه پیر استعمار» را به بریتانیا داده‌اند و هیچ وقت دل خوشی از حضور و ظهور انگلیسی‌ها در کشورشان نداشته‌اند.

از وقتی خبر حضور شما را در یزد شنیده‌ایم، در این فکر هستیم که باز چه نقشه‌ای در کار است؟! جک استراو چرا به ایران و آن هم به یزد سفر کرده است؟! چه فتنه‌ای قرار است سر پی -عنصر او رخ دهد؟؛ و این به -خاطر سابقه منفی و نفرتی است که از فتنه‌گری‌های انگلستان در حافظه تاریخی ما نهادینه شده است.

این روزها ما جوانان حسینیه ایران، عزادار حضرت سیدالشهدا(ع) هستیم و درس و رسالت تاریخی ایشان به شیعیان‌شان را مرور می‌کنیم و هر روز و شب «هیهات منا الذله» حسین(ع) را درون خود فریاد می‌زنیم.

چشمان تیزبین فرزندان معنوی امام خامنه‌ای به روی دسیسه‌های پلید آمریکا و انگلیس و رژیم غاصب صهیونیستی باز است. خیال نکنید فضای سیاسی حاکم بر ایران و پذیرش توافق هسته‌ای می‌تواند روزنه‌های نفوذ شما و یاران‌تان را به این نظام باز کند. سربازان خامنه‌ای این روزها به پیروی از رهبری صبر انقلابی می‌کنند و با جهاد فرهنگی و سیاسی خود راه‌های استحاله انقلاب امام خمینی را خواهند بست.

بدانید که ما بغض و کینه‌مان علیه دشمنان این انقلاب اسلامی را در دل نگه داشته‌ایم تا در موعد مقرر بر سرشان خالی کنیم و مطمئن باشید آن روز، روباه پیر استعمار هم از این کینه در امان نخواهد ماند.

هیات انصار ولایت دارالعباده یزد	بسیج دانشجویی دانشگاه یزد	جامعه اسلامی دانشجویان دانشگاه یزد
موسسه فرهنگی عروج دارالعباده	موسسه فرهنگی مدرسه عشق	گروه شهید مجاهد سیدعباس موسوی
موسسه حضرت منجی	فرهنگسرای امام مهدی(ع)	موسسه فرهنگی اجتماعی ۹ دی دارالعباده
هیات انصار امیرالمومنین(ع)	موسسه راه آینده	موسسه سیمای خورشید
موسسه اندیشه و فرهنگ اسلامی یزد	کانون اندیشه مطهر	هیات بچه‌های فاطمه
موسسه فرهنگی بهشت دارالعباده	کانون جوانان مسجد الزهرا یزد	هیات شهدای گمنام یزد
مرکز پژوهشی سید شهیدان اهل قلم	مجمع هم‌اندیشی نخبگان استان یزد	کانون فرهنگی شهید بهشتی
دبیرخانه اندیشه ناب یزد	کانون شهید مفتح یزد	موسسه فرهنگی هنری طریقت
موسسه طلوع جوان	هیات طهورا	موسسه قرآنی مصباح الهدی نور یزد

۲

ACKNOWLEDGEMENTS

After my first visit as Foreign Secretary to Iran in late September 2001, I thought that this country was so pivotal to international peace and security, and so little comprehended in the West, that I needed better to understand it. At the suggestion of my wife, Alice Perkins, the Foreign Office organised a series of seminars for me. It was through these that I began to know a number of the UK's great experts on Iran, and my abiding interest in the country, which has led to this book, was born.

Amongst those were Professor Ali Ansari, director of St Andrews' Institute for Iranian Studies and author of some important works, including *Modern Iran Since 1921: The Pahlavis and After* and *Confronting Iran: The Failure of American Foreign Policy and the Roots of Mistrust*.

Professor Ansari has had an important influence on my approach to Iran (in office and out of it), and so did the late Dr Michael Axworthy. Dr Axworthy began his professional life in the FCO and was posted to Tehran between 1998 and 2000, but he was an academic at heart. From 2005, he taught Iranian studies at the University of Exeter and authored a number of influential works on Iran, including *Iran: Empire of the Mind – A History from Zoroaster to the Present Day* and *Revolutionary Iran: A History of the Islamic Republic*. Tragically, he died on 16 March 2019, from cancer, at the age of fifty-six. I pay tribute to Michael as a brilliant expert on Iran and a good friend.

The historian and author Professor Michael Burleigh, neighbour and friend, was incredibly helpful, lending me various works on Iran and commenting on the whole of my manuscript.

Unlike most domestic government departments, the FCO has paid attention to its collective memory. It has a team of expert research analysts and historians. I am greatly indebted to them, and to all the diplomats who have been or are still dealing with Iran. Some of those were happy to be quoted by name; others more reluctant. In the event, I decided it would be best not to name any of them – apart from other considerations, I have no wish to make their lives difficult if they do return to serve in our Tehran Embassy. It's been a privilege to talk to them about this book, and it's been a reminder of the excellence of the British diplomatic corps. I can, however, express my thanks by name to Sir Dominick Chilcott, his wife Jane, and to Jane Marriott – each of whom were in Tehran during the frightening invasion of our Embassy in November 2011 and have provided me with extensive notes (see Chapter 19). I should like to add thanks to the staff of the FCO Knowledge Management Department at their base at Hanslope Park, who carefully assembled files for me to read through.

I had indirectly used the London Library many times when I was an MP; if the Commons Library doesn't have a book in its own stock, it invariably is able to borrow it from the London Library. I joined this library when I left the Commons in 2015. Its services, and its vast range of works under 'History – Persia', have proved invaluable. So too the resources, and staff, of the National Archives at Kew.

Some of the senior diplomats with whom I worked on Iran as Foreign Secretary have now retired from the FCO, and I can name them. I am very grateful to Sir John Sawers, Sir Peter Westmacott and his Iranian wife Susie Nemazee, Sir David Reddaway, Lord Ricketts, Sir Simon Gass, Sir Richard Dalton, Edward Chaplin – and to many other former diplomats.

Former US Secretaries of State Colin Powell and Condoleezza Rice gave me great assistance with the section about the so-called Grand Bargain (Chapter 16) and valuable insights on other matters.

I am greatly indebted to Dr Karin von Hippel, director-general of the Royal United Services Institute (RUSI), to deputy director Professor Malcolm Chalmers and to research fellow Dr Aniseh Bassiri Tabrizi and other RUSI colleagues for all their work on Iran, which has made this book a better one. I am also very grateful to the chairman of RUSI, Lord (William) Hague, for his support and a very generous endorsement of the book, as I am to Bridget Kendall, former BBC diplomatic correspondent, now Master of Peterhouse College, Cambridge.

Lord (Norman) Lamont has always spoken out courageously to seek a more balanced international understanding of Iran. I've travelled with him twice to Tehran, and I am very grateful to him for his friendship and for his acute comments on much of my draft.

In my last parliament (2010–15), I took on a very bright graduate student, Kasra Aarabi, whose parents are Iranian and who speaks good Persian, to work with me on Iran. In the past two years, Kasra has helped me immensely with the writing of the book – and I owe its title to him. I am most grateful to him.

I have many other British-Iranian and Iranian friends who have helped me with this book in various ways. However, given that some of them travel back to Iran and some live there, and given the paranoia of the Iranian regime, I have thought it best not to name any of them – and to change their names where I do refer to them in the text.

Many thanks, too, to my literary agent, Georgina Capel, and to the team at Biteback – James Stephens, Suzanne Sangster, Ellen Heaney, Namkwan Cho and my editor, Olivia Beattie, who's been quite brilliant. She combined a great strategic overview of my manuscript together with a forensic eye on my syntax and grammar. I have enjoyed working with them all.

This book is dedicated to my two children, William and Charlotte, now in their thirties with families of their own. They are wonderful – ever loyal, yet ready in private to challenge me. Both read and commented on large sections of the draft. My dedication comes with love and respect.

My final thanks are for my wife of forty years, Alice, who endured that ill-fated 'holiday' in Iran with me in October 2015. She brought all her skills as a former senior civil servant to work through draft after draft. I could not have written the book without her.

If I have omitted thanks where they are due, my apologies. I am extremely grateful to everyone who has helped with this book. But its views, and any errors, are entirely mine.

Jack Straw
June 2019

ENDNOTES

Chapter 1: 'English Is Not the Enemy'
1   From the epic poem *Shahnameh* by the Persian poet Abu 'I-Qasim Ferdowsi, quoted by Abbas Amanat in *Iran: A Modern History* (Yale, 2017), p. 5.

Chapter 2: It's Always an English Job
1   Ali Shamkhani, the Secretary of the Supreme National Security Council, said that the US, the UK and Saudi Arabia were inciting these protests by their use of hashtags and social media campaigns. See, for instance, 'Iran's Supreme Leader blames "enemies" for protests, death toll hits 21', CNN, 2 January 2018.
2   'Iran elections: Reformists make gains in Assembly of Experts', BBC News, 29 February 2016.
3   Story relayed to the author by Sir David Logan, former UK Ambassador to Turkey.
4   Originally published as a novel in Iran in 1973, and in English translation by the Modern Library, New York, in 2006. The book was banned under the Islamic Republic but it, and videos of the TV series, thrive underground.
5   *Financial Times*, 24 May 2008.

Chapter 3: From Fire to Allah
1   Bernard Lewis, *Iran in History* (Tel Aviv University).
2   Tom Holland, *Persian Fire* (Abacus, 2005), p. xxii.
3   Gerard Russell, *Heirs to Forgotten Kingdoms* (Simon & Schuster, 2014), p. 112.
4   Friedrich Nietzsche, *Ecce Homo*, 'Why I Am a Destiny', §3. Available in Penguin Classics, 2005, translated by R. J. Hollingdale. Nietzsche devoted a whole work to this subject, *Thus Spake Zarathustra* (1883). Available in Penguin Classics, 1974, translated by R. J. Hollingdale.
5   *Oxford Concise Dictionary of World Religions* (Oxford University Press, 2005), p. 660.
6   Michael Axworthy, *Iran: Empire of the Mind: A History from Zoroaster to the Present Day* (Penguin, 2008), p. 87.

Chapter 4: Shah Ismail I – Iran's Henry VIII
1   Amanat, op. cit., p. 37.
2   Vali Nasr, *The Shia Revival: How Conflicts Within Islam Will Shape the Future* (W. W. Norton & Co., 2006), p. 57.
3   Preamble to the Act.
4   Nasr, op. cit., pp. 38–9.
5   Amanat, op. cit., p. 98.
6   David Blow (ed.), *Persia: Through Writers' Eyes* (Eland, 2007), pp. 93–4.
7   *Sir Anthony Sherley: His Relation of his Travels into Persia* (1613), Bodleian Library, Oxford.
8   See Amanat, op. cit., p. 99.

Chapter 5: The British Monopolies That Triggered Democracy
1   *Etemad* (a moderate newspaper), 13 August 2018, 'Rouhani's Government and Iran's Share of Caspian Sea: A Convention which is not Turkmenchay'.
2   Published by Adam and Charles Black in 1893, republished by Forgotten Books in 2012.
3   *The Times*, 2 March 1931.
4   Geoffrey Jones, *Entrepreneurship and Multinationals: Global Business and the Making of the Modern World* (Edward Elgar Publishing, 2013), p. 111.
5   René de Balloy, French archives, quoted by Nikki R. Kiddie, *Religion and Rebellion in Iran* (Cass, 1966), p. 100.
6   The Controller-General of Persia estimated domestic production at 5.4 million kilos and exports at 4 million kilos. See Edward Granville Browne, *The Persian Revolution of 1905–1909* (Cambridge University Press, 1910), p. 47.
7   Ibid., p. 35.
8   Ibid., p. 15.
9   Guildhall Banquet, 8 March 1890.

10 Quoted in full in Browne, op. cit., pp. 15–21.
11 Amanat, op. cit., p. 205.
12 Browne, op. cit., p. 57.

Chapter 6: How Oil Trumped Democracy

1 FO 416/28, Grant Duff to Foreign Secretary, 18 June 1906.
2 FO 416/28, telegrams Duff to Grey and Grey to Duff, 15 August 1906.
3 Ibid.
4 Article 2 of the Supplementary Fundamental Laws of 7 October 1907. These provisions, and the Fundamental Laws of 30 December 1906 and 7 October 1907, and two Electoral Laws, are set out in full in Browne, op. cit., pp. 355–400.
5 Browne, op. cit., p. 195.
6 *The Times*, 25 June 1908.
7 Clarmont Skrine, *World War in Iran* (Constable, 1962), pp. xv, 37.
8 Ibid., pp. 25, 26.
9 President Wilson's Address to Congress, 11 February 1918.
10 See *Documents on British Foreign Policy 1919–39*, First Series, Vol. IV, Chapter V, p. 1120 (HMSO, 1952). (Quoted in Skrine, op. cit., p. 59.)
11 FO 371/3862, quoted in Gilmore, *Curzon* (Farrar, Straus & Giroux, 1994), p. 515.
12 J. M. Balfour, *Recent Happenings in Persia* (Blackwood, 1922), p. 130.
13 Quoted in Skrine, op. cit., p. 62.
14 Balfour, op. cit., p. 189.
15 Minute from Curzon, 26 October 1922, FO 371/7810, quoted in David Gilmour, *Curzon: Imperial Statesman* (Farrar, Straus & Giroux, 1994), p. 519.
16 FO 371/7810, quoted in Gilmour, ibid., p. 518.
17 FO 416/68, Norman to Curzon, 8 January 1921.

Chapter 7: Sergeant to Shah – with British Help

1 Sir Edmund Ironside, *High Road to Command: The Diaries of Major-General Sir Edmund Ironside* (Leo Cooper, 1972), p. 117.
2 Ibid., p. 145.
3 Ibid.
4 Ibid., p. 149.
5 Balfour, op. cit., p. 211.
6 FO 416/68, 7 January 1921.
7 Balfour, op. cit., p. 214.
8 Ironside, op. cit., pp. 161, 177–8.
9 FO 416/68, Norman to Curzon, 21 February 1921.
10 Balfour, op. cit., p. 228.
11 FO371/6401, 1 March 1921.
12 Harold Nicolson, *Curzon: The Last Phase, 1919–1925* (Constable, 1934), p. 134.
13 Amanat, op. cit., p. 418.
14 Ibid., p. 417.
15 Ibid., p. 461.

Chapter 8: The British (and Soviets) Take Over

1 FO E5519/3326/34.
2 Skrine, op. cit., p. 87.
3 Stephen L. McFarland, 'Anatomy of an Iranian Political Crowd: The Tehran Bread Riot of December 1942', *International Journal of Middle East Studies*, Vol. 17, No. 1, February 1985, pp. 51–65.
4 Arthur C. Millspaugh, *Americans in Persia* (Brookings Institution, 1946), pp. 59–60.
5 Mohammad Reza Shah Pahlavi, *Mission for My Country* (Hutchinson, 1961), p. 86.
6 FO EP 1016/54.
7 CAB 79/12/41, 9 July 1941.

Chapter 9: Abadan – Britain's Humiliation

1 Rohan Butler, 'British Policy in the Relinquishment of Abadan in 1951'. This was an internal history, written by the FCO's historian in 1966 and originally classified secret. See p. 289.
2 Daniel Yergin, *The Prize: The Epic Quest for Oil, Money and Power* (Simon & Schuster, 2008), p. 403.
3 Butler, op. cit., pp. 24–5. Figures are for 1949.
4 Mohammad Reza Shah Pahlavi, op. cit., p. 65.
5 Butler, op. cit., p. 106.
6 FO E 7357/583/34.
7 Cmd 8425, 2 May 1951, p. 32.
8 FO EP1531/129.
9 Ibid.
10 Christopher de Bellaigue, *Patriot of Persia: Muhammad Mossadegh and a very British coup* (Bodley Head, 2012), p. 145.
11 FO EP 1531/47.

12   Yergin, op. cit., p. 447.
13   Francis Williams, *A Prime Minister Remembers* (Heinemann, 1961), pp. 178–9.
14   Yergin, op. cit., p. 439.
15   FO EP 1531/204.
16   FO EP 1531/294.
17   Butler, op. cit., p. 99.
18   FO EP 1015/9.
19   Butler, op. cit., p. 79.
20   De Bellaigue, op. cit., p. 152.
21   Butler, op. cit., p. 80.
22   John Bew, *Citizen Clem: A Biography of Attlee* (Riverrun, 2016), p. 504.
23   Ibid., p. 504.
24   Letter, Stokes to Attlee, 14 September 1951, quoted in Williams, op. cit., pp. 249–50.
25   FO EP 1536/29.
26   De Bellaigue, op. cit., p. 179.
27   Hansard, 30 July 1951, vol. 491, col. 998–9.
28   *The Times*, 6 October 1951.
29   Butler, op. cit., p. 295.

Chapter 10: Spooks and Coups

1   Keith Jeffery, *MI6: The History of the Secret Intelligence Service, 1909–1949* (Bloomsbury, 2010), p. 421.
2   See Adrian O'Sullivan, *Espionage and Counter-Intelligence in Occupied Persia (Iran): The Success of the Allied Secret Services, 1941–45* (Palgrave Macmillan, 2015), pp. ix–xi.
3   Jeffery, op. cit., p. 436.
4   Butler, op. cit., p. 3.
5   Ibid., p. 171. FO EP1531/958.
6   Section 7, Intelligence Services Act 1994.
7   Butler, op. cit., p. 129. EP 1681/1G, 26 May 1951.
8   FO EP 1531/136.
9   FO 1531/1171 G.
10   Stephen Kinzer, *All the Shah's Men: An American Coup and the Roots of Middle East Terror* (Wiley, 2003), p. 159.
11   FO EP 1531/1429.
12   FO EP 1051/17.
13   Hansard, 30 July 1951, vol. 491, col. 995.
14   FO EP 1015/251.
15   Dr Donald Wilber, 'Overthrow of Premier Mossadeq of Iran, November 1952–August 1953' (CIA Clandestine Service History, March 1954), p. v.
16   Butler, op. cit., pp. 303, 304.
17   C. M. Woodhouse, *Something Ventured* (Granada, 1982).
18   Kermit Roosevelt, *Countercoup: The Struggle for the Control of Iran* (McGraw-Hill, 1979).
19   See https://nsarchive2.gwu.edu/NSAEBB/NSAEBB435/#britDocs
20   Wilber, op. cit.
21   Ibid., Appendix B, p. 1; main document, p. 18.
22   Ibid., Appendix B, p. 4.
23   Ibid., Main document, p. vii.
24   Ibid., Main document, pp. 16–17.
25   Ibid., Appendix B, p. 21.
26   Kenneth Love, *New York Times*, quoted in Kinzer, op. cit., p. 187.
27   Darioush Bayandor, *Iran and the CIA: The Fall of Mosaddeq Revisited* (Palgrave Macmillan, 2010), p. 154.
28   Wilber, op. cit., pp. 82–3.
29   Yergin, op. cit., pp. 456–60.
30   Wilber, op. cit., p. 82.
31   From a now declassified internal review by Sir Nicholas Browne, 'Iran and the fall of the Shah' (FCO, 1981), p. 14.
32   Kinzer, op. cit., p. 215.
33   Quoted in Bew, op. cit., p. 505.

Chapter 11: The Shah in His Element

1   Wright, op. cit.
2   See also the BBC 4 documentary *Decadence and Downfall: The Shah of Iran's Ultimate Party* (2016).
3   Touraj Daryaee (ed.), *The Oxford Handbook of Iranian History* (Oxford University Press, 2012), p. 360.
4   Michael Axworthy, *Revolutionary Iran: A History of the Islamic Republic* (Allen Lane, 2013), p. 60.
5   See Amanat, op. cit., p. 600.
6   Source: AA Motoring Trust, 'Petrol Prices 1896–2005'.
7   Source: World Bank, www.tradingeconomics.com
8   World Health Organization, 'Global Status Report on Road Safety 2015', Data Table A2.
9   Axworthy, *Revolutionary Iran*, op. cit., p. 90.
10   Ibid., p. 90, quoting Ali Ansari, *Modern Iran Since 1921: The Pahlavis and After* (Longman, 2003), p. 186.
11   Mohammad Reza Shah Pahlavi, op. cit., p. 178.

12 Mohammad Reza Pahlavi, *The Shah's Story* (Michael Joseph, 1980), pp. 149, 155.
13 Ibid., p. 173.
14 Axworthy, *Revolutionary Iran*, op. cit., p. 113.
15 Nicholas Browne, 'British Policy on Iran 1974–78' (FCO, 8/3601, confidential, subsequently declassified), p. 68, and conversation with Sir Peter.
16 Browne, ibid.

Chapter 12: Khomeini Returns
1 James G. Blight et al., *Becoming Enemies: US–Iran Relations and the Iran–Iraq War, 1979–1988* (Rowman & Littlefield, 2012), p. 185.
2 Inner Temple, 'The Social Context of Law', *Inner Temple Yearbook 2018–2019*, p. 20.
3 Article 2 of the Supplementary Fundamental Laws of 7 October 1907; see Chapter 6.
4 Quoted in Axworthy, *Revolutionary Iran*, op. cit., p. 138.
5 Ibid., p. 157.
6 Ibid., p. 158.
7 Bruce Laingen to Cyrus Vance, 28 July 1979, quoted in Blight, op. cit., pp. 299–300.

Chapter 13: The Imposed War
1 Pierre Razoux, *The Iran–Iraq War*, translated by Nicholas Elliott (Harvard University Press, 2015).
2 Christopher Lee, *Carrington: An Honourable Man* (Viking, 2018), p. 394.
3 Hansard, 22 June 1982, vol. 26, col. 215.
4 Geoffrey Howe, *Conflict of Loyalty* (Macmillan, 1994), pp. 512, 544, 545–6, 558.
5 Charles Moore, *Margaret Thatcher: The Authorized Biography*, Vols 1 and 2 (Allen Lane, 2013, 2015).
6 Source: note to author by Edward Chaplin, December 2018.
7 Patrick R. H. Wright, *Behind Diplomatic Lines: Relations with Ministers* (Biteback, 2018), entry for 28 May 1987. The statistical basis for Wright's belief about the scale of UK trade with Iran is unclear.
8 Ibid., entry for 2 June 1987.
9 AFP, 6 April 1980.
10 Dilip Hiro, *The Longest War: The Iran–Iraq Military Conflict* (Routledge, 1990).
11 Alexander Haig, 'Talking points for a meeting with the President', April 1981, quoted in Blight, op. cit., p. 305.
12 Razoux, op. cit., p. 69.
13 United Nations Security Council Resolution 479, 28 September 1980.
14 Quoted in Blight, op. cit., p. 267.
15 Ibid., Bruce Reidel, p. 90.
16 Razoux, op. cit., p. 243.
17 Ibid., p. 349.
18 Ibid., p. 240.
19 Ibid., Appendix F, Foreign Military Assistance, pp. 546–56.
20 Blight, op. cit., pp. 121–2.
21 Ibid., p. 101.
22 *Sunday Herald*, 8 September 2002.
23 Blight, op. cit., p. 180.
24 Ibid., p. 181.
25 Razoux, op. cit., p. 398.
26 Ibid., p. 109.
27 Blight, op. cit., p. 188.
28 Letter to Speaker of the House of Representatives from the President, 4 July 1988.
29 Hansard, 22 June 1982, vol. 26, col. 221.
30 Now in Article 64 of the constitution.
31 Blight, op. cit., p. 89.
32 Razoux, op. cit., p. 115.
33 Blight, op. cit., pp. 90–91.
34 Ibid., p. 142.
35 Razoux, op. cit., p. 384.
36 Tom Cooper and Farzad Bishop, *Iran–Iraq War in the Air 1980–1988* (Schiffer, 2000), p. 225.
37 Quoted in Razoux, op. cit., pp. 465–6.
38 Razoux, op. cit., p. 467.
39 Blight, op. cit., p. 220.

Chapter 14: The Aftermath – *The Satanic Verses* and Violence
1 Axworthy, *Revolutionary Iran*, op. cit., p. 298.
2 *Daily Mirror*, 16 February 1989.
3 Article 110 of the amended 1989 constitution.
4 Baqer Moin, *Khomeini: Life of the Ayatollah* (I. B. Tauris, 1999), p. 270.

Chapter 15: The Reformers Break Out
1 Interview with the author.

2 Trita Parsi, *Losing an Enemy: Obama, Iran, and the Triumph of Diplomacy* (Yale, 2017), p. 24.
3 Yitzhak Rabin, Reuters, 12 September 1994.
4 Ghoncheh Tazmini, *Khatami's Iran: The Islamic Republic and the Turbulent Path to Reform* (I. B. Tauris, 2013), p. 136.
5 Ibid., p. 73.

Chapter 16: 9/11 and Nukes
1 Details of my trip to Israel can be found in my memoirs, *Last Man Standing: Memoirs of a Political Survivor* (Macmillan, 2012), pp. 433–9.
2 Parsi, op. cit., pp. 39–45.
3 Condoleezza Rice, *No Higher Honor: A Memoir of My Years in Washington* (Crown, 2011), p. 150.
4 BBC Radio 4, *Bridging the Gulf with Tehran*, 6 December 2015.
5 Conversation with the author.
6 Rice, op. cit., p. 313.
7 Mohammad Reza Pahlavi, *The Shah's Story*, op. cit., p. 67.
8 CIA, 'Prospects for Further Proliferation of Nuclear Weapons', Special National Intelligence Estimate, SNIE 4-1-74, 23 August 1974.
9 Seyed Hossein Mousavian, *The Iranian Nuclear Crisis: A Memoir* (Carnegie, 2012), pp. 62–5.
10 See Axworthy, *Revolutionary Iran*, op. cit., p. 361, and Parsi, op. cit., p. 60.
11 Email to the author, 29 October 2018.
12 Email to the author, 2 November 2019.

Chapter 17: 'Chocolates, Jack, Chocolates'
1 Mousavian, op. cit., p. 69, and see Chapter 5 above.
2 Mousavian, ibid., p. 73.
3 Ibid., p. 102.
4 Donald Rumsfeld, *Known and Unknown: A Memoir* (Sentinel, 2011), p. 639.
5 Author's notes.
6 Mousavian, op. cit., p. 139.
7 BBC Radio 4, *Today*, 4 November 2004.
8 IAEA Information Circular INFCIRC/637, 26 November 2004.
9 Mousavian, op. cit., p. 150.
10 Author's notes.

Chapter 18: The Halo of Light
1 From the hardline Iranian website Baztab on 27 September 2005, reporting on a speech to the Assembly of Experts.
2 Ali Rahnema, *Superstition as Ideology in Iranian Politics: Majlesi and Ahmadinejad* (Cambridge University Press, 2011), p. 17.
3 Quoted in Rahnema, ibid., p. 72.
4 Etemad, 22 Mordad 1388 (12 August 2005), quoted in Rahnema, ibid., p. 20.
5 Official translation, Permanent Mission to the UN, Islamic Republic of Iran, 17 September 2005.
6 Fatemeh Rajabi, *Ahmadinejad: The Third Millennium Miracle* (Nashr-e Danesh Amouz, 2006), p. 300.
7 Rahnema, op. cit., p. 59.
8 Karl Marx, *Critique of Hegel's Philosophy of Right* (1843).
9 Rice, op. cit., pp. 461–4. The announcement was made on 31 May 2006.
10 Rice, op. cit., pp. 625–7.
11 *The Economist*, 22 March 2008.

Chapter 19: The Sedition of '88
1 *Haaretz*, 13 June 2009.
2 Ken Ballen and Patrick Doherty, 'The Iranian People Speak', *Washington Post*, 15 June 2009.
3 Afshon Ostovar, *Vanguard of the Imam: Religion, Politics, and Iran's Revolutionary Guards* (Oxford University Press, 2016), p. 181.
4 Rahbord e Danesh.
5 Axworthy, *Revolutionary Iran*, op. cit., pp. 402–3.
6 Ostovar, op. cit., p. 181.
7 www.amontazeri.com. Montazeri died on 19 December 2009, aged eighty-seven.
8 Mousavian, op. cit., p. 341; www.khabaonline.ir/news-79407.aspx
9 'Iranian general blames water woes on Israeli "cloud theft"', *Times of Israel*, 2 July 2018.
10 Hillary Clinton, *Hard Choices: A Memoir* (Simon & Schuster, 2014), p. 423.
11 Ibid.
12 https://www.theguardian.com/world/blog/2009/sep/25/nuclear-ultimatum-iran
13 *Time*, 12 March 2016.
14 https://www.theguardian.com/uk/2010/oct/28/sir-john-sawers-speech-full-text
15 Mousavian, op. cit., p. 423.
16 Hansard, 30 November 2011, vol. 536, col. 959 et seq.
17 Aftab News, 16 November 2005, quoted in Rahnema, op. cit., p. 60.

Chapter 20: The Guy in Your Earpiece

1 https://www.youtube.com/watch?v=q6-gJ1zI3D4
2 IPOS poll, 3–6 June 2013.
3 John Kerry, *Every Day Is Extra* (Simon & Schuster, 2018), p. 495.
4 Ibid., p. 493.
5 Ibid., p. 504.
6 Ibid., p. 523.
7 Hansard, 11 March 2014, vol. 577, col. 103 WH.
8 Source: World Bank.
9 UN population projections.
10 See, for instance, Associated Press, 6 January 2018.
11 Tabnak, 31 December 2017.
12 *The Guardian*, 2 January 2018.
13 NBC, 16 August 2016.
14 CNN, 22 March 2016.
15 *New York Times*, 8 May 2018.
16 The Intercept, 23 March 2018.

Chapter 21: The Deep State and Iran's Security

1 Ostovar, op. cit., p. 242.
2 Speech to Tehran's Supreme National Defense University, 28 January 2019. Salami was deputy chief of the IRGC when he made those remarks. He has since been appointed chief.
3 Bloomberg News, 30 May 2019.
4 BBC, 22 April 2019.
5 EnergyReporters.com, 30 May 2019.
6 Reuters, 6 May 2019.
7 Article 26, Sanctions section of the JCPOA, and Article 36.
8 Article 143.
9 https://www.dni.gov/files/documents/Newsroom/Reports%20and%20Pubs/20071203_release.pdf
10 IAEA, 2 December 2015. Gov/2015/68, para 85.
11 Speech to Air Force Officers on 8 February 2019, marking Air Force Day.
12 For example, speech by General Yahya Rahim Safavi, military adviser to the Supreme Leader, former IRGC chief, 28 January 2019, National Conference of the Defence Security Architecture.
13 *Haaretz*, 4 June 2019.
14 See, for example, Kasra Arabi, 'The Fundamentals of Iran's Islamic Revolution', Tony Blair Institute for Global Change, https://institute.global/insight/co-existence/fundamentals-irans-islamic-revolution
15 *Foreign Policy*, Winter 2019.
16 Narjas Zatat, 'Iranian protesters unveil countdown showing 8,411 days "to the destruction of Israel"', *The Independent*, 24 June 2017; Ali Arouzi and F. Brinley Bruton, 'Iran launches missiles at Syria, but message is aimed at US, Israel, Saudi Arabia', NBC News, 1 October 2018.
17 Speech to 4th National Congress of the Reformist Nedaye Iranian Party, 14 December 2018.
18 Jack Watling, 'Iran's Objectives and Capabilities: Deterrence and Subversion', RUSI Occasional Paper, February 2019.

Conclusion: Iran's Future

1 Ramita Navai, *City of Lies: Love, Sex, Death and the Search for Truth in Tehran* (Weidenfeld & Nicolson, 2014), p. xiii.
2 Article 96.
3 Fereshteh Sadeghi, Twitter, 12 May 2019.
4 BBC, 15 February 2011.
5 *New York Daily News*, 24 June 2014; BBC Persian, 6 December 2014; Misagh Parsa, *Democracy in Iran: Why It Failed and How It Might Succeed* (Harvard, 2016), p. 23.
6 Parsa, ibid., p. 22.
7 https://iranintl.com/en/iran-in-brief/ghanoon-news-paper-was-shut-down-referring-assad-%E2%80%-9Cuninvited-guest%E2%80%9D
8 Parsa, op. cit., p. 22.
9 https://observers.france24.com/en/20180919-ferraris-pet-tigers-instagram-posts-kids-iran%E2%80%99-elite-touch-nerve
10 https://www.rferl.org/a/khomeini-s-great-grandson-fends-off-firestorm-over-luxurious-lifestyle/29648424.html
11 https://thearabweekly.com/iranian-oligarchs-bask-wealth-while-others-suffer
12 Christopher de Bellaigue, *In the Rose Garden of the Martyrs: A Memoir of Iran* (HarperCollins, 2004), p. 111 et seq.
13 *The Guardian*, 11 July 2015.
14 *The Economist*, 18 August 2012.
15 *The Economist*, 9 February 2019.
16 Ibid.
17 Video posted on 22 March 2019.

INDEX

All places are in Iran, unless stated otherwise.
Jack Straw is JS throughout.